W9-BNR-795

West's Law School
Advisory Board

JESSE H. CHOPER
Professor of Law,
University of California, Berkeley

DAVID P. CURRIE
Professor of Law, University of Chicago

YALE KAMISAR
Professor of Law, University of San Diego
Professor of Law, University of Michigan

MARY KAY KANE
Chancellor, Dean and Distinguished Professor of Law,
University of California,
Hastings College of the Law

LARRY D. KRAMER
Dean and Professor of Law, Stanford Law School

WAYNE R. LaFAVE
Professor of Law, University of Illinois

JONATHAN R. MACEY
Professor of Law, Yale Law School

ARTHUR R. MILLER
Professor of Law, Harvard University

GRANT S. NELSON
Professor of Law,
University of California, Los Angeles

JAMES J. WHITE
Professor of Law, University of Michigan

ANTI-TERRORISM AND CRIMINAL ENFORCEMENT

ABRIDGED EDITION

Second Edition

For use as a supplement to courses and in seminars

By

Norman Abrams
Professor of Law, University of California, Los Angeles

AMERICAN CASEBOOK SERIES®

THOMSON
—————— TM
WEST

Mat # 40339174

Thomson/West have created this publication to provide you with accurate and authoritative information concerning the subject matter covered. However, this publication was not necessarily prepared by persons licensed to practice law in a particular jurisdiction. Thomson/West are not engaged in rendering legal or other professional advice, and this publication is not a substitute for the advice of an attorney. If you require legal or other expert advice, you should seek the services of a competent attorney or other professional.

American Casebook Series and West Group are trademarks
registered in the U.S. Patent and Trademark Office.

© West, a Thomson business, 2003
© 2005 Thomson/West
      610 Opperman Drive
      P.O. Box 64526
      St. Paul, MN 55164–0526
      1–800–328–9352
Printed in the United States of America

ISBN 0–314–15930–4

TEXT IS PRINTED ON 10% POST
CONSUMER RECYCLED PAPER

To my mother

IN MEMORIAM

GERTRUDE ABRAMS HIGHTON z"l

1902–2004

*

Preface to the Abridged Edition

This abridged version of the *Anti-terrorism and Criminal Enforcement* casebook, published in July, 2005, is intended for use as a Supplement to courses in Criminal Law, Criminal Procedure, Constitutional Criminal Procedure, Federal Criminal Law, or any similar course where the instructor wishes to teach a unit on, or address legal, constitutional or policy issues raised by current anti-terrorism enforcement. It can also be used as teaching materials in a Seminar on Anti-terrorism Enforcement. Like the full version of the casebook, it can be used to teach an undergraduate course in fields such as political science, public policy, criminal justice, criminology and sociology.

The emphasis in this abridged edition is on issues arising since September 11, 2001, and materials have been retained from the full version with that primary focus in mind. Because this volume is an abridgement, it includes less background material, is leaner, is less expensive and accordingly, is more practicable for use as a Supplement for courses where another casebook is being used. As in the full volume, the book "develops and plays off of the tension between a criminal enforcement or law enforcement approach, on the one hand, and wartime, military and intelligence basis, on the other.... [T]he book is not restricted to a treatment of substantive criminal issues, although it certainly includes them; nor is it restricted to process and procedure and issues of criminal law administration, ... An effort has been made to adopt an approach that brings together all of these different emphases in a coherent, integrated package."

In the course of abridgement of the full casebook, some chapters have been omitted, others have been pared down; cases have been edited still further, and full versions of the underlying statutes have not been included. In addition to a Table of Contents for this edition, the Table of Contents from the full version is reprinted. This should make it convenient to identify what from the full volume has been omitted and to use it, where desired, as a source of valuable background material.

The abridged version contains significant material on issues relating to:

> prosecutions under 18 U.S.C. § 2339B (providing material support to a designated foreign terrorist organization);
>
> discussion of what kind of war the antiterrorism effort is;
>
> extended detention as material witnesses, under immigration laws, and as an unlawful combatants;
>
> military tribunals;

the Classified Information Procedures Act;

the Foreign Intelligence Surveillance Act; and

targeted killings by U.S. agents acting abroad.

N.A.

August, 2005

Acknowledgments

I am grateful to Ayan Kayal, UCLA Law, '06, for his able assistance with the research on this volume, and I again want to thank Phillip Carter, a 2004 UCLA Law graduate, now in private practice, who continues to forward to me items that help to keep this book abreast of the latest developments in the field.

I would also like to thank the following individuals and organizations for the permission each has granted to reprint excerpts from their publications.

ABA, TASK FORCE ON TERRORISM AND THE LAW, REPORT AND RECOMMEDNDATION ON MILITARY COMMISSIONS (Jan. 4, 2002) Copyright © (2002) By the American Bar Association. Reprinted by permission.

ABA, TASK FORCE ON TREATMENT OF ENEMY COMBATANTS, PRELIMINARY REPORT (Aug. 8, 2002) Copyright © (2002) By the American Bar Association. Reprinted by permission.

Floyd Abrams, *The First Amendment and the War Against Terrorism*, 5 U. PA. J. CONST. L. 1 (2002) Copyright © (2002) By the University of Pennsylvania Journal of Constitutional Law. Reprinted by permission.

Bruce Ackerman, *The Emergency Constitution*, 113 YALE L.J. 1029 (2004) Copyright © 2004 By the Yale Law Journal Company. Reprinted by permission of the Yale Law Journal Company and William S. Hein Company from the Yale Law Journal, Vol. 113, pages 1029–1091.

Bruce Ackerman, *Response, This Is Not a War*, 113 YALE L.J. 1871 (2004) Copyright © 2004 By the Yale Law Journal Company. Reprinted by permission of the Yale Law Journal Company and William S. Hein Company from the Yale Law Journal, Vol. 113, pages 1871–1907.

Kenneth Anderson, *What To Do With Bin Laden and Al Qaeda Terrorists?: A Qualified Defense of Military Commissions and United States Policy on Detainees At Guantanamo Bay Naval Base*, 25 HARV. J.L. & PUB POL'Y 591 (2002) Copyright © (2002) By the Harvard Journal of Law & Public Policy. Reprinted by permission.

Curtis A. Bradley & Jack L. Goldsmith, *The Constitutional Validity of Military Commissions*, 5 GREEN BAG 2d 249 (2002) Copyright © (2002) By the Green Bag. Reprinted by permission.

Phillip Carter, *Why Can the Army Help Cops Catch the D.C. Sniper?*, SLATE, Oct. 17, 2002 Copyright © (2002) By Slate Magazine. Reprinted by permission.

Erwin Chemerinsky *Losing Liberties: Applying a Foreign Intelligence Model to Domestic Law Enforcement*, 51 UCLA L. REV. 1619 (2004) Copyright © 2004 By the Regents of the University of California. Reprinted by permission originally published in 51 UCLA Law Rev. 1619 (2004).

David Cole, *The Priority of Morality: the Emergency Constitution's Blind Spot*, 113 YALE L.J. 1753 (2004) Copyright © 2004 By the Yale Law Journal Company. Reprinted by permission of the Yale Law Journal Company and William S. Hein Company from the Yale Law Journal, Vol. 113, pages 1753–1800.

Major Kirk L. Davies, *The Imposition of Martial Law In The United States*, 49 A.F. L. REV. 67 (2000) Copyright © 2000 By the Air Force Judge Advocate General School. Reprinted by permission.

Christina Deconcini & Kareem Shora, Panel Discussion, *Perversities and Prospects: Whither Immigration Enforcement and Detention in the Anti-Terrorism Aftermath?*, 9 GEO. J. ON POVERTY L. & POL'Y 1 (2002) Reprinted with permission of the publisher, Georgetown Journal on Poverty Law & Policy © 2002.

INGRID DETTER DE LUPIS, THE LAW OF WAR (1987) Copyright © (1987) By the Cambridge University Press. Reprinted with the permission of the Cambridge University Press.

Alan M. Dershowitz, *The Torture Warrant: A Response to Professor Strauss*, 48 N.Y.L. SCH. L.REV. 275 (2003) Copyright © 2003 By the New York Law School Law Review. Reprinted by permission.

John T. Elliff, *The Attorney General's Guidelines for FBI Investigations*, 69 CORNELL L. REV. 785 (1984) Copyright © (1984) By the Cornell Law Review. Reprinted by permission.

FEDERALIST SOCIETY, WHITE PAPER ON THE USA PATRIOT ACT OF 2001; CRIMINAL PROCEDURE SECTIONS (2001) Copyright © (2001) By the Federalist Society. Reprinted by permission.

George P. Fletcher, *The Military Tribunal Order: On Justice and War: Contradictions in the Proposed Military Tribunals*, 25 HARV. J.L. & PUB. POL'Y 635 (2002) Copyright © 2002 By the Harvard Society for Law & Public Policy, Inc. Reprinted by permission from FindLaw.com. This column originally appeared on FindLaw.com (www.FindLaw.com).

George P. Fletcher, *War Crimes Proceedings in Iraq? The Bush Administration's Dilemma*, April 4, 2003, at http://writ.news.findlaw.com/commentary/20030404_fletcher.html Copyright © 2003 By FindLaw. Reprinted by permission.

Eric M. Freedman, *The Bush Military Tribunals: Where Have We Been? Where Are We Going?*, 17 CRIM. JUST. 14, 17 (2002) Copyright © (2002) By the American Bar Association. Reprinted by permission.

Michael J. Glennon, *The Fog of Law: Self–Defense, Inherence, and Incoherence in Article 51 of the United Nations Charter*, 25 HARV. J.L. & PUB. POL'Y 539 (2002) Copyright © 2002 By the Harvard Society for Law & Public Policy, Inc. Reprinted by permission.

Matthew Carlton Hammond, Note, *The Posse Comitatus Act: A Principle in Need of Renewal*, 75 WASH. U. L.Q. 953 (1997) Copyright © (1997) By the Washington University Law Quarterly. Reprinted by permission.

Neal K. Katyal & Laurence H. Tribe, *Waging War, Deciding Guilt: Trying the Military Tribunals*, 111 YALE L.J. (2002). Reprinted by permission of the Yale Law Journal Company and William S. Hein Company from The Yale Law Journal Vol. 111, pages 1259-1310.

Orrin S. Kerr, *Internet Surveillance Law after the USA PATRIOT Act: The Big Brother that Isn't*, 97 Nw. U.L. REV. 607 (2003) Copyright © 2003 By the Northwestern University Law Review. Reprinted by special permission of Northwestern University School of Law, Northwestern University Law Review.

Harold Hongju Koh, *The Case Against Military Commissions*, 96 AM. J. INT'L L. 337 (2002) Reproduced with permission from 96 AJIL 337 (2002), © The American Society of International Law.

Laurie L. Levenson, *Detention, Material Witnesses and the War on Terrorism*, 35 LOY. L.A. L. REV. 1217 (2002) Copyright © (2002) By the Loyola of Los Angeles Law Review. Reprinted by permission.

Kathryn Martin, *Note, The USA PATRIOT Act's Application to Library Patron Records*, 29 J.LEGIS. 283 (2003) Copyright © 2003 By the Journal of Legislation. Reprinted by permission.

Note: Responding to Terrorism: Crime, Punishment, and War, 115 HARV. L. REV. 1217 (2002) Copyright © 2002 By the Harvard Law Review Association. Reprinted by permission.

David M. Park, Note, *Re-Examining the Attorney General's Guidelines for FBI Investigations of Domestic Groups*, 39 ARIZ. L. REV. 769 (1997) Copyright © (1997) by the Arizona Board of Regents. Reprinted by permission.

Jordan J. Paust, *Antiterrorism Military Commissions: Courting Illegality*, 23 MICH. J. INT'L L. 1 (2001) Copyright © (2001) By Jordan J. Paust. Reprinted by permission.

Heidee Stoller, Tahlia Townsend, Rashad Hussain, and Marcia Yablon, *Developments in Law and Policy: The Costs of Post-9/11 National Security Strategy*, 22 YALE L. & POL'Y REV. 197 (2004) Copyright © 2004 By the Yale Law & Policy Review. Reprinted by permission.

Brian Z. Tamanaha, *A Critical Review of the Classified Information Procedures Act*, 13 AM. J. CRIM. L. 277 (1987) Copyright © (1987) By the Company American Journal of Criminal Law. Reprinted by permission.

Laurence H. Tribe and Patrick O. Gudridge, *The Anti-Emergency Constitution*, 113 YALE.L.J. 1801 (2004) Copyright © 2004 By the Yale Law Journal Company. Reprinted by permission of the Yale Law Journal and William S. Hein Company from the Yale Law Journal, Vol. 113, pages 1801–1870.

*

Table of Contents
Abridged Edition

Table of Contents
Unabridged Edition

PART III. ACTIONS BY GOVERNMENTAL AGENTS IN THE UNITED STATES AND ABROAD

Table of Cases

The principal cases are in bold type. Cases cited or discussed in the text are in roman type. References are to pages. Cases cited in principal cases and within other quoted materials are not included.

Table of Statutes

*

ANTI-TERRORISM AND CRIMINAL ENFORCEMENT

ABRIDGED EDITION

Second Edition

*

Chapter 1

INTRODUCTION

This book focuses on the use of the criminal process as a means to enforce the U.S. government's "war" on terrorism. In this "war," a regimen of crimes and special approaches to criminal procedure (including detention and secrecy) is being used that differs from much of ordinary criminal process. Much of the book is devoted to these special approaches—e.g. labeling individuals as "enemy combatants"—and the special substantive terrorism crimes which are being used in anti-terrorism enforcement. Problems of application, legality, constitutionality and the appropriateness of using particular policy approaches are addressed. In some of the legal areas studied in the book, the case law is burgeoning but still somewhat sparse. Where few judicial opinions are available, every new case takes on special significance. Examples are the recent district court cases addressing the constitutionality of the military commission process and examining the processes being used to review the cases of the enemy combatants at Guantanamo Bay. In areas where case law is lacking, we examine the available legal source materials, legislation, executive orders and administrative regulations.

* * *

To an unusual extent in a casebook focused on criminal enforcement, issues of law addressed in this volume turn on the application of special concepts not generally dealt with in the ordinary criminal law. Thus, the U.S. government's current "war" on terrorism may be said to have begun more than two decades ago, triggered by major acts of terrorism at home and against U.S. personnel and property abroad. However, the terrorist attacks on September 11, 2001, involving the destruction of the twin towers of the World Trade Center and a portion of the Pentagon caused a paradigm shift in this war. Prior to these events, the government's actions in this sphere may have been described as a "war," but the use of that term was largely metaphorical and without any particular legal consequences.

Following the September 11th attacks, the concept of "war" in a more traditional sense came to be relied on by the government as providing legal authority for various kinds of enforcement actions. The

1

authority of the President as Commander-in-Chief was invoked, and the rules applicable in wartime were said to come into play. Accordingly, among the many issues that are addressed, the volume includes materials that help to illuminate the legal concept of ''war'' and the government's rationale for its ''wartime'' actions; addresses the question whether the kind of war in which we are engaged has the legal significance that the government would give to it—specifically whether governmental action that exceeds the traditional limits imposed by statute or the Constitution can be justified under the present circumstances; and presents views and commentary relevant to that question.

* * *

There is, of course, an overriding, powerful more general theme reflected in questions repeatedly explored in different contexts in this volume, sometimes made explicit, sometimes not—whether particular governmental steps are necessary to maintain our security and how much and to what extent will those steps take away from us elements of our traditional civil liberties and cause a potential change in the nature of our society. The purpose of this book is to make available through original and secondary sources and analytical and discussion text and questions the raw material for addressing this theme in an informed, balanced way—presenting, to the extent possible, relevant information on both sides of the many issues, hopefully without prejudgment or bias.

Chapter 2

BACKGROUND: ANTI–TERRORISM LEGISLATIVE PACKAGES

A. Introduction

The modern history of anti-terrorism legislation dates back at least to the early 1960's when the hijacking of commercial airliners by politically motivated individuals triggered the enactment in the United States of a criminal statute dealing with air piracy. Anti-terrorism legislation was usually enacted in reaction to a specific terrorism event or series of events and usually took one of two forms—either a specific statute addressing a relatively narrow terrorism problem or a comprehensive legislative package containing a multiplicity of specific pieces of legislation dealing with various aspects of anti-terrorism activity by the government.

In all, in the past two decades, five such broad legislative packages have been enacted—the Omnibus Diplomatic Security and Antiterrorism Act of 1986—triggered by increasing violence against U.S. installations and personnel abroad (by one estimate, in the decade prior to 1985, there were 2500 terrorist acts directed against Americans worldwide. S. Res. 190, 99th Cong., 1st Sess., 131 Cong. Rec. 8999 (1985)); the Antiterrorism and Effective Death Penalty Act of 1996—largely responding to the 1993 World Trade Center bombing, the 1995 bombing of a training center in Riyadh, Saudi Arabia, and the 1995 Oklahoma City bombing; the USA PATRIOT Act of 2001; the Homeland Security Act of 2002, both enacted in the wake of the attacks of September 11, 2001; (of course, during these same decades, additional terrorist events played a role in precipitating these congressional responses—including the 1998 destruction of embassies in Tanzania and Kenya, the bombing in the year 2000 of the USS Cole in a harbor in Yemen, the smuggling of materials into the United States from Canada for a planned bombing at millennium celebrations in Los Angeles, as well as miscellaneous additional attacks or attempts); and the Intelligence Reform and Terrorism Prevention Act of 2004, drafted largely in response to the report of the 9/11 Commission.

3

While these packages of legislation shared the general feature that they were aimed at addressing the problems of terrorism, they also were each a collection of statutes dealing with many different issues, each having a broad theme or character reflected in a majority of its provisions. Each of the last four also share an additional feature in common: they contain provisions designed to fill in gaps or make amendments to one or more of the earlier packages.

* * *

C.   The major legislative packages

* * *

2.   The Antiterrorism and Effective Death Penalty Act

* * *

The AEDPA ... is the first legislative package that begins to develop a series of federal crimes that are aimed at terrorist acts generally and the interdicting of support for terrorist organizations.

* * *

3.   The USA PATRIOT Act

Public Law 107–56, the USA PATRIOT ACT ("Uniting and Strengthening America by Providing Appropriate Tools Required to Intercept and Obstruct Terrorism") was signed into law on Oct. 26, 2001—just six weeks after the attacks on the World Trade Center and Pentagon. Because of the national trauma created by the September 11th attacks and the mood in Congress to take some legislative action in response, the Act received limited substantive consideration in the two houses of the Congress. The congressional enactment process was very abbreviated, quite unusual given the complexity, the range, and the far-reaching nature of some of the provisions of the Act. Limited committee hearings were held, and there was very little debate on the floor of the Congress. * * *

Unlike the AEDPA, the PATRIOT Act did not add very much to the body of anti-terrorism crimes. The main thrust of the Act was rather directed to broadening and strengthening law enforcement tools of investigation and procedures and methods that can be used to attack terrorist groups and activities. While many of the Act's provisions are restricted to being used in terrorism-related investigations, some of the tools can be used as well against ordinary criminals and criminal activity. The Act includes provisions that loosen the restrictions on the government's use of electronic surveillance, loosen the secrecy that attaches to grand jury deliberations, add to its authority to address money laundering, give it additional procedural power in certain kinds of immigration matters, and facilitate cooperation between government agents focused on intelligence gathering and those whose goal is arrest and prosecution. It also modifies definitions of terrorism that are used for various purposes in the criminal and immigration fields and provides a new definition of "domestic terrorism."

Several sections of the Act build on existing money laundering provisions to provide additional authority to deal with foreign money laundering.

* * *

The PATRIOT Act, much more than any of its predecessors, has been the center of controversy and a lightening rod for criticism. We reproduce below some reports of the public's reaction to the PATRIOT Act and some of the criticisms of particular provisions and some responses to the criticisms, particularly relating to the provisions of the Act dealing with surveillance of the internet, and the subpoenaing of library records.

Erwin Chemerinsky, Losing Liberties: Applying a Foreign Intelligence Model to Domestic Law Enforcement, 51 UCLA L. Rev. 1619, 1621 (2004):

> The [PATRIOT] Act contains many very troubling provisions. As evidence of this, over 150 cities and three states have passed resolutions criticizing the law.

Orrin S. Kerr, Internet Surveillance Law after the USA PATRIOT Act: The Big Brother that Isn't, 97 Nw. U.L. Rev. 607, 623–624 (2003):

> The ACLU declared that the Act gave law enforcement "extraordinary new powers." Another civil liberties group, the Electronic Frontier Foundation, announced that "the civil liberties of ordinary Americans have taken a tremendous blow with this law." The website of the Electronic Privacy Information Center featured a drawing of a tombstone that stated "The Fourth Amendment: 1789–2001." Major media outlets agreed. The New York Times viewed the Act as an overreaction to September 11th, and concluded that the law gave the government unjustified "broad new powers." The Washington Post also opposed the Act: its editorial board described the Patriot Act as "panicky legislation" that "reduced the healthy oversight of the courts."

In an article in the Wall Street Journal, Nov. 12, 2004, a former Congressman, Bob Barr, who sat on the Judiciary Committee when the PATRIOT Act was passed, expressed the view that only about a dozen of the Act's 150 provisions need to be reformed, and he described section 213 (the sneak and peek provision) and section 215 (the seizure of tangible things, such as library records) codified at 50 U.S.C. § 1861 as representing the "most significant problems."

His criticism of section 213 was that it expanded the grounds for delaying notice to the occupants of homes or businesses of the fact that a search of their premises had occurred—that prior to enactment of the PATRIOT Act, in certain categories of cases judges might delay the giving of notice where it would threaten life or safety, involve witness intimidation, endanger evidence or allow flight from prosecution. The effect of section 213 was to codify the afore-mentioned grounds for delaying notice that judges applied and also add a new ground, "seriously jeopardizing an investigation or unduly delaying a trial."

* * *

Barr's criticism of section 215 was that it expanded the category of what could be seized under FISA authority from business records to "any tangible thing" from any third party record holder and lowered the standard from "specific and articulable facts" to relevant to an investigation. The language of section 215 reads as follows:

> The Director of the ... [FBI] or a designee ... may make an application for an order requiring the production of any tangible things ... for an investigation to protect against international terrorism or clandestine intelligence activities, provided that such investigation of a United States person is not conducted solely upon the basis of activities protected by the first amendment to the Constitution.

Erwin Chemerinsky, Losing Liberties: Applying a Foreign Intelligence Model to Domestic Law Enforcement, 51 UCLA L. Rev. 1619, 1623–1628 (2004):

> The Patriot Act was adopted on October 26, 2001. It is 342 pages long and is difficult to read because it is filled with references to other provisions of the United States Code. Many of its provisions are innocuous. For example, section 219 amends Rule 41(a) of the Federal Rules of Criminal Procedure to allow magistrate judges to authorize nationwide search warrants wherever terrorist activities "may" have occurred (not limited to that judicial district). The prior requirement that a warrant be issued in each district was unduly cumbersome, and this national procedure simplifies the process of conducting investigations.
>
> ...
>
> The [Foreign Intelligence Surveillance] Act [enacted in 1978] applies only to "foreign powers" or their "agents" in order to obtain "foreign intelligence information." A key aspect of the law is that it relaxes the usual probable cause standard followed under the Fourth Amendment. The Act provides that an order can be issued if there is "probable cause to believe that the target of the [electronic] surveillance is a foreign power or an [agent] of a foreign power."
>
> ...
>
> As originally enacted, FISA applied only to electronic surveillance, but was amended in 1995 to include physical searches.
>
> ...

The Patriot Act marks a significant shift by expanding FISA to include domestic law enforcement so long as a purpose is also foreign intelligence gathering.

. . .

The broad definition of terrorism and the government's power to use FISA for law enforcement is especially troubling because the Patriot Act gives the government significant new powers to gather information. Section 216 allows the use of pen/traps to monitor internet activity (e-mail and web browsing) on a showing that the information "likely to be obtained" is "relevant to an ongoing criminal investigation." This provision allows the government to monitor the e-mail addresses that a person sends to or receives from, as well as the web sites a person visits, by showing that it is "relevant to a criminal investigation." This standard is much easier to meet than "probable cause" or even "reasonable suspicion." The government already has this authority for telephones, but expanding it to electronic communications is troubling because a great deal of information can be learned about a person, some of it misleading, based on a list of web sites visited.

. . .

Section 206 authorizes the FISA court to authorize intercepts on any phones or computers that the target may use. This authority for roving wiretaps means that the police no longer need to list the phone numbers to be tapped; the police can listen to any phone that a person might use. This means that the police can listen to all phones where a person works, or shops, or visits. . . . The argument for roving wiretaps is that suspected terrorists might repeatedly change cell phones. The problem with this argument is that the government, by definition, cannot listen to a phone until they know that it exists. Once they know, they could just add the new number to an existing warrant. In debates with FBI agents, the response always has been that it takes too long to add a new number to existing warrants. But this calls for a faster procedure to do so, not roving wiretaps.

One of the most troubling and controversial provisions of the Act is section 215, which provides the Director of the FBI broad authority to obtain records "to protect against international terrorism or clandestine intelligence activities." This allows the FISA Court to issue orders for "production of any tangible things (including books, records, papers, documents, and other items)." When such information is provided, "no person shall disclose to any other person . . . that the [FBI] has sought or obtained tangible things under this section." . . .

Under this provision the government has broad access to records about a person. For example, the government can obtain from libraries a list of the books that a person has borrowed. No probable cause or even reasonable suspicion is required. Nor must the government meet the usual Fourth Amendment requirement to list with specification what is sought; the Act authorizes orders for "production of any tangible thing." A library, or other institution, ordered to produce the information cannot disclose to the person that the request has been made.

* * *

Kathryn Martin, Note, The USA PATRIOT Act's Application to Library Patron Records, 29 J.Legis. 283, 288 (2003):

> There are rumors that the government has used its USA PATRIOT Act special powers to search libraries across the country. The gag order in the Act prevents librarians from sharing with the public the extent and nature of the secret warrants' use.

Orrin S. Kerr, Internet Surveillance Law after the USA PATRIOT Act: The Big Brother that Isn't, 97 Nw. U.L. Rev. 607, 607–608, 624–637, 639, 641–643 (2003):

> The Patriot Act has been widely understood as a "sweeping" anti-terrorism law that gave the government "vast new powers" to conduct electronic surveillance over the Internet. The Act's surveillance provisions proved so controversial that Congress added a sunset provision that will nullify several of its key provisions after four years, on December 31, 2005. To many legislators, the vast law enforcement authorities unleashed by the Patriot Act seemed too dangerous to extend indefinitely.

> The Patriot Act triggered tremendous anxiety in part because few understood exactly what it did. At the time of its passage, even many key legislators seemed to have little idea of the laws governing electronic surveillance, both before the Patriot Act and following it. Did the Act go too far? How much privacy did Internet users have, and how much were they giving away? No one seemed to know, and because the legislation rushed through Congress with remarkable speed, little in the way of Committee reports or other legislative history existed to help explain it. . . .

> . . .

> When we focus on the Internet surveillance provisions that passed into law, however, it becomes clear that the popular understanding of the Patriot Act is substantially wrong. The Patriot Act did not tilt the balance between Internet privacy and security strongly in favor of security. Most of the Patriot Act's key changes reflected reasonable compromises that updated antiquated laws. Some of these changes advance law enforcement interests, but others advance privacy interests, and several do both at the same time. . . .

* * *

Questions

1.   Many criticisms have been leveled at the PATRIOT Act. As some of the preceding textual materials suggest, some of these criticisms may not be meritorious. For example, as Professor Kerr noted, the PATRIOT Act has been criticized for expanding the authority of the government to engage in internet surveillance. Compare the amount of information that the government obtains from placing a pen register on a telephone, which provides information on what numbers were called by a user of that telephone, with the placement of a pen register on an email account which provides a similar type of information, that is, the email addresses to which emails were sent from the targeted account. Does the government learn more or less from the internet surveillance of email addresses to which communications are sent than from the surveillance of telephone numbers which are called? For example, in regard to phone calls emanating from a particular telephone number, does the government learn the location of the caller from the fact that the call was made? Does the government learn the location of the sender of an email from the fact that the email was sent from a particular email address? See Professor Kerr's article on internet surveillance, op. cit. supra, p. at p.. Also see Professor Chemerinsky's comment about the fact that section 216 of the PATRIOT Act authorizes the government to monitor the fact that an individual has visited particular websites:

> The government already has this authority for telephones, but expanding it to electronic communications is troubling because a great deal of information can be learned about a person, some of it misleading, based on a list of web sites visited. 51 UCLA L. Rev. 1619, 1627.

How is information learned about websites visited different from information learned about email addresses to which communications are sent? In light of your consideration of these various questions, what conclusions do you reach about the validity of the criticisms that are being made regarding the provisions of the PATRIOT Act relating to internet surveillance?

2.   How much of an answer is it to criticism of a particular provision that the criticized provision existed in the law prior to the enactment of the PATRIOT Act but was narrowly applicable until the PATRIOT Act expanded its application. See, e.g. the discussion, supra, p. of the so-called sneak and peek provision, section 213 of the Act, authorizing the delaying of notice to a person that his/her premises have been secretly searched. It is not commonly noted in the criticisms of the sneak and peek provision that prior to the PATRIOT Act, judicial practice was to authorize delaying notice of the search in a number of situations, and the effect of section 213 was to provide additional grounds for which the giving of notice could be delayed. How much of an extension of government authority is involved in adding new grounds for delaying notice of a search?

* * *

Chapter 3

DEFINITIONS OF TERRORISM
AND TERRORISM CRIMES

* * *

B. Terrorism: Definitions and definitional approaches

1. In general

Definitions of terrorism that are relevant to the federal criminal enforcement process can be found in various sources and may serve different functions. The most important source for our purposes is statutory: Some statutes contain specific definitions of terrorism; some do not. The concept that makes a crime terrorism is sometimes contained in the elements of the offense even though there is no specific definition of terrorism in the statute. Some non-criminal statutes also contain definitions of terrorism, and these may be incorporated by reference into certain criminal enforcement contexts. Further, one finds examples of definitions of the concept in federal administrative regulations and administrative policy, formal or informal, articulated by various government agencies.

In the United States, both at the federal level and in the states, in the criminal enforcement context, different definitions of the term "terrorism" may be used, but the definitions tend to fall within a certain range and within certain parameters; differences in the definitions are matters of detail. In some other countries and on the international level, however, one finds much less consensus on what constitutes "terrorism" and what definition should be used. The differences lie at a basic level and tend to reflect varying political outlooks and ideological concerns. See Gabriel Soll, Terrorism: The Known Element No One Can Define, 11 Willamette J. Int'l L. & Disp. Resol. 123 (2004); Yonah Alexander, Terrorism in the Twenty-First Century: Threats and Responses, 12 DePaul Bus.L.J. 59 (2004), and see generally, Yonah Alexander & Edgar H. Brenner, Legal Aspects of Terrorism in the United States (2000).

The most common approach in the federal system is one which relies on a general definition formulated in the form of something like, "a purpose to coerce a government to do something or to retaliate against a government." There are variations in the exact terms used in these general definitions, but these differences tend to be matters of degree and detail. Is there anything which commends one variation in preference to the others?

A second category is one which combines the first approach with a list of statutory offenses, with the combination of the two being the marker for terrorism. See, e.g., 18 U.S.C. § 2332b.

A third category simply uses a list of offenses that are deemed terrorism-related offenses. Variation among the approaches that use a listing of offenses may occur as a result of differences in the offenses that are listed. Compare, e.g., 18 U.S.C. § 2339, with § 2339A, and with § 2332b.

A fourth category is one which does not use a definition as such. The fact that the offense is viewed as terrorism flows from the nature of the harmful conduct engaged in. Illustrative are §§ 2332a and 2332f, offenses involving the use of weapons of mass destruction and bombing of public facilities, respectively.

A fifth category is one which arguably uses a surrogate concept for the concept of terrorism—for example, the transcending national boundaries formula found in § 2332b.

Finally, in administrative policy formulations relating to terrorist activity, one finds formulations that tend to be less analytically tight and may combine elements of several of the categories described above as well as others. Of course, some of the administrative formulations simply cross-reference to and rely upon one of the statutory definitions.

The purpose of, or use to which the concept of terrorism is put may vary, and one might expect the definition or definitional approach to that concept to be geared to the relevant purpose or use. For example, the concept of a terrorist purpose may be incorporated into the mens rea of an offense as a measure of its seriousness, or even as an element of the actus reus of the offense indicating the type of conduct that is prohibited, or as a basis for jurisdiction. Or the fact that an offense involved a terrorist element may be relied upon as a sentence enhancing factor under the federal Sentencing Guidelines.

Does the theory of the relevance of the purpose or use help to explain why in some provisions a general definition of terrorism is used while in others a general definition is combined with a listing of specific offenses deemed terrorism-related?

* * *

In a number of instances, criminal or crime-related statutes refer to and incorporate by reference a definition used in another area of the law—for example, the immigration laws. See, e.g., § 2339B. Clearly here a definition originally formulated for one purpose is being used for another.

Not only definitions of terrorism simpliciter are found in these materials. Other terrorism-related concepts are also used, for example, "terrorist activity"; "terrorist organization"; "international terrorism"; and "domestic terrorism." Issues similar to those involving the definition of terrorism also arise regarding the use of these phrases.

In connection with the definitions that are borrowed, the determination of whether a phrase such as "terrorist organization," applies to a particular group or entity may be initially made in an administrative proceeding rather than in the course of the judicial proceedings in which it is later used. In effect, the procedures for applying the definition as well as the definition itself have been borrowed from another area of the law. As we shall see, in Chapter 4, special issues are raised by this type of approach.

2. Statutory definitions of terrorism

... Section 2331, in Title 18, U.S.C. contains definitions that are to be used in Chapter 113B, which contains most of the general terrorism statutes....

* * *

18 U.S.C. § 2331. Definitions

As used in this chapter—

(1) the term "international terrorism" means activities that—

(A) involve violent acts or acts dangerous to human life that are a violation of the criminal laws of the United States or of any State, or that would be a criminal violation if committed within the jurisdiction of the United States or of any State;

(B) appear to be intended—

(i) to intimidate or coerce a civilian population;

(ii) to influence the policy of a government by intimidation or coercion; or

(iii) to affect the conduct of a government by mass destruction, assassination, or kidnapping; and

(C) occur primarily outside the territorial jurisdiction of the United States, or transcend national boundaries in terms of the means by which they are accomplished, the persons they appear intended to intimidate or coerce, or the locale in which their perpetrators operate or seek asylum;

...

(5) the term "domestic terrorism" means activities that—

(A) involve acts dangerous to human life that are a violation of the criminal laws of the United States or of any State;

(B) appear to be intended—

(i) to intimidate or coerce a civilian population;

(ii) to influence the policy of a government by intimidation or coercion; or

(iii) to affect the conduct of a government by mass destruction, assassination, or kidnapping; and

(C) occur primarily within the territorial jurisdiction of the United States.

* * *

4.   Definitions of terrorism: What difference does it make?

Erwin Chemerinsky, Losing Liberties: Applying a Foreign Intelligence Model to Domestic Law Enforcement, 51 UCLA L. Rev. 1619, 1623–1624 (2004):

Section 802 of the Patriot Act provides a definition of "domestic terrorism," which is the predicate for the application of many provisions of the law. The term is defined as activities occurring primarily within the territorial jurisdiction of the United States and involving acts dangerous to human life that are a violation of the criminal laws of the United States or any state and that appear to be intended to either "intimidate or coerce a civilian population," "influence the policy of a government by intimidation or coercion," or "affect the conduct of a government by mass destruction, assassination or kidnaping."

This is an incredibly broad definition. Many lawful protests might be seen as trying to coerce or intimidate government or civilian populations. If they are large enough, they might even be seen as dangerous to human life. An antiwar protest rally where windows are intentionally broken in a federal building could be prosecuted as terrorist activity. Most crimes—from assault to robbery to rape to kidnapping to extortion—are intended to coerce. The result is that the broad powers granted to the government by the Patriot Act are not limited to what common understanding would define as terrorism.

Problems

a.   On July 4, 2002, an Egyptian citizen who was living in Irvine, California but had recently returned from a visit to Egypt pulled a gun at the El Al counter at Los Angeles International Airport, started shooting and killed two people and wounding others before he himself was killed by a security guard. The FBI investigated and, as reported in public statements, concluded it was not a terrorist act. Several newspaper articles discussed the issue. See, e.g. Joe Mathews & Henry Weinstein, A Matter for Debate: Was This a Terrorist Attack? Semantics: To the Israelis, It Seems Clear That It Was. But U.S. Government Officials—from the White House to the FBI—Take a More Cautious Approach, L.A. Times, July 6, 2002 at A17; Greg Kirkorian, LAX Shooter Motivated by Personal Woes, Probe Finds; Investigation: Federal Agents Say Egyptian Man acted Alone When He Opened Fire at El Al Counter on July 4, L.A. Times, Sept. 5, 2002 at Metro section 1. Do you think that under the definition of terrorism that is applied by the FBI, supra, it arguably was a terrorist act? Under any of the other definitions of terrorism presented in these materials, supra? What difference does it make whether the FBI treats it as a terrorist act or not? How important is it to determine whether a criminal act that has been perpetrated was a terrorist act? What difference does it make in the way the crime is treated statistically (and how important is the question of statistical treatment)? Might it affect the crimes with which the perpetrator could have been charged if he had survived?

* * *

c. A terrorism statute enacted by the Virginia legislature in 2002 provides the death penalty for killings committed with "the intent to intimidate or coerce a civilian population or influence the policy, conduct or activities of the government ... through intimidation or coercion." This statute was used to prosecute John Lee Malvo and John Allen Muhammad, accused as snipers who terrorized the Washington D.C. area and made demands for a 10 million dollar ransom. Do you think that the actions of the snipers constitute terrorism, as a general proposition? Under the Virginia statute? Does this mean that any one who engages in an extended crime spree in Virginia might be subject to being prosecuted under the state's terrorism statute?

* * *

Chapter 4

STATUTORY OFFENSES IN TERRORISM PROSECUTIONS; THE CRIMES OF PROVIDING MATERIAL SUPPORT FOR USE IN TERRORIST OFFENSES AND MATERIAL SUPPORT TO A FOREIGN TERRORIST ORGANIZATION: 18 U.S.C. § 2339A AND § 2339B

A. Introduction: Statutory offenses used in prosecuting terrorism cases

Over the course of recent decades, while there had been a number of major terrorism events in, or directly involving the United States, prior to September 11, 2001, there had not been a large number of prosecutions arising out of such events nor a very large body of accumulated criminal case law related to such matters. Among the most well-known of the recent major instances of terrorism prior to September 11, 2001, and some of the prosecutions instituted in their wake were the 1995 Oklahoma City bombing [See United States v. McVeigh, 153 F.3d 1166 (10th Cir.1998)]; the first World Trade Center bombing in 1993 [see, e.g., United States v. Salameh, et al., 261 F.3d 271 (2d Cir. 2001) and see the earlier opinion in the same case, 152 F.3d 88 (1998)]; the 1998 bombings of U.S. embassies in Nairobi, Kenya and Dar Es Salaam, Tanzania [see United States v. Bin Laden et al., 92 F.Supp. 2d 225 (S.D.N.Y.2000)].

Post 9/11, some of the more prominent prosecutions of persons directly or indirectly involved in terrorism-related conduct included: the trial of Zacarias Moussaoui, in the Eastern District of Virginia, 2001, alleged to have been intended to be the so-called 20th terrorist in the 9/11 bombing of the World Trade Center, and the prosecutions of Richard Reid, the so-called shoe bomber; John Walker Lindh, the so-

15

called American Taliban; the so-called Lackawanna six in upstate New York; and James Earnest Ujaama in the state of Washington.

Additionally, several defendants, including Ramzi Yousef were prosecuted and convicted of conspiring to bomb commercial airlines in Southeast Asia, and attorney Lynne Stewart, and others were charged with facilitating the sending of messages between an incarcerated convicted terrorist leader and his cohorts around the world.

Both terrorism crimes as well as more traditional federal crimes are often charged in such cases. These cases also illustrate a recurring phenomenon in federal criminal prosecutions—the charging in a single case of a multiplicity of different offenses, made possible by the overlapping nature of many crimes in the federal criminal code.

McVeigh, for example, was convicted of charges involving use of a weapon of mass destruction, 18 U.S.C. § 2332a, destruction by explosives, 18 U.S.C. § 844, and homicide offenses, 18 U.S.C. §§ 1111 and 1114. The convictions in the Salameh case similarly were based in 18 U.S.C. § 844 as well as using explosives to bomb automobiles used in interstate commerce, with reckless disregard for human life, 18 U.S.C. § 33, assaulting federal officers, § 111, using a destructive device in a crime of violence, 18 U.S.C. § 924, and traveling in interstate commerce with intent to commit certain crimes, 18 U.S.C. § 1952. In the Bin Laden prosecution, the charged offenses involved conspiring to kill U.S. nationals under 18 U.S.C. § 2332 and destruction of national defense facilities, 18 U.S.C. § 2155 as well as offenses that had been used in the earlier cases, namely, Title 18, U.S.C. §§ 844, 2332a and 1111, 1114.

* * *

B.   18 U.S.C. § 2339A and § 2339B

Recognizing that many different statutory offenses can be used in prosecuting conduct relating to terrorism, in this section we focus on two anti-terrorism crimes—18 U.S.C. §§ 2339A and 2339B—that have been charged in the post–9/11 period more frequently than any other terrorism-related offenses. These offenses share certain special characteristics: they are among the most doctrinally innovative of the new terrorism offenses; they can be used to prosecute a wide variety of different kinds of conduct; and they can be invoked relatively early in the chronology of steps toward a completed terrorist act. The government views these offenses as especially important tools in the effort to prevent terrorism.

1.   The statutory provisions

[Ed. Note: Language in the Intelligence Reform and Terrorism Prevention Act of 2004 amended the definition of material support found in § 2339A(b), added another section that both complements and supplements the concept of material support under these statutes, and amended the mens rea language applicable to § 2339B. We reproduce below the pre-IRTPA language of §§ 2339A and 2339B. The new IRTPA language is reproduced infra, pp. ___ – ___.]

§ 2339A. *Providing material support to terrorists*

(a) Offense.—Whoever provides material support or resources or conceals or disguises the nature, location, source, or ownership of material support or resources, knowing or intending that they are to be used in preparation for, or in carrying out, a violation of section 32, 37, 81, 175, 229, 351, 831, 842(m) or (n), 844(f) or (i), 930(c), 956, 1114, 1116, 1203, 1361, 1362, 1363, 1366, 1751, 1992, 1993, 2155, 2156, 2280, 2281, 2332, 2332a, 2332b, 2332c, or 2340A of this title, section 236 of the Atomic Energy Act of 1954 (*42 U.S.C. 2284*), or section 46502 or 60123(b) of title 49, or in preparation for, or in carrying out, the concealment or an escape from the commission of any such violation, or attempts or conspires to do such an act, shall be fined under this title, imprisoned not more than 15 years, or both, and, if the death of any person results, shall be imprisoned for any term of years or for life. A violation of this section may be prosecuted in any Federal judicial district in which the underlying offense was committed, or in any other Federal judicial district as provided by law.

(b) Definition.—In this section, the term "material support or resources" means currency or monetary instruments or financial securities, financial services, lodging, training, expert advice or assistance, safehouses, false documentation or identification, communications equipment, facilities, weapons, lethal substances, explosives, personnel, transportation, and other physical assets, except medicine or religious materials.

§ 2339B. *Providing material support or resources to designated foreign terrorist organizations*

(a) Prohibited activities.—

(1) Unlawful conduct.—Whoever, within the United States or subject to the jurisdiction of the United States, knowingly provides material support or resources to a foreign terrorist organization, or attempts or conspires to do so, shall be fined under this title or imprisoned not more than 15 years, or both, and, if the death of any person results, shall be imprisoned for any term of years or for life.

* * *

. . .

(g) Definitions.—As used in this section—

* * *

(4) the term "material support or resources" has the same meaning as in section 2339A;

. . .

(6) the term "terrorist organization" means an organization designated as a terrorist organization under section 219 of the Immigration and Nationality Act.

* * *

2. The concept of material support as used in § 2339A and § 2339B and the mens rea for § 2339A

While the crimes defined in § 2339A and § 2339B differ in a number of respects, they share in common the concept of material support which is defined in § 2339A(b) for purposes of § 2339A but is then also incorporated by reference into § 2339B.

§ 2339A makes it a federal crime to provide material support knowing that the support is to be used in aid of committing any of the listed offenses. This offense thus resembles liability for complicity in the listed offenses. One of the ways in which 2339A is different from complicity is that it creates a separate substantive offense rather than relying on derivative liability from the principal's offense.

§ 2339B makes it a federal crime knowingly to provide material support or resources to a foreign terrorist organization. This provision establishes a means of attacking terrorist conduct that is largely indirect, albeit through criminal prosecution. Section 2339B is primarily aimed at cutting off the supply of money and other resources to terrorist groups. As we shall see, this offense is also being used to attack the participants or would-be participants in a terrorist organization's activities. Because this criminal offense relies, as one of its elements, on an administrative designation under 8 U.S.C. § 1189 that a foreign organization is a "foreign terrorist organization," it also raises some special issues of administrative law and constitutionality.

In most instances, § 2339B is not relied upon in cases that involve a charge of 2339A and vice versa. On occasion, however, both sections may become involved in the same prosecution, as in the following case.

UNITED STATES v. SATTAR

314 F.Supp.2d 279 (S.D.N.Y. 2004).

Koetl, District Judge.

The defendants—Ahmed Abdel Sattar ("Sattar"), Lynne Stewart ("Stewart"), and Mohammed Yousry ("Yousry")—were charged in a seven-count superseding indictment ("S1 Indictment") filed on November 19, 2003. Count One of the S1 Indictment charges Sattar, Stewart, and Yousry with conspiring to defraud the United States in violation of 18 U.S.C. § 371. Count Two charges Sattar with conspiring to murder and kidnap persons in a foreign country in violation of 18 U.S.C. § § 956(a)(1) and (a)(2)(A). Count Three charges Sattar with soliciting persons to engage in crimes of violence in violation of 18 U.S.C. § 373. Count Four charges Stewart and Yousry with conspiring, in violation of

18 U.S.C. § 371, to provide and conceal material support to be used in preparation for, and in carrying out, the conspiracy alleged in Count Two. Count Five charges Stewart and Yousry with a substantive count of providing and concealing material support to the Count Two conspiracy, in violation of 18 U.S.C. § § 2339A and 2. Counts Six and Seven charge Stewart with making false statements in violation 18 U.S.C. § 1001.

The S1 Indictment supersedes a five-count indictment filed on April 8, 2002 ("original indictment"). Count One of the original indictment charged Sattar, Stewart, Yousry, and Yassir Al–Sirri, a defendant not charged in the S1 Indictment, with conspiring to provide material support and resources to a foreign terrorist organization ("FTO") in violation of 18 U.S.C. § 2339B. Count Two charged the same defendants with providing and attempting to provide material support and resources to an FTO in violation of 18 U.S.C. § § 2339B and 2. Count Three charged Sattar and Al–Sirri with soliciting persons to engage in crimes of violence in violation of 18 U.S.C. § 373. Count Four charged Sattar, Stewart, and Yousry with conspiring to defraud the United States in violation of 18 U.S.C. § 371. And Count Five charged Stewart with making false statements in violation of 18 U.S.C. § § 1001 and 2. *United States v. Sattar,* 272 F.Supp.2d 348, 352–53 (S.D.N.Y.2003). [Ed: Sattar I.]

Sattar, Stewart, and Yousry moved to dismiss the original indictment on various grounds. The defendants argued, among other things, that Counts One and Two were unconstitutionally vague as applied to the conduct alleged against them in the original indictment. Counts One and Two charged the defendants with conspiring to provide, and providing, material support and resources to the Islamic Group, an organization led by Sheikh Abdel Rahman that had been designated an FTO by the Secretary of State. __ Section 2339B of Title 18 incorporates the definition of "material support or resources" from § 2339A, and the definition includes, among other things, "personnel" and "communications equipment." In an Opinion and Order dated July 22, 2003, the Court granted the defendants' motion to dismiss Counts One and Two of the original indictment as void for vagueness as applied to the allegations in the original indictment, where the defendants were alleged in part to have "provided" material support by providing themselves as "personnel" and to have provided "communications equipment" by using their own telephones.

The Government filed the S1 Indictment on November 19, 2003. Sattar and Stewart now move to dismiss the S1 Indictment on numerous grounds. They also move for a bill of particulars and various other relief.

I

A

The S1 Indictment alleges the following facts. From at least the early 1990's until in or about April 2002, Omar Ahmad Ali Abdel Rahman, a/k/a "the Sheikh," a/k/a "Sheikh Omar" ("Sheikh Abdel

Rahman''), an unindicted alleged co-conspirator in Counts One and Two, was an influential and high-ranking member of terrorist organizations based in Egypt and elsewhere. . . .

Sheikh Abdel Rahman allegedly supported and advocated jihad to, among other things: (1) overthrow the Egyptian government and replace it with an Islamic state; (2) destroy the nation of Israel and give the land to the Palestinians; and (3) oppose those governments, nations, institutions, and individuals, including the United States and its citizens, whom he perceived as enemies of Islam and supporters of Egypt and Israel.

Sheikh Abdel Rahman allegedly endorsed terrorism to accomplish his goals. . . . * * *

. . . In October 1995, Sheikh Abdel Rahman was convicted of engaging in a seditious conspiracy to wage a war of urban terrorism against the United States, including the 1993 World Trade Center bombing and a plot to bomb other New York City landmarks. He was also found guilty of soliciting crimes of violence against the United States military and Egyptian president Hosni Mubarak. In 1996 Sheikh Abdel Rahman was sentenced to life imprisonment. His conviction was affirmed on appeal, and became final on January 10, 2000 when the United States Supreme Court refused to hear his case.

The S1 Indictment alleges that both prior to and after his arrest and imprisonment, Sheikh Abdel Rahman was a spiritual leader of an international terrorist group based in Egypt and known as the Islamic Group, a/k/a "Gama'a al-Islamiyya," a/k/a "IG," . . . Sheikh Abdel Rahman allegedly played a key role in defining and articulating the goals, policies, and tactics of the Islamic Group.

Since in or about 1997, Sheikh Abdel Rahman has been incarcerated in various facilities operated by the United States Bureau of Prisons, including the Federal Medical Center in Rochester, Minnesota. The S1 Indictment alleges that, following his arrest, Sheikh Abdel Rahman urged his followers to wage jihad to obtain his release from custody. Sheikh Abdel Rahman's followers, including those associated with the Islamic Group, allegedly shared his views about the reasons for jihad, including the goal of obtaining Sheikh Abdel Rahman's release from United States custody. . . .

The S1 Indictment charges that, after Sheikh Abdel Rahman's arrest, a coalition of alleged terrorists, supporters, and followers, including leaders and associates of the Islamic Group, al Qaeda, the Egyptian Islamic Jihad, and the Abu Sayyaf terrorist group in the Philippines threatened and committed acts of terrorism directed at obtaining the release of Sheikh Abdel Rahman from prison. The Islamic Group allegedly released, in response to the sentence of life imprisonment imposed on Sheikh Abdel Rahman, a statement that warned: "All American interests will be legitimate targets for our struggle until the release of Sheikh Omar Abdel Rahman and his brothers. As the American Government has opted for open confrontation with the Islamic movement and the

Islamic symbols of struggle, [the Islamic Group] swears by God to its irreversible vow to take an eye for any eye." . . .

On or about November 17, 1997, six assassins shot and stabbed a group of tourists visiting an archaeological site in Luxor, Egypt, killing fifty-eight foreign tourists and four Egyptians. The S1 Indictment charges that, before making their exit, the assassins scattered leaflets espousing their support for the Islamic Group and calling for release of Sheikh Abdel Rahman, and inserted one of the leaflets into one victim's slit torso. Following this attack, the Islamic Group allegedly issued a statement that blamed the high number of fatalities on Egyptian government security forces, and warned that the Islamic Group would "continue its military operations as long as the regime does not respond to our demands," which included "the establishment of God's law, cutting relations with the Zionist entity (Israel) . . . and the return of our sheik[h] and emir to his land."

. . . The S1 Indictment further charges that on or about September 21, 2000, an Arabic television station, Al Jazeera, televised a meeting of Taha, Usama Bin Laden (leader of the al Qaeda terrorist organization), and Ayman Al–Zawahiri (former leader of the Egyptian Islamic Jihad organization and one of Bin Laden's top lieutenants). Sitting under a banner that read, "Convention to Support Honorable Omar Abdel Rahman," the three alleged terrorist leaders allegedly pledged jihad to free Sheikh Abdel Rahman from incarceration in the United States. . . .

The S1 Indictment charges that at various times starting in or about July 1997, certain Islamic Group leaders and factions called for an "initiative," or cease-fire, in which the Islamic Group would suspend terrorist operations in Egypt in a tactical effort to persuade the Egyptian government to release Islamic Group leaders, members, and associates who were in prison in Egypt. The S1 Indictment further charges that, in or about February 1998, Usama Bin Laden and Taha, among others, issued a fatwah, a legal ruling issued by an Islamic scholar, that stated, among other things, "We in the name of God, call on every Muslim who believes in God and desires to be rewarded, to follow God's order and kill Americans and plunder their wealth wherever and whenever they find it." . . .

The S1 Indictment alleges that, beginning in or about April 1997, United States authorities, in order to protect the national security, limited certain of Sheikh Abdel Rahman's privileges in prison, including his access to the mail, the media, the telephone, and visitors. At that time, the Bureau of Prisons, at the direction of the Attorney General, imposed Special Administrative Measures ("SAMs") upon Sheikh Abdel Rahman. The alleged purpose of the SAMs was to protect "persons against the risk of death or serious bodily injury" that could result if Sheikh Abdel Rahman were free "to communicate (send or receive) terrorist information." Under the SAMs, Sheikh Abdel Rahman was permitted to call and receive visits only from his immediate family members or his attorneys and their translator. SAMs prohibited communication with any member or representative of the news media, and they required all of Sheikh Abdel Rahman's mail to be screened by federal authorities. The SAMs specifically provided that Sheikh Abdel Rahman's attorneys, before being allowed access to Sheikh Abdel Rahman, were obliged to sign an affirmation acknowledging that that they and their staff would abide fully by the SAMs. The attorneys agreed in the affirmations, among other things, to "only be accompanied by translators for the purpose of communicating with inmate Abdel Rahman concerning legal matters.") Since at least in or about May 1998, the attorneys also agreed not to use "meetings, correspondence, or phone calls with Abdel Rahman to pass messages between third parties (including, but not limited to, the media) and Abdel Rahman."

Stewart was one of Sheikh Abdel Rahman's attorneys during his 1995 criminal trial and continued to act as one of his attorneys following his conviction. Yousry testified as a defense witness at Sheikh Abdel Rahman's 1995 criminal trial and, starting in or about 1997, acted as an Arabic interpreter for communications between Sheikh Abdel Rahman and his attorneys. The S1 Indictment charges that Sattar is a longtime associate of and surrogate for Sheikh Abdel Rahman. The S1 Indictment alleges that, following Sheikh Abdel Rahman's arrest, conviction, sentence, and the imposition of the SAMs, Sattar coordinated efforts to keep Sheikh Abdel Rahman in contact with his co-conspirators and followers. It also alleges that Stewart, through her continued access to Sheikh Abdel Rahman, enabled him to remain in contact with his co-conspirators and followers. And it alleges that Yousry, through his continued access to Sheikh Abdel Rahman and facilitated by Stewart, enabled Sheikh Abdel Rahman to remain in contact with his co-conspirators and followers.

B

Count One of the S1 Indictment alleges that, from in or about June 1997 through in or about April 2002, defendants Sattar, Stewart, and Yousry, as well as Sheikh Abdel Rahman and Taha, together with others known and unknown, in violation of 18 U.S.C. § 371, conspired to defraud the United States by obstructing the Department of Justice and the Bureau of Prisons in the administration and enforcement of the SAMs imposed on Sheikh Abdel Rahman. The S1 Indictment alleges a series of overt acts committed in furtherance of the alleged conspiracy. For example, the S1 Indictment charges that, following a March 1999 prison visit to Sheikh Abdel Rahman by Stewart and Yousry, Sattar disseminated to an unnamed Islamic Group leader, a statement issued by Sheikh Abdel Rahman and directed to Islamic Group leader Taha, a statement that instructed Taha to adhere to the initiative and to make no changes without consulting or informing Sheikh Abdel Rahman. The S1 Indictment also charges that, following a September 1999 prison visit to Sheikh Abdel Rahman by Yousry and one of Sheikh Abdel Rahman's attorneys other than Stewart, Sattar told Taha that Sheikh Abdel Rahman had issued a statement from jail calling for an end to the initiative in response to reports that a raid by Egyptian law enforcement officials that month had resulted in the deaths of four members of the Islamic Group.

On or about May 16, 2000, Stewart signed an affirmation in which she agreed to abide by the terms of the SAMs then in effect on Sheikh Abdel Rahman. The S1 Indictment alleges that during a May 2000 prison visit to Sheikh Abdel Rahman by Stewart and Yousry, Yousry told Sheikh Abdel Rahman and Stewart about the kidnappings by the Abu Sayyaf terrorist group in the Philippines and the group's demand to free Sheikh Abdel Rahman. Stewart allegedly responded, "Good for them." During the same prison visit, Yousry allegedly read Sheikh Abdel Rahman an inflammatory statement by Taha that had recently been published in an Egyptian newspaper. Yousry also allegedly read to Sheikh Abdel Rahman, at Stewart's urging, a letter from Sattar. Sattar's letter allegedly sought Sheikh Abdel Rahman's comments on Sattar's communications with certain Islamic Group leaders, and it also allegedly sought Sheikh Abdel Rahman's endorsement of "the formation of a team that calls for cancellation of the peace initiative or makes threats or escalates things."

The S1 Indictment alleges that while Yousry read Taha's statement and Sattar's letter to Sheikh Abdel Rahman, Stewart actively concealed that fact from the prison guards, in part by instructing Yousry to make it look as if Stewart were communicating with Sheikh Abdel Rahman and Yousry were merely translating, by having Yousry look periodically at Stewart and Sheikh Abdel Rahman in turn, and by pretending to be participating in the conversation with Sheikh Abdel Rahman by making extraneous comments like "chocolate" and "heart attack." Stewart allegedly observed to Yousry that she could "get an award for" her acts, and Yousry allegedly agreed that Stewart should "get an award in acting." On the second day of the May 2000 prison visit, Stewart again allegedly actively concealed the conversation between Yousry and Sheikh Abdel Rahman in which Sheikh Abdel Rahman dictated letters to Yousry about the cease-fire.

Following the May 2000 prison visit, Sattar is alleged to have had telephone conversations with Islamic Group leaders in which he stated that Sheikh Abdel Rahman did not object to a return to "work" (which the S1 Indictment describes as "terrorist operations"), that Sheikh Abdel Rahman agreed that the Islamic Group should escalate the issues in the media, that he advised the Islamic Group to avoid division in its leadership, and that he instructed the Islamic Group to hint at a military operation even if the Islamic Group was not ready for military action. The S1 Indictment also alleges that on or about June 14, 2000, Stewart released a statement to the press that quoted Sheikh Abdel Rahman as stating that he "is withdrawing his support for the cease-fire that currently exists." The S1 Indictment further alleges that on or about June 20, 2002, Sattar advised Mohammed Abdel Rahman by telephone that Sheikh Abdel Rahman had had a conference call with some of his attorneys that morning and that Sheikh Abdel Rahman had issued a new statement clarifying that he was not unilaterally ending the initiative, but rather was withdrawing his support and stated that it was up to the "brothers" in the Islamic Group to reconsider the issue.

The S1 Indictment also alleges that in October 2000, Taha and Sattar discussed a fatwah that Taha had written under Sheikh Abdel Rahman's name in response to recent events in the Middle East, and that Sattar made revisions to the fatwah. A In a subsequent phone call on or about October 11, 2000, Yousry allegedly told Stewart that Sheikh Abdel Rahman did not want his attorneys to deny that he had issued the fatwah. And during an attorney telephone call to Sheikh Abdel Rahman on or about October 20, 2000, Sheikh Abdel Rahman told Yousry that he did not personally issue the fatwah, but did not want anyone to deny he had made it because "it is good."

On or about October 25, 2000, the S1 Indictment charges, Sattar spoke by telephone to Taha, who told Sattar that "an Egyptian male" was involved in the bombing of the U.S.S. Cole, and that Sattar should assist in delivering a message to the United States government suggesting that similar attacks would occur unless Sheikh Abdel Rahman were freed from prison.

On or about May 7, 2001, Stewart signed an affirmation in which she agreed to abide by the terms of the SAMs then in effect on Sheikh Abdel Rahman. The S1 Indictment charges that, on or about July 13, 2001, during a prison visit to Sheikh Abdel Rahman by Stewart and Yousry, Yousry told Sheikh Abdel Rahman that Sattar had been informed that the U.S.S. Cole had been bombed on Sheikh Abdel Rahman's behalf and that Sattar was asked to convey to the United States government that more terrorist acts would follow if the United States government did not release Sheikh Abdel Rahman from custody. While Yousry was speaking to Sheikh Abdel Rahman, Stewart allegedly actively concealed the conversation between Sheikh Abdel Rahman and Yousry from prison guards by, among other things, shaking a water jar and tapping on the table while stating that she was "just doing covering noise." The S1 Indictment further charges that on a second day of the prison visit by Stewart and Yousry, Yousry read letters to Sheikh Abdel Rahman and Sheikh Abdel Rahman dictated responsive letters to Yousry.

The S1 Indictment also alleges that on or about January 8, 2001, Sattar informed Stewart by telephone that a prison administrator where Sheikh Abdel Rahman was incarcerated had pleaded with Sheikh Abdel Rahman's wife to tell Sheikh Abdel Rahman to take insulin for his diabetes. Sattar and Stewart allegedly agreed that Sattar would issue a public statement falsely claiming that the Bureau of Prisons was denying medical treatment to Sheikh Abdel Rahman, even though Sattar and Stewart allegedly knew that Sheikh Abdel Rahman was voluntarily refusing to take insulin for his diabetes. Stewart allegedly expressed the opinion that this misrepresentation was "safe" because no one on the "outside" would know the truth. The S1 Indictment further alleges that

Sattar and Al–Sirri thereafter wrote a statement falsely claiming that Sheikh Abdel Rahman was being denied insulin by the United States Government, a statement that Sattar and Al–Sirri disseminated to several news organizations, including Reuters, and on a website.

. . .

Count Four charges that, from in or about September 1999 through in or about April 2002, defendants Stewart and Yousry, together with others, conspired, in violation of 18 U.S.C. § 371, to violate 18 U.S.C. § 2339A. The alleged object of the conspiracy was to provide material support and resources, in the form of personnel, by making Sheikh Abdel Rahman available as a co-conspirator, and to conceal and disguise the nature, location, and source of personnel by concealing and disguising that Sheikh Abdel Rahman was a co-conspirator. The S1 Indictment charges that Stewart and Yousry carried out this conspiracy knowing and intending that such material support and resources were to be used in preparation for, and in carrying out, the conspiracy charged in Count Two of the S1 Indictment—namely, the conspiracy to kill and kidnap persons in a foreign country—and in preparation for, and in carrying out, the concealment of such violation. Count Four realleges various overt acts in furtherance of the alleged conspiracy. Count Five charges defendants Stewart and Yousry with committing the substantive offense of violating 18 U.S.C. §§ 2339A and that was the object of the conspiracy charged in Count Four.

Counts Six and Seven charge defendant Stewart with having made false statements in her affirmations submitted to the United States Attorney's Office for the Southern District of New York, in May 2000 and May 2001, respectively, stating that she would abide by the terms of the SAMs imposed on Sheikh Abdel Rahman, that the translators accompanying her on prison visits would be used only for communications concerning legal matters, and that she would not use any communication with Sheikh Abdel Rahman to pass messages between Sheikh Abdel Rahman and third parties, including, but not limited to, the media. The May 2001 affirmation is also alleged to be false in stating that Stewart "will only allow the meetings to be used for legal discussion between Abdel Rahman and [her]."

C

* * *

II

Stewart moves to dismiss Counts Four and Five on a number of grounds. Counts Four and Five charge Stewart and Yousry with conspiring to violate, and violating, 18 U.S.C. § 2339A.

. . .

Counts Four and Five charge that Stewart and Yousry conspired to provide, and did in fact provide, material support knowing or intending that it would be used in preparation for, or in carrying out, the conspiracy charged in Count Two—the conspiracy to kill and kidnap persons in a foreign country in violation of 18 U.S.C. § 956—by making Sheikh Abdel Rahman available as a co-conspirator in the Count Two conspiracy. The Counts also charge that Stewart and Yousry conspired to, and did in fact, conceal and disguise the nature, location, and source of Sheikh Abdel Rahman as personnel preparing for, or carrying out, the conspiracy charged in Count Two. The S1 Indictment alleges, among other things, that Stewart and Yousry used prison visits with Sheikh Abdel Rahman to pass messages between Sheikh Abdel Rahman and his alleged Count Two co-conspirators, including Sattar. It also alleges that Stewart and Yousry took steps to conceal their efforts to pass messages between Sheikh Abdel Rahman and the alleged Count Two co-conspirators.

The charges in Counts Four and Five of the S1 Indictment differ from those in Counts One and Two in the original indictment that the Court previously dismissed. While the factual allegations are similar, the critical statute is different, the elements of the offense, including scienter, are different, and the allegations as to how the defendants' conduct violated the statute are different.

Counts One and Two of the original indictment charged that Sattar, Stewart, and Yousry conspired to violate 18 U.S.C. § 2339B and committed a substantive violation of that statute by, among other means, providing themselves as "personnel" to a designated FTO and by providing "communications equipment" to an FTO by using their own telephones to further the goals of an FTO. Title 18 U.S.C. § 2339B, which was enacted about a year and a half after 18 U.S.C. § 2339A was enacted, makes it a crime to, in relevant part, "knowingly provide[ ] material support or resources to a foreign terrorist organization." Section 2339B incorporates the definition of "material support or resources" from 18 U.S.C. § 2339A, and that definition includes, among other things, "personnel" and "communications equipment." Title 18 U.S.C. § 2339A, at issue in the S1 Indictment, and which Stewart and Yousry are alleged to have violated, does not penalize the provision of material support or resources to an FTO, but rather makes it a crime to provide material support or resources or conceal or disguise the nature, location, or source of such material support or resources "knowing or intending that they are to be used in preparation for, or in carrying out, a violation" of specific violent crimes—in this case, a violation of 18 U.S.C. § 956, which prohibits a conspiracy to kill or kidnap persons in a foreign country. In the opinion dismissing Counts One and Two of the original indictment, the Court contrasted the intent requirements of the two statutes: "Section 2339B, which is alleged to have been violated [in the original indictment], requires only that a person 'knowingly' 'provides' 'material support or resources' to a 'foreign terrorist organization.' Section 2339A criminalizes the provision of 'material support or resources' 'knowing or intending that they are to be used in preparation for, or in carrying out,' a violation of various criminal statutes."

The Court dismissed Counts One and Two of the original indictment as unconstitutionally vague as applied to the conduct alleged in those counts. Concerning the "provision" of "communications equipment," the Court held that "by criminalizing the mere use of phones and other means of communication the statute provides neither notice nor standards for its application such that it is unconstitutionally vague as applied." The Court further concluded that by prohibiting the "provision" of "personnel," including oneself, to a "foreign terrorist organization," § 2339B could conceivably apply to someone engaging in advocacy on behalf of such an organization, conduct protected by the First Amendment. The Court noted that mere membership in an organization could not be prohibited without a requirement that the Government prove the defendants' specific intent to further the FTO's unlawful ends, . . . but the statute provided no means to distinguish providing oneself to an organization from mere membership in the organization.

The S1 Indictment, on the other hand, which charges a violation of 18 U.S.C. § 2339A rather than § 2339B, no longer charges Stewart and Yousry with providing themselves as personnel to an FTO, but rather with providing and conspiring to provide personnel—by making Sheikh Abdel Rahman, not themselves, available as a co-conspirator—to the conspiracy alleged in Count Two, namely the conspiracy to kill and kidnap persons in a foreign country. It also charges them with concealing and disguising the nature, location, and source of that personnel by disguising that Sheikh Abdel Rahman was a co-conspirator. These actions were allegedly done with the knowledge and intent that such personnel was to be used in preparation for, or in carrying out, the conspiracy to kill and kidnap persons in a foreign country. This is the heightened specific intent required by § 2339A.

Stewart argues that, despite the changes from the original indictment, the charges in Counts Four and Five of the S1 Indictment should be dismissed because 18 U.S.C. § 2339A should not be interpreted to reach the conduct alleged in Counts Four and Five, because § 2339A is unconstitutionally vague as applied to the allegations in the S1 Indictment, and because the statute is unconstitutionally overbroad.

A

Stewart argues initially that 18 U.S.C. § 2339A does not cover the conduct in which she allegedly engaged. The S1 Indictment charges that Stewart and Yousry "provided" "personnel" by "making Abdel Rahman available" as a co-conspirator in the conspiracy to kill and kidnap persons in a foreign country. Stewart alleges that "provides" should not be interpreted to include "makes available" and that "personnel" should not include Sheikh Abdel Rahman. Stewart contends that the term "making available" does not define the term "provides," but rather represents an impermissible attempt by the Government to expand the statute's reach. Stewart would limit the word "provides" to the physical transfer of an item.

The term "provides" is not defined in § 2339A. Where words in a statute are not defined, they "must be given their ordinary meaning." ... The plain and ordinary meaning of the transitive verb "provide" is "[t]o furnish; supply ... [t]o make ready ... [t]o make available; afford." *Webster's II: New Riverside University Dictionary* 948 (1994); *see also The American Heritage Dictionary of the English Language* 1411 (4th ed.2000) (defining "provide" to include such meanings as "[t]o furnish; supply" and "[t]o make available; afford").

Moreover, statutory terms are to be interpreted in their context in light of their "placement and purpose in the statutory scheme. In this case, "provides" is the verb used for a variety of items defined as "material support or resources," including "financial services, lodging, training, ... [and] transportation...." 18 U.S.C. § 2339A(b). A defendant would reasonably be providing material support or resources by making these items or services available with the requisite knowledge or intent. Limiting the definition of "provides" to the physical transfer of an asset would result in a strained and untenable reading of the statute. Thus, there is no basis to limit the meaning of "provides ... personnel" to the physical transfer of personnel, and not to include making personnel available—which is in accord with the ordinary and natural use of the term "provide," and which is consistent with its placement in the statute and the purpose of proscribing the provision of resources to be used for a prohibited purpose.

. . .

Stewart also raises questions whether the meaning of "personnel" in the statute can be interpreted to include Sheikh Abdel Rahman. However, the Government is correct that, in using the term "personnel" in § 2339A, Congress plainly intended to refer to persons engaged in "prepar[ing] for" or "carry[ing] out" one of the crimes specified in § 2339A, or in "prepar[ing] for" or "carry[ing] out[ ] the concealment or an escape from the commission of any such" crime—that is, persons who are jointly involved in participating in those crimes. This meaning comports with the plain meaning of "personnel," which is defined as "[t]he body of persons employed by or active in an organization, business, or service." *Webster's II: New Riverside University Dictionary* 877 (1994)....

Stewart also argues that the rule of lenity should be used to avoid the application of the statute to her alleged provision of Sheikh Abdel Rahman as personnel to the alleged conspiracy to kill and kidnap persons in a foreign country. However, the language and context of the terms in the statute, "provides" and "personnel" are not ambiguous terms in the statute, and the ordinary meaning of those terms in the context of the statute covers making Sheikh Abdel Rahman available to the conspiracy to kill and kidnap persons in a foreign country. The rule of lenity provides no argument to the contrary. . . .

* * *

B

Stewart also argues that § 2339A is unconstitutionally vague in its proscription of "provid[ing]" material support or resources in the form of "personnel," and in its proscription of "conceal[ing] or disguis[ing] the nature, location, [or] source" of "personnel." Stewart contends that § 2339A does not provide fair notice of the acts that are prohibited by its proscription of providing personnel.

. . .

In light of the plain meaning of the term "personnel" as used in the context of § 2339A, Stewart's reliance on cases, including this Court's prior opinion, that have found the term "personnel" in 18 U.S.C. § 2339B unconstitutionally vague is misplaced. Section 2339B makes it a crime to "provide[ ] material support or resources to a foreign terrorist organization" that has been designated as such by the Secretary of State. 18 U.S.C. § 2339B(a)(1), (g)(6). The statute's potential reach raises significant First Amendment concerns, because § 2339B's ban on providing personnel to a "foreign terrorist organization" could trench upon associational and expressive freedoms—including pure advocacy—protected by the First Amendment. The statute, as this Court explained, was particularly problematic as applied to the conduct of persons allegedly providing themselves as personnel to the organization. . . . The Court of Appeals for the Ninth Circuit has held that these concerns are not displaced even when 18 U.S.C.§ 2339B is construed to include a requirement that the accused knew of the organization's designation as an FTO or of the organization's unlawful activities that caused it to be so designated. *See Humanitarian Law Project v. U.S. Dept. of Justice*, 352 F.3d 382, 404–05 (9th Cir.2003).[11]

The First Amendment concerns raised by the use of "personnel" in § 2339B, as applied to persons who provided themselves as "personnel" to an organization, are simply not present in this case. Section 2339A is being applied to persons who allegedly provided other personnel "knowing and intending that [it is] to be used in preparation for, or in carrying out" a violation of specific statutes, in this case a conspiracy to kill or kidnap persons in a foreign country. The allegations in this case do not concern the scope of membership in an organization or the permissible extent of advocacy. . . .

* * * A defendant cannot complain about a lack of notice when the statute requires a high level of specific intent for a violation. . . . Section

---

11. The meaning of "personnel" is clear in the context of § 2339A when applied to personnel who are to be used in preparation for, or in carrying out, specific crimes. Moreover, the Government in this case has not sought to apply § 2339A to the provision by a person of himself or herself to such activity, and § 2339A does not raise the issues of providing "personnel" to an organization. . . .

2339A applies only to those people who provide material support or resources "knowing or intending" that the support or resources are to be used in preparation for, or in carrying out, a violation of enumerated criminal statutes, in this case a conspiracy to kill and kidnap persons in a foreign country. . . .

Stewart contends that the statute is unconstitutionally vague because a conscientious lawyer representing her client could not avoid "making her client 'available' through . . . services that a lawyer regularly and lawfully performs." Lawyers, including defense lawyers, are not immune from criminal liability arising out of offenses committed while representing clients, and indeed defense counsel conceded at argument that lawyers have no license to violate generally applicable criminal laws.

. . .

In this case, Stewart has not demonstrated that § 2339A, on its face or in actual fact, prohibits any constitutionally protected expression, much less that any possible overbreadth is "substantial" when judged in relation to the statute's plainly legitimate sweep. The motion to dismiss on overbreadth grounds is therefore denied.

Notes and Questions

* * *

c.   What advantages, if any, did the government gain by changing the offense charged from 2339B to 2339A?

d.   Why do you think the government changed its theory of "material support"? What was the exact nature of the change?

* * *

5.   Does Sattar II extend criminal liability based on a mens rea of knowledge too far? See generally, Norman Abrams, The Material Support Terrorism Offenses: Perspectives Derived from the (Early) Model Penal Code, 1 J.Nat Sec.L. & Policy 5 (2005).

* * *

3.   The mens rea for § 2339B

Note: After the issuance of the following opinion in the Humanitarian Law Project case, a motion to rehear the matter en banc was granted and the following opinion was vacated. The instruction accompanying the notice that the case was to be reheard en banc indicated the three judge opinion was not to be cited except to the extent it was adopted by the court. 382 F. 3d 1154 (9th Cir. 2004). Despite the fact that it has been vacated, it is useful to read the following opinion. The en banc opinion is reproduced following the case at p. ___.

HUMANITARIAN LAW PROJECT v. U.S. DEPARTMENT OF JUSTICE

352 F.3d 382 (9th Cir. 2003)(vacated by 382 F.3d 1154).

Appeal from the United States District Court for the Central District of California Audrey B. Collins, District Judge, Presiding.

Before: PREGERSON, THOMAS, and RAWLINSON, Circuit Judges.

PREGERSON, Circuit Judge.

In 1996, President Clinton signed into law the Antiterrorism and Effective Death Penalty Act of 1996 ("AEDPA"). Two provisions of AEDPA, section 302 and section 303, codified at 8 U.S.C. § 1189 and 18 U.S.C. § 2339B, authorize the Secretary of State ("Secretary") to designate an organization as a "foreign terrorist organization," and make it a crime with a maximum penalty of life in prison for a person to provide "material support or resources" [hereinafter "material support"] to a designated organization, respectively. This case addresses the question whether a criminal prosecution under 18 U.S.C. § 2339B requires the government to prove as an element of the offense that the defendant knew the organization had been designated by the Secretary as a foreign terrorist organization, or at least knew of the organization's unlawful activities leading to its designation.

Plaintiffs are legal and social service organizations and two individuals who seek to provide "material support" to the non-violent humanitarian and political activities of Kurdish and Tamil organizations the Secretary designated as "foreign terrorist organizations." Each of the plaintiffs has a history of donating money and services to support the designated organizations' humanitarian work, which assists refugees and ethnic minorities displaced by decades of conflict in securing the basic necessities for human life. Plaintiffs no longer provide such support in fear of criminal sanctions under 18 U.S.C. § 2339B.

Except for a recently asserted Fifth Amendment due process claim, this is the second time that the constitutional issues raised by plaintiffs are before us. In 2000, we decided *Humanitarian Law Project v. Reno,* 205 F.3d 1130 (9th Cir.2000), *cert. denied,* 532 U.S. 904 (2001) ("*Humanitarian Law Project II*"). . . . We agreed with the district court that 18 U.S.C. § 2339B did not violate the First Amendment by allegedly imposing guilt by association and restricting symbolic speech. We also rejected, as did the district court, the plaintiffs' argument that the designation process set forth in 8 U.S.C. § 1189 ran afoul of the First and Fifth Amendments by granting the Secretary overbroad discretion to designate organizations as "foreign terrorist organizations." In addition, we affirmed the district court's partial grant of preliminary injunctive relief that restrained the government's enforcement of two terms included in the definition of "material support," found in 18 U.S.C. § 2339A, i.e., "personnel" and "training." On remand, the district court reaffirmed its prior rulings and issued a permanent injunction that restrained the government from enforcing 18 U.S.C. § 2339B against plaintiffs were they to provide material support in the form of "training" and "personnel" to designated organizations. The government appeals and plaintiffs cross-appeal.

We hold that *Humanitarian Law Project II* is the law of the case; therefore, we decline to revisit the plaintiffs' constitutional challenges to 8 U.S.C. § 1189 and 18 U.S.C. § 2339B, that we previously resolved. We will, however, address plaintiffs' recently asserted Fifth Amendment due process challenge on this appeal, and hold that 18 U.S.C. § 2339B, by not requiring proof of personal guilt, raises serious Fifth Amendment due process concerns. But we conclude that there is no need to address those constitutional concerns because we construe 18 U.S.C. § 2339B to require proof that a person charged with violating the statute had knowledge of the organization's designation or knowledge of the unlawful activities that caused it to be so designated. In addition, we reaffirm our decision in *Humanitarian Law Project II* that the prohibition on providing "training" and "personnel" in § 2339B is impermissibly overbroad, and thus void for vagueness under the First and Fifth Amendments.

. . .

* * *

HUMANITARIAN LAW PROJECT
v. UNITED STATES DOJ

393 F.3d 902 (9th Cir. 2004) (en banc).

JUDGES: Before: SCHROEDER, Chief Judge, KOZINSKI, KLEINFELD, THOMAS, GRABER, McKEOWN, WARDLAW, GOULD, TALLMAN, CALLAHAN, and BEA, Circuit Judges.

With respect to the appellants' First Amendment challenge to sections 302 and 303 of the Antiterrorism and Effective Death Penalty Act of 1996, we affirm the district court's order dated October 2, 2001, for the reasons set out in Humanitarian Law Project v. Reno, 205 F.3d 1130 (9th Cir. 2000). In light of Congress's recent amendment to the challenged statute, the Intelligence Reform and Terrorism Prevention Act of 2004, Pub. L. No. 108–458, 118 Stat. 3638, we affirm the judgment in part, as set forth above, vacate the judgment and injunction regarding the terms "personnel" and "training," and remand to the district court for further proceedings, if any, as appropriate. We decline to reach any other issue urged by the parties.

Notes and Questions

1. The decision in Humanitarian Law Project v. Reno, 205 F.3d 1130 (labeled in Judge Pregerson's opinion, supra, as Humanitarian Law Project II, but in the Al-Arian case, infra, as Humanitarian Law Project I) and

referred to in the en banc opinion supra, was written by Judge Kozinski. After rejecting several first amendment claims made by the plaintiffs, Judge Kozinski went on to state:

> Finally, Plaintiffs challenge AEDPA on vagueness grounds. In the district court, they alleged that "foreign terrorist organization" and "material support," as defined in AEDPA, were void for vagueness. The district court agreed in part, finding that two of the components included within the definition of material support, "training" and "personnel," were impermissibly vague. It enjoined the prosecution of any of the plaintiffs' members for activities covered by these terms. The district court did not abuse its discretion in doing so.
>
> When a criminal law implicates First Amendment concerns, the law must be "sufficiently clear so as to allow persons of 'ordinary intelligence a reasonable opportunity to know what is prohibited.'" It is easy to see how someone could be unsure about what AEDPA prohibits with the use of the term "personnel," as it blurs the line between protected expression and unprotected conduct. ... Someone who advocates the cause of the PKK could be seen as supplying them with personnel; it even fits under the government's rubric of freeing up resources, since having an independent advocate frees up members to engage in terrorist activities instead of advocacy. But advocacy is pure speech protected by the First Amendment.
>
> In order to keep the statute from trenching on such advocacy, the government urges that we read into it a requirement that the activity prohibited be performed "under the direction or control" of the foreign terrorist organization. While we construe a statute in such a way as to avoid constitutional questions, we are not authorized to rewrite the law so it will pass constitutional muster....
>
> The term "training" fares little better. Again, it is easy to imagine protected expression that falls within the bounds of this term. For example, a plaintiff who wishes to instruct members of a designated group on how to petition the United Nations to give aid to their group could plausibly decide that such protected expression falls within the scope of the term "training." The government insists that the term is best understood to forbid the imparting of skills to foreign terrorist organizations through training. Yet, presumably, this definition would encompass teaching international law to members of designated organizations. The result would be different if the term "training" were qualified to include only military training or training in terrorist activities. Because plaintiffs have demonstrated that they are likely to succeed on the merits of their claim with respect to the terms "training" and "personnel," we conclude that the district court did not abuse its discretion in issuing its limited preliminary injunction.[5]

* * *

---

5. The government invites us to cure any possible vagueness problems with the statute by including the term "knowingly" in it. However, the term "knowingly" modifies the verb "provides," meaning that the only scienter requirement here is that the accused violator have knowledge of the fact that he has provided something, not knowl-

UNITED STATES v. AL–ARIAN

308 F.Supp.2d 1322 (M.D. Fla. 2004).

JAMES S. MOODY, JR., UNITED STATES DISTRICT JUDGE.

This is a criminal action against alleged members of the Palestinian Islamic Jihad–Shiqaqi Faction (the "PIJ") who purportedly operated and directed fundraising and other organizational activities in the United States for almost twenty years. The PIJ is a foreign organization that uses violence, principally suicide bombings, and threats of violence to pressure Israel to cede territory to the Palestinian people. On February 19, 2003, the government indicted the defendants in a 50 count indictment that included counts for: (1) conspiracy to commit racketeering (Count 1); (2) conspiracy to commit murder, maim, or injure persons outside the United States (Count 2); (3) conspiracy to provide material support to or for the benefit of foreign terrorists (Counts 3 and 4); (4) violations of the Travel Act (Counts 5 through 44); (5) violation of the immigration laws of the United States (Counts 45 and 46); (6) obstruction of justice (Count 47); and (7) perjury (Counts 48 through 50).

. . .

In X–Citement Video, the Supreme Court faced almost the same statutory interpretation issues faced in this case. There, the Supreme Court considered the Protection of Children Against Sexual Exploitation Act, 18 U.S.C. § 2252. 513 U.S. at 65–66. Section 2252 of that Act made it unlawful for any person to "knowingly" transport, ship, receive, distribute, or reproduce a visual depiction involving a "minor engaging in sexually explicit conduct." The Ninth Circuit had interpreted "knowingly" to only modify the surrounding verbs, like transport or ship. See id. Under this construction, whether a defendant knew the minority of the performer(s) or even knew whether the material was sexually explicit was inconsequential. The Supreme Court reversed, concluding that, while the Ninth Circuit's construction of Section 2252 complied with the plain meaning rule, the construction caused absurd results. Under the Ninth Circuit's construction, the Court noted that a Federal Express courier who knew that there was film in a package could be convicted even though the courier had no knowledge that the film contained child pornography. To avoid such results, the Court utilized the cannons of statutory construction to imply a "knowing" requirement to each element, including the age of the performers and the sexually explicit nature of the material. . . .

. . .

. . . [In Humanitarian II,] the Ninth Circuit reconsidered its interpretation of the *mens rea* requirement in Humanitarian I. Under its new interpretation, the Ninth Circuit concluded that Section 2339B also required proof that a person either knew: (a) that an organization was a

edge of the fact that what is provided in fact constitutes material support.

FTO; or (b) of an organization's unlawful activities that caused it to be designated as a FTO. The Ninth Circuit then reaffirmed its prior holding on the vagueness of "personnel" and "training" without analyzing how the change in the *mens rea* requirement affected its prior vagueness analysis.

. . .

[L]ike Humanitarian II, this Court agrees that this construction renders odd results and raises serious constitutional concerns. For example under Humanitarian I, a donor could be convicted for giving money to a FTO without knowledge that an organization was a FTO or that it committed unlawful activities, and without an intent that the money be used to commit future unlawful activities.

Humanitarian II attempted to correct this odd result and accompanying constitutional concerns by interpreting "knowingly" to mean that a person knew: (a) an organization was a FTO; or (b) an organization committed unlawful activities, which caused it to be designated a FTO. But, Humanitarian II's construction of Section 2339B only cures some of the Fifth Amendment concerns. First, Humanitarian II fails to comply with X–Citement Video's holding that a *mens rea* requirement "should apply to each of the statutory elements that criminalize otherwise innocent conduct." Humanitarian II implies only a *mens rea* requirement to the FTO element of Section 2339B(a)(1) and not to the material support element. Under Humanitarian II's construction, a cab driver could be guilty for giving a ride to a FTO member to the UN, if he knows that the person is a member of a FTO or the member or his organization at sometime conducted an unlawful activity in a foreign country. Similarly, a hotel clerk in New York could be committing a crime by providing lodging to that same FTO member under similar circumstances as the cab driver. Because the Humanitarian II's construction fails to avoid potential Fifth Amendment concerns, this Court rejects its construction of Section 2339B.

Second, the Humanitarian II construction does not solve the constitutional vagueness concerns of Section 2339B(a)(1), which can be avoided by implying a *mens rea* requirement to the "material support or resources" element of Section 2339B(a)(1). If this Court accepted the Humanitarian II construction, it would likely have to declare many more categories of "material support" (in addition to "training" and "personnel" determined to be unconstitutionally vague in the Humanitarian cases) unconstitutionally vague for impinging on advocacy rights, including "financial services," "lodging," "safe houses," "communications equipment," "facilities," "transportation" and "other physical assets." Using the Ninth Circuit's vagueness example on "training," the statute could likewise punish other innocent conduct, such as where a person in New York City (where the United Nations is located) gave a FTO member a ride from the airport to the United Nations before the member petitioned the United Nations. Such conduct could be punished as providing "transportation" to a FTO under Section 2339B. The end result of the Ninth Circuit's statutory construction in Humanitarian II is to render a substantial portion of Section 2339B unconstitutionally vague.

But, it is not necessary to do such serious damage to the statute if one follows the analysis used by the United States Supreme Court in X–Citement Video. This Court concludes that it is more consistent with Congress's intent, which was to prohibit material support from FTOs to the "fullest possible basis," to imply a *mens rea* requirement to the "material support" element of Section 2339B(a)(1). Therefore, this Court concludes that to convict a defendant under Section 2339B(a)(1) the government must prove beyond a reasonable doubt that the defendant knew that: (a) the organization was a FTO or had committed unlawful activities that caused it to be so designated; and (b) what he was furnishing was "material support." To avoid Fifth Amendment personal guilt problems, this Court concludes that the government must show more than a defendant knew something was within a category of "material support" in order to meet (b). In order to meet (b), the government must show that the defendant knew (had a specific intent) that the support would further the illegal activities of a FTO.

This Court does not believe this burden is that great in the typical case. Often, such an intent will be easily inferred. For example, a jury could infer a specific intent to further the illegal activities of a FTO when a defendant knowingly provides weapons, explosives, or lethal substances to an organization that he knows is a FTO because of the nature of the support. Likewise, a jury could infer a specific intent when a defendant knows that the organization continues to commit illegal acts and the defendant provides funds to that organization knowing that money is fungible and, once received, the donee can use the funds for any purpose it chooses. That is, by its nature, money carries an inherent danger for furthering the illegal aims of an organization. Congress said as much when it found that FTOs were "so tainted by their criminal conduct that any contribution to such an organization facilitates that conduct."

This opinion in no way creates a safe harbor for terrorists or their supporters to try and avoid prosecution through utilization of shell "charitable organizations" or by directing money through the memo line of a check towards lawful activities.[35] This Court believes that a jury can quickly peer through such facades when appropriate. This is especially true if other facts indicate a defendant's true intent, like where defendants or conspirators utilize codes or unusual transaction practices to transfer funds. Instead, this Court's holding works to avoid potential constitutional problems and fully accomplish congressional intent.

---

35. For example, a donation to a suicide bomber's family given with the intent to encourage others to engage in such activities or support such activities would satisfy this specific intent requirement.

Notes and Questions

1. Congress passed the following legislation on the subject of material support as part of the Intelligence Reform and Terrorism Protection Act of 2004:

Subtitle G—Providing Material Support to Terrorism

SEC. 6601. SHORT TITLE.

This subtitle may be cited as the "Material Support to Terrorism Prohibition Enhancement Act of 2004".

SEC. 6602. RECEIVING MILITARY–TYPE TRAINING FROM A FOREIGN TERRORIST ORGANIZATION.

Chapter 113B of title 18, United States Code, is amended by adding after section 2339C the following new section:

Sec. 2339D. Receiving military-type training from a foreign terrorist organization

(a) Offense.—Whoever knowingly receives military-type training from or on behalf of any organization designated at the time of the training by the Secretary of State under section 219(a)(1) of the Immigration and Nationality Act as a foreign terrorist organization shall be fined under this title or imprisoned for ten years, or both. To violate this subsection, a person must have knowledge that the organization is a designated terrorist organization (as defined in subsection (c)(4)), that the organization has engaged or engages in terrorist activity (as defined in section 212 of the Immigration and Nationality Act), or that the organization has engaged or engages in terrorism (as defined in section 140(d)(2) of the Foreign Relations Authorization Act, Fiscal Years 1988 and 1989).

* * *

SEC. 6603. ADDITIONS TO OFFENSE OF PROVIDING MATERIAL SUPPORT TO TERRORISM.

(a) In General.—Chapter 113B of title 18, United States Code, is amended—

. . .

(b) Definitions.—Section 2339A(b) of title 18, United States Code, is amended to read as follows:

(b) Definitions.—As used in this section—

(1) the term 'material support or resources' means any property, tangible or intangible, or service, including currency or monetary instruments or financial securities, financial services, lodging, training, expert advice or assistance, safehouses, false documentation or identification, communications equipment, facilities, weapons, lethal substances, explosives, personnel (1 or more individuals who may be or include oneself), and transportation, except medicine or religious materials;

(2) the term 'training' means instruction or teaching designed to impart a specific skill, as opposed to general knowledge; and

(3) the term 'expert advice or assistance' means advice or assistance derived from scientific, technical or other specialized knowledge.

(c) Terrorist Organizations.—Section 2339B(a)(1) of title 18, United States Code, is amended—

. . .

(2) by adding at the end the following: "To violate this paragraph, a person must have knowledge that the organization is a designated terrorist organization (as defined in subsection (g)(6)), that the organization has engaged or engages in terrorist activity (as defined in section 212(a)(3)(B) of the Immigration and Nationality Act), or that the organization has engaged or engages in terrorism (as defined in section 140(d)(2) of the Foreign Relations Authorization Act, Fiscal Years 1988 and 1989).

* * *

(e) Definition.—Section 2339B(g)(4) of title 18, United States Code, is amended to read as follows:

(4) the term 'material support or resources' has the same meaning given that term in section 2339A (including the definitions of 'training' and 'expert advice or assistance' in that section).

(f) Additional Provisions.—Section 2339B of title 18, United States Code, is amended by adding at the end the following:

(h) Provision of Personnel.—No person may be prosecuted under this section in connection with the term 'personnel' unless that person has knowingly provided, attempted to provide, or conspired to provide a foreign terrorist organization with 1 or more individuals (who may be or include himself) to work under that terrorist organization's direction or control or to organize, manage, supervise, or otherwise direct the operation of that organization. Individuals who act entirely independently of the foreign terrorist organization to advance its goals or objectives shall not be considered to be working under the foreign terrorist organization's direction and control.

(i) Rule of Construction.—Nothing in this section shall be construed or applied so as to abridge the exercise of rights guaranteed under the First Amendment to the Constitution of the United States.

(j) Exception.—No person may be prosecuted under this section in connection with the term 'personnel', 'training', or 'expert advice or assistance' if the provision of that material support or resources to a foreign terrorist organization was approved by the Secretary of State with the concurrence of the Attorney General. The Secretary of State may not approve the provision of any material support that may be used to carry out terrorist activity (as defined in section 212(a)(3)(B)(iii) of the Immigration and Nationality Act).

(g) Sunset Provision.—

(1) In general.—Except as provided in paragraph (2), this section and the amendments made by this section shall cease to be effective on December 31, 2006.

* * *

3. Persons receiving military training from a foreign terrorist organization were subject to criminal prosecution and were indeed prosecuted under § 2339B before the enactment of the specific provisions dealing with that subject contained in the IRTPA statute, supra. Which particular language in the definition of material support in § 2339A was relied upon in prosecuting such conduct before the enactment of IRTPA?

4. In the future, individuals who receive military training provided by a foreign terrorist organization will be subject to prosecution under the new offense. Will they also continue to be subject to prosecution for such conduct under § 2339B, so that now they will have committed two offenses rather than just one?

* * *

6. Is the interpretative theory relied on by the government in the second indictment in Sattar affected at all by the new legislation?

7. Are you persuaded by the reasoning of the court in the Al-Arian case? How does § 6603(c) relate to that decision? Is Al Arian still good law after the enactment of 6603?

4. Administrative designation as a "Foreign Terrorist Organization" for purposes of § 2339B; hearing procedure and judicial review under 8 U.S.C. § 1189

Subsection (g)(6) of § 2339B refers to a "terrorist organization" designated under section 219 of the Immigration and Nationality Act. Section 219 is 8 U.S.C. § 1189. § 1189 was substantially amended by the Intelligence Reform and Terrorism Prevention Act of 2004.

* * *

NATIONAL COUNCIL OF RESISTANCE OF IRAN v. DEPARTMENT OF STATE

251 F.3d 192 (D.C.Cir.2001).

Opinion for the Court filed by Circuit Judge SENTELLE.

SENTELLE, Circuit Judge:

Two organizations, the National Council of Resistance of Iran and the People's Mojahedin of Iran, petition for review of the Secretary's designation of the two as constituting a "foreign terrorist organization" under the Anti–Terrorism and Effective Death Penalty Act of 1996, raising both statutory and constitutional arguments. While we determine that the designation was in compliance with the statute, we further determine that the designation does violate the due process rights of the petitioners under the Fifth Amendment, and we therefore remand the case for further proceedings consistent with this opinion.

. . .

* * *

The Petitions

By notice of October 8, 1999, the Secretary of State, inter alia, redesignated petitioner People's Mojahedin of Iran ("PMOI") as a foreign terrorist organization pursuant to 8 U.S.C. § 1189. 64 Fed.Reg. 55,112 (1999). The two-year redesignation of the PMOI extended the October 8, 1997 designation of the same group as a terrorist organization. This court rejected a petition for review of the 1997 designation in People's Mojahedin Org. of Iran v. Dep't of State, 182 F.3d 17 (D.C.Cir. 1999). In the 1999 designation, then Secretary Madeleine Albright for the first time included the designation of the second petitioner before us, the National Council of Resistance of Iran ("NCRI"). The Secretary found that the NCRI is an alter ego or alias of the PMOI. Both petitioners argue that the Secretary's designation deprives them of constitutionally protected rights without due process of law. NCRI argues additionally that the Secretary had no statutory authority to find that it was an alias or alter ego of PMOI. For the reasons set forth below, we agree with the due process argument, while rejecting the statutory claim.

. . .

B. The Due Process Claim

Both petitioners assert that by designating them without notice or hearing as a foreign terrorist organization, with the resultant interference with their rights to obtain and possess property and the rights of their members to enter the United States, the Secretary deprived them of "liberty, or property, without due process of law," in violation of the Fifth Amendment of the United States Constitution. We agree. The United States's defense against the constitutional claims of the petitioners is two-fold: (1) that the petitioners have no protected constitutional rights and (2) that even if they have such rights, none are violated. Both lines of defense fail.

. . .

The government admits that the record before us reflects that the NCRI "has an overt presence within the National Press Building in Washington, D.C.," and further recognizes that the NCRI claims an interest in a small bank account. The government attempts to blow this away by saying that foreign entities " 'receive constitutional protections [only] when they have come within the territory of the United States and developed substantial connections within this country.' " Brief of the Secretary at 39 (quoting United States v. Verdugo–Urquidez, 494 U.S.

259, 271, 110 S.Ct. 1056, 108 L.Ed.2d 222 (1990)) (bracketed material and emphasis added by the Secretary).

. . .

In any event, we are not undertaking to determine, as a general matter, how "substantial" an alien's connections with this country must be to merit the protections of the Due Process Clause or any other part of the Constitution. Rather, we have reviewed the entire record including the classified information and determine that NCRI can rightly lay claim to having come within the territory of the United States and developed substantial connections with this country. We acknowledge that in reviewing the whole record, we have included the classified material. As we noted above and in People's Mojahedin, we will not and cannot disclose the contents of the record. We note further that the PMOI has made little serious assertion of an independent presence in the United States. Unfortunately for the cause of the Secretary, the PMOI does not need one. Insofar as PMOI's claimed presence is concerned, the United States is now hoist with its own petard. The Secretary concluded in her designation, which we upheld for the reasons set forth above, that the NCRI and the PMOI are one. The NCRI is present in the United States. If A is B, and B is present, then A is present also.

. . .

The PMOI and NCRI have entered the territory of the United States and established substantial connections with this country. The cases distinguished by the Verdugo–Urquidez Court make plain that both organizations therefore are entitled to the protections of the Constitution. See, e.g., Kwong Hai Chew v. Colding, 344 U.S. at 596, 73 S.Ct. 472 (holding that an alien who permanently resided in the United States was "a person within the protection of the Fifth Amendment" and therefore was entitled to due process); Bridges v. Wixon, 326 U.S. at 148, 65 S.Ct. 1443 (holding that a permanent alien resident was entitled to the First Amendment's guarantees of free speech and press); Russian Volunteer Fleet v. United States, 282 U.S. at 489, 491–92, 51 S.Ct. 229 (holding that a Russian corporation whose property was taken by the United States was "an alien friend," and hence deserved protection under the Fifth Amendment's Takings Clause); Wong Wing v. United States, 163 U.S. at 238, 16 S.Ct. 977 (holding that permanent alien residents were entitled to due process under the Fifth Amendment, and indictment by grand jury under the Sixth Amendment); and Yick Wo v. Hopkins, 118 U.S. at 369, 6 S.Ct. 1064 (holding that permanent alien residents deserved protection under the Fourteenth Amendment's Due Process Clause). We therefore proceed to consider whether the PMOI and NCRI have been deprived of a constitutional right.

. . .

The most obvious rights to be impaired by the Secretary's designation are the petitioners' property rights. Specifically, there is before us at least a colorable allegation that at least one of the petitioners has an interest in a bank account in the United States. As they are one, if one does, they both do. We have no idea of the truth of the allegation, there never having been notice and hearing, but for the present purposes, the colorable allegation would seem enough to support their due process claims. Russian Volunteer Fleet v. United States, 282 U.S. 481, 491–92, 51 S.Ct. 229, 75 L.Ed. 473 (1931), makes clear that a foreign organization that acquires or holds property in this country may invoke the protections of the Constitution when that property is placed in jeopardy by government intervention. This is not to say that the government cannot interfere with that and many other rights of foreign organizations present in the United States; it is only to say that when it does so it is subject to the Due Process Clause.

. . .

. . . [W]e need not decide as an initial matter whether those consequences invade Fifth Amendment protected rights of liberty, because the invasion of the Fifth Amendment protected property right in the first consequence is sufficient to entitle petitioners to the due process of law.

b.   When process is due

As petitioners argue, the fundamental norm of due process clause jurisprudence requires that before the government can constitutionally deprive a person of the protected liberty or property interest, it must afford him notice and hearing. Therefore, petitioners argue that the Secretary was obligated to give them notice of her intent to make the declarations of terrorist status and previous nature, and afford them the opportunity to respond to the evidence upon which she proposed to make those declarations and to be heard on the proper resolution of the questions. Indeed, "[the Supreme] Court consistently has held that some form of hearing is required before an individual is finally deprived of a property interest."

* * *

When analyzing the petitioners' claims, and the government's defenses, we are mindful that two distinct questions remain for us to determine. We have dispensed with the issue as to whether petitioners are entitled to due process; the questions remaining for us are what due process, and when. That is, to what procedural devices must the petitioners have access in order to protect their interests against the deprivations worked by the statute, and must that access be afforded before the Secretary's declaration, or is it sufficient under the circumstances that such access be available post-deprivation? The government rightly reminds us that the Supreme Court established in Mathews v. Eldridge and indeed even before that decision, that identification of the specific dictates of due process generally requires consideration of three distinct factors: first, the private interests that will be affected by the official action; second, the risk of an erroneous deprivation of such interest of the procedure used, and the probable value, if any, of additional or substitute procedural safeguards; and finally, the government's interest, including the function involved and the fiscal and administrative burdens that the additional or substitute procedural requirements would entail.

* * *

. . .

As to the third . . . factor—"the government's interest, including the function involved in the fiscal and administrative burdens that the additional or substitute procedural requirement would entail,"—the Secretary rightly reminds us that "no governmental interest is more compelling than the security of the nation." It is on this very point that the Secretary most clearly has failed to distinguish between the what of the Due Process Clause and the when. Certainly the United States enjoys a privilege in classified information affecting national security so strong that even a criminal defendant to whose defense such information is relevant cannot pierce that privilege absent a specific showing of materiality. As we will discuss further infra, that strong interest of the government clearly affects the nature—the "what" of the due process which must be afforded petitioners. It is not immediately apparent how that affects the "when" of the process—that is, whether due process may be effectively provided post-deprivation as opposed to pre-deprivation.

In support of the argument that the foreign-policy/national-security nature of the evidence supports the constitutional adequacy of a post-deprivation remedy, the Secretary offers our decision in Palestine Information Office v. Shultz, 853 F.2d 932 (D.C.Cir.1988). The Secretary is correct that in that case, we held that where the Secretary of State had ordered the closing of an office (arguably, a foreign ministry) in this country in response to and in an attempt to curb alleged terrorist activities, the "burden on the government of requiring a hearing before the closing of [the] foreign mission" was sufficient to warrant dispensing with any otherwise available pre-deprivation hearing. Id. at 942. We did so recognizing the " 'changeable and explosive nature of contemporary international relations, and the fact that the executive is immediately privy to information which cannot be swiftly presented to, evaluated by, and acted upon by the legislature. . . .' " We remain committed to, and indeed bound by, that same reasoning. It is simply not the case, however, that the Secretary has shown how affording the organizations whatever due process they are due before their designation as foreign terrorist organizations and the resulting deprivation of right would interfere with the Secretary's duty to carry out foreign policy.

To oversimplify, assume the Secretary gives notice to one of the entities that:

> We are considering designating you as a foreign terrorist organization, and in addition to classified information, we will be using the following summarized administrative record. You have the right to come forward with any other evidence you may have that you are not a foreign terrorist organization.

It is not immediately apparent how the foreign policy goals of the government in general and the Secretary in particular would be inherently impaired by that notice. It is particularly difficult to discern how such a notice could interfere with the Secretary's legitimate goals were it presented to an entity such as the PMOI concerning its redesignation. We recognize, as we have recognized before, that items of classified information which do not appear dangerous or perhaps even important to judges might "make all too much sense to a foreign counterintelligence specialist who could learn much about this nation's intelligence-gathering capabilities from what these documents revealed about sources and methods." Yunis, 867 F.2d at 623. We extend that recognition to the possibility that alerting a previously undesignated organization to the impending designation as a foreign terrorist organization might work harm to this county's foreign policy goals in ways that the court would not immediately perceive. We therefore wish to make plain that we do not foreclose the possibility of the Secretary, in an appropriate case, demonstrating the necessity of withholding all notice and all opportunity to present evidence until the designation is already made. The difficulty with that in the present case is that the Secretary has made no attempt at such a showing.

We therefore hold that the Secretary must afford the limited due process available to the putative foreign terrorist organization prior to the deprivation worked by designating that entity as such with its attendant consequences, unless he can make a showing of particularized need.

c.   What process is due

We have no doubt foreshadowed our conclusion as to what process the Secretary must afford by our discussion of when the Secretary must afford it. That is, consistent with the full history of due process jurisprudence, as reflected in Mathews v. Eldridge, "[t]he fundamental requirement of due process is the opportunity to be heard 'at a meaningful time and in a meaningful manner.'" 424 U.S. at 333, 96 S.Ct. 893 (quoting Armstrong v. Manzo, 380 U.S. 545, 552, 85 S.Ct. 1187, 14 L.Ed.2d 62 (1965)). To make plain what we have assumed above, those procedures which have been held to satisfy the Due Process Clause have "included notice of the action sought," along with the opportunity to effectively be heard. Id. at 334, 96 S.Ct. 893. This, we hold, is what the Constitution requires of the Secretary in designating organizations as foreign terrorist organizations under the statute. The Secretary must afford to the entities under consideration notice that the designation is impending. Upon an adequate showing to the court, the Secretary may provide this notice after the designation where earlier notification would impinge upon the security and other foreign policy goals of the United States.

The notice must include the action sought, but need not disclose the classified information to be presented in camera and ex parte to the court under the statute. This is within the privilege and prerogative of the executive, and we do not intend to compel a breach in the security which that branch is charged to protect. However, the Secretary has shown no reason not to offer the designated entities notice of the administrative record which will in any event be filed publicly, at the very latest at the time of the court's review. We therefore require that as soon as the Secretary has reached a tentative determination that the designation is impending, the Secretary must provide notice of those unclassified items upon which he proposes to rely to the entity to be designated. There must then be some compliance with the hearing requirement of due process jurisprudence—that is, the opportunity to be heard at a meaningful time and in a meaningful manner recognized in Mathews, Armstrong, and a plethora of other cases. We do not suggest "that a hearing closely approximating a judicial trial is necessary." Mathews, 424 U.S. at 333, 96 S.Ct. 893. We do, however, require that the Secretary afford to entities considered for imminent designation the opportunity to present, at least in written form, such evidence as those entities may be able to produce to rebut the administrative record or otherwise negate the proposition that they are foreign terrorist organizations.

It is for this reason that even in those instances when post-deprivation due process is sufficient, our review under § 1189(b) is not sufficient to supply the otherwise absent due process protection. The statutory judicial review is limited to the adequacy of the record before the court to support the Secretary's executive decision. That record is currently compiled by the Secretary without notice or opportunity for any meaningful hearing. We have no reason to presume that the petitioners in this particular case could have offered evidence which might have either changed the Secretary's mind or affected the adequacy of the record. However, without the due process protections which we have outlined, we cannot presume the contrary either.

Remedy

We recognize that a strict and immediate application of the principles of law which we have set forth herein could be taken to require a revocation of the designations before us. However, we also recognize the realities of the foreign policy and national security concerns asserted by the Secretary in support of those designations. We further recognize the timeline against which all are operating: the two-year designations before us expire in October of this year. We therefore do not order the vacation of the existing designations, but rather remand the questions to the Secretary with instructions that the petitioners be afforded the opportunity to file responses to the nonclassified evidence against them, to file evidence in support of their allegations that they are not terrorist organizations, and that they be afforded an opportunity to be meaningfully heard by the Secretary upon the relevant findings.

While not within our current order, we expect that the Secretary will afford due process rights to these and other similarly situated entities in the course of future designations.

Conclusion

For the reasons set forth above, we order that the Secretary's designation of the National Council of Resistance of Iran and the People's Mojahedin of Iran as being one foreign terrorist organization be remanded to the Secretary for further proceedings consistent with this opinion.

Notes and Questions

1. In the National Council case, the court did not find that the government's argument (the foreign policy and national security nature of the evidence) for dispensing with pre-deprivation notice and opportunity to present evidence was supported by an adequate showing, while recognizing that such a showing possibly could be made in an appropriate case. Are there other kinds of factors in a proceeding under § 1189 that might support dispensing with pre-deprivation process? Consult Notes and Comments: Designation of Foreign Terrorist Organization under the AEDPA: The National Council Court Erred in Requiring Pre-designation Process, 2002 B.Y.U.L.Rev. 675 (2002).

2. The court in National Council ordered as a remedy that "the petitioners be afforded the opportunity to file responses to the nonclassified evidence against them, to file evidence in support of their allegations that they are not terrorist organizations, and that they be afforded an opportunity to be meaningfully heard by the Secretary upon the relevant findings." In the National Council case, there was both classified and nonclassified evidence in the administrative record. Suppose that the record consisted only of classified evidence. (The language of § 1189 does not appear to preclude such a possibility.) How meaningfully would the due process right granted by the Nat'l Council court be in such a context? Is it arguable that the most important due process protection needed by an affected organization is adequate judicial review of the Secretary's finding?

3. Section 1189 provides that classified information may be considered in deciding whether to designate an organization as a foreign terrorist organization. It does not apply the provisions of the Classified Information Procedures Act to this type of proceeding. Should it? You will wish to reconsider this question after detailed consideration of that Act, in Chapter 9, infra.

4. The procedures ordered by the court in National Council to remedy the constitutional flaw in the process are, of course, not found in the statute. Is it permissible for the court to read such procedural requirements into the statute when they are not found there, or, alternatively, simply to order them so as to avoid voiding the statute on the ground that it violates due process?

5. What would you advise the Secretary of State to do in the wake of the decision in the National Council case? Seek review in the Supreme Court? Provide to the organizations involved in National Council the procedural protections ordered by the court? Provide such procedural protections in all subsequent designation cases? Go back and reopen all previous designation cases and provide the prescribed procedural protections? Seek an

amendment of sec. 1189 to codify by statute the procedural requirements prescribed by the court in National Council?

6. In the aftermath of the National Council case, we inquired by telephone and fax to the State Department in two different offices as to how the Department was responding to the National Council court's decision. One State Department official, in reply to a question, indicated that they were not planning to amend § 1189 procedures as a result of the National Council decision and expressed concern about notifying terrorist groups about their designation and thus allowing them to hide their assets. Query, is the concern about the possibility that assets will be hidden a sufficient reason to provide only post-designation hearings? Should the National Council court have considered this concern in its opinion?

A more formal response was received from the Office of Legal Adviser, Law Enforcement and Intelligence, in response to a faxed inquiry:

> Your facsimile ... was referred to me. You asked whether the Secretary of State is implementing or plans to implement the procedures outlined by the court in National Council ... , in other cases of designating a foreign terrorist organization.

> Without waiving its right to challenge the correctness of the decision of the court in National Council ... , the State Department has implemented such procedures where applicable. The D.C. Circuit's ruling in National Council ... made clear, however, that the threshold question is first whether a foreign entity is present within the United States and has sufficient connections with this country to bring it within our constitutional framework. If the necessary quantum of presence and connections is missing, entities can claim no rights under the Due Process Clause. Thus, where foreign entities do not have sufficient connections with the United States such that the provisions of the Constitution could be applied to them, notice and hearings and similar procedures are not provided. See, e.g., 32 County Sovereignty Comm. v. Department of State, 292 F.3d 797, 799 (D.C.Cir. 2002).

7. In 32 County Sovereignty Comm. v. Department of State, cited supra note 6, the court reported that the petitioners who had been designated as a "foreign terrorist organization" had requested "the process ordered in National Council" and that the Department of Justice attorney representing the State Department notified the petitioners that their request for the National Council procedures was denied. The court concluded that the organization had not demonstrated a property interest or a presence within the United States and therefore the Secretary did not have to provide the organization with any particular process before designating it as a foreign terrorist organization. The court went on to deny the petition for judicial review because the administrative record furnished substantial support for the designation.

8. What kind of presence in the U.S. is needed in order to qualify for due process protection? In the 32 County case supra note 7, the court stated: "[T]he affidavits petitioners submitted ... demonstrate only that some of their American 'members' personally rented post office boxes and utilized a bank account to transmit funds and information to ... [the organization] in Ireland. The affidavits do not aver that ... [the organization] possessed any

controlling interest in property located within the United States, nor do they demonstrate any other form of presence here."

9.   Are there practical problems in providing notice and other procedural opportunities to the kind of organizations that are likely to be designated as foreign terrorist organizations? Consider the type of organizations that are already listed, supra, p. ___. First, many of these organizations are by definition foreign; they are also secretive and hidden. It is as if the government were obligated to provide notice to the Mafia. How does one go about it?

* * *

Notes and Questions

1. . . . Is there any way to avoid the frequent revisiting of the designation issue given the provision for biennial redesignations? Why did the Congress provide for biennial redesignations?

2. What is the effect on the biennial redesignation process of the provisions of the IRTPA of 2004, amending § 1189, which are set forth below? Is this a better approach than biennial redesignations?

Intelligence Reform and Terrorism Prevention Act of 2004

. . .

SEC. 7119. DESIGNATION OF FOREIGN TERRORIST ORGANIZATIONS.

(a) PERIOD OF DESIGNATION—Section 219(a)(4) of the Immigration and Nationality Act (8 U.S.C. 1189(a)(4)) is amended—

(1) in subparagraph (A)—

(A) by striking 'Subject to paragraphs (5) and (6), a' and inserting 'A'; and

(B) by striking 'for a period of 2 years beginning on the effective date of the designation under paragraph (2)(B)' and inserting 'until revoked under paragraph (5) or (6) or set aside pursuant to subsection c)';

(2) by striking subparagraph (B) and inserting the following:

'(B) REVIEW OF DESIGNATION UPON PETITION—

'(i) IN GENERAL—The Secretary shall review the designation of a foreign terrorist organization under the procedures set forth in clauses (iii) and (iv) if the designated organization files a petition for revocation within the petition period described in clause (ii).

'(ii) PETITION PERIOD—For purposes of clause (I)—

'(I) if the designated organization has not previously filed a petition for revocation under this subparagraph, the petition period begins 2 years after the date on which the designation was made; or

'(II) if the designated organization has previously filed a petition for revocation under this subparagraph, the petition period begins 2 years after the date of the determination made under clause (iv) on that petition.

'(iii) PROCEDURES—Any foreign terrorist organization that submits a petition for revocation under this subparagraph must provide evidence in that petition that the relevant circumstances described in paragraph (1) are sufficiently different from the circumstances that were the basis for the designation such that a revocation with respect to the organization is warranted.

'(iv) DETERMINATION—

'(I) IN GENERAL—Not later than 180 days after receiving a petition for revocation submitted under this subparagraph, the Secretary shall make a determination as to such revocation.

'(II) CLASSIFIED INFORMATION—The Secretary may consider classified information in making a determination in response to a petition for revocation. Classified information shall not be subject to disclosure for such time as it remains classified, except that such information may be disclosed to a court ex parte and in camera for purposes of judicial review under subsection c).

'(III) PUBLICATION OF DETERMINATION—A determination made by the Secretary under this clause shall be published in the Federal Register.

'(IV) PROCEDURES—Any revocation by the Secretary shall be made in accordance with paragraph (6).'; and (3) by adding at the end the following:

'(C) OTHER REVIEW OF DESIGNATION—

'(i) IN GENERAL—If in a 5–year period no review has taken place under subparagraph (B), the Secretary shall review the designation of the foreign terrorist organization in order to determine whether such designation should be revoked pursuant to paragraph (6).

'(ii) PROCEDURES—If a review does not take place pursuant to subparagraph (B) in response to a petition for revocation that is filed in accordance with that subparagraph, then the review shall be conducted pursuant to procedures established by the Secretary. The results of such review and the applicable procedures shall not be reviewable in any court.

'(iii) PUBLICATION OF RESULTS OF REVIEW–The Secretary shall publish any determination made pursuant to this subparagraph in the Federal Register.

(b) ALIASES—Section 219 of the Immigration and Nationality Act (8 U.S.C. 1189) is amended–

(1) by redesignating subsections (b) and (c) as subsections (c) and (d), respectively; and

(2) by inserting after subsection (a) the following new subsection (b):

(b) AMENDMENTS TO A DESIGNATION—

(1) IN GENERAL—The Secretary may amend a designation under this subsection if the Secretary finds that the organization has changed its name, adopted a new alias, dissolved and then reconstituted itself under a different name or names, or merged with another organization.

(2) PROCEDURE—Amendments made to a designation in accordance with paragraph (1) shall be effective upon publication in the Federal Register. Subparagraphs (B) and (C) of subsection (a)(2) shall apply to an amended designation upon such publication. Paragraphs (2)(A)(i), (4), (5), (6), (7), and (8) of subsection (a) shall also apply to an amended designation.

(3) ADMINISTRATIVE RECORD—The administrative record shall be corrected to include the amendments as well as any additional relevant information that supports those amendments.

(4) CLASSIFIED INFORMATION—The Secretary may consider classified information in amending a designation in accordance with this subsection. Classified information shall not be subject to disclosure for such time as it remains classified, except that such information may be disclosed to a court ex parte and in camera for purposes of judicial review under subsection (c).

. . .

(d) SAVINGS PROVISION—For purposes of applying section 219 of the Immigration and Nationality Act on or after the date of enactment of this Act, the term 'designation', as used in that section, includes all redesignations made pursuant to section 219(a)(4)(B) of the Immigration and Nationality Act (8 U.S.C. 1189(a)(4)(B)) prior to the date of enactment of this Act, and such redesignations shall continue to be effective until revoked as provided in paragraph (5) or (6) of section 219(a) of the Immigration and Nationality Act (8 U.S.C. 1189(a)).

5. Criminal prosecution under § 2339B

* * * Issues relating to the designation can also arise in a criminal prosecution under 18 U.S.C. § 2339B. The following case presents such a context.

UNITED STATES v. AFSHARI

392 F.3d 1031 (9th Cir. 2004).

JUDGES: Before: Andrew J. Kleinfeld, Kim McLane Wardlaw, and William A. Fletcher, Circuit Judges.

KLEINFELD, Circuit Judge:

We review the constitutionality of a statute prohibiting financial support to organizations designated as "terrorist."

Facts

The issue here is the constitutionality of the crime charged in the indictment, that from 1997 to 2001, Rahmani and others knowingly and willfully conspired to provide material support to the Mujahedin-e Khalq ("MEK"), a designated terrorist organization, in violation of 18 U.S.C. § 2339B(a)(1).

According to the indictment, the defendants solicited charitable contributions at the Los Angeles International Airport for the "Committee for Human Rights," gave money and credit cards to the MEK, and wired money from the "Committee for Human Rights" to an MEK bank account in Turkey. They did all this after participating in a conference call with an MEK leader, in which they learned that the State Department had designated the MEK as a foreign terrorist organization. The MEK leader told them to continue to provide material support despite the designation. All told, according to the indictment in this case, the money they sent to the MEK amounted to at least several hundred thousand dollars.

The MEK was founded in the 1960s as an Iranian Marxist group seeking to overthrow the regime then ruling Iran. It participated in various terrorist activities against the Iranian regime and against the United States, including the taking of American embassy personnel as hostages in 1979. After the Iranian regime fell and was replaced by a clerical, rather than a Marxist, regime, MEK members fled to France. They later settled in Iraq, along the Iranian border. There they carried out terrorist activities with the support of Saddam Hussein's regime, as well as, if the indictment is correct, the money that the defendants sent them.

For purposes of reviewing a motion to dismiss an indictment, we assume the truth of what the indictment alleges. Thus, we take it as true that the defendants knew that they were furnishing assistance to a designated "terrorist" organization, having been informed of the designation in a conference call with an MEK leader.

The district court dismissed the indictment on the ground that the terrorist designation statute was unconstitutional. We review de novo, and reverse.

Analysis

I. Challenging the designation.

. . .

The district court found that it was a facially unconstitutional restriction on judicial review of the designation for Congress to assign such review exclusively to the D.C. Circuit. We reject that position.

Many administrative determinations are reviewable only by petition to the correct circuit court, bypassing the district court, and that procedure has generally been accepted. Many are reviewable only in the D.C. Circuit, or the Federal Circuit, and those restrictions have also been generally accepted. The congressional restriction does not interfere with the opportunity for judicial review, as the MEK's extensive litigation history shows. And this scheme avoids the awkwardness of criminalizing material support for a designated organization in some circuits but not others, as varying decisions in the different regional circuits might.

However, a holding that a restriction of judicial review of the Secretary of State's designation of a terrorist organization to the Court of Appeals for the D.C. Circuit is not facially unconstitutional does not settle the question whether a defendant may be criminally prosecuted for donating to a designated organization. A district court in which such a defendant is criminally prosecuted may bring a due process challenge to his or her prosecution for donating to such an organization. The district court properly ruled that it had jurisdiction to review this challenge. But its conclusion that § 1189 is facially unconstitutional because judicial review was assigned exclusively to the D.C. Circuit was in error.

II.   Due Process claim.

The statute assigns criminal penalties to one who "knowingly provides material support or resources to a foreign terrorist organization, or attempts or conspires to do so." The statutory phrase "terrorist organization" is a term of art, defined by Congress as "an organization designated as a terrorist organization" under 8 U.S.C. § 1189(a)(1). The defendants' central argument is that § 2339B denies them their constitutional rights because it prohibits them from collaterally attacking the designation of a foreign terrorist organization. This contention was recently rejected by the Fourth Circuit en banc.[20] We, too, reject it.

The specific section that is at issue here is 8 U.S.C. § 1189(a)(8), which states in relevant part:

> If a designation . . . or if a redesignation under this subsection has become effective . . . a defendant in a criminal action or an alien in a removal proceeding shall not be permitted to raise any question concerning the validity of the issuance of such designation or redesignation as a defense or an objection at any trial or hearing.

The defendants are right that § 1189(a)(8) prevents them from contending, in defense of the charges against them under 18 U.S.C. § 2339B, that the designated terrorist organization is not really terrorist at all. No doubt Congress was well aware that some might be of the view that "one man's terrorist is another man's freedom fighter." Congress clearly chose to delegate policymaking authority to the President and Department of State with respect to designation of terrorist organizations, and to keep such policymaking authority out of the hands of United States Attorneys and juries. Under § 2339B, if defendants pro-

20.   United States v. Hammoud, 381 F.3d 316 (4th Cir. 2004) (en banc).

vide material support for an organization that has been designated a terrorist organization under § 1189, they commit the crime, and it does not matter whether the designation is correct or not.

The question then is whether due process prohibits a prosecution under § 2339B when the predicate designation was obtained in an unconstitutional manner or is otherwise erroneous. In *Lewis v. United States,* [445 U.S. 55 (1980)], the Supreme Court held that a prior conviction could properly be used as a predicate for a subsequent conviction for a felon in possession of a firearm, even though it had been obtained in violation of the Sixth Amendment right to counsel. The Court held that it was proper to prohibit a collateral attack on the predicate during the criminal hearing because the felon-in-possession statute made no exception "for a person whose outstanding felony conviction ultimately might turn out to be invalid for any reason." The Court noted that the prohibition on collateral attack was proper because a convicted felon could challenge the validity of the conviction before he purchased his firearm.

The defendants attempt to distinguish *Lewis* from this § 2339B prosecution because the defendant in *Lewis* had the ability to challenge his predicate, whereas here the defendants, themselves, are prohibited from challenging the designation. But this does not change the principle that a criminal proceeding may go forward, even if the predicate was in some way unconstitutional, so long as a sufficient opportunity for judicial review of the predicate exists. Here there was such an opportunity, which the MEK took advantage of each time it was designated a foreign terrorist organization.

The defendants also attempt to distinguish *Lewis* by relying on *United States v. Mendoza–Lopez.* [481 U.S. 828 (1987)]. In that case, the Supreme Court held that a prosecution under 8 U.S.C. § 1326 for illegal reentry does not comport with due process if there is no judicial review of whether the predicate deportation proceeding violated the alien's rights. It is not at all clear from *Mendoza-Lopez* that the Supreme Court meant that the due process problem is in the *later* proceeding. The Court held that "where a determination made in an administrative proceeding is to play a critical role in the subsequent imposition of a criminal sanction, there must be *some* meaningful review of the administrative proceeding." Nothing in *Mendoza-Lopez* appears to require that this review be had by the defendant in the subsequent criminal proceeding.

Furthermore, it is obvious in *Lewis* and *Mendoza-Lopez* that the opportunity to seek review would be in the hands of the defendants themselves because it was *their* rights at issue in the hearing that created the predicate in the later criminal proceeding. But here, the defendants' rights were not directly violated in the earlier designation proceeding. The predicate designation was against the MEK, not the defendants. Section 1189 provides for the organizations to seek review of the predicate designation, and that review was had in this case. Therefore, due process does not require another review of the predicate by the court adjudicating the instant § 2339B criminal proceeding.

. . .

As we noted in another case where we rejected a defendant's right to challenge an export listing in a subsequent criminal proceeding, the defendants' argument here "is analogous to one by a defendant in a drug possession case that his conviction cannot stand because no specific showing has been made that the drug is a threat to society. . . . [A] showing that the drug possessed by the individual defendant has a 'detrimental effect on the general welfare' [is not] an element of the offense." Likewise, the element of the crime that the prosecutor must prove in a § 2339B case is the predicate fact that a particular organization *was* designated at the time the material support was given, not whether the government made a correct designation. Our position is consistent with that of the Fourth Circuit, which held that a defendant's inability to challenge the designation was not a violation of his constitutional rights, since the *validity* of the designation is not an element of the crime. Rather, the element is the *fact* of an organization's designation as a "foreign terrorist organization."

* * *

After the Secretary of State designated the MEK a "foreign terrorist organization" in 1997, the MEK challenged the designation in the United States Court of Appeals for the District of Columbia, and lost. When the Secretary renewed the designation in 1999, the MEK litigated it again, this time successfully. The D.C. Circuit remanded to the Secretary for renewed consideration with greater procedural protections for the MEK. When the Secretary again designated the MEK as a foreign terrorist organization on a new administrative record, the MEK brought its third challenge in the D.C. Circuit, which this time upheld the designation. The D.C. Circuit also reconsidered the 1997 designation on the merits and again upheld it, expressly anticipating the possibility of a criminal prosecution based on either designation.

. . .

Conceivably the MEK developed its practices at a time when the United States supported the previous regime in Iran, and maintained its position while harbored by the Saddam Hussein Ba'ath regime in Iraq, but will change, or has already changed, so that its interest in overturning the current regime in Iran coincides with the interests of the United States. The sometimes subtle analysis of a foreign organization's political program to determine whether it is indeed a terrorist threat is peculiarly within the expertise of the State Department and the Executive Branch. Juries could not make reliable determinations without extensive foreign policy education and the disclosure of classified materials. Leaving the determination to the Executive Branch, coupled with the procedural protections and judicial review afforded by the statute, is both a reasonable and a constitutional way to make a determination of whether a group is a "foreign terrorist organization." The Constitution does not forbid Congress from requiring individuals, whether they agree with the Executive Branch determination or not, to refrain from furnishing material assistance to designated organizations during the two year period of designation.

REVERSED.

* * *

Chapter 5

WHAT KIND OF WAR IS IT?

A. Introduction

The purpose of this chapter is to introduce and provide general materials on the subject of whether the current war against terror is a real war, that is, a war that permits invocation of the laws of war and war powers that exist under the Constitution. Because addressing the question in general whether this is a real war may not answer questions about the specific legal consequences that flow from viewing the current situation as a war, we shall return to this subject in the chapters dealing with the specific issues that arise, for example, in Chapter 7 (whether individuals can be detained for extended periods as enemy combatants), and Chapter 8 (whether individuals can be tried before military commissions).

First, we propose to examine any obvious differences between the circumstances that warrant calling our anti-terrorist efforts a war and earlier law enforcement "wars."

Second, we shall review some of the applicable sources and doctrines that are relevant in determining whether a war is being carried on that entails specific legal consequences.

Third, we examine some suggestions by scholars about how to address terrorism using approaches different from the "war" model.

The notion that the government is conducting a "war" on terrorism requires close examination. This is not the first "war" using forces of law enforcement that has been carried on by the U.S. government. A war on organized crime was announced long ago. Later it was followed by a war on drugs and, still later, by a war on white collar crime and, its first cousin, political corruption. See, for example, Norman Abrams, Assessing the Federal Government's "War" on White–Collar Crime, 53 Temple L.Q. 984 (1980). Undoubtedly, there have been other such wars announced by various administrations over the course of decades. Such wars typically have amounted to the announcement of "a new enforcement emphasis," ibid, or a statement that the enforcement area is being given "the highest investigative priority." Ibid. Viewed against this kind of background, proclamation of a war on terrorism hardly seems problematic or, even, very noteworthy. An important question, however, that is crucial in the consideration of the materials that follow in this volume is whether there are important differences between this new war and all of those which came earlier.

The use of war terminology for all of the earlier governmental programs was clearly metaphorical. This is not to say that the use of the words of war did not itself have import and impact. Announcement of the war on drugs, for example, made clear that an important focus of governmental law efforts would be targeted on drugs. Denoting this activity a war had political and administrative consequences. It affected the organization of governmental efforts in this arena, and it meant that considerable resources would be devoted to the subject. It also carried with it the entire war-related vocabulary—battles, targets, forays, collateral damage, victory, defeat, weapons, defenses, attack, enemy, etc.

Clearly, when the Bush Administration uses the vocabulary of war today in regard to terrorism, however, it is trying to do something different from those earlier rhetorical wars. It is not simply engaging in word play. In instance after instance, when it has announced a new measure or a new policy, it has made clear that when it says "war" it really means "war," one that is in some sense a real war. Similarly, in its judicial filings, it has made clear that in the judgment of the Administration, there is a war going on that has significant legal consequences.

Issues relating to the legal consequences argued for by the Administration arise in every one of the remaining chapters in this book. There is an ongoing tension between the rules applicable if the government's efforts against terror are deemed traditional law enforcement against criminal conduct or whether they are being done under wartime conditions where terrorist actions are acts of war by an enemy and the laws of war and various off-shoots are applicable. Examples abound: Can persons apprehended be treated as prisoners of war or detained as enemy combatants rather than simply ordinary arrestees? Where should accused terrorists be tried, in civilian courts or military tribunals? Can the government engage in kinds of surveillance activities that might be allowable in wartime but not in peacetime? Under what circumstances can the military be called upon for law enforcement activity within the boundaries of the United States? Is it permissible for the United States to engage abroad in targeted killing of terrorists on the theory that in wartime such actions are permissible?

B.   Comparing past metaphorical wars

The previous wars against organized crime, white collar crime, drugs, and the like all were ways to characterize a focusing of the federal law enforcement effort, a way of stating that there was going to be an emphasis on a particular kind of criminality. Drugs and white collar crime fit that model. Organized crime as the "enemy" [note how easy it is to slip into the vocabulary of war] was a variation on this theme. It targeted a category of perpetrators, and a mode of perpetration rather than a specific substantive category of crime. It also was framed, however, in a sense, in terms of a human target rather than a crime classification. But this was a distinction that made no difference. After all, behind the commission of the drug crimes were the drug lords and the drug cartels. Similarly, corporate and political officials were the true targets where the focus was on "crime in the 'suites'."

Insofar as the war was against organized crime, there has always been some uncertainty and ambivalence about the federal target. Was it the old line Mafia, ethnically Italian, or their organized ethnic group successors in our cities, whether Hispanic, African–American, Russian, Israeli, or similar ethnic groups? Did it extend to and include the street gangs in our cities or motorcycle gangs that roam over our streets and highways?

In each of these cases, the police-prosecutor enforcement effort was concerned with the commission of "ordinary" crime, and the standard mode of proceeding was to effect arrests, prosecute under the applicable criminal laws, obtain convictions and incarcerate in a correctional institution, usually for a determinate period of years.

The categories of crime targeted in these metaphorical wars typically were crimes committed for gain, crimes with an economic motive. In general, the "enemy" who was busy engaging in their particular forms of criminality was not an aggressor who engaged in aggression for its own sake although he might initiate attacks against law enforcement or the government or other targets insofar as it furthered his economic motivation; he did not see the United States as a general enemy, although, of course, its law enforcement minions were the enemy. If law enforcement would just let him alone to engage in his criminal activities, he would be satisfied. It was in his interest to keep a low profile and to be left alone so that he could maximize his desired goal of economic gain. Of course, if attacked by law enforcement, he might respond with deadly force, and, on occasion, he might initiate an attack on a law enforcement person who was too effective or retaliate or seek revenge against specific individuals.

The "war" against terror, terrorism, terrorists, al Qaeda, it can be argued, is different in a key aspect. This enemy is aggressive. He initiates attacks, by surprise, and without mercy. His goal is ultimately to defeat or overthrow the enemy, us, the government of the United States. His goal is not economic gain, at least not in any ordinary sense. The crimes committed are crimes of violence against the United States and other countries. In effect, he behaves very much like an enemy functioning on the battlefield in a traditional kind of war. We assume that if he had the armies and the weaponry, he might well initiate a traditional war to defeat us. Because he does not have those tools available, he proceeds, using whatever advantages he has, stealth, surprise, methods of achieving large scale destruction and devastation, often using the very machinery of modernity against us.

On occasion in this "war," there may be action on a battlefield in the more traditional war mode. The fighting against the Taliban, an ally of al Qaeda, in Afghanistan fit this model. Whether the war with Iraq, should be seen as part of the war against terrorism is a debatable proposition. In any event, if such battlefield wars do, on occasion, occur as part of the war against terrorism, they tend to be incidental and not central thereto. The prevailing model is one that does not include an active, traditional battlefield.

Another element of this war, however, that makes it similar to the metaphorical wars and dissimilar to the classic war model is the fact that it is hard to see how it will ever end. Traditional wars on the battlefield typically have a definitive end, a ceasing of hostilities marked perhaps by an armistice and/or a peace treaty. It seems unlikely that we shall ever be able to achieve the complete and total victory that would be the equivalent of a victory on the battlefield.

In making these comparisons, it should not be forgotten that the enemy does perpetrate acts that are crimes under our criminal laws. Often they are perpetrated within the territorial United States. The agencies that act on our behalf in addressing these crimes and trying to apprehend the perpetrators are our police agencies, with the FBI at the forefront on the federal level. And the law enforcement efforts are not very different from those that are used against ordinary crime.

Stating these comparisons, while useful, does not provide an answer to the question of whether this is the kind of war that entails application of the classic international law of war and its concomitant treaties, conventions and the like. We turn now to an examination of the sources and doctrines that are relevant to the classic law of war to see whether they are helpful in providing an answer.

C. Sources and doctrines relating to a traditional kind of war

1. The U.S. Constitution

Article I, Section 8:

"The Congress shall have Power ... To declare War ... ; To raise and support Armies ... ; ... To provide and maintain a Navy; To make Rules for the Government and Regulation of the land and naval Forces; To provide for the calling forth the Militia to execute the Laws of the Union, suppress Insurrections and repel Invasions...."

Article II, Section 2:

"The President shall be Commander in Chief of the Army and Navy of the United States, and of the militia of the several States when called into the actual Service of the United States...."

2. Reproduced below are provisions of the Third Geneva Convention that bear on the "war" issue. Other provisions of the Convention relevant to prisoner of war and enemy combatant issues will be found in Chapter 7.

Geneva Convention relative to the Treatment of Prisoners of War, 75 U.N.T.S. 135, *entered into force* Oct. 21, 1950.

PART I

General Provisions

Article 1

The High Contracting Parties undertake to respect and to ensure respect for the present Convention in all circumstances.

Article 2

In addition to the provisions which shall be implemented in peace time, the present Convention shall apply to all cases of declared war or of any other armed conflict which may arise between two or more of the High Contracting Parties, even if the state of war is not recognized by one of them.

. . .

Although one of the Powers in conflict may not be a party to the present Convention, the Powers who are parties thereto shall remain bound by it in their mutual relations. They shall furthermore be bound by the Convention in relation to the said Power, if the latter accepts and applies the provisions thereof.

Article 3

In the case of armed conflict not of an international character occurring in the territory of one of the High Contracting Parties, each party to the conflict shall be bound to apply, as a minimum, the following provisions. . . .

———————

3. In the immediate aftermath of the September 11th attacks, at the behest of the administration, Congress passed a Joint Resolution, S.J. Res. 23, 107th Cong., 115 Stat. 224 (2001), authorizing the use of military force which was signed by the President on September 18, 2001.

Public Law 107–40

107th Congress

Joint Resolution

To authorize the use of United States Armed Forces against those responsible for the recent attacks launched against the United States.

Whereas, on September 11, 2001, acts of treacherous violence were committed against the United States and its citizens; and

Whereas, such acts render it both necessary and appropriate that the United States exercise its rights to self-defense and to protect United States citizens both at home and abroad; and

Whereas, in light of the threat to the national security and foreign policy of the United States posed by these grave acts of violence; and

Whereas, such acts continue to pose an unusual and extraordinary threat to the national security and foreign policy of the United States; and

Whereas, the President has authority under the Constitution to take action to deter and prevent acts of international terrorism against the United States: Now, therefore, be it

Resolved by the Senate and House of Representatives of the United States of America in Congress assembled,

SECTION 1. SHORT TITLE.

This joint resolution may be cited as the "Authorization for Use of Military Force."

SECTION 2. AUTHORIZATION FOR USE OF UNITED STATES ARMED FORCES.

(a) IN GENERAL.—That the President is authorized to use all necessary and appropriate force against those nations, organizations, or persons he determines planned, authorized, committed, or aided the terrorist attacks that occurred on September 11, 2001, or harbored such organizations or persons, in order to prevent any future acts of international terrorism against the United States by such nations, organizations or persons.

(b) WAR POWERS RESOLUTION REQUIREMENTS.—

(1) SPECIFIC STATUTORY AUTHORIZATION.—Consistent with section 8(a)(1) of the War Powers Resolution, the Congress declares that this section is intended to constitute specific statutory authorization within the meaning of section 5(b) of the War Powers Resolution.

(2) APPLICABILITY OF OTHER REQUIREMENTS.—Nothing in this resolution supersedes any requirement of the War Powers Resolution.

Approved September 18, 2001.

4. Following the September 11th attacks, the UN Security Council expressly declared that the acts of September 11th constituted a threat

to international peace and security. S.C Res. 1368, U.N. SCOR, 56th Sess. 4370th mtg., U.N. Doc. S/RES/1368 (2001).

5. Following the September 11th attacks, some formal declarations of war were introduced into the Congress. Apparently, the administration did not want to dignify the the attacks with a formal declaration of war, indicating that "the legal implications of a declaration of war were unnecessary and even undesirable," and the Congress did not act on any of these declarations. David Abramowitz, The President, the Congress, and Use of Force: Legal and Political Considerations in Authorizing the Use of Force Against International Terrorism, 43 Harv. Int'l L.J. 71, 72 at n. 5.

6. Is a declaration of war needed for the United States to be at war?

   a. "A state of declared war offers the clearest authority for the broadest use of war powers. A state of declared war draws clear lines. It defines ... who the enemy is: another state and all the nationals of that state. It marks a beginning, and (again traditionally) an end, with some legal act or instrument marking its conclusion." ABA, Task Force on Terrorism and the Law, Report and Recommendations on Military Commissions, January 4, 2002, p. 5.

* * *

   c. Professor Turner argues that a congressional declaration of war would only be needed under the Constitution were an aggressive war initiated by the United States; it is not needed in response to a war initiated by others. He further contends that a declaration of war is now an anachronism since aggressive wars are outlawed by the UN Charter and other international documents. Robert F. Turner, The War on Terrorism and the Modern Relevance of the Congressional Power to "Declare War", 25 Harv.J.L. & Pub. Pol'y 519, 524–532 (2002).

   d. The Joint Resolution passed by Congress in the aftermath of September 11 was "the constitutional equivalent of a declaration of war," (quoting Senator Joseph Biden in Turner, op cit supra c. at p. 521).

   e. " 'War' may exist when a state of war has been declared or when activities involving the use of force rise to such a level that a state of war exists. Absent a declaration of war, there may be some uncertainty whether a state of war exists, depending on the level and nature of hostile activities.... Based on [the Joint Resolution] ... and U.S. combat operations in Afghanistan it may be concluded that the United States is at war with al Qaeda, the organization deemed responsible for the September 11 attacks." ABA, Task Force on Treatment of Enemy Combatants, Preliminary Report, August 8, 2002, 7–8 at n. 10.

   f. "War is thus a struggle by armed forces of a certain intensity between groups, of a certain size, consisting of individuals who are armed, who wear distinctive insignia, and who are subjected to military discipline under responsible command." Ingrid Detter de Lupis, The Law of War (Cambridge University Press 1987) p. 24.

g. "Between 1945 and 1999, two-thirds of the members of the United Nations—126 states out of 189—fought 291 interstate conflicts in which over 22 million people were killed.... The international system has come to subsist in a parallel universe of two systems, one de jure, the other de facto. The de jure system consists of illusory rules that would govern the use of force among states in a platonic world of forms, a world that does not exist. The de facto system consists of actual state practice in the real world...." Michael J. Glennon, The Fog of Law: Self–Defense, Inherence, and Incoherence in Article 51 of the United Nations Charter, 25 Harv. J.L. & Pub. Pol'y 539, 540 (2002).

h. "The attacks of September 11 have been described as an act of war. While the label may have political potency, it is unhelpful within the legal framework of terrorism and war. The war power being a prerogative of Congress, formal definition of war is a matter of positive law. And before September 11, the default position of positive law was to categorize terrorism as a crime, not an act of war." Note:, Responding to Terrorism: Crime, Punishment, and War, 115 Harv. L. Rev. 1217, 1225 (2002).

7. Bruce Ackerman, The Emergency Constitution, 113 Yale L.J. 1029, 1032–1037 (2004):

I. Between War and Crime

Our legal tradition provides us with two fundamental concepts—war and crime—to deal with our present predicament. Neither fits.

A. War?

The "war on terrorism" has paid enormous political dividends for President Bush, but that does not make it a compelling legal concept. War is traditionally defined as a state of belligerency between sovereigns. The wars with Afghanistan and Iraq were wars; the struggle against Osama bin Laden and al Qaeda is not. The selective adaptation of doctrines dealing with war predictably leads to sweeping incursions on fundamental liberties. It is one thing for President Roosevelt to designate a captured American citizen serving in the German army as an "enemy combatant" and try him without standard scrutiny by the civilian courts; it is quite another for President Bush to do the same thing for suspected members of al Qaeda.

The difference is obvious and fundamental: Only a very small percentage of the human race is composed of recognized members of the German military, but anybody can be suspected of complicity with al Qaeda. This means that all of us are, in principle, subject to executive detention once we treat the "war on terrorism" as if it were the legal equivalent of the war against Germany.

War between sovereign states also comes to an end; some decisive act of capitulation, armistice, or treaty takes place for all the world to see. But this will not happen in the war against terrorism. Even if bin Laden is caught, tried, and convicted, it will not be clear whether al Qaeda has survived. Even if this network disintegrates, it will likely morph into other terrorist groups. Al Qaeda is already collaborating with Hezbollah, for example, and how will anybody determine where one group ends and the other begins? There are more than six billion people in the world—more than enough to supply terrorist networks with haters, even if the West does nothing to stir the pot. So if we choose to call this a war, it will be endless. This means that we not only subject everybody to the risk of detention by the Commander in Chief, but we subject everybody to the risk of endless detention.

If the President is allowed to punish, as well as to detain, the logic of war-talk leads to the creation of a full-blown alternative system of criminal justice for terrorism suspects. This system is already emerging in the military, and we are beginning to argue about the way it should be constructed: How little evidence suffices to justify how much detention? Can detainees ever get in touch with civilian lawyers? Can these lawyers ever scrutinize the evidence, or must it remain secret?

These are important questions, but it is even more important to challenge the war-talk that makes the entire enterprise seem plausible. The only legal language presently available for making this critique—the language of the criminal law—is not entirely persuasive. But it is powerful.

B.   Crime?

For the criminal law purist, the "war on terrorism" is merely a metaphor without decisive legal significance, more like the "war on drugs" or the "war on crime" than the war against Nazi Germany. Al Qaeda is a dangerous conspiracy, but so is the Mafia, whose activities lead to the deaths of thousands through drug overdoses and gangland murders. Conspiracy is a serious crime, and crime fighters have special tools to deal with it. But nobody supposes that casual talk of a "war on crime" permits us to sweep away the entire panoply of criminal protections built up over the centuries. Why is the "war on terrorism" any different?

Recall too the experience of the Cold War. There was pervasive talk of a Communist conspiracy—and in contrast to al Qaeda, the shadowy cells of grim-faced plotters were supported by a great superpower commanding massive armies with nuclear weapons. American presidents also had substantial evidence of links between domestic Communist cells and the Soviet GRU, which was a military organization. For decades, we were only minutes away from an incident that could lead to nuclear holocaust. From a legal point of view, domestic Communist cells were virtually front-line troops in something very close to a classic war between sovereign states.

Yet no president ever suspended the normal operation of the criminal law by calling domestic Communists "enemy combatants." The

Communist conspiracy was treated as a Communist conspiracy; the accused were provided all the traditional protections of the criminal law. If Cold War anxieties did not overwhelm us, why should war-talk justify extraordinary military measures against small bands of terrorists who cannot rely on the massive assistance of an aggressive superpower?

These are powerful questions that provide a crucial context for questioning the remarkable success of the present administration in persuading the public that wartime emergency measures are appropriate responses to our present predicaments. Richard Hofstadter warned Americans long ago that they were peculiarly vulnerable to the paranoid style of political leadership. We are succumbing yet again.

Despite the excessive rhetoric and repressive practices, there is one distinctive feature of our present situation that distinguishes it from the scares of the past. Begin with the criminal law purist's normative benchmarks: the traditional legal response to the Mafia and other wide-ranging conspiracies. The purist rightfully emphasizes that the criminal law has managed to contain antisocial organizations within tolerable limits without the need for arbitrary police-state measures. Nonetheless, the reassurance such analogies offer is distinctly limited.

Even the most successful organized crime operations lack the over-weening pretensions of the most humble terrorist cell. Mafiosi are generally content to allow government officials to flaunt their symbols of legitimacy so long as gangsters control the underworld. Whatever else is happening in Palermo, the mayor's office is occupied by the duly elected representative of the Italian Republic. But the point of a terrorist bomb is to launch a distinctly political challenge to the government. The deaths caused by terrorists may be smaller in number than those caused by the drug-dealing Mafia. Nevertheless, terrorists' challenge to political authority is greater. The only way to meet this challenge is for the government to demonstrate to its terrified citizens that it is taking steps to act decisively against the blatant assault on its sovereign authority.

The political dimension of the terrorist threat makes the lessons from the McCarthy era more relevant, but once again there is a difference. For all the McCarthyite talk of the Red Menace, the danger remained abstract to ordinary people. While the Cuban Missile Crisis brought us to the brink of World War III, it did not conclude with an event, like the toppling of the Twin Towers, that dramatized America's incapacity to defend its frontiers.

The risk of nuclear devastation during the Cold War might well have been much larger than the terrorist danger today. But we were lucky, and the threat of nuclear holocaust remained a threat. In contrast, the changing technological balance in favor of terrorists means that events like September 11 will recur at unpredictable intervals, each shattering anew the ordinary citizen's confidence in the government's capacity to fend off catastrophic breaches of national security.

Paradoxically, the relative weakness of terrorists compared to the Communist conspiracy only exacerbates the political problems involved in an effective response. If the Cold War threat of nuclear annihilation had been realized, it would have meant the end of civilization as we know it. The survivors would have been obliged to build a legitimate government from the ground up. This will not be true in the new age of terrorism. It may only be a matter of time before a suitcase A-bomb obliterates a major American city, but there will be nothing like a Soviet-style rocket assault leading to the destruction of all major cities simultaneously. Despite the horror, the death, and the pain, American government will survive the day after the tragedy. And it will be obliged to establish—quickly—that it has not been thoroughly demoralized by the lurking terrorist underground.

8.   In Hamdi v. Rumsfeld, 124 S.Ct. 2633, Justice O'Connor, writing for a plurality, stated:

> We recognize that the national security underpinnings of the "war on terror," although crucially important, are broad and malleable. As the Government concedes, "given its unconventional nature, the current conflict is unlikely to end with a formal cease-fire agreement." The prospect Hamdi raises is therefore not far-fetched. If the Government does not consider this unconventional war won for two generations, and if it maintains during that time that Hamdi might, if released, rejoin forces fighting against the United States, then the position it has taken throughout the litigation of this case suggests that Hamdi's detention could last for the rest of his life.

> It is a clearly established principle of the law of war that detention may last no longer than active hostilities. See Article 118 of the Geneva Convention (III) Relative to the Treatment of Prisoners of War, Aug. 12, 1949, [1955] 6 U.S.T. 3316, 3406, T.I.A.S. No. 3364 ("Prisoners of war shall be released and repatriated without delay after the cessation of active hostilities").

> . . .

> . . . [W]e understand Congress' grant of authority for the use of "necessary and appropriate force" to include the authority to detain for the duration of the relevant conflict, and our understanding is based on longstanding law-of-war principles. If the practical circumstances of a given conflict are entirely unlike those of the conflicts that informed the development of the law of war, that understanding may unravel. But that is not the situation we face as of this date. Active combat operations against Taliban fighters apparently are ongoing in Afghanistan. . . . The United States may detain, for the duration of these hostilities, individuals legitimately determined to be Taliban combatants who "engaged in an armed conflict against the United States." If the record establishes that United States troops are still involved in active combat in Afghanistan, those detentions are part of the exercise of "necessary and appropriate force," and therefore are authorized by the AUMF.

9.   What can be inferred from the excerpt from Justice O'Connor's opinion regarding the question whether the "war" against al Qaeda is a war that invokes "longstanding law-of-war principles?"

10.   "If America is at war, did it start on September 11, 2001, or when U.S. forces invaded Afghanistan? Did it end when U.S. troops toppled the Taliban?" The Miami Herald, Herald.com, Nov. 1, 2004.

11.   See Noah Feldman, Choices of Law, Choices of War, 25 Harv. J.L. & Pub. Pol'y 457 (2002); Philip B. Heymann, Terrorism, Freedom and Security: Winning Without War (2003).

12.   David Cole, The Priority of Morality: the Emergency Constitution's Blind Spot, 113 Yale L.J. 1753, 1756–1759, 1773, (2004):

> . . . Ackerman offers preventive detention only as an example of an emergency power under his "emergency constitution." His ambition is not simply to design a preventive detention scheme; he calls for nothing less than a "sweeping revision of the emergency power provisions currently found in many of the world's constitutions." His basic idea is to give the Executive extraordinary emergency powers—including suspicionless preventive detention—while conditioning the state of emergency on a political process check—the "supermajoritarian escalator"—designed to forestall "permanent" emergencies. Inspired by South Africa's constitution, Ackerman proposes that a majority vote be required to continue the emergency for the first two to three months, that a sixty-percent vote be required to extend the emergency two more months, that seventy percent be required for the next two months, and eighty percent thereafter. Under such a scheme, emergencies would be unlikely to last more than six to seven months in the absence of truly extraordinary consensus.

> Ackerman's attempt to impose a meaningful but flexible time constraint on emergency powers is laudable: Undoubtedly one problem with "states of emergency" and their attendant powers is that they have a way of dragging on far longer than the actual emergency does. His insight that political process safeguards are critically important in checking emergency powers is perceptive and important, as is his sense that we should think about emergency powers now, before the next attack sends us into panic mode again. His solution is creative and, if adopted, might even work: The supermajoritarian escalator might actually succeed in putting an end to states of emergency in a timely manner. But time limits are only one problem with emergency powers, and a solution to the durational issue leaves unanswered the more difficult question of precisely what substantive powers ought to be assigned to the government for the duration of the emergency.

> . . .

> My Essay takes on three aspects of Ackerman's thesis—its premises, its efficacy, and its morality. Part I critiques three of Ackerman's

premises—his underestimation of courts and overestimation of legislatures as guardians of liberty, his misguided belief that the supermajoritarian escalator provides a one-size-fits-all solution to the conundrum of emergency powers, and his contention that the short-lived character of emergencies makes it sensible to cede to a minority of our popular representatives control over critically important and largely unpredictable decisions concerning the appropriate duration of emergency powers.

Part II turns to the details, and finds fatal shortcomings in the proposed implementation of Ackerman's scheme. First, the limits it prescribes would do nothing to respond to the preventive detention abuses so evident in the post-September 11 roundup; with the exception of three individuals held as "enemy combatants," all the domestic detentions were accomplished without resort to any "emergency" powers. Second, Ackerman's after-the-fact compensation scheme fails to confront the basic question of who deserves compensation and why. As a result, the scheme would not have the deterrent effect he claims and, on the contrary, would legitimate detention of innocent people. Third, despite Ackerman's purported quid pro quo of preventive detention authority for a supermajoritarian escalator check, many and perhaps most preventive detentions would never be affected by the supermajoritarian escalator, as they would typically occur in the initial weeks following the attacks, before the escalator kicks in.

Part III contends that Ackerman has failed to confront the central normative questions presented by his proposal—namely, whether it is ever justified to incarcerate innocent people without suspicion, whether reassuring a public in panic is an acceptable justification for such suspicionless detention, and whether preventive detention without prompt judicial review ought to be countenanced outside a battlefield.

... Ackerman's supermajoritarian escalator rests on an unproven and unprovable premise that emergencies are likely to be short-lived. ...

In fact, there is substantial evidence that emergencies are not likely to be as short-lived as Ackerman posits

. . .

In sum, the premises for Ackerman's proposal are open to question in three fundamental respects: He is too pessimistic about courts and too optimistic about legislatures; his "political process" one-size-fits-all solution resolves very little about the appropriate extent of emergency powers; and his view of the likely duration of emergencies is simply unrealistic.

13.   Laurence H. Tribe and Patrick O. Gudridge, The Anti–Emergency Constitution, 113 Yale.L.J. 1801, 1801–1805, 1807 (2004):

The season for talk of leaving the Constitution behind, while we grit our teeth and do what must be done in times of grave peril—the season for talk of saving the Constitution from the distortions wrought by sheer necessity, while we save ourselves from the dangers of genuine fidelity to the Constitution—is upon us. Such talk, the staple of commentary on the survival of constitutional democracies in wartime and other similarly trying periods, was to be expected in the wake of September 11.

It was once an unspeakable thought that our Constitution should have lacunae—temporal discontinuities within which nation-saving steps would be taken by those in power, blessed not by the nation's founding document but by the brute necessities of survival. But the unspeakable became more readily articulable when the inimitable pen of Robert H. Jackson gave word to the thought in his canonical dissent from the Supreme Court's justly infamous Korematsu decision, proclaiming that the great harm to liberty and equality done by the military expulsion of Japanese Americans from their homes and communities was dwarfed by the still greater harm done by bending the Constitution into a form that could rationalize that course of action. Better by far, Jackson darkly suggested, would have been a strategy whereby the military would have been left free to do what the law of necessity called for, while the courts washed their hands of the affair and did nothing to create a precedent by holding the military's actions to be constitutional.

Although Justice Jackson failed to work out a scheme that could actually achieve both of those results, there has been no dearth of commentators seeking to close the Jackson gap by dreaming up elaborate superstructures of doctrine and meta-doctrine that could essentially square the circle that the Justice left unsquared. By no means the first of these commentators but by far the most ambitious has been, not surprisingly, Bruce Ackerman, who brings to the task his special gift for provokery. His work, even (perhaps especially) for the unpersuaded reader, persists in memory—reorients resistant thought and recasts problems, working materials, even expectations. The Emergency Constitution is no exception. It is brave. Ackerman proposes that we assume the trauma of September 11 will recur often, and that we face up to the task of thinking through the work constitutional law must do given this assumption. It is startling. Ackerman believes that ordinary constitutional law in all its elaborateness (mostly "fog," he seems to think) should overtly give way in states of emergency like that occasioned by September 11. It is inventive. Ackerman proposes that in states of emergency a constitution of his own devising should instead apply.

In the United States, he thinks, this constitution would likely take the form of a framework statute. Basic procedures are clearly outlined. Each particular state of emergency would require congressional authorization; such authorizations would be subject to time limits and provisions requiring escalating supermajorities for renewals. Congress would be able, in a structured way, to obtain pertinent information developed by executive officials.

But it is not always easy to grasp more than the vaguest contours of Ackerman's scheme. For example, the content of the powers granted to executive officials by a declaration of emergency seems to be left to improvisation by unspecified institutions and at unspecified times (whether by Congress ex ante, or by Congress at the time of the emergency's invocation, or by the emergency-invoking Executive at that time). Ackerman often talks as though authority to engage in wide-scale preventive detention will be the principal power conferred. On this assumption, individuals would be afforded a limited set of procedural and substantive rights, including time limits on detention, a ban on torture, and a right to compensation for those ultimately determined to have been wrongly incarcerated. But at other points, especially in This Is Not a War, Ackerman suggests that any of a seemingly open-ended list of counterterrorism measures might come into play. As a result, this Essay at times must proceed in the alternative, yielding a regrettable cumbersomeness that may make it especially helpful to identify at the outset the broad themes we pursue in the pages that follow.

Our first concern is pragmatic: Is Ackerman's "emergency constitution" a remotely plausible way to organize government action? To the extent that the scheme sets itself up outside ordinary constitutional law—as freestanding—it warrants a particularly searching examination to test for unexpected implications or byproducts, including any that may be so troubling as to bring the entire enterprise into doubt. Based on that examination, we believe the grounds are overwhelming for rejecting the Ackerman proposal as anything beyond an interesting thought experiment—a useful reminder of the reasons for not following the sirens that beckon us in times of crisis to set the Constitution aside and to live by another code altogether.

Second, we worry about the enormity of what proposals like Ackerman's would have us give up in order to create bracketed times and spaces within which we might do terrible things without thereby becoming terrible people. Ackerman, it often appears, genuinely means to jettison much of ordinary constitutional law during the brightly demarked periods within which his emergency constitution is in force. It therefore becomes important to evaluate how the propositions of constitutional law that are retained by—or, more properly, incorporated by reference in—the Ackerman emergency constitution will work in their new context. Beyond that, there is the large question of what Ackerman is willing to abandon, however temporarily....

    . . .

Do we think Ackerman's proposal is unconstitutional within the terms of ordinary constitutional law? In an important sense, the question answers itself. Of course we do:

    . . .

The issue, ... is whether constitutional law, as we experience it (make it, interpret it, teach it, deploy it) in all its ordinary complexity, should in important respects be set to the side and suspended during certain defined episodes that will punctuate our lives as we engage in the grave business of fighting terrorism.

14. Bruce Ackerman, Response, This Is Not a War, 113 Yale L.J. 1871, 1871–1874, 1876–1878 (2004).

"I know that some people question if America is really in a war at all. They view terrorism more as a crime, a problem to be solved mainly with law enforcement and indictments. After the World Trade Center was first attacked in 1993, some of the guilty were indicted and tried and convicted and sent to prison. But the matter was not settled. The terrorists were still training and plotting in other nations and drawing up more ambitious plans. After the chaos and carnage of September the 11th, it is not enough to serve our enemies with legal papers. The terrorists and their supporters declared war on the United States, and war is what they got." [Applause.]

—President George W. Bush, State of the Union, January 20, 2004

The Cold War. The War on Poverty. The War on Crime. The War on Drugs. The War on Terrorism. Apparently, it isn't enough to call a high-priority initiative a High–Priority Initiative. If it's really important, only a wimp refuses to call it war, almost without regard to its relationship to the real thing.

* * *

While it is easy enough to condemn this tendency toward war-talk, the State of the Union suggests that more than moralizing will be required to check the presidential dynamic. Consider the artful way that the speech sets up a sharp dichotomy as the foundation for its martial conclusion. The only alternative to war, President Bush suggests, is to "view terrorism more as a crime, a problem to be solved mainly with law enforcement and indictments." So far as he is concerned, September 11 demonstrated the futility of "serving our enemies with legal papers." According to the President, that leaves us with a single remaining alternative: "The terrorists and their supporters declared war on the United States, and war is what they got."

I want to prevent this rhetorical slide to war by creating a third framework that disrupts the President's false dichotomy: This is not a war, but a state of emergency. I build upon ideas and practices that are already in common use. The newscasts constantly report declarations of emergency by governors responding to natural disasters—and though this is less familiar to ordinary citizens, presidents regularly declare emergencies in response to foreign crises and terrorist threats.My aim is to develop these well-established practices further and construct a new bulwark against the presidential war-dynamic. When the next terrorist strike occurs, we should not turn to our television sets to see the President of the United States heating up the war-talk to an even higher pitch. It would be far better to see him go before Congress and somberly request its support for a declaration of a limited state of emergency.

* * *

Chapter 6

EXTENDED DETENTION I:
MATERIAL WITNESSES
AND ALIENS

A. Introduction

The power to detain an individual for an extended period can be used as a potent enforcement tool. A period of extended detention can be utilized to interrogate and obtain information—whether to be used against the person being detained or to assist in the apprehension and prosecution of others. Extended for a long enough period, detention may itself serve as a kind of sanction, albeit without the sanctioned person having had a trial or having been convicted. The conditions under which a person is detained and what goes on during the detention have implications for the issue of whether the detention amounts to punishment. The conditions and what goes on are also relevant to the legality of any interrogation that takes place. Issues relating to the processes used in interrogating detainees held in Guantanamo Bay post–9/11, for prisoners seized in the military action in Afghanistan, and in military prisons in Iraq have taken center stage: the treatment of these prisoners has raised questions about whether torture may in some circumstances be permissible, and about prisoner abuse, apart from interrogation. Detention extended long enough, may also viewed as an effective means to incapacitate and prevent the commission of crimes.

Absent a legal basis, the detention of an individual by the government in this country would violate his or her constitutional rights. There are a number of different legal bases for detaining people in the United States. Post-arrest, prior-to-charge detention that does not have any other basis is usually limited in length. Post-charge, pre-trial detention can be quite lengthy if the accused is denied bail or cannot make the bail that is set. The use of preventive detention pending trial, on the ground that the accused is dangerous, is a relatively recent development in the federal system based on specific statutory authorization. See United States v. Salerno, 481 U.S. 739 (1987). Also see 18 U.S.C. § 3142 (e) and (f), and section 6952 of the Intelligence Reform and Terrorism Prevention Act of 2004 (extending the presumption of preventive detention in a certain category of cases to additional offenses). Some other categories of persons subject to extended detention: juveniles; sex offenders; and mental illness-public deviance, are not usually relevant to the anti-terrorist enforcement effort.

Another basis for detention that can last in certain circumstances up to one year, or possibly two, is the citing for contempt and detaining of a recalcitrant witness, who refuses to testify before the grand jury, for the period during which the grand jury sits. The focus in section B. below is on a related basis for extended detention, namely, holding a person as a material witness, even though charges have not yet been filed against anyone. In section C. we review the post–9/11 experience with detaining aliens in aid of terrorism investigations through the use of immigration laws and also examine legislative provisions for detaining aliens on the ground that they are suspected terrorists. Chapter 7 continues the detention theme, treating the detention of individuals on the ground that they are enemy combatants, examining the incidents of the different types of hearings being conducted regarding the Guantanamo detainees, and also dealing with issues relating to the conditions of detention, including interrogation and the legality of harsh methods including torture.

Following the events of September 11, 2001, federal agents arrested and detained over 1000 individuals, many of whom remained under detention for an extended period, in some cases for more than a year. Generally, either of two legal justifications was offered for these detentions. One basis was that individuals were being held as material witnesses. The second, more frequently invoked basis was that the individuals were aliens and had committed immigration law violations and could be held pending disposition of the alleged violations.

The Department of Justice declined to provide information about who was being detained, where these individuals were being detained and how many persons were being detained.

* * *

B.   Material witness detention

* * *

The federal material witness statute is 18 U.S.C. § 3144.

18 U.S.C.

§ 3144.   Release or detention of a material witness

If it appears from an affidavit filed by a party that the testimony of a person is material in a criminal proceeding, and if it is shown that it may become impracticable to secure the presence of the person by subpoena, a judicial officer may order the arrest of the person and treat the person in accordance with the provisions of section 3142 of this title. No material witness may be detained because of inability to comply with any condition of release if the testimony of such witness can adequately be secured by deposition, and if further detention is not necessary to prevent a failure of justice. Release of a material witness may be delayed for a reasonable period of time until the deposition of the witness can be taken pursuant to the Federal Rules of Criminal Procedure.

Also see Rule 46 of the Federal Rules of Criminal Procedure:

Rule 46. Release from Custody; Supervising Detention

(a) Before Trial. The provisions of 18 U.S.C. §§ 3142 and 3144 govern pretrial release.

. . .

(h) Supervising Detention Pending Trial.

(1) *In General.* To eliminate unnecessary detention, the court must supervise the detention within the district of any defendants awaiting trial and of any persons held as material witnesses.

(2) *Reports.* An attorney for the government must report bi-weekly to the court, listing each material witness held in custody for more than 10 days pending indictment, arraignment, or trial. For each material witness listed in the report, an attorney for the government must state why the witness should not be released with or without a deposition being taken under Rule 15(a).

. . .

Notes and Questions

1. Under certain conditions, section 3144 authorizes the arrest and detention of a person whose testimony is material in a criminal proceeding:

a. An affidavit must be filed by the government alleging that the testimony of the person to be detained is "material in a criminal proceeding."

b. A showing must be made that it is impractical do secure the presence of the person by subpoena.

c. If the testimony of the material witness can be adequately secured by deposition and if detention is not necessary to prevent a failure of justice, he/she may not be detained.

2. The basic showing that needs to be made is that the testimony of the witness is material in a criminal proceeding. The government has taken the position that they can arrest individuals and hold them as material witnesses even in the absence of a relevant criminal prosecution having been initiated, provided that the grand jury was sitting and investigating criminal matters. The government's theory is that the grand jury proceeding is a "criminal proceeding" within the meaning of section 3144. How sound is this theory? Acceptance of the government's theory (see the Awadallah case below) seems to permit the government to hold the individual at least for the period in which the instant grand jury continued to sit. (Compare the doctrine applicable to a witness called before the grand jury to testify who

refuses to do so, is held in contempt and can be detained for the duration during which that grand jury sits.)

3. The material witness provision, 18 U.S.C. § 3144 refers to § 3142, which deals with conditions of release and hearing requirements for defendants. § 3142 is discussed infra in Awadallah.

4. Rule 46 of the Federal Rules of Criminal Procedure deals with material witness matters. An amendment of Rule 46 promulgated in 2002 is relevant to the issue of whether a grand jury proceeding is a criminal proceeding within the meaning of § 3144. See the discussion in Awadallah, infra.

UNITED STATES v. AWADALLAH

349 F.3d 42 (2d Cir. 2003)
cert. denied, Awadallah v. United States, 125 S.Ct. 861 (2005).

Before: JACOBS and STRAUB, Circuit Judges, and CARMAN, Chief Judge. Judge STRAUB concurs in the opinion except as to Part II.C.3, and has filed a separate concurrence.

JACOBS, Circuit Judge.

This appeal, which arises from the government's investigation of the September 11, 2001 terrorist attacks, presents questions about the scope of the federal material witness statute and the government's powers of arrest and detention thereunder. See 18 U.S.C. § 3144. The district court (Scheindlin, J.) ruled that the statute cannot be applied constitutionally to a grand jury witness such as the defendant-appellee, Osama Awadallah, and dismissed the perjury indictment against him as fruit of an illegal detention. . . . We conclude that these rulings must be reversed and the indictment reinstated. . . .

In the days immediately following September 11, 2001, the United States Attorney for the Southern District of New York initiated a grand jury investigation into the terrorist attacks. Investigators quickly identified Nawaf Al–Hazmi and Khalid Al–Mihdhar as two of the hijackers on American Airlines Flight 77, which crashed into the Pentagon. The Justice Department released the identities of all nineteen hijackers on Friday, September 14, 2001, and news media around the country publicized their names and photographs the following day. A search of the car Al–Hazmi abandoned at Dulles Airport in Virginia produced a piece of paper with the notation, "Osama 589–5316." Federal agents tracked this number to a San Diego address at which the defendant, Osama Awadallah, had lived approximately eighteen months earlier. Al–Hazmi and Al–Mihdhar also had lived in the San Diego vicinity around that time. The district court made extensive factual findings concerning the ensuing events of September 20 and 21, 2001. See United States v. Awadallah, 202 F.Supp.2d 82, 85–96 (S.D.N.Y.2002) ("Awadallah IV"). With two minor exceptions, the court credited Awadallah's testimony over that of the FBI agents. . . . However, the government "has elected not to appeal Judge Scheindlin's credibility findings and does not contest them here."

For purposes of this appeal, then, the government accepts and relies on the facts found by the district court, as does Awadallah. Our recitation of the facts conforms to the district court's findings. . . .

Throughout the questioning . . ., the FBI agents in San Diego had been in contact with an Assistant United States Attorney ("AUSA") in New York. At approximately 2:00 p.m. Eastern time, the AUSA instructed the agents to arrest Awadallah as a material witness. The agents handcuffed Awadallah and took him to the San Diego correctional center for booking. Meanwhile, prosecutors and agents in New York prepared an application for a material witness warrant. In the supporting affidavit, FBI Special Agent Ryan Plunkett recounted how the FBI found the phone number in Al–Hazmi's car, Awadallah's admission that he knew Al–Hazmi, and the results of the agents' searches, including the "box-cutter" and the photographs of bin Laden. Agent Plunkett stated that it might become difficult to secure Awadallah's grand jury testimony because he had extensive family ties in Jordan and might be a flight risk. The affidavit did not say when Awadallah said he had last seen Al–Hazmi (over a year earlier); that Awadallah had moved eighteen months earlier from the address associated with the phone number; that Awadallah had used the "box-cutter" recently to install a new carpet in his apartment; that Awadallah had been (ostensibly) cooperative with the FBI agents in San Diego; or that Awadallah had three brothers who lived in San Diego, one of whom was an American citizen. Also, the affidavit stated that the "box-cutter" had been found in Awadallah's apartment when, in fact, it had been found in his inoperative second car. Shortly before 6:00 p.m. Eastern time, Agent Plunkett and an AUSA presented the material witness warrant application to Chief Judge Mukasey of the United States District Court for the Southern District of New York. Based solely on the contents of Agent Plunkett's affidavit, Chief Judge Mukasey issued a warrant to arrest Awadallah as a material witness pursuant to 18 U.S.C. § 3144. The court was unaware that Awadallah had already been arrested as a material witness three hours earlier.

On September 25, 2001, Awadallah appeared before a Magistrate Judge Ruben B. Brooks in the Southern District of California, who declined to release him on bail and ordered that he be removed to New York. On October 2, 2001, the day after he arrived in New York, Awadallah appeared before Chief Judge Mukasey for a second bail hearing. Chief Judge Mukasey also declined to release Awadallah on bail, finding his continued detention to be "reasonable under the circumstances."

During the period of his detention, Awadallah spent time in four prisons as he was transferred to the New York correctional center by way of Oklahoma City. He alleges that he received harsh and improper treatment during this period. Because these allegations of abuse and mistreatment were immaterial to the issues before the district court, Judge Scheindlin expressly declined to make "findings of fact on disputed issues regarding the conditions of confinement... On October 10, 2001, twenty days after his arrest as a material witness, Awadallah testified before the grand jury in the Southern District of New York. The prosecutor questioned him for most of the day. In the course of his testimony, Awadallah denied knowing anyone named Khalid Al–Mihdhar or Khalid.... On October 15, 2001, when Awadallah again appeared before the grand jury, he stated that his recollection of Khalid's name had been refreshed by his October 10 testimony and that the disputed writing in the exam booklet was in fact his own. However, he did not admit to making false statements in his first grand jury appearance.

The United States Attorney for the Southern District of New York filed charges against Awadallah on two counts of making false statements to the grand jury in violation of 18 U.S.C. § 1623: falsely denying that he knew Khalid Al–Mihdhar (Count One); and falsely denying that the handwriting in the exam booklet was his own (Count Two).

On November 27, 2001, the district court (Scheindlin, *J.*) granted Awadallah's bail application. He satisfied the bail conditions and was released approximately two weeks later. In December 2001, Awadallah moved to dismiss the indictment....

On April 30, 2002, after an evidentiary hearing and further briefing, the district court issued two orders dismissing the indictment against Awadallah. In *Awadallah III,* the court ruled that the federal material witness statute, 18 U.S.C. § 3144, did not apply to grand jury witnesses. 202 F.Supp.2d at 61–79. This ruling evidently was made without briefing or argument. The court held that Awadallah's arrest and detention were therefore unlawful. ... Judge Scheindlin ruled that Awadallah's perjured grand jury testimony had to be suppressed as fruit of this illegal arrest and detention....

The government filed a timely notice of appeal. ... Awadallah remains free on bail at this time.

We consider the issues presented on appeal in the order in which the district court developed them: (1) whether the federal material witness statute, 18 U.S.C. § 3144, may be applied to grand jury witnesses like Awadallah; ...

Applicability of 18 U.S.C. § 3144

The first issue presented is whether the federal material witness statute, 18 U.S.C. § 3144, allows the arrest and detention of grand jury witnesses. In *Awadallah III,* the district court determined that it did not. Shortly thereafter, however, on July 11, 2002, Chief Judge Mukasey issued an opinion in an unrelated case that declined to follow the reasoning and holding of *Awadallah III.* Specifically, Judge Mukasey held that 18 U.S.C. § 3144 applies to grand jury witnesses. *See In re Material Witness Warrant,* 213 F.Supp.2d 287, 288 (S.D.N.Y.2002). Thus there is now a split of authority within the Circuit on this question.

... Both parties to this appeal, as well as the amici, persuasively urge us to decide whether § 3144 may properly be applied to grand jury witnesses. The issue is squarely presented, has been fully briefed, and will tend to evade review in future cases where the detention is brief or matters take a different procedural course.

18 U.S.C. § 3144 ... is cast in terms of a material witness in "a criminal proceeding." The decisive question here is whether that term encompasses proceedings before a grand jury. Based on its study of the statutory wording, context, legislative history, and case law, the district court held that "Section 3144 only allows the detention of material witnesses in the pretrial (as opposed to the grand jury) context." We have found no other decision that has arrived at this conclusion .

The only prior case that squarely considered the issue held that 18 U.S.C. § 3149, the precursor to today's material witness statute, allowed detention of grand jury witnesses. *See Bacon v. United States,* 449 F.2d 933, 936–41 (9th Cir.1971). The Ninth Circuit conceded that "[t]he term 'criminal proceeding,' absent a clear context, [was] ambiguous," but held that the relevant statutes and Federal Rules of Criminal Procedure, "[t]aken as a whole," were "clearly broad enough in scope to encompass grand jury investigations".

Other courts, including this one, have assumed that the material witness statute authorizes detention of grand jury witnesses. ...

Two judges have also declined to follow the district court's ruling in this case. In *In re Material Witness Warrant,* 213 F.Supp.2d 287 (S.D.N.Y.2002), Chief Judge Mukasey "decline[d] to follow the reasoning and holding in *Awadallah,*" holding instead:

> Given the broad language of the statute, its legislative history ..., the substantial body of case law indicating that there is no constitutional impediment to detention of grand jury witnesses, and the unquestioned application of the statute to grand jury witnesses over a period of decades before *Awadallah,* to perceive a Congressional intention that grand jury witnesses be excluded from the reach of section 3144 is to perceive something that is not there.

> [S]ee also In re Grand Jury Material Witness Detention, 271 F.Supp.2d 1266, 1268 (D.Or.2003) (concluding that "a grand jury proceeding constitutes a 'criminal proceeding,' as the term is used in § 3144"). Having the benefit of thorough opinions on both sides of the question, we conclude that the district court's ruling in this case must be reversed.

...

B. Language of the Statute

As noted above, § 3144 applies to witnesses whose testimony is material in "a criminal proceeding." 18 U.S.C. § 3144. "Criminal proceeding" is a broad and capacious term, and there is good reason to conclude that it includes a grand jury proceeding. First, it has long been recognized that "[t]he word 'proceeding' is not a technical one, and is aptly used by courts to designate an inquiry before a grand jury." Second, the term "criminal proceeding" has been construed in other statutes to encompass grand jury proceedings....

Notwithstanding this support for the general view that "criminal proceedings" encompass grand jury proceedings, however, we cannot say that the statutory wording alone compels that conclusion. Black's Law Dictionary defines a "criminal proceeding" as "[a] proceeding instituted to determine a person's guilt or innocence or to set a convicted person's punishment; a criminal hearing or trial." *Black's Law Dictionary* 1221 (7th ed.1999). It defines a "grand jury" as "[a] body of ... people ... who, in ex parte proceedings, decide whether to issue indictments. If the grand jury decides that evidence is strong enough to hold a suspect for trial, it returns a bill of indictment ... charging the suspect with a specific crime." Defined this way, a grand jury proceeding is not a "proceeding instituted to determine a person's guilt or innocence or to set a convicted person's punishment," but rather a proceeding to "decide whether to issue indictments." ... A grand jury proceeding is certainly a stage of criminal justice; and it is certainly a proceeding. As a proceeding, it is certainly not civil, administrative, arbitral, commercial, social, or any type of proceeding other than (or as much as) criminal. Even so, the dictionary entries could suggest that grand jury proceedings lie outside the scope of § 3144.

. . .

The statutory context does not allay all uncertainty. Under § 3144, a judge "may order the arrest of the person and treat the person in accordance with the provisions of section 3142 of this title." 18 U.S.C. § 3144. Section 3142, which sets conditions for the "[r]elease or detention of a defendant pending trial," uses terms not normally associated with grand juries. It provides: Upon the appearance before a judicial officer of a person *charged with an offense,* the judicial officer shall issue an order that, *pending trial,* the person be—(1) released on personal recognizance or upon execution of an unsecured appearance bond ...; (2) released on a condition or combination of conditions ...; (3) temporarily detained to permit revocation of conditional release, deportation, or exclusion ...; or (4) detained....

By its own terms, § 3142 applies during the post-indictment ("a person charged with an offense") and pretrial ("pending trial") phase of criminal prosecution. The section also goes on to identify factors to be considered "in determining whether there are conditions of release that will reasonably assure the appearance of the person as required and the safety of any other person and the community." 18 U.S.C. § 3142(g). Two of the four listed considerations have little bearing on the situation of an individual detained as a material witness in a grand jury proceeding. *See* 18 U.S.C. § 3142(g)(1) ("[t]he nature and circumstances of the offense charged"); *id.* § 3142(g)(2) ("the weight of the evidence against the person"). For these reasons, we must look beyond the text of § 3144 to discern the meaning of "criminal proceeding."

C. Legislative History

The legislative history of § 3144 makes clear Congress's intent to include grand jury proceedings within the definition of "criminal proceeding." Congress enacted § 3144 in its current form as part of the Bail Reform Act of 1984. *See* Pub.L. No. 98–473, 98 Stat. 1837, 1976–81 (1984). Its language is nearly identical to the text of its predecessor statute, 18 U.S.C. § 1349 (1966), which the Ninth Circuit construed to encompass grand juries. *See Bacon,* 449 F.2d at 939–41....

The most telling piece of legislative history appears in the Senate Judiciary Committee Report that accompanied the 1984 enactment of § 3144. The Report stated that, "[i]f a person's testimony is material in any criminal proceeding, and if it is shown that it may become impracticable to secure his presence by subpoena, the government is authorized to take such person into custody." S.Rep. No. 98–225, at 28 (1983), *reprinted in* 1984 U.S.C.C.A.N. 3182, 3211. A footnote to this statement advised categorically that "[a] grand jury investigation is a 'criminal proceeding' within the meaning of this section. *Bacon v. United States,* 449 F.2d 933 (9th Cir.1971)." *Id.* at 25 n. 88, 1984 U.S.C.C.A.N. at 3208. The approving citation to *Bacon* by the Senate Committee with responsibility for this bill is as indicative as the text of the footnote....

In surveying legislative history we have repeatedly stated that the authoritative source for finding the Legislature's intent lies in the Committee Reports on the bill, which "represen[t] the considered and collective understanding of those Congressmen involved in drafting and studying proposed legislation."

Here, the Senate committee report states in so many words the intent to include grand jury proceedings within the ambit of the statute—an intent that is consistent with the statute's language, even if not compelled by it.

This statement of congressional intent is particularly telling, because the Bail Reform Act of 1984 reenacted the provisions of the former § 3149 in nearly identical language. "Congress is presumed to be aware of an administrative or judicial interpretation of a statute and to adopt that interpretation when it re-enacts a statute without change."...

* * *

D. Constitutional Considerations...

As a threshold matter, the detention of material witnesses for the purpose of securing grand jury testimony has withstood constitutional challenge.

... [W]e see no serious constitutional problem that would warrant the exclusion of grand jury proceedings from the scope of § 3144.

...

The essential purpose of the proscriptions in the Fourth Amendment is to impose a standard of "reasonableness" upon the exercise of discretion by government officials, including law enforcement agents, in order "to safeguard the privacy and security of individuals against arbitrary invasions...." Thus, the permissibility of a particular law enforcement practice is judged by balancing its intrusion on the individual's Fourth Amendment interests against its promotion of legitimate governmental interests.

. . . Thus we must consider both "the nature and quality of the intrusion on the individual's Fourth Amendment interests" and "the importance of the governmental interests alleged to justify the intrusion." . . . In its balancing analysis, the district court found that "[t]he only legitimate reason to detain a grand jury witness is to aid in 'an ex parte investigation to determine whether a crime has been committed and whether criminal proceedings should be instituted against any person.' ". . . This is no small interest. . . . The district court noted (and we agree) that it would be improper for the government to use § 3144 for other ends, such as the detention of persons suspected of criminal activity for which probable cause has not yet been established. However, the district court made no finding (and we see no evidence to suggest) that the government arrested Awadallah for any purpose other than to secure information material to a grand jury investigation. Moreover, that grand jury was investigating the September 11 terrorist attacks. The particular governmental interests at stake therefore were the indictment and successful prosecution of terrorists whose attack, if committed by a sovereign, would have been tantamount to war, and the discovery of the conspirators' means, contacts, and operations in order to forestall future attacks.

On the other side of the balance, the district court found in essence that § 3144 was not calibrated to minimize the intrusion on the liberty of a grand jury witness. According to the district court, several procedural safeguards available to trial witnesses are not afforded in the grand jury context. We agree with the district court, of course, that arrest and detention are significant infringements on liberty, but we conclude that § 3144 sufficiently limits that infringement and reasonably balances it against the government's countervailing interests.

The first procedural safeguard to be considered is § 3144's provision that "[n]o material witness may be detained because of inability to comply with any condition of release *if the testimony of such witness can adequately be secured by deposition,* and if further detention is not necessary to prevent a failure of justice." 18 U.S.C. § 3144 (emphasis added). The district court agreed with the government that this deposition provision does not apply to grand jury witnesses. The government's altered position on appeal is that "Congress intended depositions to be available as a less restrictive alternative to detaining a grand jury witness." Such a pivot by the government on appeal is awkward, but we accept the government's explanation that it was persuaded by Chief Judge Mukasey's view in *In re Material Witness Warrant,* 213 F.Supp.2d at 296.

We conclude that the deposition mechanism is available for grand jury witnesses detained under § 3144. At the time of Awadallah's detention, the Federal Rule of Criminal Procedure that governs depositions provided:

If a witness is detained pursuant to [§ 3144], the court on written motion of the witness and upon notice to the parties may direct that the witness' deposition be taken. After the deposition has been subscribed the court may discharge the witness.

The district court is thereby authorized to order a deposition and to release the witness once it has been taken. Awadallah and the NYCDL argue that this provision cannot apply to grand jury witnesses because there can be no "party" or "trial" prior to indictment. The prosecutor and the witness may broadly be deemed parties, however, in the sense that each has interests to advance or protect before the grand jury. Thus, the rule governing the issuance of subpoenas—which indisputably applies during grand jury proceedings—refers to "the party requesting" a subpoena. Fed.R.Crim.P. 17(a).

The district court found the deposition provision inapplicable in the grand jury context in part because a conventional deposition is inconsistent with the procedural and evidentiary rules of a grand jury hearing. ... [T]he district court may set additional conditions for the conduct of a deposition. *Compare* Fed.R.Crim.P. 15(d) (1987) ("[s]ubject to such additional conditions as the court shall provide"), *with* Fed.R.Crim.P. 15(e) (2003) ("[u]nless these rules or a court order provides otherwise"). The court thus can limit the deposition according to grand jury protocol, for example by limiting the witness's right to have counsel present during the deposition or by permitting the use of hearsay.

Rule 46 of the Federal Rules of Criminal Procedure, which governs detention and release, further supports the view that depositions are available to grand jury witnesses detained under § 3144. The version of Rule 46 in effect at the time of Awadallah's detention provided that "[t]he attorney for the government shall make a biweekly report to the court listing *each* defendant and *witness* who has been *held in custody pending indictment,* arraignment or trial for a period in excess of ten days," and as to "each witness so listed," state "the reasons why such witness should not be released with or without the taking of a *deposition* pursuant to Rule 15(a)." Fed.R.Crim.P. 46(g) (1993) (emphasis added). The new version of the rule, which omits the reference to defendants, is even more explicit:

> An attorney for the government must report biweekly to the court, listing each material witness held in custody for more than 10 days pending indictment, arraignment, or trial. For each material witness listed in the report, an attorney for the government must state why the witness should not be released with or without a deposition being taken under Rule 15(a).

Fed. R. Crim. P. 46(h)(2) (2003) (emphasis added).

Both versions of the rule expressly contemplate the deposition of a "witness held in custody ... pending indictment." It follows that the deposition mechanism of § 3144 is a safeguard available to grand jury witnesses.

The second procedural safeguard at issue is § 3144's express invocation of the bail and release provisions set forth in 18 U.S.C. § 3142. Section 3144 directs that "a judicial officer may . . . treat the [detained] person in accordance with the provisions of section 3142 of this title." 18 U.S.C. § 3144. As noted above, § 3142 sets conditions for the "[r]elease or detention of a defendant pending trial," as follows:

Upon the appearance before a judicial officer of a person charged with an offense, the judicial officer shall issue an order that, pending trial, the person be—(1) released on personal recognizance or upon execution of an unsecured appearance bond . . .; (2) released on a condition or combination of conditions . . .; (3) temporarily detained to permit revocation of conditional release, deportation, or exclusion . . .; or (4) detained. . . . 18 U.S.C. § 3142(a).

As the district court observed, some of the terms used in § 3142— namely, "a person charged with an offense" and "pending trial"—do not comport with the structure of grand jury proceedings. However, we do not deduce (as the district court did) that "it is plain that section 3142 cannot apply to grand jury proceedings." We agree with Chief Judge Mukasey that the provisions of § 3142 govern insofar as they are applicable in the grand jury setting:

[T]he common sense reading of section 3144 is that it refers to section 3142 only insofar as that section is applicable to witnesses, in making available such alternatives to incarceration as release on bail or on conditions, in suggesting standards such as risk of flight, likelihood that the person will appear, and danger to the community, and in providing for a detention hearing. Not every provision of section 3142 applies to witnesses, but some do, and those govern. *In re Material Witness Warrant,* 213 F.Supp.2d at 295.

Thus, a person detained as a material witness in a grand jury investigation may obtain a hearing on the propriety of his continued detention and the conditions, if any, which will allow his release.

The district court also observed that the closed nature of a grand jury investigation limits the court's ability to assess the materiality of a witness's testimony. This may be true at the margins, because the materiality of the testimony given by a trial witness can be assessed on the basis of the indictment, discovery materials, and trial evidence, whereas grand jury secrecy requires the judge to rely largely on the prosecutor's representations about the scope of the investigation and the materiality of the witness's testimony. However, as Chief Judge Mukasey observed, "courts make similar determinations all the time, based on sealed submissions, when deciding whether a subpoena calls for relevant information, whether such information is privileged, and the like." Moreover, "the hypothesized difficulty of the materiality decision can be just as great, or greater, when a court must determine if a trial witness must be detained, because the decision likely will have to be made before the trial begins and thus before it is possible to fit the witness's testimony into the grid of other evidence." The materiality determination called for by § 3144 lies within the district court's competence.

Finally, Awadallah and the NYCDL argue that § 3144 provides no limit on how long a grand jury witness may be detained, whereas the detention of a trial witness is implicitly limited (or speeded) by the time limits on prosecution contained in the Speedy Trial Act, 18 U.S.C. § 3161 *et seq.* However, the Speedy Trial Act permits delay for various reasons, *see* 18 U.S.C. § 3161(h), which may have the collateral effect of extending the detention of a material witness; and nothing in the Speedy Trial Act requires a court to consider the effect of a continuance or delay on a detained witness. The Act therefore provides cold comfort to a detained trial witness.

While § 3144 contains no express time limit, the statute and related rules require close institutional attention to the propriety and duration of detentions: "[n]o material witness may be detained because of inability to comply with any condition of release if the testimony of such witness can adequately be secured by deposition, and if further detention is not necessary to prevent a failure of justice." 18 U.S.C. § 3144. The court must "treat the person in accordance with the provisions of section 3142," which provides a mechanism for release. And release may be delayed only "for a reasonable period of time until the deposition of the witness can be taken pursuant to the Federal Rules of Criminal Procedure." Perhaps most important, Rule 46 requires the government to make a "biweekly report" to the court listing each material witness held in custody for more than ten days and justifying the continued detention of each witness. Fed.R.Crim.P. 46(g) (1993); *see also* Fed.R.Crim.P. 46(h)(2) (2003). These measures tend to ensure that material witnesses are detained no longer than necessary.

In light of the foregoing analysis, we must ask whether Awadallah was properly detained when he was held for several weeks without being allowed to give his deposition and obtain release. Such a detention constitutes a significant intrusion on liberty, since a material witness can be arrested with little or no notice, transported across the country, and detained for several days or weeks. Under the circumstances of this case, however, we are satisfied that Awadallah's detention was not unreasonably prolonged. . . .

As indicated above, the deposition mechanism invoked in § 3144 is available to grand jury witnesses, but it is not required in every instance. Section 3144 requires release after deposition only if "the testimony of such witness can *adequately* be secured by deposition" and "further detention is not necessary to prevent a failure of justice." 18 U.S.C. § 3144 (emphasis added). Similarly, § 3142 provides that a person may be detained if, "after a hearing . . ., the judicial officer finds that no condition or combination of conditions will reasonably assure the appearance of the person as required and the safety of any other person and the community." 18 U.S.C. § 3142(e).

The procedural history demonstrates that Awadallah received adequate process to ensure that the duration of his detention was reasonable. Awadallah was arrested on Friday, September 21, 2001. He first appeared before a magistrate judge in San Diego for a bail hearing on Monday, September 24. That hearing was adjourned until the following day in order for Awadallah's counsel to obtain a translator. When Awadallah appeared before the magistrate judge the next day, the court received testimony from his witnesses and heard argument from counsel. Awadallah's attorney argued, among other things, that a deposition should be taken pursuant to § 3144. The court found that, under § 3142, there were no conditions of release that would reasonably assure Awadallah's appearance before the grand jury. The court denied bail and ordered that Awadallah be removed to New York. The government transported Awadallah across the country, and he arrived in New York on Monday, October 1. The next day, he appeared for a second bail hearing before Chief Judge Mukasey in the Southern District of New York. Chief Judge Mukasey also declined to release Awadallah from detention, finding that, "given the facts alleged in the application[,] he may well have incentive to leave," and that "[t]here is no way to prevent him from leaving, no effective way, unless he is detained." The court found that his continued detention was "reasonable under the circumstances." During this hearing, the government informed the court that the grand jury met only on Mondays and Wednesdays, that the following Monday was a holiday, and that the next opportunity to present Awadallah to the grand jury would be Wednesday, October 10. The court therefore set October 11 as a control date for further hearings.

When Awadallah appeared before the grand jury on Wednesday, October 10, he made statements that resulted in perjury charges being filed against him. He testified before the grand jury a second time on Monday, October 15, and he was arrested on the perjury charges on Friday, October 19. All told, Awadallah spent 20 days in detention as a material witness before testifying before the grand jury and uttering the allegedly perjurious statements. The undisputed facts establish that he received two bail hearings pursuant to § 3142 within days of his arrest, and that the judges in both hearings found his continued detention to be both reasonable and necessary. Under these circumstances, Awadallah's detention as a material witness was a scrupulous and constitutional use of the federal material witness statute.

Notes and Questions

1. Is it a misuse of the material witness statute to hold individuals because you want to be certain, that at least for the period of the detention, they are not free to engage in terrorist acts? Is this a proper basis on which to invoke the materials witness statute? What does Awadallah say about that practice? Suppose that the Attorney General has more than one purpose, for example, to be certain that the witness is available to testify ... and to ensure that the individual will not be able to engage in terrorism?

2. Others have suggested that the use of statutes like the material witness law to detain individuals for extended periods can be used to coerce information. See, e.g., Christian Science Monitor, June 19, 2002, p. 1. Is this an improper reason to detain an individual under the material witness statute? Compare the use of a contempt citation and detention of a person who declines to answer questions before the grand jury. Is the use of the material witness statute for this purpose different? How?

3. Sometimes arresting a person as a material witness is a temporizing action, while the prosecutor gathers enough evidence to charge the individual with a crime. Others originally detained as material witnesses and then later charged with a crime include Zacarias Moussauoi, who is being tried as a co-conspirator in the September 11th attacks. Jose Padilla, on the other hand, was originally detained as a material witness, and then the government switched his status to that of an "enemy combatant." See Chapter 7, infra.

4. Is the problem in the use of the material witness statute for such purposes as suggested in notes 1–3, supra, the government's goal, or in the use of the material witness statute to accomplish the goal? Could Congress constitutionally authorize what the Attorney General was trying to accomplish? Would you vote for such legislation? Is it important for the Executive Branch to obtain the imprimatur of the Congress on such matters, before undertaking to act in new ways that push the legal envelope? Consult generally, Roberto Iraola, Terrorism, Grand Juries, and the Federal Material Witness Statute, 34 St. Mary's L.J. 401 (2003); Stacey M. Studnicki & John P. Apol, Witness Detention and Intimidation: The History and Future of Material Witness Law, 76 St. John's L. Rev. 483 (2002).

5. The exact number of persons who have been held as material witnesses in the anti-terrorism investigation since September 11th has not been made public. The Washington Post has reported that "at least 44 persons" have been detained under this heading since September 11, 2002. Washington Post, November 24, 2002, p. AO1.

6. In the district court opinion in Center for National Security Studies v. U.S. DOJ, 215 F.Supp. 2d 94, 106 (D.D.C. 2002), Judge Kessler stated:

> The Government's reliance on grand jury secrecy rules to justify withholding the identities of material witnesses is fundamentally wrong as a matter of law. First, on its face, Fed. R. Crim. P. 6(e) does not bar disclosure of the identities of persons detained as material witnesses. Fed. R. Crim. P. 6(e) (2) prohibits disclosure of "matters occurring before the grand jury." Fed. R. Crim. P. 6(e) (6) provides that "records, orders and subpoenas relating to grand jury proceedings shall be kept under seal to the extent and for such time as is necessary to prevent disclosure of matters occurring before a grand jury."

Compare, however, Judge Mukasey's view expressed in footnote 1 in the In re Material Witness Warrant, 213 F.Supp. 2d 287, 288 (S.D.N.Y. 2002):

> The witness who has filed the current motion was taken into custody pursuant to a warrant issued in aid of a grand jury subpoena, and the docket and the record of all appearances in this matter have been sealed as proceedings ancillary to grand jury proceedings. See Fed. R. Crim. P.

6(e)(2), (5) and (6) (setting forth general rule of secrecy and rules for closing of hearings and sealing of records). Accordingly, neither the witness's name nor any identifying facts about him or this matter are set forth in this opinion, except to the extent necessary to treat the legal issues presented.

* * *

Can you reconcile the Kessler and Mukasey views about the relevance of grand jury secrecy to material witness status in these matters? Is it an implication of the Mukasey view that government can keep secret the identities of any persons taken into custody as material witnesses on the theory that their testimony before a grand jury is needed?

7. It has also been suggested that a built-in safeguard in connection with the detaining of a person as a material witness is the fact that a judge always supervises the matter, although some former prosecutors do not believe that judges offer much supervision in such matters. Washington Post, November 24, 2002, p. AO1.

* * *

C. Detention of aliens

1. Introduction

The law regarding the detention and removal (i.e., deportation or exclusion) of aliens is complex. In the immediate wake of the events of September 11, 2001, the government rounded up and detained over 1000 persons, most of whom were aliens of Middle Eastern or South Asian origin. (In addition, shortly after September 11, the government announced a plan to have the FBI interview approximately 5000 men between the ages of 18 and 33 who were from countries with "an al Qaeda terrorist presence." See Kenneth L. Wainstein, Final Report on Interview Project, Office of the Director, Executive Office for United States Attorneys, February 26, 2002 at 2.) A small number of those detained were held under the material witness statute. Most, however, were detained in connection with violations of the immigration laws. Subsection 2, below, describes different categories of detention of aliens under the immigration laws and relevant statistics, wholly apart from terrorism matters. Subsection 3 examines the use of the immigration laws in aid of an anti-terrorism law enforcement purpose in the aftermath of 9/11. Subsection 4 presents recent decisions barring indefinite detention of persons slated for removal (removal (i.e. deportation) where a receiving country cannot be found, but providing for a possible exception where terrorism is involved. Finally, in subsection 5, we focus on the provisions of the immigration laws that by their very terms are directed against terrorists and that establish special procedures for both their detention and their removal from the U.S (including some provisions enacted in 2001 as part of the USA PATRIOT Act).

* * *

3. Post 9/11/01 detentions and removals based on immigration law violations

a. The use of authority to detain aliens in violation of the immigration laws as an aid to terrorism investigation and as a form of preventive detention

David Cole, The Priority of Morality, The Emergency Constitution's Blind Spot, 113 Yale L.J. 1753, 1777–1778 (2004):

> ... [T]he Attorney General ... has been able to subject over 5000 foreign nationals to preventive detention ... by ... using preexisting immigration and criminal law authorities. Many of those detainees were arrested and held without charges for much longer than seven days. And many were held for months on end without any judicial review. Under preexisting immigration law, the Attorney General has discretion to detain foreign nationals charged with immigration violations pending the outcome of their removal proceedings, although such detention generally requires proof that the individual poses either a risk of flight or a danger to the community. The Justice Department used that discretionary detention authority to deny bond to all immigration detainees deemed "of interest" to the September 11 investigation, without regard to whether it had any evidence whatsoever that they were dangerous, a flight risk, or in any way connected to terrorism. It interfered with their access to attorneys and sought delays and continuances in bond hearings to disguise the fact that it had no evidence justifying detention without bond. It promulgated a rule, subsequently declared unconstitutional by five federal judges, that permits immigration prosecutors to keep foreign nationals detained even after an immigration judge rules that there is no basis for denying bond. And it kept individuals in detention for months after their immigration charges were fully resolved, not because it had any affirmative evidence that they posed any danger, but simply because the FBI had not gotten around to "clearing" them.

> Where a person "of interest" could not be charged with an immigration violation, prosecutors searched for a criminal charge—any charge. Individuals were charged with lying to FBI agents and the grand jury, credit card fraud, "trespassing" in a hotel room they were renting, and carrying a knife one-quarter inch longer than permitted under state law. Where neither a criminal nor an immigration charge was available, the Justice Department invoked the material witness statute. ...

> Through these tactics, all relying on preexisting immigration and criminal authority, the Attorney General was able to effectuate a mass preventive detention campaign....

* * *

c. Is indefinite, open-ended detention possible in connection with efforts to remove an individual from the United States?

In the following case, the Supreme Court addressed the question of how long an alien as to whom removal had been ordered could be detained if removal could not be effected, if, for example, the government could not find a country willing to accept the person.

ZADVYDAS v. DAVIS

533 U.S. 678 (2001).

JUDGES: BREYER, J., delivered the opinion of the Court, in which STEVENS, O'CONNOR, SOUTER, and GINSBURG, JJ., joined. SCALIA, J., filed a dissenting opinion, in which THOMAS, J., joined. KENNEDY, J., filed a dissenting opinion, in which REHNQUIST, C.J., joined, and in which SCALIA and THOMAS, JJ., joined as to Part I.

JUSTICE BREYER delivered the opinion of the Court.

When an alien has been found to be unlawfully present in the United States and a final order of removal has been entered, the Government ordinarily secures the alien's removal during a subsequent 90–day statutory "removal period," during which time the alien normally is held in custody.

A special statute authorizes further detention if the Government fails to remove the alien during those 90 days. It says:

"An alien ordered removed [1] who is inadmissible ... [2] [or] removable [as a result of violations of status requirements or entry conditions, violations of criminal law, or reasons of security or foreign policy] or [3] who has been determined by the Attorney General to be a risk to the community or unlikely to comply with the order of removal, may be detained beyond the removal period and, if released, shall be subject to [certain] terms of supervision...." 8 U.S.C. § 1231(a)(6) (1994 ed., Supp. V).

In these cases, we must decide whether this post-removal-period statute authorizes the Attorney General to detain a removable alien *indefinitely* beyond the removal period or only for a period *reasonably necessary* to secure the alien's removal. We deal here with aliens who were admitted to the United States but subsequently ordered removed. Aliens who have not yet gained initial admission to this country would present a very different question. Based on our conclusion that indefinite detention of aliens in the former category would raise serious constitutional concerns, we construe the statute to contain an implicit "reasonable time" limitation, the application of which is subject to federal court review.

The post-removal-period detention statute is one of a related set of statutes and regulations that govern detention during and after removal proceedings. While removal proceedings are in progress, most aliens may be released on bond or paroled. 66 Stat. 204, as added and amended, 110 Stat. 3009–585, 8 U.S.C. §§ 1226 (a)(2), (c) (1994 ed., Supp. V). After entry of a final removal order and during the 90–day removal period, however, aliens must be held in custody. § 1231(a)(2). Subsequently, as the post-removal-period statute provides, the Government "may" continue to detain an alien who still remains here or release that alien under supervision. § 1231(a)(6).

. . .

We consider two separate instances of detention. The first concerns Kestutis Zadvydas, a resident alien who was born, apparently of Lithuanian parents, in a displaced persons camp in Germany in 1948. When he was eight years old, Zadvydas immigrated to the United States with his parents and other family members, and he has lived here ever since.

Zadvydas has a long criminal record, involving drug crimes, attempted robbery, attempted burglary, and theft. He has a history of flight, from both criminal and deportation proceedings. Most recently, he was convicted of possessing, with intent to distribute, cocaine; sentenced to 16 years' imprisonment; released on parole after two years; taken into INS custody; and, in 1994, ordered deported to Germany. See 8 U.S.C. § 1251(a)(2) (1988 ed., Supp. V) (delineating crimes that make alien deportable).

In 1994, Germany told the INS that it would not accept Zadvydas because he was not a German citizen. Shortly thereafter, Lithuania refused to accept Zadvydas because he was neither a Lithuanian citizen nor a permanent resident. In 1996, the INS asked the Dominican Republic (Zadvydas' wife's country) to accept him, but this effort proved unsuccessful. In 1998, Lithuania rejected, as inadequately documented, Zadvydas' effort to obtain Lithuanian citizenship based on his parents' citizenship; Zadvydas' reapplication is apparently still pending.

The INS kept Zadvydas in custody after expiration of the removal period. In September 1995, Zadvydas filed a petition for a writ of habeas corpus under 28 U.S.C. § 2241 challenging his continued detention. In October 1997, a Federal District Court granted that writ and ordered him released under supervision. In its view, the Government would never succeed in its efforts to remove Zadvydas from the United States, leading to his permanent confinement, contrary to the Constitution. The Fifth Circuit reversed this decision. *Zadvydas* v. *Underdown,* 185 F.3d 279 (1999). It concluded that Zadvydas' detention did not violate the Constitution because eventual deportation was not "impossible," good faith efforts to remove him from the United States continued, and his detention was subject to periodic administrative review. The Fifth Circuit stayed its mandate pending potential review in this Court.

* * *

The post-removal-period detention statute applies to certain categories of aliens who have been ordered removed, namely inadmissible aliens, criminal aliens, aliens who have violated their nonimmigrant status conditions, and aliens removable for certain national security or foreign relations reasons, as well as any alien "who has been determined by the Attorney General to be a risk to the community or unlikely to comply with the order of removal." 8 U.S.C. § 1231(a)(6) (1994 ed., Supp. V). . . . It says that an alien who falls into one of these categories "may be detained beyond the removal period and, if released, shall be subject to [certain] terms of supervision."

The Government argues that the statute means what it literally says. It sets no "limit on the length of time beyond the removal period that an alien who falls within one of the Section 1231(a)(6) categories may be detained." Hence, "whether to continue to detain such an alien and, if so, in what circumstances and for how long" is up to the Attorney General, not up to the courts.

. . .

A statute permitting indefinite detention of an alien would raise a serious constitutional problem. The Fifth Amendment's Due Process Clause forbids the Government to "deprive" any "person . . . of . . . liberty . . . without due process of law." Freedom from imprisonment—from government custody, detention, or other forms of physical restraint—lies at the heart of the liberty that Clause protects, see *Foucha* v. *Louisiana*, 504 U.S. 71, 80, 118 L. Ed. 2d 437, 112 S. Ct. 1780 (1992). And this Court has said that government detention violates that Clause unless the detention is ordered in a *criminal* proceeding with adequate procedural protections, see *United States* v. *Salerno*, 481 U.S. 739, 746, 95 L. Ed. 2d 697, 107 S. Ct. 2095 (1987), or, in certain special and "narrow" non-punitive "circumstances," *Foucha, supra,* at 80, where a special justification, such as harm-threatening mental illness, outweighs the "individual's constitutionally protected interest in avoiding physical restraint." *Kansas* v. *Hendricks*, 521 U.S. 346, 356, 138 L. Ed. 2d 501, 117 S. Ct. 2072 (1997).

The proceedings at issue here are civil, not criminal, and we assume that they are nonpunitive in purpose and effect. There is no sufficiently strong special justification here for indefinite civil detention—at least as administered under this statute. The statute, says the Government, has two regulatory goals: "ensuring the appearance of aliens at future immigration proceedings" and "preventing danger to the community." Brief for Respondents in No. 99–7791, p. 24. But by definition the first justification—preventing flight—is weak or nonexistent where removal seems a remote possibility at best. . . .

The second justification—protecting the community—does not necessarily diminish in force over time. But we have upheld preventive detention based on dangerousness only when limited to specially dangerous individuals and subject to strong procedural protections. Compare *Hendricks, supra,* at 368 (upholding scheme that imposes detention upon "a small segment of particularly dangerous individuals" and provides "strict procedural safeguards") and *Salerno, supra,* at 747, 750–752 (in upholding pretrial detention, stressing "stringent time limitations," the fact that detention is reserved for the "most serious of crimes," the requirement of proof of dangerousness by clear and convincing evidence, and the presence of judicial safeguards), with *Foucha, supra,* at 81–83 (striking down insanity-related detention system that placed burden on detainee to prove nondangerousness). In cases in which preventive detention is of potentially *indefinite* duration, we have also demanded that the dangerousness rationale be accompanied by some other special circumstance, such as mental illness, that helps to create the danger. See *Hendricks, supra,* at 358, 368.

The civil confinement here at issue is not limited, but potentially permanent. Cf. *Salerno, supra,* at 747 (noting that "maximum length of pretrial detention is limited" by "stringent" requirements).... The provision authorizing detention does not apply narrowly to "a small segment of particularly dangerous individuals," *Hendricks, supra,* at 368, say suspected terrorists, but broadly to aliens ordered removed for many and various reasons, including tourist visa violations cf. *Hendricks,* 521 U.S. at 357–358 (only individuals with "past sexually violent behavior and a present mental condition that creates a likelihood of such conduct in the future" may be detained). And, once the flight risk justification evaporates, the only special circumstance present is the alien's removable status itself, which bears no relation to a detainee's dangerousness.

Moreover, the sole procedural protections available to the alien are found in administrative proceedings, where the alien bears the burden of proving he is not dangerous, without (in the Government's view) significant later judicial review. ... This Court has suggested, however, that the Constitution may well preclude granting "an administrative body the unreviewable authority to make determinations implicating fundamental rights." ... The serious constitutional problem arising out of a statute that, in these circumstances, permits an indefinite, perhaps permanent, deprivation of human liberty without any such protection is obvious.

The Government argues that, from a constitutional perspective, alien status itself can justify indefinite detention, and points to *Shaughnessy* v. *United States ex rel. Mezei,* 345 U.S. 206, 97 L. Ed. 956, 73 S. Ct. 625 (1953), as support. That case involved a once lawfully admitted alien who left the United States, returned after a trip abroad, was refused admission, and was left on Ellis Island, indefinitely detained there because the Government could not find another country to accept him. The Court held that Mezei's detention did not violate the Constitution. Id. at 215–216.

Although *Mezei,* like the present cases, involves indefinite detention, it differs from the present cases in a critical respect. As the Court emphasized, the alien's extended departure from the United States required him to seek entry into this country once again. His presence on Ellis Island did not count as entry into the United States. Hence, he was "treated," for constitutional purposes, "as if stopped at the border." And that made all the difference.

. . .

In light of this critical distinction between *Mezei* and the present cases, *Mezei* does not offer the Government significant support, and we need not consider the aliens' claim that subsequent developments have undermined *Mezei*'s legal authority.

The Government also looks for support to cases holding that Congress has "plenary power" to create immigration law, and that the judicial branch must defer to executive and legislative branch decision-making in that area. . . . But that power is subject to important constitutional limitations. . . . Rather, the issue we address is whether aliens that the Government finds itself unable to remove are to be condemned to an indefinite term of imprisonment within the United States.

. . .

Nor do the cases before us require us to consider the political branches' authority to control entry into the United States. Hence we leave no "unprotected spot in the Nation's armor. Neither do we consider terrorism or other special circumstances where special arguments might be made for forms of preventive detention and for heightened deference to the judgments of the political branches with respect to matters of national security. The sole foreign policy consideration the Government mentions here is the concern lest courts interfere with "sensitive" repatriation negotiations. But neither the Government nor the dissents explain how a habeas court's efforts to determine the likelihood of repatriation, if handled with appropriate sensitivity, could make a significant difference in this respect.

Finally, the Government argues that, whatever liberty interest the aliens possess, it is "greatly diminished" by their lack of a legal right to "live at large in this country." . . . The choice, however, is not between imprisonment and the alien "living at large." . . .

Despite this constitutional problem, if "Congress has made its intent" in the statute "clear, 'we must give effect to that intent.' " . . . We cannot find here, however, any clear indication of congressional intent to grant the Attorney General the power to hold indefinitely in confinement an alien ordered removed. And that is so whether protecting the community from dangerous aliens is a primary or (as we believe) secondary statutory purpose. After all, the provision is part of a statute that has as its basic purpose effectuating an alien's removal. Why should we assume that Congress saw the alien's dangerousness as unrelated to this purpose?

. . .

The Government points to similar related statutes that *require* detention of criminal aliens during removal proceedings and the removal period, and argues that these show that mandatory detention is the rule while discretionary release is the narrow exception. But the statute before us applies not only to terrorists and criminals, but also to ordinary visa violators, and, more importantly, post-removal-period detention, unlike detention pending a determination of removability or during the subsequent 90–day removal period, has no obvious termination point.

In early 1996, Congress explicitly expanded the group of aliens subject to mandatory detention, eliminating provisions that permitted release of criminal aliens who had at one time been lawfully admitted to the United States. Antiterrorism and Effective Death Penalty Act of 1996, § 439(c), 110 Stat. 1277. And later that year Congress enacted the present law, which liberalizes pre-existing law by shortening the removal period from six months to 90 days, mandates detention of certain criminal aliens during the removal proceedings and for the subsequent 90–day removal period, and adds the post-removal-period provision here at issue. Illegal Immigration Reform and Immigrant Responsibility Act of 1996, Div. C, §§ 303, 305, 110 Stat. 3009–585, 3009–598 to 3009–599; 8 U.S.C. §§ 1226(c), 1231(a) (1994 ed., Supp. V).

We have found nothing in the history of these statutes that clearly demonstrates a congressional intent to authorize indefinite, perhaps permanent, detention. Consequently, interpreting the statute to avoid a serious constitutional threat, we conclude that, once removal is no longer reasonably foreseeable, continued detention is no longer authorized by statute.

The Government seems to argue that, even under our interpretation of the statute, a federal habeas court would have to accept the Government's view about whether the implicit statutory limitation is satisfied in a particular case, conducting little or no independent review of the matter. In our view, that is not so.

In answering that basic question, the habeas court must ask whether the detention in question exceeds a period reasonably necessary to secure removal. It should measure reasonableness primarily in terms of the statute's basic purpose, namely assuring the alien's presence at the moment of removal. Thus, if removal is not reasonably foreseeable, the court should hold continued detention unreasonable and no longer authorized by statute. In that case, of course, the alien's release may and should be conditioned on any of the various forms of supervised release that are appropriate in the circumstances, and the alien may no doubt be returned to custody upon a violation of those conditions... And if removal is reasonably foreseeable, the habeas court should consider the risk of the alien's committing further crimes as a factor potentially justifying confinement within that reasonable removal period.

We recognize, as the Government points out, that review must take appropriate account of the greater immigration-related expertise of the Executive Branch, of the serious administrative needs and concerns inherent in the necessarily extensive INS efforts to enforce this complex statute, and the Nation's need to "speak with one voice" in immigration matters. But we believe that courts can take appropriate account of such matters without abdicating their legal responsibility to review the law-fulness of an alien's continued detention.

. . .

We realize that recognizing this necessary Executive leeway will often call for difficult judgments. In order to limit the occasions when courts will need to make them, we think it practically necessary to recognize some presumptively reasonable period of detention.

. . .

While an argument can be made for confining any presumption to 90 days, we doubt that when Congress shortened the removal period to 90 days in 1996 it believed that all reasonably foreseeable removals could be accomplished in that time. We do have reason to believe, however, that Congress previously doubted the constitutionality of detention for more than six months. . . . Consequently, for the sake of uniform administration in the federal courts, we recognize that period. After this 6–month period, once the alien provides good reason to believe that there is no significant likelihood of removal in the reasonably foreseeable future, the Government must respond with evidence sufficient to rebut that showing. And for detention to remain reasonable, as the period of prior post-removal confinement grows, what counts as the "reasonably foreseeable future" conversely would have to shrink. This 6–month presumption, of course, does not mean that every alien not removed must be released after six months. To the contrary, an alien may be held in confinement until it has been determined that there is no significant likelihood of removal in the reasonably foreseeable future.

. . . [W]e vacate the decisions below and remand both cases for further proceedings consistent with this opinion.

It is so ordered.

Notes and Questions

1. On the one hand, Zadvydas provides some comfort for those who are concerned that the government is detaining people for too long based on too little evidence. The case establishes that indefinite, open-ended detention is impermissible for persons ordered to be removed from the U.S in circum-stances where no country will accept them. Zadvydas thus is a strong statement against detention that extends too long, even for alien criminals.

2. On the other hand, Zadvydas several times seems to recognize that the detention of terrorists may be a possible exception to the restriction on indefinite detention. How many times does Justice Breyer mention the matter of detaining terrorists? Does the court majority clearly opine on the question of extended detention of terrorists? What do you read into the majority's mention of terrorists in this context? Are the Court's statements mentioning terrorists restricted to alien terrorists?

3. In the wake of the Zadvydas decision, Congress enacted legislation as part of the USA PATRIOT Act that provided that aliens whose release

"will threaten the security of the United States or the safety of the community or any person" may be detained for additional periods of six months. 8 U.S.C. § 1226a (6). The full § 1226a is reproduced infra.

* * *

6. The question of how to deal with aliens who had not yet been admitted into this country but ended up in U.S. custody and were otherwise in the same situation as Zadvydas soon came before the Supreme Court [in Clark v. Martinez, 125 S.Ct. 716 (2005), and the Court applied the same rules applied in Zadvydas.]

* * *

d. Detention and removal provisions directed specifically toward terrorists under the USA PATRIOT Act and other immigration law provisions

The USA PATRIOT Act (P.L. 107–56, Oct. 26, 2001) added Section 1226a to Title 8, United States Code, which contains the codified parts of the Immigration and Nationality Act of 1952. It adds another tool to the array of immigration law provisions that could be used in alien terrorist cases.

§ 1226a. Mandatory detention of suspected terrorists; habeas corpus; judicial review

(a) Detention of terrorist aliens.

(1) Custody.—The Attorney General shall take into custody any alien who is certified under paragraph (3).

(2) Release.—Except as provided in paragraphs (5) and (6), the Attorney General shall maintain custody of such an alien until the alien is removed from the United States. Except as provided in paragraph (6), such custody shall be maintained irrespective of any relief from removal for which the alien may be eligible, or any relief from removal granted the alien, until the Attorney General determines that the alien is no longer an alien who may be certified under paragraph (3). If the alien is finally determined not to be removable, detention pursuant to this subsection shall terminate.

(3) Certification.—The Attorney General may certify an alien under this paragraph if the Attorney General has reasonable grounds to believe that the alien—

(A) is described in section 212(a)(3)(A)(i), 212(a)(3)(A)(iii), 212(a)(3)(B), 237(a)(4)(A)(i), 237(a)(4)(A)(iii), or 237(a)(4)(B) [8 USC §§ 1182(a)(3)(A)(i), 1182(a)(3)(A)(iii), 1182(a)(3)(B), 1227(a)(4)(A)(i), 1227(a)(4)(A)(iii), or 1227(a)(4)(B)]; or

(B) is engaged in any other activity that endangers the national security of the United States.

(4) Nondelegation.—The Attorney General may delegate the authority provided under paragraph (3) only to the Deputy Attorney General. The Deputy Attorney General may not delegate such authority.

(5) Commencement of proceedings.—The Attorney General shall place an alien detained under paragraph (1) in removal proceedings, or shall charge the alien with a criminal offense, not later than 7 days after the commencement of such detention. If the requirement of the preceding sentence is not satisfied, the Attorney General shall release the alien.

(6) Limitation on indefinite detention.—An alien detained solely under paragraph (1) who has not been removed under section 241(a)(1)(A) [8 USC § 1231(a)(1)(A)], and whose removal is unlikely in the reasonably foreseeable future, may be detained for additional periods of up to six months only if the release of the alien will threaten the national security of the United States or the safety of the community or any person.

(7) Review of certification.—The Attorney General shall review the certification made under paragraph (3) every 6 months. If the Attorney General determines, in the Attorney General's discretion, that the certification should be revoked, the alien may be released on such conditions as the Attorney General deems appropriate, unless such release is otherwise prohibited by law. The alien may request each 6 months in writing that the Attorney General reconsider the certification and may submit documents or other evidence in support of that request.

* * *

Notes and Questions

1. Provisions in the immigration laws dealing with persons suspected of being terrorists and providing for their removal (i.e. deportation) were on the books prior to September 11th. See below sections 1531–1537, 1227, Title 8, U.S.C. What does section 1226a add?

* * *

3. The language of subsection (a)(2) in 1226a is confusing. Consider the following commentaries on this provision.

a) Panel Discussion, Perversities and Prospects, op. cit. supra, note 1, supra, p. __, at 21:

> Because we are in the post-September 11 climate and because an anti-terrorism bill was passed today, I do want to briefly touch on the topic of terrorism and the legislation as it relates to indefinite detention,.... The new legislation grants the Attorney General the power to detain immigrants, including long-time legal permanent residents, indefinitely without any meaningful judicial review. This new law must be read in light of the Zadvydas holding, and will likely be challenged based on this. While the Zadvydas decision did mention that terrorism or other special circumstances might justify preventative detention, it made clear that adequate procedural safe-

guards would be required in order to avoid running afoul of the Constitution, safeguards that are not present in the current review process. Under the anti-terrorist law passed today, a person could be indefinitely detained for an immigration related violation if he or she is "certified" as a terrorist. This certification requires the minimal "reasonable grounds to believe" standard, used in stop and frisk cases, and the government has no obligation to provide the detainee with a trial or a hearing in which the government must prove that he is, in fact, a terrorist. It seems doubtful that such a process would meet the constitutional requirements for indefinite detention as outlined by the court in Zadvydas.

b) Federalist Society, White Paper on the USA PATRIOT Act of 2001, Criminal Procedure Sections 13 (2001):

The final language [of 1226a] is confusing and possibly contradictory in subdivision (a)(2) regarding the effect of the outcome of the removal proceedings. The second sentence retains language from the original Senate bill that "custody should be maintained irrespective . . . of any relief from removal granted the alien. . . ." Yet the last sentence added in the final stages says, "If the alien is finally determined not to be removable, detention pursuant to this subsection shall terminate." If the basis of detention was also the ground for the removal and if the ground has been finally adjudicated to be false, continued detention would raise serious constitutional questions. It seems likely the courts would avoid the questions by relying on the last sentence.

c) Testimony of David Cole on Civil Liberties and Proposed Anti-terrorism Legislation, Subcommittee on Constitution, Federalism and Property Rights, Senate Judiciary Committee, October 3, 2001 [Note: This testimony was given prior to the passage of the PATRIOT Act, but this excerpt addresses the language that appears in the Act.]

The mandatory detention provision is a form of preventive detention prior to trial. But the Supreme Court has held that "[i]n our society, liberty is the norm, and detention prior to trial or without trial is the carefully limited exception." United States v. Salerno, 481 U.S. 739, 755 (1987). Preventive detention is constitutional only in very limited circumstances, where there is a demonstrated need for the detention— because of current dangerousness or risk of flight—and only where there are adequate procedural safeguards.

. . .

. . . [T]he detention authority proposed would allow the INS to detain aliens indefinitely, even where they have prevailed in their removal proceedings. This, too, is patently unconstitutional. Once an alien has prevailed in his removal proceeding, and has been granted relief from removal, he has a legal right to remain here. Yet the Administration proposal would provide that even aliens granted relief from removal would still be detained. At that point, however, the INS has no legitimate basis for detaining the individual. The INS's authority to detain is only incident to its removal authority. If it cannot remove an individual, it has no basis for detaining him. Zadvydas v. INS, 121 S.Ct. 2491 (holding that INS could not detain indefinitely even aliens ruled deportable where there was no reasonable likelihood that they could be deported because no country would take them).

* * *

4.   The special provisions providing for removal of persons believed to be terrorists, enacted in 1996 as part of the AEDPA, [see 8 U.S.C. § 1531 et. seq.] included provision for the establishment of a special court to deal with such cases where classified information is involved and some in camera proceedings are needed. General authority to remove persons because of terrorist activity is contained in other provisions of the immigration laws (see section 1227, Title 8, U.S.C.). As far as is known, the provisions dealing with the removal court have not yet been used. (Note that the same judges appointed to the special Foreign Intelligence Surveillance Court, see infra, Chapter 10, may be appointed to the removal court.)

* * *

Chapter 7

EXTENDED DETENTION II: ENEMY COMBATANTS

A. Introduction: The recent case law

The material in this chapter is closely tied to the "war" issue discussed in Chapter 5 and involves, inter alia, another legal basis for extended detention to be compared with material witness and alien detention in Chapter 6. Enemy combatant detention issues typically arise with respect to non-citizens seized on the battlefield, e.g., the detainees in Guantanamo, although battlefield captures included some American citizens, Lindh and Hamdi. The category of enemy combatant has also been applied by the government to citizens arrested in the United States, Padilla and Al–Marri and to persons seized in toher countries. In the first part of this chapter, we examine three recent Supreme Court cases and one district court decision that address issues relating to enemy combatants. Next, we review other materials relevant to the categorization of detainees as "enemy combatants" rather than prisoners of war or ordinary criminal prisoners. We then examine the different kinds of reviews of enemy combatant status available to the Guantanamo prisoners. Finally, we examine certain issues relating the to terms and conditions of detention, focusing first on interrogation techniques and the possible uses of torture to gain information....

RASUL v. BUSH

124 S.Ct. 2686 (2004).

[STEVENS, J., delivered the opinion of the Court, in which O'CONNOR, SOUTER, GINSBURG, and BREYER, JJ., joined. KENNEDY, J., filed an opinion concurring in the judgment. SCALIA, J., filed a dissenting opinion, in which REHNQUIST, C.J., and THOMAS, J., joined.]

Justice STEVENS delivered the opinion of the Court.

These two cases present the narrow but important question whether United States courts lack jurisdiction to consider challenges to the legality of the detention of foreign nationals captured abroad in connection with hostilities and incarcerated at the Guantanamo Bay Naval Base, Cuba.

I

. . .

Petitioners in these cases are 2 Australian citizens and 12 Kuwaiti citizens who were captured abroad during hostilities between the United States and the Taliban. Since early 2002, the U.S. military has held them—along with, according to the Government's estimate, approximately 640 other non-Americans captured abroad—at the Naval Base at Guantanamo Bay. The United States occupies the Base, which comprises 45 square miles of land and water along the southeast coast of Cuba, pursuant to a 1903 Lease Agreement executed with the newly independent Republic of Cuba in the aftermath of the Spanish–American War. Under the Agreement, "the United States recognizes the continuance of the ultimate sovereignty of the Republic of Cuba over the [leased areas]," while "the Republic of Cuba consents that during the period of the occupation by the United States . . . the United States shall exercise complete jurisdiction and control over and within said areas." In 1934, the parties entered into a treaty providing that, absent an agreement to modify or abrogate the lease, the lease would remain in effect "[s]o long as the United States of America shall not abandon the . . . naval station of Guantanamo."

In 2002, petitioners, through relatives acting as their next friends, filed various actions in the U.S. District Court for the District of Columbia challenging the legality of their detention at the Base. All alleged that none of the petitioners has ever been a combatant against the United States or has ever engaged in any terrorist acts. They also alleged that none has been charged with any wrongdoing, permitted to consult with counsel, or provided access to the courts or any other tribunal.

The two Australians, Mamdouh Habib and David Hicks, each filed a petition for writ of habeas corpus, seeking release from custody, access to counsel, freedom from interrogations, and other relief. Fawzi Khalid Abdullah Fahad Al Odah and the 11 other Kuwaiti detainees filed a complaint seeking to be informed of the charges against them, to be allowed to meet with their families and with counsel, and to have access to the courts or some other impartial tribunal. They claimed that denial of these rights violates the Constitution, international law, and treaties of the United States. Invoking the court's jurisdiction under 28 U.S.C. §§ 1331 and 1350, among other statutory bases, they asserted causes of action under the Administrative Procedure Act, 5 U.S.C. §§ 555, 702, 706; the Alien Tort Statute, 28 U.S.C. § 1350; and the general federal habeas corpus statute, §§ 2241–2243.

Construing all three actions as petitions for writs of habeas corpus, the District Court dismissed them for want of jurisdiction. The court held, in reliance on our opinion in *Johnson v. Eisentrager,* 339 U.S. 763,

70 S.Ct. 936, 94 L.Ed. 1255 (1950), that "aliens detained outside the sovereign territory of the United States [may not] invok[e] a petition for a writ of habeas corpus." ... The Court of Appeals affirmed ... We granted certiorari, ... and now reverse.

* * *

The question now before us is whether the habeas statute confers a right to judicial review of the legality of Executive detention of aliens in a territory over which the United States exercises plenary and exclusive jurisdiction, bu not "ultimate sovereignty."

III

Respondents' primary submission is that the answer to the jurisdictional question is controlled by our decision in *Eisentrager*. In that case, we held that a Federal District Court lacked authority to issue a writ of habeas corpus to 21 German citizens who had been captured by U.S. forces in China, tried and convicted of war crimes by an American military commission headquartered in Nanking, and incarcerated in the Landsberg Prison in occupied Germany.... In reversing ... [the court of appeals decision], this Court summarized the six critical facts in the case:

> "We are here confronted with a decision whose basic premise is that these prisoners are entitled, as a constitutional right, to sue in some court of the United States for a writ of *habeas corpus*. To support that assumption we must hold that a prisoner of our military authorities is constitutionally entitled to the writ, even though he (a) is an enemy alien; (b) has never been or resided in the United States; (c) was captured outside of our territory and there held in military custody as a prisoner of war; (d) was tried and convicted by a Military Commission sitting outside the United States; (e) for offenses against laws of war committed outside the United States; (f) and is at all times imprisoned outside the United States." 339 U.S., at 777, 70 S.Ct. 936.

On this set of facts, the Court concluded, "no right to the writ of *habeas corpus* appears.

Petitioners in these cases differ from the *Eisentrager* detainees in important respects: They are not nationals of countries at war with the United States, and they deny that they have engaged in or plotted acts of aggression against the United States; they have never been afforded access to any tribunal, much less charged with and convicted of wrongdoing; and for more than two years they have been imprisoned in territory over which the United States exercises exclusive jurisdiction and control.

Not only are petitioners differently situated from the *Eisentrager* detainees, but the Court in *Eisentrager* made quite clear that all six of the facts critical to its disposition were relevant only to the question of the prisoners' *constitutional* entitlement to habeas corpus. The court had far less to say on the question of the petitioners' *statutory* entitlement to habeas review. Its only statement on the subject was a passing reference to the absence of statutory authorization: "Nothing in the text of the Constitution extends such a right, nor does anything in our statutes."

. . .

Because subsequent decisions of this Court have filled the statutory gap that had occasioned *Eisentrager's* resort to "fundamentals," persons detained outside the territorial jurisdiction of any federal district court no longer need rely on the Constitution as the source of their right to federal habeas review. of developments that "had a profound impact on the continuing vitality of that decision." . . . These developments included, notably, decisions of this Court in cases involving habeas petitioners "confined overseas (and thus outside the territory of any district court)," in which the Court "held, if only implicitly, that the petitioners' absence from the district does not present a jurisdictional obstacle to the consideration of the claim." . . .

IV

. . . [R]espondents contend that we can discern a limit on § 2241 through application of the "longstanding principle of American law" that congressional legislation is presumed not to have extraterritorial application unless such intent is clearly manifested. Whatever traction the presumption against extraterritoriality might have in other contexts, it certainly has no application to the operation of the habeas statute with respect to persons detained within "the territorial jurisdiction" of the United States. . . . By the express terms of its agreements with Cuba, the United States exercises "complete jurisdiction and control" over the Guantanamo Bay Naval Base, and may continue to exercise such control permanently if it so chooses. 1903 Lease Agreement, Art. III; 1934 Treaty, Art. III. Respondents themselves concede that the habeas statute would create federal-court jurisdiction over the claims of an American citizen held at the base. Considering that the statute draws no distinction between Americans and aliens held in federal custody, there is little reason to think that Congress intended the geographical coverage of the statute to vary depending on the detainee's citizenship. Aliens held at the base, no less than American citizens, are entitled to invoke the federal courts' authority under § 2241.

Application of the habeas statute to persons detained at the base is consistent with the historical reach of the writ of habeas corpus. At common law, courts exercised habeas jurisdiction over the claims of aliens detained within sovereign territory of the realm, as well as the claims of persons detained in the so-called "exempt jurisdictions," where ordinary writs did not run, and all other dominions under the sovereign's control. aliens). . . .

In the end, the answer to the question presented is clear. Petitioners contend that they are being held in federal custody in violation of the laws of the United States. No party questions the District Court's jurisdiction over petitioners' custodians. Section 2241, by its terms, requires nothing more. We therefore hold that § 2241 confers on the District Court jurisdiction to hear petitioners' habeas corpus challenges to the legality of their detention at the Guantanamo Bay Naval Base.

* * *

Whether and what further proceedings may become necessary after respondents make their response to the merits of petitioners' claims are matters that we need not address now. What is presently at stake is only whether the federal courts have jurisdiction to determine the legality of the Executive's potentially indefinite detention of individuals who claim to be wholly innocent of wrongdoing. Answering that question in the affirmative, we reverse the judgment of the Court of Appeals and remand for the District Court to consider in the first instance the merits of petitioners' claims.

It is so ordered.

[Justice KENNEDY, concurred in the judgment and wrote a separate opinion.]

* * *

Justice SCALIA, with whom THE CHIEF JUSTICE and Justice THOMAS join, dissenting.

. . .

The Commander in Chief and his subordinates had every reason to expect that the internment of combatants at Guantanamo Bay would not have the consequence of bringing the cumbersome machinery of our domestic courts into military affairs. Congress is in session. If it wished to change federal judges' habeas jurisdiction from what this Court had previously held that to be, it could have done so. And it could have done so by intelligent revision of the statute, instead of by today's clumsy, countertextual reinterpretation that confers upon wartime prisoners greater habeas rights than domestic detainees. The latter must challenge their present physical confinement in the district of their confinement, see *Rumsfeld v. Padilla,* ___ U.S. ___, [124] S.Ct. [2711], [159] L.Ed.2d [513], 2004 WL 1432135 (2004), whereas under today's strange holding Guantanamo Bay detainees can petition in any of the 94 federal judicial districts. The fact that extraterritorially located detainees lack the district of detention that the statute requires has been converted from a factor that precludes their ability to bring a petition at all into a factor that frees them to petition wherever they wish—and, as a result, to forum shop. For this Court to create such a monstrous scheme in time of war, and in frustration of our military commanders' reliance upon clearly stated prior law, is judicial adventurism of the worst sort. I dissent.

HAMDI v. RUMSFELD

542 U.S. 507 (2004).

[O'CONNOR, J., announced the judgment of the Court and delivered an opinion, in which REHNQUIST, C.J., and KENNEDY and BREYER, JJ., joined. SOUTER, J., filed an opinion concurring in part, dissenting in part, and concurring in the judgment, in which GINSBURG, J., joined. SCALIA, J., filed a dissenting opinion, in which STEVENS, J., joined. THOMAS, J., filed a dissenting opinion.]

Justice O'CONNOR announced the judgment of the Court and delivered an opinion, in which THE CHIEF JUSTICE, Justice KENNEDY, and Justice BREYER join.

At this difficult time in our Nation's history, we are called upon to consider the legality of the Government's detention of a United States citizen on United States soil as an "enemy combatant" and to address the process that is constitutionally owed to one who seeks to challenge his classification as such. The United States Court of Appeals for the Fourth Circuit held that petitioner's detention was legally authorized and that he was entitled to no further opportunity to challenge his enemy-combatant label. We now vacate and remand. We hold that although Congress authorized the detention of combatants in the narrow circumstances alleged here, due process demands that a citizen held in the United States as an enemy combatant be given a meaningful opportunity to contest the factual basis for that detention before a neutral decisionmaker.

I

On September 11, 2001, the al Qaeda terrorist network used hijacked commercial airliners to attack prominent targets in the United States. Approximately 3,000 people were killed in those attacks. One week later, in response to these "acts of treacherous violence," Congress passed a resolution authorizing the President to "use all necessary and appropriate force against those nations, organizations, or persons he determines planned, authorized, committed, or aided the terrorist attacks" or "harbored such organizations or persons, in order to prevent any future acts of international terrorism against the United States by such nations, organizations or persons." Authorization for Use of Military Force ("the AUMF"), 115 Stat. 224. Soon thereafter, the President ordered United States Armed Forces to Afghanistan, with a mission to subdue al Qaeda and quell the Taliban regime that was known to support it.

This case arises out of the detention of a man whom the Government alleges took up arms with the Taliban during this conflict. His name is Yaser Esam Hamdi. Born an American citizen in Louisiana in 1980, Hamdi moved with his family to Saudi Arabia as a child. By 2001, the parties agree, he resided in Afghanistan. At some point that year, he was seized by members of the Northern Alliance, a coalition of military groups opposed to the Taliban government, and eventually was turned over to the United States military. The Government asserts that it initially detained and interrogated Hamdi in Afghanistan before transferring him to the United States Naval Base in Guantanamo Bay in January 2002. In April 2002, upon learning that Hamdi is an American citizen, authorities transferred him to a naval brig in Norfolk, Virginia, where he remained until a recent transfer to a brig in Charleston, South Carolina. The Government contends that Hamdi is an "enemy combatant," and that this status justifies holding him in the United States indefinitely—without formal charges or proceedings—unless and until it makes the determination that access to counsel or further process is warranted.

. . .

II

The threshold question before us is whether the Executive has the authority to detain citizens who qualify as "enemy combatants." There is some debate as to the proper scope of this term, and the Government has never provided any court with the full criteria that it uses in classifying individuals as such. It has made clear, however, that, for purposes of this case, the "enemy combatant" that it is seeking to detain is an individual who, it alleges, was " 'part of or supporting forces hostile to the United States or coalition partners' " in Afghanistan and who " 'engaged in an armed conflict against the United States' " there. We therefore answer only the narrow question before us: whether the detention of citizens falling within that definition is authorized.

The Government maintains that no explicit congressional authorization is required, because the Executive possesses plenary authority to detain pursuant to Article II of the Constitution. We do not reach the question whether Article II provides such authority, however, because we agree with the Government's alternative position, that Congress has in fact authorized Hamdi's detention, through the AUMF.

Our analysis on that point, set forth below, substantially overlaps with our analysis of Hamdi's principal argument for the illegality of his detention. He posits that his detention is forbidden by 18 U.S.C. § 4001(a). Section 4001(a) states that "[n]o citizen shall be imprisoned or otherwise detained by the United States except pursuant to an Act of Congress." Congress passed § 4001(a) in 1971 as part of a bill to repeal the Emergency Detention Act of 1950, 50 U.S.C. § 811 *et seq.*, which provided procedures for executive detention, during times of emergency, of individuals deemed likely to engage in espionage or sabotage. Congress was particularly concerned about the possibility that the Act could be used to reprise the Japanese internment camps of World War II. H.R.Rep. No. 92–116 (1971); *id.,* at 4, U.S.Code Cong. & Admin.News 1971, 1435, 1438 ("The concentration camp implications of the legislation render it abhorrent"). The Government again presses two alternative positions. First, it argues that § 4001(a), in light of its legislative history and its location in Title 18, applies only to "the control of civilian prisons and related detentions," not to military detentions .. Second, it maintains that § 4001(a) is satisfied, because Hamdi is being detained "pursuant to an Act of Congress"—the AUMF. Again, because we conclude that the Government's second assertion is correct, we do not address the first. In other words, for the reasons that follow, we conclude that the AUMF is explicit congressional authorization for the detention of individuals in the narrow category we describe (assuming, without deciding, that such authorization is required), and that the AUMF satisfied § 4001(a)'s requirement that a detention be "pursuant to an Act of Congress" (assuming, without deciding, that § 4001(a) applies to military detentions).

The AUMF authorizes the President to use "all necessary and appropriate force" against "nations, organizations, or persons" associated with the September 11, 2001, terrorist attacks. 115 Stat. 224. There can be no doubt that individuals who fought against the United States in Afghanistan as part of the Taliban, an organization known to have supported the al Qaeda terrorist network responsible for those attacks, are individuals Congress sought to target in passing the AUMF. We conclude that detention of individuals falling into the limited category we are considering, for the duration of the particular conflict in which they were captured, is so fundamental and accepted an incident to war as to be an exercise of the "necessary and appropriate force" Congress has authorized the President to use.

The capture and detention of lawful combatants and the capture, detention, and trial of unlawful combatants, by "universal agreement and practice," are "important incident[s] of war." *Ex parte Quirin,* 317 U.S., at 28, 63 S.Ct. 2. The purpose of detention is to prevent captured individuals from returning to the field of battle and taking up arms once again.... cf. *In re Territo,* 156 F.2d 142, 145 (C.A.9 1946) ("The object of capture is to prevent the captured individual from serving the enemy. He is disarmed and from then on must be removed as completely as practicable from the front, treated humanely, and in time exchanged, repatriated, or otherwise released".

There is no bar to this Nation's holding one of its own citizens as an enemy combatant. In *Quirin,* one of the detainees, Haupt, alleged that he was a naturalized United States citizen. 317 U.S., at 20, 63 S.Ct. 2. We held that "[c]itizens who associate themselves with the military arm of the enemy government, and with its aid, guidance and direction enter this country bent on hostile acts, are enemy belligerents within the meaning of ... the law of war.... A citizen, no less than an alien, can be "part of or supporting forces hostile to the United States or coalition partners" and "engaged in an armed conflict against the United States," ... such a citizen, if released, would pose the same threat of returning to the front during the ongoing conflict.

In light of these principles, it is of no moment that the AUMF does not use specific language of detention. Because detention to prevent a combatant's return to the battlefield is a fundamental incident of waging war, in permitting the use of "necessary and appropriate force," Congress has clearly and unmistakably authorized detention in the narrow circumstances considered here.

Hamdi objects, nevertheless, that Congress has not authorized the *indefinite* detention to which he is now subject. The Government responds that "the detention of enemy combatants during World War II was just as 'indefinite' while that war was being fought." We take Hamdi's objection to be not to the lack of certainty regarding the date on which the conflict will end, but to the substantial prospect of perpetual detention. We recognize that the national security underpinnings of the "war on terror," although crucially important, are broad and malleable. As the Government concedes, "given its unconventional nature, the current conflict is unlikely to end with a formal cease-fire agreement." The prospect Hamdi raises is therefore not far-fetched. If the Government does not consider this unconventional war won for two generations, and if it maintains during that time that Hamdi might, if released, rejoin forces fighting against the United States, then the position it has taken throughout the litigation of this case suggests that Hamdi's detention could last for the rest of his life.

It is a clearly established principle of the law of war that detention may last no longer than active hostilities. See Article 118 of the Geneva Convention (III) Relative to the Treatment of Prisoners of War, Aug. 12, 1949, [1955] 6 U.S.T. 3316, 3406, T.I.A.S. No. 3364 ("Prisoners of war shall be released and repatriated without delay after the cessation of active hostilities"). See also ... Praust, Judicial Power to Determine the Status and Rights of Persons Detained without Trial, 44 Harv. Int'l L.J. 503, 510–511 (2003) (prisoners of war "can be detained during an armed conflict, but the detaining country must release and repatriate them 'without delay after the cessation of active hostilities,' unless they are being lawfully prosecuted or have been lawfully convicted of crimes and are serving sentences" ...

Hamdi contends that the AUMF does not authorize indefinite or perpetual detention. Certainly, we agree that indefinite detention for the purpose of interrogation is not authorized. Further, we understand Congress' grant of authority for the use of "necessary and appropriate force" to include the authority to detain for the duration of the relevant conflict, and our understanding is based on longstanding law-of-war principles. If the practical circumstances of a given conflict are entirely unlike those of the conflicts that informed the development of the law of war, that understanding may unravel. But that is not the situation we face as of this date. Active combat operations against Taliban fighters apparently are ongoing in Afghanistan.... The United States may detain, for the duration of these hostilities, individuals legitimately determined to be Taliban combatants who "engaged in an armed conflict against the United States." If the record establishes that United States troops are still involved in active combat in Afghanistan, those detentions are part of the exercise of "necessary and appropriate force," and therefore are authorized by the AUMF.

Ex parte Milligan, 4 Wall. 2, 125, 18 L.Ed. 281 (1866), does not undermine our holding about the Government's authority to seize enemy combatants, as we define that term today. In that case, the Court made repeated reference to the fact that its inquiry into whether the military tribunal had jurisdiction to try and punish Milligan turned in large part on the fact that Milligan was not a prisoner of war, but a resident of Indiana arrested while at home there. That fact was central to its conclusion. Had Milligan been captured while he was assisting Confederate soldiers by carrying a rifle against Union troops on a Confederate battlefield, the holding of the Court might well have been different. The Court's repeated explanations that Milligan was not a prisoner of war suggest that had these different circumstances been present he could have been detained under military authority for the duration of the conflict, whether or not he was a citizen.[1]

. . .

Quirin was a unanimous opinion. It both postdates and clarifies *Milligan,* providing us with the most apposite precedent that we have on the question of whether citizens may be detained in such circumstances. Brushing aside such precedent—particularly when doing so gives rise to a host of new questions never dealt with by this Court—is unjustified and unwise.

. . .

III

Even in cases in which the detention of enemy combatants is legally authorized, there remains the question of what process is constitutionally due to a citizen who disputes his enemy-combatant status. Hamdi argues that he is owed a meaningful and timely hearing and that "extrajudicial detention [that] begins and ends with the submission of an affidavit based on third-hand hearsay" does not comport with the Fifth and Fourteenth Amendments. The Government counters that any more process than was provided below would be both unworkable and "constitutionally intolerable." Our resolution of this dispute requires a careful examination both of the writ of habeas corpus, which Hamdi now seeks to employ as a mechanism of judicial review, and of the Due Process Clause, which informs the procedural contours of that mechanism in this instance.

---

1. Here the basis asserted for detention by the military is that Hamdi was carrying a weapon against American troops on a foreign battlefield; that is, that he was an enemy combatant. The legal category of enemy combatant has not been elaborated upon in great detail. The permissible bounds of the category will be defined by the lower courts as subsequent cases are presented to them.

A

Though they reach radically different conclusions on the process that ought to attend the present proceeding, the parties begin on common ground. All agree that, absent suspension, the writ of habeas corpus remains available to every individual detained within the United States. U.S. Const., Art. I, § 9, cl. 2 ("The Privilege of the Writ of Habeas Corpus shall not be suspended, unless when in Cases of Rebellion or Invasion the public Safety may require it").... At all other times, it has remained a critical check on the Executive, ensuring that it does not detain individuals except in accordance with law.... All agree suspension of the writ has not occurred here. Thus, it is undisputed that Hamdi was properly before an Article III court to challenge his detention under 28 U.S.C. § 2241. Further, all agree that § 2241 and its companion provisions provide at least a skeletal outline of the procedures to be afforded a petitioner in federal habeas review. Most notably, § 2243 provides that "the person detained may, under oath, deny any of the facts set forth in the return or allege any other material facts," and § 2246 allows the taking of evidence in habeas proceedings by deposition, affidavit, or interrogatories.

The simple outline of § 2241 makes clear both that Congress envisioned that habeas petitioners would have some opportunity to present and rebut facts and that courts in cases like this retain some ability to vary the ways in which they do so as mandated by due process. The Government recognizes the basic procedural protections required by the habeas statute, but asks us to hold that, given both the flexibility of the habeas mechanism and the circumstances presented in this case, the presentation of the Mobbs Declaration to the habeas court completed the required factual development. It suggests two separate reasons for its position that no further process is due.

B

First, the Government urges the adoption of the Fourth Circuit's holding below—that because it is "undisputed" that Hamdi's seizure took place in a combat zone, the habeas determination can be made purely as a matter of law, with no further hearing or factfinding necessary. This argument is easily rejected. As the dissenters from the denial of rehearing en banc noted, the circumstances surrounding Hamdi's seizure cannot in any way be characterized as "undisputed," as "those circumstances are neither conceded in fact, nor susceptible to concession in law, because Hamdi has not been permitted to speak for himself or even through counsel as to those circumstances." Further, the "facts" that constitute the alleged concession are insufficient to support Hamdi's detention. Under the definition of enemy combatant that we accept today as falling within the scope of Congress' authorization, Hamdi would need to be "part of or supporting forces hostile to the United States or coalition partners" and "engaged in an armed conflict against the United States" to justify his detention in the United States for the duration of the relevant conflict. The habeas petition states only that "[w]hen seized by the United States Government, Mr. Hamdi resided in Afghanistan." An assertion that one *resided* in a country in which combat operations are taking place is not a concession that one was "*captured* in a zone of active combat operations in a foreign theater of war," and certainly is not a concession that one was "part of or supporting forces hostile to the United States or coalition partners" and "engaged in an armed conflict against the United States." Accordingly, we reject any argument that Hamdi has made concessions that eliminate any right to further process.

C

The Government's second argument requires closer consideration. This is the argument that further factual exploration is unwarranted and inappropriate in light of the extraordinary constitutional interests at stake. Under the Government's most extreme rendition of this argument, "[r]espect for separation of powers and the limited institutional capabilities of courts in matters of military decision-making in connection with an ongoing conflict" ought to eliminate entirely any individual process, restricting the courts to investigating only whether legal authorization exists for the broader detention scheme. At most, the Government argues, courts should review its determination that a citizen is an enemy combatant under a very deferential "some evidence" standard. *Id.*, at 34 ("Under the some evidence standard, the focus is exclusively on the factual basis supplied by the Executive to support its own determination") (citing *Superintendent, Mass. Correctional Institution at Walpole v. Hill*, 472 U.S. 445, 455–457, 105 S.Ct. 2768, 86 L.Ed.2d 356 (1985) (explaining that the some evidence standard "does not require" a "weighing of the evidence," but rather calls for assessing "whether there is any evidence in the record that could support the conclusion")). Under this review, a court would assume the accuracy of the Government's articulated basis for Hamdi's detention, as set forth in the Mobbs Declaration, and assess only whether that articulated basis was a legitimate one. . . .

In response, Hamdi emphasizes that this Court consistently has recognized that an individual challenging his detention may not be held at the will of the Executive without recourse to some proceeding before a neutral tribunal to determine whether the Executive's asserted justifications for that detention have basis in fact and warrant in law. . . . He argues that the Fourth Circuit inappropriately "ceded power to the Executive during wartime to define the conduct for which a citizen may be detained, judge whether that citizen has engaged in the proscribed conduct, and imprison that citizen indefinitely," and that due process demands that he receive a hearing in which he may challenge the Mobbs Declaration and adduce his own counter evidence. The District Court, agreeing with Hamdi, apparently believed that the appropriate process would approach the process that accompanies a criminal trial. It therefore disapproved of the hearsay nature of the Mobbs Declaration and anticipated quite extensive discovery of various military affairs. Anything less, it concluded, would not be "meaningful judicial review."

Both of these positions highlight legitimate concerns. And both emphasize the tension that often exists between the autonomy that the Government asserts is necessary in order to pursue effectively a particular goal and the process that a citizen contends he is due before he is deprived of a constitutional right. The ordinary mechanism that we use for balancing such serious competing interests, and for determining the procedures that are necessary to ensure that a citizen is not "deprived of life, liberty, or property, without due process of law," is the test that we articulated in *Mathews v. Eldridge,* 424 U.S. 319, 96 S.Ct. 893, 47 L.Ed.2d 18 (1976).... *Mathews* dictates that the process due in any given instance is determined by weighing "the private interest that will be affected by the official action" against the Government's asserted interest, "including the function involved" and the burdens the Government would face in providing greater process.... The *Mathews* calculus then contemplates a judicious balancing of these concerns, through an analysis of "the risk of an erroneous deprivation" of the private interest if the process were reduced and the "probable value, if any, of additional or substitute safeguards." We take each of these steps in turn.

It is beyond question that substantial interests lie on both sides of the scale in this case. Hamdi's "private interest ... affected by the official action," is the most elemental of liberty interests—the interest in being free from physical detention by one's own government....

Nor is the weight on this side of the *Mathews* scale offset by the circumstances of war or the accusation of treasonous behavior, for "[i]t is clear that commitment for *any* purpose constitutes a significant deprivation of liberty that requires due process protection,".... Moreover, as critical as the Government's interest may be in detaining those who actually pose an immediate threat to the national security of the United States during ongoing international conflict, history and common sense teach us that an unchecked system of detention carries the potential to become a means for oppression and abuse of others who do not present that sort of threat.... We reaffirm today the fundamental nature of a citizen's right to be free from involuntary confinement by his own government without due process of law, and we weigh the opposing governmental interests against the curtailment of liberty that such confinement entails.

On the other side of the scale are the weighty and sensitive governmental interests in ensuring that those who have in fact fought with the enemy during a war do not return to battle against the United States. As discussed above, ... the law of war and the realities of combat may render such detentions both necessary and appropriate, and our due process analysis need not blink at those realities. Without doubt, our Constitution recognizes that core strategic matters of warmaking belong in the hands of those who are best positioned and most politically accountable for making them. * * *

The Government also argues at some length that its interests in reducing the process available to alleged enemy combatants are heightened by the practical difficulties that would accompany a system of trial-like process. In its view, military officers who are engaged in the serious work of waging battle would be unnecessarily and dangerously distracted by litigation half a world away, and discovery into military operations would both intrude on the sensitive secrets of national defense and result in a futile search for evidence buried under the rubble of war. To the extent that these burdens are triggered by heightened procedures, they are properly taken into account in our due process analysis.

Striking the proper constitutional balance here is of great importance to the Nation during this period of ongoing combat. But it is equally vital that our calculus not give short shrift to the values that this country holds dear or to the privilege that is American citizenship. It is during our most challenging and uncertain moments that our Nation's commitment to due process is most severely tested; and it is in those times that we must preserve our commitment at home to the principles for which we fight abroad. . . .

With due recognition of these competing concerns, we believe that neither the process proposed by the Government nor the process apparently envisioned by the District Court below strikes the proper constitutional balance when a United States citizen is detained in the United States as an enemy combatant. That is, "the risk of erroneous deprivation" of a detainee's liberty interest is unacceptably high under the Government's proposed rule, while some of the "additional or substitute procedural safeguards" suggested by the District Court are unwarranted in light of their limited "probable value" and the burdens they may impose on the military in such cases.

We therefore hold that a citizen-detainee seeking to challenge his classification as an enemy combatant must receive notice of the factual basis for his classification, and a fair opportunity to rebut the Government's factual assertions before a neutral decisionmaker. . . . These essential constitutional promises may not be eroded.

At the same time, the exigencies of the circumstances may demand that, aside from these core elements, enemy combatant proceedings may be tailored to alleviate their uncommon potential to burden the Executive at a time of ongoing military conflict. Hearsay, for example, may need to be accepted as the most reliable available evidence from the Government in such a proceeding. Likewise, the Constitution would not be offended by a presumption in favor of the Government's evidence, so long as that presumption remained a rebuttable one and fair opportunity for rebuttal were provided. Thus, once the Government puts forth credible evidence that the habeas petitioner meets the enemy-combatant criteria, the onus could shift to the petitioner to rebut that evidence with more persuasive evidence that he falls outside the criteria. A burden-shifting scheme of this sort would meet the goal of ensuring that the errant tourist, embedded journalist, or local aid worker has a chance to prove military error while giving due regard to the Executive once it has put forth meaningful support for its conclusion that the detainee is in fact an enemy combatant.

We think it unlikely that this basic process will have the dire impact on the central functions of warmaking that the Government forecasts. The parties agree that initial captures on the battlefield need not receive the process we have discussed here; that process is due only when the determination is made to *continue* to hold those who have been seized. The Government has made clear in its briefing that documentation regarding battlefield detainees already is kept in the ordinary course of military affairs. Any factfinding imposition created by requiring a knowledgeable affiant to summarize these records to an independent tribunal is a minimal one. Likewise, arguments that military officers ought not have to wage war under the threat of litigation lose much of their steam when factual disputes at enemy-combatant hearings are limited to the alleged combatant's acts. This focus meddles little, if at all, in the strategy or conduct of war, inquiring only into the appropriateness of continuing to detain an individual claimed to have taken up arms against the United States. While we accord the greatest respect and consideration to the judgments of military authorities in matters relating to the actual prosecution of a war, and recognize that the scope of that discretion necessarily is wide, it does not infringe on the core role of the military for the courts to exercise their own time-honored and constitutionally mandated roles of reviewing and resolving claims like those presented here.

In sum, while the full protections that accompany challenges to detentions in other settings may prove unworkable and inappropriate in the enemy-combatant setting, the threats to military operations posed by a basic system of independent review are not so weighty as to trump a citizen's core rights to challenge meaningfully the Government's case and to be heard by an impartial adjudicator.

D

* * *

Because we conclude that due process demands some system for a citizen detainee to refute his classification, the proposed "some evidence" standard is inadequate. Any process in which the Executive's factual assertions go wholly unchallenged or are simply presumed correct without any opportunity for the alleged combatant to demonstrate otherwise falls constitutionally short. As the Government itself has recognized, we have utilized the "some evidence" standard in the past as a standard of review, not as a standard of proof.... This standard therefore is ill suited to the situation in which a habeas petitioner has received no prior proceedings before any tribunal and had no prior opportunity to rebut the Executive's factual assertions before a neutral decisionmaker.

Today we are faced only with such a case. Aside from unspecified "screening" processes, and military interrogations in which the Government suggests Hamdi could have contested his classification, Hamdi has received no process. An interrogation by one's captor, however effective an intelligence-gathering tool, hardly constitutes a constitutionally adequate factfinding before a neutral decisionmaker.... Plainly, the "process" Hamdi has received is not that to which he is entitled under the Due Process Clause.

There remains the possibility that the standards we have articulated could be met by an appropriately authorized and properly constituted military tribunal. Indeed, it is notable that military regulations already provide for such process in related instances, dictating that tribunals be made available to determine the status of enemy detainees who assert prisoner-of-war status under the Geneva Convention. See Enemy Prisoners of War, Retained Personnel, Civilian Internees and Other Detainees, Army Regulation 190–8, § 1–6 (1997). In the absence of such process, however, a court that receives a petition for a writ of habeas corpus from an alleged enemy combatant must itself ensure that the minimum requirements of due process are achieved. Both courts below recognized as much, focusing their energies on the question of whether Hamdi was due an opportunity to rebut the Government's case against him. The Government, too, proceeded on this assumption, presenting its affidavit and then seeking that it be evaluated under a deferential standard of review based on burdens that it alleged would accompany any greater process. As we have discussed, a habeas court in a case such as this may accept affidavit evidence like that contained in the Mobbs Declaration, so long as it also permits the alleged combatant to present his own factual case to rebut the Government's return. We anticipate that a District Court would proceed with the caution that we have indicated is necessary in this setting, engaging in a factfinding process that is both prudent and incremental. We have no reason to doubt that courts faced with these sensitive matters will pay proper heed both to the matters of national security that might arise in an individual case and to the constitutional limitations safeguarding essential liberties that remain vibrant even in times of security concerns.

IV

Hamdi asks us to hold that the Fourth Circuit also erred by denying him immediate access to counsel upon his detention and by disposing of the case without permitting him to meet with an attorney. Since our grant of certiorari in this case, Hamdi has been appointed counsel, with whom he has met for consultation purposes on several occasions, and with whom he is now being granted unmonitored meetings. He unquestionably has the right to access to counsel in connection with the proceedings on remand. No further consideration of this issue is necessary at this stage of the case.

* * *

The judgment of the United States Court of Appeals for the Fourth Circuit is vacated, and the case is remanded for further proceedings.

It is so ordered.

Justice SOUTER, with whom Justice GINSBURG joins, concurring in part, dissenting in part, and concurring in the judgment.

. . . .

IV

Because I find Hamdi's detention forbidden by § 4001(a) and unauthorized by the Force Resolution, I would not reach any questions of what process he may be due in litigating disputed issues in a proceeding under the habeas statute or prior to the habeas enquiry itself. For me, it suffices that the Government has failed to justify holding him in the absence of a further Act of Congress, criminal charges, a showing that the detention conforms to the laws of war, or a demonstration that § 4001(a) is unconstitutional. I would therefore vacate the judgment of the Court of Appeals and remand for proceedings consistent with this view.

Since this disposition does not command a majority of the Court, however, the need to give practical effect to the conclusions of eight members of the Court rejecting the Government's position calls for me to join with the plurality in ordering remand on terms closest to those I would impose. Although I think litigation of Hamdi's status as an enemy combatant is unnecessary, the terms of the plurality's remand will allow Hamdi to offer evidence that he is not an enemy combatant, and he should at the least have the benefit of that opportunity.

It should go without saying that in joining with the plurality to produce a judgment, I do not adopt the plurality's resolution of constitutional issues that I would not reach. It is not that I could disagree with the plurality's determinations (given the plurality's view of the Force Resolution) that someone in Hamdi's position is entitled at a minimum to notice of the Government's claimed factual basis for holding him, and to a fair chance to rebut it before a neutral decision maker . . .; nor, of course, could I disagree with the plurality's affirmation of Hamdi's right to counsel, ... On the other hand, I do not mean to imply agreement that the Government could claim an evidentiary presumption casting the burden of rebuttal on Hamdi, or that an opportunity to litigate before a military tribunal might obviate or truncate enquiry by a court on habeas . . . .

Subject to these qualifications, I join with the plurality in a judgment of the Court vacating the Fourth Circuit's judgment and remanding the case.

Justice SCALIA, with whom Justice STEVENS joins, dissenting.

. . . This case brings into conflict the competing demands of national security and our citizens' constitutional right to personal liberty. Although I share the Court's evident unease as it seeks to reconcile the two, I do not agree with its resolution.

Where the Government accuses a citizen of waging war against it, our constitutional tradition has been to prosecute him in federal court for treason or some other crime. Where the exigencies of war prevent that, the Constitution's Suspension Clause, Art. I, § 9, cl. 2, allows Congress to relax the usual protections temporarily. Absent suspension, however, the Executive's assertion of military exigency has not been thought sufficient to permit detention without charge. No one contends that the congressional Authorization for Use of Military Force, on which the Government relies to justify its actions here, is an implementation of the Suspension Clause. Accordingly, I would reverse the decision below.

. . .

Many think it not only inevitable but entirely proper that liberty give way to security in times of national crisis—that, at the extremes of military exigency, *inter arma silent leges*. Whatever the general merits of the view that war silences law or modulates its voice, that view has no place in the interpretation and application of a Constitution designed precisely to confront war and, in a manner that accords with democratic principles, to accommodate it. Because the Court has proceeded to meet the current emergency in a manner the Constitution does not envision, I respectfully dissent.

Justice THOMAS, dissenting.

The Executive Branch, acting pursuant to the powers vested in the President by the Constitution and with explicit congressional approval, has determined that Yaser Hamdi is an enemy combatant and should be detained. This detention falls squarely within the Federal Government's war powers, and we lack the expertise and capacity to second-guess that decision. As such, petitioners' habeas challenge should fail, and there is no reason to remand the case. The plurality reaches a contrary conclusion by failing adequately to consider basic principles of the constitutional structure as it relates to national security and foreign affairs and by using the balancing scheme of *Mathews v. Eldridge*, 424 U.S. 319, 96 S.Ct. 893, 47 L.Ed.2d 18 (1976). I do not think that the Federal Government's war powers can be balanced away by this Court. Arguably, Congress could provide for additional procedural protections, but until it does, we have no right to insist upon them. But even if I were to agree with the general approach the plurality takes, I could not accept the particulars. The plurality utterly fails to account for the Government's compelling interests and for our own institutional inability to weigh competing concerns correctly. I respectfully dissent.

Notes and Questions

1. In the aftermath of the Supreme Court's decision in the Hamdi case, the government and Hamdi reached a negotiated settlement. (The Supreme Court opinion was handed down on June 28, 2004; the settlement was

finalized on September 17, 2004.) Under the terms of the settlement, Hamdi was released and transported to Saudi Arabia; the U.S. agreed to make no request that he be detained by the Saudis; he agreed that he would not engage in any combat activities against the U.S. nor engage in terrorism or aid or affiliate with al Qaeda, the Taliban or any terrorist organization, and he would inform Saudi officials and the U.S. embassy if he were solicited to engage in such activities; he also agreed to renounce his U.S. nationality; he agreed not to travel outside of the Saudi Arabian kingdom for a period of five years, never to travel to Afghanistan, Iraq, Israel, Pakistan, Syria, the West Bank or the Gaza Strip, nor to travel to the United States for ten years and then only having obtained express permission from named high U.S. government officials, and for 15 years to notify the U.S. Embassy of any plans to travel outside of Saudi Arabia. Hamdi also agreed that if he failed to fulfill the conditions of the agreement, he was subject to being detained immediately "insofar as consistent with the law of armed conflict." Finally, the settlement provided for dismissal of the action, Hamdi v. Rumsfeld, with prejudice.

* * *

3. Following announcement of the settlement in the Hamdi case, lawyers for John Walker Lindh, see supra, p. , filed a request for clemency. LA Times, Sept. 29, 2004, p.A1. Lindh had pleaded guilty to supplying services to the Taliban and carrying firearms and destructive devices and received a 20 year sentence. With the exception of the life sentence given to Richard Reid, see infra, p. , his is the most severe sentence meted out in anti-terrorism cases, post–9/11. Both Lindh and Hamdi were seized in the same general area of Afghanistan. Both are American citizens. Does the Hamdi settlement warrant granting clemency to Lindh?

* * *

5. Review carefully the positions taken in each of the opinions in the Hamdi case and the lineup of the various justices in support of each position. How many justices supported the government's position in the case? How many justices would have released Hamdi? How many justices were of the view that the preferred outcome was that which actually occurred? If you were to compare opinions, which would you characterize as polar opposites?

6. A third case, Rumsfeld v. Padilla, 124 S.Ct. 2711 (2004), was decided along with the Rasul and Hamdi cases, supra. In Padilla, the Supreme Court reversed the court of appeals decision, 352 F.3d 695 (2d Cir. 2003), which in turn had reversed the district court decision. Padilla was an American citizen arrested at Chicago's O'Hare Airport, as a material witness in connection with an alleged plot to detonate a dirty bomb (i.e. an explosive device sheathed in radioactive material). Subsequently, the President issued an order declaring Padilla an enemy combatant and he was transferred to military jurisdiction and detained in a military brig. From that point forward, he was denied access to counsel and had no contact with anyone on the outside. His attorney, retained earlier when he was still in material witness status, filed suit on his behalf in New York against the Secretary of Defense.

In the Supreme Court, a majority of the justices concluded that the Secretary of Defense was not the proper respondent in the case; the appropriate respondent was the commander of the naval brig where Padilla was detained. Further, the district court in the Southern District of New York did not have jurisdiction over the commander of the brig. Accordingly, the court of appeals decision was reversed, and the case was dismissed "without prejudice." The Court majority (Rehnquist, C.J. joined by Justices O'Connor, Scalia, Kennedy and Thomas) did not reach the question whether the President had authority to detain Padilla militarily. The four dissenting justices (Stevens J. joined by Justices Souter, Ginsburg and Breyer) voted to uphold the district court's jurisdiction and, reaching the merits, stated:

> Whether respondent is entitled to immediate release is a question that reasonable jurists may answer in different ways.[8] There is, however, only one possible answer to the question whether he is entitled to a hearing on the justification for his detention.[9]

> At stake in this case is nothing less than the essence of a free society. Even more important than the method of selecting the people's rulers and their successors is the character of the constraints imposed on the Executive by the rule of law. Unconstrained Executive detention for the purpose of investigating and preventing subversive activity is the hallmark of the Star Chamber.[10] Access to counsel for the purpose of protecting the citizen from official mistakes and mistreatment is the hallmark of due process.

> Executive detention of subversive citizens, like detention of enemy soldiers to keep them off the battlefield, may sometimes be justified to prevent persons from launching or becoming missiles of destruction. It may not, however, be justified by the naked interest in using unlawful procedures to extract information. Incommunicado detention for months on end is such a procedure. Whether the information so procured is more or less reliable than that acquired by more extreme forms of torture is of no consequence. For if this Nation is to remain true to the ideals symbolized by its flag, it must not wield the tools of tyrants even to resist an assault by the forces of tyranny. . . .

7. Four justices reached the merits in the Padilla case and concluded that the government did not have legal authority to hold him. The court majority did not, however, reach the merits. Is there a fifth vote in support

---

8. Consistent with the judgment of the Court of Appeals, I believe that the Non–Detention Act, 18 U.S.C. § 4001(a), prohibits—and the Authorization for Use of Military Force Joint Resolution, 115 Stat. 224, adopted on September 18, 2001, does not authorize—the protracted, incommunicado detention of American citizens arrested in the United States.

9. Respondent's custodian has been remarkably candid about the Government's motive in detaining respondent: " '[O]ur interest really in his case is not law enforcement, it is not punishment because he was a terrorist or working with the terrorists.

Our interest at the moment is to try and find out everything he knows so that hopefully we can stop other terrorist acts.' " 233 F.Supp.2d 564, 573–574 (S.D.N.Y.2002) (quoting News Briefing, Dept. of Defense (June 12, 2002), 2002 WL 22026773).

10. See *Watts v. Indiana,* 338 U.S. 49, 54, 69 S.Ct. 1347, 93 L.Ed. 1801 (1949) (opinion of Frankfurter, J.). "There is torture of mind as well as body; the will is as much affected by fear as by force. And there comes a point where this Court should not be ignorant as judges of what we know as men." *Id.,* at 52, 69 S.Ct. 1347.

of Padilla's position on the merits, to be found among the court majority in the case? That is, when the Padilla case again reaches the Supreme Court, is there likely to be a fifth vote in his favor (assuming no changes in the makeup of the Court in the meantime)? Consider the position taken by Justice Scalia in the Hamdi case. Does it suggest that he would vote in favor of Padilla when the Court finally faces the issue on the merits in the case?

8. Justice Stevens wrote for the four dissenters in Padilla and he joined with Justice Scalia in dissent in Hamdi. Are those two votes and the supporting positions consistent? Justice Stevens also wrote in footnote 8 in his dissent in Padilla that the relevant statutes do not authorize protracted, incommunicado detention of an American citizen, but he also wrote in the text:

> Executive detention of subversive citizens, like detention of enemy soldiers to keep them off the battlefield, may sometimes be justified to prevent persons from launching or becoming missiles of destruction.

Are the statements in the text and in footnote 8 reconcilable? Where would the authority to take the action described in the text come from? Might the government's protracted detention of Padilla possibly be justified on the ground that he was involved in plans to detonate a "dirty bomb"; that his detention was necessary to keep him from launching a "missile of destruction"?

9. The import of the Supreme Court's decision in Rumsfeld v. Padilla was that Padilla had sued the wrong defendant in the wrong court. Soon thereafter, on July 2, 2004, Padilla filed a new habeas corpus action in the U.S. District Court for the District of South Carolina against the commander of the brig in which he was being detained. Padilla filed a motion for summary judgment on October 20, 2004; a hearing on the motion was held on January 5, 2005, Padilla v. Hanft, Civil No. 2:04CV2221, and the district court handed down its decision, which is reproduced below, on February 28, 2005.

10. Another detainee, in a situation similar to Padilla's—that is, a U.S. citizen arrested in the U.S. and detained as an "enemy combatant—filed his petition for habeas corpus against Commander Hanft on July 8, 2005. Al–Marri v. Hanft, Civil No. 2:04CV2257. Al–Marri then filed a motion to allow him to hold unmonitored conversations with his attorney. Subsequently, a settlement was entered in which Al–Marri agreed to a Special Administrative Measures (SAM) regarding his contacts with his attorneys, a protective order was entered into, and his attorneys agreed that they would act to obtain security clearance. . . .

PADILLLA v. HANFT

2005 WL 465691 (D.S.C. 2005).

Floyd, Henry F., District Judge

MEMORANDUM OPINION AND ORDER

This is a 28 U.S.C. § 2241 *habeas corpus* action. . . . Pending before the Court is Petitioner's Motion for Summary Judgment as to Counts

One and Two. The sole question before the Court today is whether the President of the United States (President) is authorized to detain a United States citizen as an enemy combatant under the unique circumstances presented here.

. . .

This case was commenced on July 2, 2004, with the filing of the petition discussed herein. Respondent filed his Answer on August 30, 2004.

On October 20, 2004, Petitioner filed a Motion for Summary Judgment to Counts One and Two of his Petition, as well as his Memorandum of Law in Support of the Motion (Petitioner's Motion). The parties jointly submitted their Stipulations of Fact on the same day. Subsequently, on November 22, 2004, Respondent filed his Opposition to Petitioner's Motion (Respondent's Opposition). Petitioner filed a Reply to Respondent's Opposition on December 13, 2004. Oral arguments were held on January 5, 2005. The case is now ripe for adjudication.

. . .

Rule 56(c) of the Federal Rules of Civil Procedure provides that summary judgment "shall be rendered forthwith if the pleadings, depositions, answers to interrogatories and admissions on file, together with affidavits, if any, show that there is no genuine issue as to any material fact and that the moving party is entitled to a judgment as a matter of law."

* * *

Petitioner maintains that Congress has not authorized the indefinite detention without trial of citizens arrested in the United States. He also argues that the President's inherent constitutional powers do not allow him to subject United States citizens who are arrested in the United States to indefinite military detention.

Conversely, respondent contends that the President has the constitutional authority to detain Petitioner as an enemy combatant without charging him criminally. Furthermore, according to Respondent, the Non–Detention Act, 18 U.S.C. § 4001(a), does not constrain the President's authority to detain Petitioner as an enemy combatant.

. . .

Respondent maintains that the decisions of the Supreme Court in *Hamdi v. Rumsfeld,* 124 S.Ct. 2633 (2004) and *Quirin,* 317 U.S. 1 "reaffirm the military's long-settled authority—independent of and distinct from the criminal process—to detain enemy combatants for the duration of a given armed conflict, including the current conflict against al Qaeda.". According to Respondent, "[t]hose decisions squarely apply to this case." Petitioner, on the other hand, maintains that *Ex parte Milligan,* 71 U.S. (4 Wall) 2 (1866) is controlling. The Court will consider each case in turn.

The petitioner in *Hamdi* was an American citizen captured while on the battlefield in Afghanistan. In that case, the Supreme Court had before it the threshold question of "whether the Executive has the authority to detain citizens who qualify as 'enemy combatants.'"

While the Court noted that there was some debate and no full exposition by the Government of the proper scope of the term "enemy combatant," it was clear in *Hamdi* that, the "enemy combatant that [the Government was] seeking to detain [was] an individual who, it allege[d], was part of or supporting forces hostile to the United States or coalition partners in Afghanistan and who engaged in an armed conflict against the United States there." The Court also noted that, "the basis asserted for detention by the military is that Hamdi was *carrying a weapon against American troops on a foreign battlefield;* that is, that he was an enemy combatant."

Against this backdrop, the Supreme Court found that authority existed to detain Mr. Hamdi. The Court reasoned,

> [t]here is no bar to this Nation's holding one of its own citizens as an enemy combatant. . . . A citizen, no less than an alien, can be "part of or supporting forces hostile to the United States or coalition partners" and "engaged in an armed conflict against the United States"; such a citizen, if released, would pose the same threat of returning to the front during the ongoing conflict.

> In light of these principles, it is of no moment that the AUMF does not use specific language of detention. Because detention to prevent a combatant's return to the battlefield is a fundamental incident of waging war, in permitting the use of "necessary and appropriate force," Congress has clearly and unmistakably authorized detention *in the narrow circumstances considered here.*

Hamdi, 124 S.Ct. at 2640–41 (emphasis added).

Thus, it is true that, under some circumstances, such as those present in *Hamdi,* the President can indeed hold an United States citizen as an enemy combatant. Just because something is sometimes true, however, does not mean that it is always true. The facts in this action bear out that truth.

In the instant case, Respondent would have this Court find more similarities between Petitioner here and the petitioner in *Hamdi* than actually exist. As two other courts have already found, however, the differences between the two are striking.

The first to distinguish the difference was Judge Wilkinson when he noted that "[t]o compare this battlefield capture [in *Hamdi]* to the domestic arrest in *Padilla v. Rumsfeld* is to compare apples and oranges." *Hamdi v. Rumsfeld,* 337 F.3d 335, 344 (4th Cir. 2003) (Wilkinson, J., concurring). Not long thereafter, the Supreme Court, in responding to Justice Scalia's dissent, specifically noted "Justice Scalia largely ignores the context of *[Hamdi]*: a United States citizen captured in a *foreign* combat zone." [8]

Nevertheless, Respondent would have the Court find that the place of capture is of no consequence in determining whether the President can properly hold Petitioner as an enemy combatant. According to that view, it would be illogical to find that Petitioner could evade his detention as an enemy combatant status just because he returned to the United States before he could be captured. The cogency of this argument eludes the Court.

In *Hamdi,* the petitioner was an American citizen who was captured on the battlefield. Petitioner is also an American citizen, but he was captured in an United States airport. He is, in some respects, being held for a crime that he is alleged to have planned to commit in this country. [9] No one could rightfully argue that "[t]he exigencies of military action on the battlefield present an entirely different set of circumstances than the arrest of a citizen arriving at O'Hare International Airport." Brief of *Amici Curiae* Janet Reno et al. at 5, *Padilla.*

It cannot be disputed that the circumstances in *Hamdi* comport with the requirement of the AUMF, which provides that "the President is authorized to use all *necessary and appropriate force* against those . . . persons, in order to prevent attacks by al Qaeda on the United States." That is, the President's use of force to capture Mr. Hamdi was necessary and appropriate. Here, that same use of force was not.

Again, Petitioner in this action was captured in the United States. His alleged terrorist plans were thwarted at the time of his arrest. There were no impediments whatsoever to the Government bringing charges against him for any one or all of the array of heinous crimes that he has been effectively accused of committing. Also at the Government's dispos-

---

8. In fact, in the plurality opinion, Justice O'Connor noted at least nine additional times that the Court's holding that Mr. Hamdi's detention as an enemy combatant was constitutionally permissible was limited to the facts of that case. *Id.* at 2635 ("Congress authorized the detention of combatants in the *narrow circumstances* alleged here."); *Id.* at 2639 ("We therefore answer only the *narrow question* before us."); *Id.* at 2639–40 ("[W]e conclude that the AUMF is explicit congressional authorization for the detention of individuals in the *narrow category* we describe.") (emphasis added); *Id.* at 2640 ("We conclude that the detention of individuals falling within the *limited category* we are considering . . . is an exercise of the 'necessary and appropriate force' Congress has authorized the President to use."); *Id.* at 2641 ("Congress has clearly and unmistakably authorized detention in the *narrow circumstances* considered here."); *Id.* at 2642 ("*Ex parte Milligan* . . . does not undermine our holding about the Government's authority to seize enemy combatants, *as we define that term today.*"); *Id.* at 2642 n.1 ("Here the basis asserted for detention by the military is that Hamdi was *carrying a weapon against American troops on a foreign battlefield;* that is, that he was an enemy combatant."); *Id.* at 2643 (noting with disapproval that "Justice Scalia finds the *fact of battlefield capture* irrelevant. . . ."); *Id.* ("Justine Scalia can point to no case or other authority for the proposition that those *captured on a foreign battlefield* . . . cannot be detained outside the criminal process.").

9. The Court finds Respondent's argument concerning whether Petitioner had actually entered the country unavailing. Respondent has not provided, and this Court has not found, any case law that supports Respondent's position that an United States citizen, is not "in" the United States when he or she is "in" a United States airport. Such a failure is fatal to the claim.

al was the material witness warrant. In fact, the issuance of a material witness warrant was the tool that the law enforcement officers used to thwart Petitioner's alleged terrorist plans. Therefore, since Petitioner's alleged terrorist plans were thwarted when he was arrested on the material witness warrant, the Court finds that the President's subsequent decision to detain Petitioner as an enemy combatant was neither necessary nor appropriate.

. . .

Quirin involves the *habeas* petitions of seven German soldiers, all of whom had lived in the United States at some point in their lives. The soldiers came to the United States bent on engaging in military sabotage. One of the seven, Haupt, claimed to be an American citizen.

In denying the soldiers' petitions, the Supreme Court held that "Citizenship in the United States of an enemy belligerent does not relieve him from the consequences of a belligerency which is unlawful because in violation of the law of war."

Respondent maintains that that *Quirin* is wholly on point and, thus, for purposes of this motion, is controlling. The Court is unconvinced.

Although seemingly similar to the instant case, it is, in fact, like *Hamdi,* starkly different. As the Second Circuit has already noted, "the *Quirin* Court's decision to uphold military jurisdiction rested on the express congressional authorization of the use of military tribunals to try combatants who violated the law."

> From the very beginning of its history this Court has recognized and applied the law of war as including that part of the law of nations which prescribes, for the conduct of war, the status, rights and duties of enemy nations as well as of enemy individuals. By the Articles of War, and especially Article 15, Congress has explicitly provided, so far as it may constitutionally do so, that military tribunals shall have jurisdiction to try offenders or offenses against the law of war in appropriate cases. Congress, in addition to making rules for the government of our Armed Forces, has thus exercised its authority to define and punish offenses against the law of nations by sanctioning, within constitutional limitations, the jurisdiction of military commissions to try persons for offenses which, according to the rules and precepts of the law of nations, and more particularly the law of war, are cognizable by such tribunals. And the President, as Commander in Chief, by his Proclamation in time of war has invoked that law. By his Order creating the present Commission he has undertaken to exercise the authority conferred upon him by Congress, and also such authority as the Constitution itself gives the Commander in Chief, to direct the performance of those functions which may constitutionally be performed by the military arm of the nation in time of war.

Quirin, 317 U.S. at 27–28.

Respondent goes to great lengths to argue that the Court is *Quirin* did not rest its decision on a "clear statement from Congress." The Court is unconvinced.

Contrary to Respondent's argument, it is clear from *Quirin* that the Court found that Congress had "explicitly provided, so far as it may constitutionally do so, that military tribunals shall have jurisdiction to try offenders or offenses against the law of war in appropriate cases." Therefore, since no such Congressional authorization is present here, Respondent's argument as to the application of *Quirin* must fail.[10]

. . .

Ex parte Milligan involves a United States citizen during the Civil War who was neither a resident of one of the Confederate states, nor a prisoner of war, but a citizen of Indiana for twenty years. He had never been in the military or naval service. Milligan was arrested while at home.

The Court held in *Milligan* that the military commission lacked any jurisdiction to try Milligan when the civilian "courts are open and their process unobstructed." The President may not unilaterally establish military commissions in wartime "because he is controlled by law, and has his appropriate sphere of duty, which is to execute, not to make, the laws."[11]

While not directly on point, and limited by *Quirin, Milligan's* greatest import to the case at bar is the same as that found in *Quirin:* the detention of a United States citizen by the military is disallowed without explicit Congressional authorization.

. . .

The Non–Detention Act, also referred to as the "Railsback Amendment," after its author Representative Railsback, provides that "No

---

10. Other differences include, but are not limited to, the fact that:

1) In *Quirin*, Mr. Quirin was charged with a crime and tried by a military tribunal. In the instant case, Petitioner has not been charged and has not been tried.

2) *Quirin* involves a prisoner whose detention was punitive whereas Petitioner's detention is purportedly preventative.

3) *Quirin* is concerned more with whether the petitioner was going to be tried by a military tribunal or a civilian court. The case at bar is concerned with whether Petitioner is going to be charged and tried at all.

4) The decision in *Quirin* preceded the Non–Detention Act.

5) *Quirin* involved a war that had a definite ending date. The present war on terrorism does not.

11. The court in *Hamdi,* 124 S.Ct. at 2642, observed, however, that the *Milligan* court made repeated reference to the fact that its inquiry into whether the military tribunal had jurisdiction to try and punish Milligan turned in large part on the fact that Milligan was not a prisoner of war, but a resident of Indiana arrested while at home there. That fact was central to its conclusion. Had Milligan been captured while he was assisting Confederate soldiers by carrying a rifle against Union troops on a Confederate battlefield, the holding of the Court might well have been different. The Court's repeated explanations that Milligan was not a prisoner of war suggest that had these different circumstances been present he could have been detained under military authority for the duration of the conflict, whether or not he was a citizen.

citizen shall be imprisoned or otherwise detained by the United States except pursuant to an Act of Congress." 18 U.S.C. § 4001(a).

Respondent asserts that the Non–Detention Act does not constrain the President's authority to detain Petitioner as an enemy combatant. He contends that 1) the Joint Resolution for Authorization for Use of Miliary Force (AUMF), passed by Congress on September 18, 2001, is an "Act of Congress" authorizing Petitioner's detention and 2) the Non–Detention Act does not apply to the military's detention of the military's wartime detention of enemy combatants to fulfill this statute [sic?]. The Court finds these contentions to be without merit. The AUMF provides, in relevant part, that

> [t]he President is authorized to use all *necessary and appropriate* force against those nations, organizations, or persons he determines planned, authorized, committed, or aided the terrorist attacks that occurred on September 11, 2001, or harbored such organizations or persons, in order to prevent any future acts of international terrorism against the United States by such nations, organizations or persons.

Joint Resolution § 2(a).

. . . In clear and unambiguous language, the Non–Detention Act forbids *any* kind of detention of an United States citizen, except that which is specifically allowed by Congress. *Howe v. Smith*, 452 U.S. 473, 479 n.3 (1981) ("[T]he plain language of § 4001(a) proscrib[es] detention of *any kind* by the United States, absent a congressional grant of authority to detain.") (emphasis in original). Contrary to Respondent's contentions otherwise, the Court finds that 1) the AUMF does not authorize Petitioner's detention and 2) Petitioner's present confinement is in direct contradiction to the mandate of the Non–Detention Act.

As the Second Circuit stated,

> While it may be possible to infer a power of detention from the Joint Resolution in the battlefield context where detentions are necessary to carry out the war, there is no reason to suspect from the language of the Joint Resolution that Congress believed it would be authorizing the detention of an American citizen already held in a federal correctional institution and not arrayed against our troops in the field of battle.

Padilla, 352 F.3d at 723.

To be more specific, whereas it may be a necessary and appropriate use of force to detain a United States citizen who is captured on the battlefield, this Court cannot find, in narrow circumstances presented in this case, that the same is true when a United States citizen in arrested in a civilian setting such as an United States airport.

* * * In the case *sub judice,* there is no language in the AUMF that "clearly and unmistakably" grants the President the authority to hold

Petitioner as an enemy combatant. Therefore, Respondent's argument must fail.

* * *

In arguing that the Non–Detention Act has no application to Petitioner, Respondent first maintains that the placement the Act—in Title 18 ("Crimes and Criminal Procedure"), with directions regarding the Attorney General's control over federal prisons, and not in Title 10 ("Armed Forces") or Title 50 ("War and National Defense")—indicates that it speaks only to civilian detentions. Second, Respondent argues that the legislative history of the Non–Detention Act renders the same result. The Court is unpersuaded by either argument. Simply stated, the statute is clear, simple, direct and ambiguous. It forbids *any* kind of detention of an United States citizen, except that it be specifically allowed by Congress. Therefore, since Petitioner's detention has not been authorized by Congress, Respondent's argument must again fail.

Having found that the Non–Detention Act expressly forbids the President from holding Petitioner as an enemy combatant, and that the AUMF does not authorize such detention, neither explicitly nor by implication, the Court turns to the question of whether the President has the inherent authority to hold Petitioner.

Respondent states that

> The Commander-in-Chief Clause grants the President the power to defend the Nation when it is attacked, and he "is bound to accept the challenge without waiting for any special legislative authority." *The Prize Cases,* 67 U.S. (2 Black) 635, 668 (1862). An essential aspect of the President's authority in this regard is to "determine what degree of force the crisis demands." *Id.* at 670; see *Campbell* v. *Clinton,* 203 F.3d 19, 27 (D.C. Cir.) (Silberman, J., concurring) ("[T]he President has independent authority to repel aggressive acts by third parties even without specific congressional authorization, and courts may not review the level of force selected."), cert. denied, 531 U.S. 815 (2000). The President's decision to detain petitioner as an enemy combatant represents a basic exercise of his authority as Commander in Chief to determine the level of force needed to prosecute the conflict against al Qaeda.

Respondent's Opposition at 10.

As a preliminary matter, the Court strongly agrees that "great deference is afforded the President's exercise of his authority as Commander-in-Chief." However, "[w]here the exercise of Commander-in-Chief powers, no matter how well intentioned, is challenged on the ground that it collides with the powers assigned by the Constitution to Congress, a fundamental role exists for the courts." *Hamdi,* 352 F.3d at 713 (citing *Marbury v. Madison,* 5 U.S. (1 Cranch) 137, 2 L.Ed. 60 (1803).

Pursuant to the seminal case of *Youngstown Sheet & Tube v. Sawyer,* 343 U.S. 579 (1952), in a case such as this, where the President has taken steps that are inconsistent with the will of Congress—both express and implied—the President's authority is "at its lowest ebb, for then he can rely only upon his own constitutional powers minus any constitutional powers of Congress over the matter." *Youngstown,* 343 U.S. at 637.

Simply stated, Respondent has not provided, and this Court has not found, any law that supports the contention that the President enjoys the inherent authority pursuant to which he claims to hold Petitioner. The *Prize* cases are chiefly concerned with enemy property, not enemy combatants, and *Campbell* concerns air strikes in another country. Obviously, neither of those issues are present here. Thus, the Court finds the two cases of little guidance.

As Justice Jackson stated, "Congress, not the Executive, should control utilization of the war power as an instrument of domestic policy." *Youngstown,* 343 U.S. at 644 (Jackson, J., concurring). "There are indications that the Constitution did not contemplate that the title Commander-in-Chief of the Army and Navy will constitute [the President] also Commander-in-Chief of the country, its industries and its inhabitants." *Id.* at 643–44.

Accordingly, and limited to the facts of this case, the Court is of the firm opinion that it must reject the position posited by Respondent. To do otherwise would not only offend the rule of law and violate this country's constitutional tradition, but it would also be a betrayal of this Nation's commitment to the separation of powers that safeguards our democratic values and individual liberties.

* * * Pursuant to its interpretation, the Court finds that the President has no power, neither express nor implied, neither constitutional nor statutory, to hold Petitioner as an enemy combatant.

. . .

It is true that there may be times during which it is necessary to give the Executive Branch greater power than at other times. Such a granting of power, however, is in the province of the legislature and no one else–not the Court and not the President. * * *

Simply stated, this is a law enforcement matter, not a military matter. The civilian authorities captured Petitioner just as they should have. At the time that Petitioner was arrested pursuant to the material arrest warrant, any alleged terrorist plans that he harbored were thwarted. From then on, he was available to be questioned—and was indeed questioned—just like any other citizen accused of criminal conduct. This is as it should be.

There can be no debate that this country's laws amply provide for the investigation, detention and prosecution of citizen and non-citizen terrorists alike. For example, in his dissenting opinion in *Hamdi,* 124 S.Ct. at 2664, Justice Scalia lists the following criminal statutes that are available to the Government in fighting terrorism: 18 U.S.C. § 2381(the modern treason statute which essentially tracks the language of the constitutional provision); 18 U.S.C. § 32 (destruction of aircraft or aircraft facilities); 18 U.S.C. § 2332a (use of weapons of mass destruction); 18 U.S.C. § 2332b (acts of terrorism transcending national boundaries); 18 U.S.C. § 2339A (providing material support to terrorists); 18 U.S.C. § 2339B (providing material support to certain terrorist organizations); 18 U.S.C. § 2382 (misprision of treason); 18 U.S.C. § 2383 (rebellion or insurrection); § 2384 (seditious conspiracy); 18 U.S.C. § 2390 (enlistment to serve in armed hostility against the United States); 31 CFR § 595.204 (2003) (prohibiting the "making or receiving of any contribution of funds, goods, or services" to terrorists); and 50 U.S.C. § 1705(b) (criminalizing violations of 31 CFR § 595.204). In his concurrence, in addition to these statutes, Justice Souter lists 18 U.S.C. § 3142(e) (pretrial detention).

> [I]n declaring Padilla an enemy combatant, the President relied upon facts that would have supported charging Padilla with a variety of offenses. The government thus had the authority to arrest, detain, interrogate, and prosecute Padilla apart from the extraordinary authority it claims here. The difference between invocation of the criminal process and the power claimed by the President here, however, is one of accountability. The criminal justice system requires that defendants and witnesses be afforded access to counsel, imposes judicial supervision over government action, and places congressionally imposed limits on incarceration.

Amici Curiae at 3.

"The Privilege of the Writ of *Habeas Corpus* shall not be suspended, unless when in Cases of Rebellion or Invasion the public Safety may require it." Const. Art. 1, § 9, cl. 2. This power belongs solely to Congress. Since Congress has not acted to suspend the writ, and neither the President nor this Court have the ability to do so, in light of the findings above, Petitioner must be released.

If the law in its current state is found by the President to be insufficient to protect this country from terrorist plots, such as the one alleged here, then the President should prevail upon Congress to remedy the problem. For instance, if the Government's purpose in detaining Petitioner as an enemy combatant is to prevent him from "returning to the field of battle and taking up arms once again[,]" *Hamdi,* 124 S.Ct. at 2640, but the President thinks that the laws do not provide the necessary and appropriate measures to provide for that goal, then the President should approach Congress and request that it make proper modifications to the law. As Congress has already demonstrated, it stands ready to carefully consider, and often accommodate, such significant requests.

    . . .

Accordingly, in light of the foregoing discussion and analysis, it is the judgment of this Court that Petitioner's Motion for Summary Judgment on Counts One and Two of the Petition, as well as his Petition for a writ of *habeas corpus* must be **GRANTED.** Accordingly, Respondent is hereby directed to release Petitioner from his custody within forty-five (45) days of the entry of this Order.[14] **IT IS SO ORDERED.**

B.   What status to accord to detainees at Guantanamo? "Enemy Combatants"?

Notes and Questions

1.   Early in 2002, the issue of what status to accord to al Qaeda and Taliban captives was being debated in the Department of Justice, and the Department of State. White House memos and letters from that period reveal the nature of the debate. On February 1, 2002, Attorney General Ashcroft sent a letter to the President describing "two basic theories" that supported the conclusion that Taliban combatants are not legally entitled to Geneva Convention protections as prisoners of war: a) Afghanistan was a failed state; as such the treaty's protections do not apply because it has lost its status as party to the treaty able to fulfill its obligations; b) if during the relevant times Afghanistan was a party to the treaty, Taliban combatants were not entitled to Geneva Convention III prisoner of war status because they were unlawful combatants. The letter went on to detail the risks of adopting the one theory or the other, namely, under theory a) "no court would subsequently entertain charges that U.S. officials had violated the War Crimes Act through a violation of the Geneva Convention, whereas theory b) would not "accord American officials the same protection from legal consequences."

2.   A week before, on January 25, 2002, a draft memorandum for the President had been prepared by the Alberto Gonzales, then Counsel to the President (now Attorney General) noting that on January 18, 2002, he had advised the President that the Department of Justice had issued a formal legal opinion concluding that the Geneva Convention III on the Treatment of Prisoners (GPW) does not apply to the conflict with al Qaeda; also that there are reasonable grounds for concluding that the Convention does not apply to the Taliban; and noting that the President had decided that the Convention does not apply and that al Qaeda and Taliban detainees are not POWs under the Convention. This was the key decision made regarding the Guantanamo detainees. The January 25 memorandum went on to state that the Secretary of State had requested that the President reconsider that decision and that the Legal Adviser to the State Department had reached conclusions different from the Department of Justice. In this memorandum, Mr. Gonzales presented arguments in support of reconsideration and reversal of the decision that the GPW does not apply to either al Qaeda or the Taliban as well as the arguments opposed. Some of the arguments presented for reversing the decision were as follows:

- The United States could not invoke the GPW if enemy forces threatened to mistreat . . . U.S. or coalition forces captured during operations in Afghanistan, or if they denied Red Cross access or other POW privileges.

---

14.   Of course, if appropriate, the Government can bring criminal charges against   Petitioner or it can hold him as a material witness.

. . .

- Our position would likely provoke widespread condemnation among our allies and in some domestic quarters, even if we make clear that we will comply with the core humanitarian principles of the treaty as a matter of policy.

. . .

- Other countries may be less inclined to turn over terrorists or provide legal assistance to us if we do not recognize a legal obligation to comply with the GPW.

- A determination that GPW does not apply to al Qaeda and the Taliban could undermine U.S. military culture which emphasizes maintaining the highest standards of conduct in combat, and could introduce an element of uncertainty in the status of adversaries.

Mr. Gonzalez then stated his belief that "on balance" these arguments were unpersuasive and presented responses to them:

- . . . [Y]our [i.e the President's] policy of providing humane treatment to enemy detainees gives us the credibility to insist on like treatment for our soldiers.

- . . . [O]ur adversaries in several recent conflicts have not been deterred by GPW in their mistreatment of captured U.S. personnel, and terrorists will not follow GPW in any event.

. . .

- The statement that other nations would criticize the U.S. because we have determined that GPW does not apply is undoubtedly true . . . [W]e can facilitate cooperation with other nations by reassuring them that we fully support GPW where it is applicable and by acknowledging that in this conflict the U.S. continues to respect other recognized standards.

. . .

- . . . [T]he argument based on military culture fails to recognize that our military remain bound to apply the principles of GPW because that is what you [i.e the President] have directed them to do.

3. In July 2004, the Government adopted the following definition of enemy combatant, which has been applied to foreign nationals held at Guantanamo:

[A]n individual who was part of or supporting Taliban or al Qaeda forces, or associated forces that are engaged in hostilities against the United States or its coalition partners. This includes any person who has committed a belligerent act or has directly supported hostilities in aid of enemy armed forces.

See Deputy Secretary of Defense Paul Wolfowitz, Memorandum for the Secretary of the Navy, *Order Establishing Combatant Status Review Tribunal* (July 7, 2004) (hereinafter "CSRT Order"), cited in Khalid v. Bush, 2005 WL 100924 (D.D.C. 2005).

4. Relevant provisions from the Geneva Convention Relative to the Treatment of Prisoners of War appear below:

Geneva Convention III Relative to the Treatment of Prisoners
of War, 75 U.N.T.S. 135, *entered into force* Oct. 21, 1950.

General Provisions

Article 1

The High Contracting Parties undertake to respect and to ensure respect for the present Convention in all circumstances.

Article 2

In addition to the provisions which shall be implemented in peace time, the present Convention shall apply to all cases of declared war or of any other armed conflict which may arise between two or more of the High Contracting Parties, even if the state of war is not recognized by one of them.

The Convention shall also apply to all cases of partial or total occupation of the territory of a High Contracting Party, even if the said occupation meets with no armed resistance.

Although one of the Powers in conflict may not be a party to the present Convention, the Powers who are parties thereto shall remain bound by it in their mutual relations. They shall furthermore be bound by the Convention in relation to the said Power, if the latter accepts and applies the provisions thereof.

. . .

Article 4

A. Prisoners of war, in the sense of the present Convention, are persons belonging to one of the following categories, who have fallen into the power of the enemy:

1. Members of the armed forces of a Party to the conflict as well as members of militias or volunteer corps forming part of such armed forces.

2. Members of other militias and members of other volunteer corps, including those of organized resistance movements, belonging to a Party to the conflict and operating in or outside their own territory, even if this territory is occupied, provided that such militias or volunteer corps, including such organized resistance movements, fulfill the following conditions:

(a) That of being commanded by a person responsible for his subordinates;

(b) That of having a fixed distinctive sign recognizable at a distance;

(c) That of carrying arms openly;

(d) That of conducting their operations in accordance with the laws and customs of war.

3. Members of regular armed forces who profess allegiance to a government or an authority not recognized by the Detaining Power.

. . .

6.   Inhabitants of a non-occupied territory, who on the approach of the enemy spontaneously take up arms to resist the invading forces, without having had time to form themselves into regular armed units, provided they carry arms openly and respect the laws and customs of war.

. . .

Article 5

The present Convention shall apply to the persons referred to in Article 4 from the time they fall into the power of the enemy and until their final release and repatriation.

Should any doubt arise as to whether persons, having committed a belligerent act and having fallen into the hands of the enemy, belong to any of the categories enumerated in Article 4, such persons shall enjoy the protection of the present Convention until such time as their status has been determined by a competent tribunal.

. . .

Article 9

The provisions of the present Convention constitute no obstacle to the humanitarian activities which the International Committee of the Red Cross or any other impartial humanitarian organization may, subject to the consent of the Parties to the conflict concerned, undertake for the protection of prisoners of war and for their relief.

Article 10

. . .

When prisoners of war do not benefit or cease to benefit, no matter for what reason, by the activities of a Protecting Power or of an organization provided for in the first paragraph above, the Detaining Power shall request a neutral State, or such an organization, to undertake the functions performed under the present Convention by a Protecting Power designated by the Parties to a conflict.

If protection cannot be arranged accordingly, the Detaining Power shall request or shall accept, subject to the provisions of this Article, the offer of the services of a humanitarian organization, such as the International Committee of the Red Cross, to assume the humanitarian functions performed by Protecting Powers under the present Convention.

Any neutral Power or any organization invited by the Power concerned or offering itself for these purposes, shall be required to act with a sense of responsibility towards the Party to the conflict on which persons protected by the present Convention depend, and shall be required to furnish sufficient assurances that it is in a position to undertake the appropriate functions and to discharge them impartially.

Article 11

In cases where they deem it advisable in the interest of protected persons, particularly in cases of disagreement between the Parties to the conflict as to the application or interpretation of the provisions of the present Convention, the Protecting Powers shall lend their good offices with a view to settling the disagreement.

For this purpose, each of the Protecting Powers may, either at the invitation of one Party or on its own initiative, propose to the Parties to the conflict a meeting of their representatives, and in particular of the authorities responsible for prisoners of war, possibly on neutral territory suitably chosen. The Parties to the conflict shall be bound to give effect to the proposals made to them for this purpose. The Protecting Powers may, if necessary, propose for approval by the Parties to the conflict a person belonging to a neutral Power, or delegated by the International Committee of the Red Cross, who shall be invited to take part in such a meeting.

PART II

General Protection of Prisoners of War

. . .

Article 13

Prisoners of war must at all times be humanely treated. Any unlawful act or omission by the Detaining Power causing death or seriously endangering the health of a prisoner of war in its custody is prohibited, and will be regarded as a serious breach of the present Convention. In particular, no prisoner of war may be subjected to physical mutilation or to medical or scientific experiments of any kind which are not justified by the medical, dental or hospital treatment of the prisoner concerned and carried out in his interest.

Likewise, prisoners of war must at all times be protected, particularly against acts of violence or intimidation and against insults and public curiosity

Measures of reprisal against prisoners of war are prohibited.

Article 14

Prisoners of war are entitled in all circumstances to respect for their persons and their honour.

Women shall be treated with all the regard due to their sex and shall in all cases benefit by treatment as favourable as that granted to men.

Prisoners of war shall retain the full civil capacity which they enjoyed at the time of their capture. The Detaining Power may not restrict the exercise, either within or without its own territory, of the rights such capacity confers except in so far as the captivity requires.

Article 15

The Power detaining prisoners of war shall be bound to provide free of charge for their maintenance and for the medical attention required by their state of health.

Article 16

Taking into consideration the provisions of the present Convention relating to rank and sex, and subject to any privileged treatment which may be accorded to them by reason of their state of health, age or professional qualifications, all prisoners of war shall be treated alike by the Detaining Power, without any adverse distinction based on race, nationality, religious belief or political opinions, or any other distinction founded on similar criteria.

Captivity

Section I

Beginning of Captivity

Article 17

Every prisoner of war, when questioned on the subject, is bound to give only his surname, first names and rank, date of birth, and army, regimental, personal or serial number, or failing this, equivalent information.

If he wilfully infringes this rule, he may render himself liable to a restriction of the privileges accorded to his rank or status.

Each Party to a conflict is required to furnish the persons under its jurisdiction who are liable to become prisoners of war, with an identity card showing the owner's surname, first names, rank, . . .

No physical or mental torture, nor any other form of coercion, may be inflicted on prisoners of war to secure from them information of any kind whatever. Prisoners of war who refuse to answer may not be threatened, insulted, or exposed to any unpleasant or disadvantageous treatment of any kind.

. . . .

5. Numerous questions are raised by the administration's position on the prisoner of war versus enemy combatant issue. Insofar as the provisions of the Geneva Convention, supra, are deemed relevant, the administration apparently relies on the four-part test of Article 4 A.2., supra. This test includes in the category of prisoners of war, those members of militia or organized resistance forces who have serve under a commander, with a "fixed distinctive sign recognizable at a distance", who carry "arms openly," and who observe the laws of war in their conduct. The administration argues, inter alia, that members of the al Qaeda and the Taliban do not wear uniforms or the equivalent; therefore they do not qualify for prisoner of war status. Of course, the issue of whether prisoner of war status is warranted under the terms of the Convention may vary depending on which group of captives is being considered. For example, should members of the Taliban qualify under Article 4 A. 1. as, "Members of the armed forces of a Party to the conflict"? There appears to be no requirement for a distinctive insignia under that provision. Even if the Taliban do not qualify under the first clause of 4 A. 1, might they qualify under the second clause "as members of militias or volunteer corps forming part of such armed forces"? Further, might any members of al Qaeda captured on the Afghanistan battlefield qualify under that same second clause of Article 4 A.1.?

6. Consider what difference it would make if Geneva Convention-prisoner of war status is given to the detainees? Among other things, would it make it difficult for the government to interrogate and, possibly, obtain information from them, given the terms of Article 17 of the Convention? The Convention also contemplates repatriation at the end of hostilities. While the government has released a number of the detainees to their home countries, it appears to contemplate indefinite detention of some of them. *See* LA

Times, Dec. 1, 2002, A1, A36, quoting John C. Yoo, a Deputy Assistant Attorney General, in a speech at the College of William and Mary Law School of Law: "Does it make sense to ever release them if you think they are going to continue to be dangerous, even though you can't convict them of a crime?"

* * *

9. "But there is genuine reason for concern about a President's—or anyone's—power to unilaterally declare that an American citizen who is arrested in the United States or elsewhere far from any battlefield or combat arena is part of the enemy and thus may be treated in the same way as an enemy seized in battle." ABA Task Force on Treatment of Enemy Combatants, Preliminary Report, 18 (Aug. 8, 2002).

10. "However, even if the detainees were not covered by the Third Geneva Convention, a person may not be held forever without charges or trial. At some point, in some manner, . . . the question of indefinite and possibly permanent detention without trial must eventually arise . . . Moreover, one could argue—decisively, in my view—that as long as operations are carried out against Al Qaeda, the organization whose destruction is one of the war aims of the United States, the United States is perfectly entitled . . . to detain fighters whom it determines to be a security risk. . . . It probably could not do so with respect to an endless and essentially metaphorical 'war on terrorism' dealing with targets wholly unrelated to Al Qaeda—a war which might indeed have no end—but it is certainly entitled to do so with fighters . . . connected even loosely with Al Qaeda, wherever they may be." Kenneth Anderson, What To Do with Bin Laden and Al Qaeda Terrorists? A Qualified Defense of Military Commissions and United States Policy on Detainees at Guantanamo Bay Naval Base, 25 Harv. J.L. & Pub Pol'y 591, 625–626 (2002).

C. Administrative process reviews for the Guantanamo detainees

1. Introduction

The decisions in Rasul and Hamdi triggered different kinds of responses to the question of how to review the status of the enemy combatant detainees at Guantanamo. Recall that Justice O'Connor, writing for a plurality of the Court in Hamdi stated:

> . . . [D]ue process demands that a citizen held in the United States as an enemy combatant be given a meaningful opportunity to contest the factual basis for that detention before a neutral decision-maker.
>
> . . .
>
> There remains the possibility that the standards we have articulated could be met by an appropriately authorized and properly constituted military tribunal. Indeed, it is notable that military regulations already provide for such process in related instances, dictating that tribunals be made available to determine the status of enemy

detainees who assert prisoner-of-war status under the Geneva Convention ... In the absence of such process, however, a court that receives a petition for a writ of habeas corpus from an alleged enemy combatant must itself ensure that the minimum requirements of due process are achieved.... We anticipate that a District Court would proceed with the caution that we have indicated is necessary in this setting, engaging in a factfinding process that is both prudent and incremental.

Of course, in Hamdi, Justice O'Connor was dealing with a citizen-detainee. Should the same considerations be fully applicable to non-citizen detainees?

The government had been working on establishing a formal review procedure for all of the Guantanamo detainees before the decisions in Rasul and Hamdi, and, indeed, had informally reviewed and released a couple hundred detainees to their home countries. In the wake of the Hamdi and Rasul decisions, the New York Times reported that the Pentagon and private attorneys acting on behalf of some of the detainees were battling in a sort of race—the military quickly setting up military boards to review the status of the detainees and the private lawyers rushing to the courthouse to try to obtain relief there. NY Times, July 17, 2004, p. A1.

2. Administrative reviews: enemy combatant status; continuing dangerousness or intelligence value

Notes and Questions

1. Following the decisions in Rasul and Hamdi, the government quickly established two kinds of administrative reviews of detainees' status—Combatant Status Review Tribunals (CSRT's) and Administrative Review Boards (ARB's). Information about these two types of reviews, their purposes, makeup, and some information about the process in proceedings before them has been provided by the government—see, e.g., Special Department of Defense Briefing by Gordon England, Secretary of the Navy, December 20, 2004, reported by Federal News Service—but very little information has been obtained directly from observation of the proceedings. In a limited number of instances, the press was given access to some of the CSRT hearings, but they have not been able to attend most of the hearings, and, as of this writing, they have not been given permission to attend any of the ARB hearings.

2. The issue in the CSRT review is whether or not the particular detainee is an enemy combatant. The issue in the ARB review is whether the individual (who has previously gone through a CSRT proceeding which determined him to an enemy combatant) continues to be a threat or has intelligence information which would be of value.

3. The CSRT hearings have been heard by three person boards of military officers. They have been characterized as neutral (recall Justice O'Connor's statement in Hamdi, requiring review before a "neutral decision-

maker") since the officers serving on them would not have any interest in the fate of the detainees appearing before them. See NY Times, July 17, 2004, A1.

4. A military officer who acts as a representative, not as his attorney or advocate, is made available to each of the detainees whose case is reviewed by the CSRT. Because the representative is not acting as the detainee's lawyer, the attorney-client privilege does not cover their conversations. Ibid.

* * *

6. Each detainee is given a written document with those accusations that do not reveal classified information that bear on the question of the detainee's status as an enemy combatant. The CSRT may also consider classified information not contained in the document provided to the detainee. These tribunals are not barred from considering evidence obtained by torture in foreign countries. See AP dispatch, posted on CNN.com, December 30, 2004, quoting Principal Deputy Associate Attorney General, Brian Doyle.

7. At the hearing, the detainee is allowed to testify, and his family and home nation may submit written testimony. Reportedly, almost half the detainees have refused to participate in the proceedings. Transcripts of the hearings have not been released. The Associated Press has filed a Freedom of Information Act action seeking the transcripts. AP dispatch, dated Jan. 14, 2005, available through Findlaw.com.

8. Following completion of the CSRT hearing, it is reviewed administratively to make sure that it was conducted properly and then sent to an Admiral who has been delegated authority to make the final decision in these cases. The recommendations of the ARB'S are reviewed by the Secretary of the Navy. Special Department of Defense Briefing conducted by Gordon England, Secretary of the Navy, Federal News Service, December 20, 2004.

9. Determination in a CSRT hearing that a detainee was not an enemy combatant results in the release of the individual and arrangement by the State Department to return him to his home country. Determination that he was an enemy combatant results in continued detention but subsequent annual review in the ARB procedure. In the ARB proceeding, any of three dispositions is possible: release of the detainee and transportation to his home country; transfer of the detainee to his home country with conditions as negotiated with that country; or continued detention at Guantanamo. Ibid.

10. The final CSRT hearing was held on January 22, 2005. In all, the cases of 558 detainees were reviewed in the CSRT procedure. As of February 3, 2005, six detainees had been released as the outcome of a CSRT hearing, and 387 ordered detained as enemy combatants. LA Times, Feb. 4, 2005, A17. The rest of the cases, as of this writing, are still under review. Also see AP dispatch, January 22, 2005, posted on Findlaw.com reporting 11 ARB proceedings had been held thus far.

11. Prior to the creation of the CSRT procedure, approximately 200 detainees had been released and the government believes that at least 12 of these have returned to terrorist activity. Special Department of Defense

Briefing conducted by Gordon England, Secretary of the Navy, Federal News Service, December 20, 2004.

12.   The government has stated that all detainees in the custody of the Department of Defense are being put through the CSRT procedure and the annual ARB reviews. There have been newspaper reports, however, suggesting that a small number of detainees are being held off the books, possibly by the CIA to allow intelligence officials to continue interrogations. See LA Times, July 9, 2004, p. A1.

13.   How does the CSRT procedure compare with requirements of the Geneva Convention that are applicable to prisoners of war? Have the requirements of the Convention been met regarding the process for determining whether a detainee falls into the category of prisoner of war, even though we have not recognized the detainees as prisoners of war. Consider the following materials:

a.   Article 5 of the Convention provides:

Should any doubt arise as to whether persons, having committed a belligerent act and having fallen into the hands of the enemy, belong to any of the categories enumerated in Article 4, such persons shall enjoy the protection of the present Convention until such time as their status has been determined by a competent tribunal.

b.   Footnote 16 in Khalid v. Bush, infra, provides:

"... In *Hamdi,* the Court considered the process that is owed under the Constitution for United States citizens detained as enemy combatants .. A plurality of the Court held that Due Process for even United States citizens requires only "notice of the factual basis for the [detainee's] classification, and a fair opportunity to rebut the Government's factual assertion before a neutral decisionmaker." *Id.* In this regard, even assuming, arguendo, that the petitioners do possess constitutional rights, which they do not, the Court notes that the CSRTs provide each petitioner with much of the same process afforded by Article 5 of the Geneva Conventions."

c.   Secretary of the Navy England addressing the comparison between the CSRT procedure and what is contemplated by Article 5 of the Geneva Convention for prisoners of war stated: "... [W]e've actually gone beyond Article 5.... So we actually provide an expanded hearing for all the detainees beyond what you would do for a prisoner of war." Special Department of Defense Briefing conducted by Gordon England, Secretary of the Navy, Federal News Service, December 20, 2004.

d.   Secretary England in the same briefing meeting stated regarding the ARB process that "there's no Geneva requirement, there's no precedent for this type of process." Ibid.

e.   It has been reported that human rights groups and defense attorneys complain that the procedures being used do not "afford the protections assured a prisoner of war." AP dispatch, Jan. 14, 2005, Findlaw; and that the procedures are a sham because the detainees are not permitted to have counsel represent them at the hearings and secret evidence can be used against them. AP dispatch, Jan. 22, 2005, Findlaw.com.

14.   The military seems to have won the battle to establish and conduct administrative hearings before private lawyers representing some of the detainees could obtain judicial hearings on the legality of the detention of their clients, but query whether they have won the war. See below. In Khalid v. Bush, see infra, Judge Leon was able to refer to "the military review process already in place."

3.   Judicial consideration of the status of the detainees

KHALID v. BUSH

355 F.Supp.2d 311, (D.D.C. 2005).

LEON, District J.

Petitioners are seven foreign nationals who were seized by United States forces and have been detained at the United States naval base at Guantanamo Bay, Cuba ("Guantanamo") pursuant to military orders arising out of the ongoing war against terror initiated in the aftermath of September 11, 2001 ("9/11"). Based on the Supreme Court's decision in Rasul v. Bush, each detainee has filed a petition for a writ of habeas corpus with this Court seeking to challenge the lawfulness of his continued detention. Each petitioner claims, in essence, that he is being held in violation of the United States Constitution, certain federal laws and United States treaties, and certain international laws. In stark contrast, the respondents ("United States") have moved to dismiss these petitions claiming, in essence, that there is no viable legal theory by which this Court could issue such a writ because: (1) non-resident aliens detained under these circumstances have no rights under the Constitution; (2) no existing federal law renders their custody unlawful; (3) no legally binding treaty is applicable; and (4) international law is not binding under these circumstances.

Thus, these cases pose the novel issue of whether there is any viable legal theory under which a federal court could issue a writ of habeas corpus challenging the legality of the detention of non-resident aliens captured abroad and detained outside the territorial sovereignty of the United States, pursuant to lawful military orders, during a Congressionally authorized conflict.

After due consideration of the respondents' Motion, the petitioners' individual and joint oppositions, oral arguments and various supplemental briefs, the Court, for the following reasons, concludes that no viable legal theory exists by which it could issue a writ of habeas corpus under these circumstances. Accordingly, the Court grants the respondents' Motion to Dismiss or for Judgment as a Matter of Law, and, therefore, will not issue the writs of habeas corpus.

    . . .

At present, the Department of Defense ("DoD") is holding nearly 550 ... foreign nationals at Guantanamo, although recent media reports indicate that the DoD intends to release or transfer hundreds in the near future.

Seven of these foreign nationals are the petitioners in this case . None are United States citizens or have any connection to the United States, other than their current status as detainees at a U.S. military base. To the contrary, the petitioners are non-resident aliens captured outside of Afghanistan. They include five Algerian–Bosnian citizens (Lakhdar Boumediene, Mohammed Nechle, Hadj Boudella, Belkacem Bensayah, and Mustafa Ait Idir); one Algerian citizen with permanent Bosnian residency (Saber Lahmar); and one French citizen (Ridouane Khalid), All, with the exception of Khalid, were captured in Bosnia around October 2001. Khalid was seized in Pakistan sometime during the early fall of 2001. In January 2001, shortly after they were captured and transferred to United States military authorities, the petitioners were transported to Guantanamo, where they currently remain.

In the wake of the Supreme Court's ruling in *Rasul,* petitioners filed writs of habeas corpus on their own behalf and through certain relatives as their "next friend" (collectively, petitioners and their relatives are referred to herein as "petitioners"). Both petitions raise nearly identical claims, in that they challenge the legality of their detention and the conditions of their confinement under the Constitution, certain federal statutes and regulations, and international law.

In particular, the petitions challenge the President's authority to issue the November 13, 2001 Detention Order, and, even if legal, they claim it is unconstitutional as applied to them because they have been or are being denied their constitutional rights, Finally, even if those rights are not being violated, they claim their continued detention violates certain federal statutes and international law. In the final analysis, the petitioners are asking this Court to do something no federal court has done before: evaluate the legality of the Executive's capture and detention of non-resident aliens, outside of the United States, during a time of armed conflict.

. . .

The petitioners have essentially mounted a two-front attack on the legality of their detention. In the first instance, they challenge the President's authority, under either the Constitution or the AUMF, to issue the Detention Order pursuant to which they are detained. Next, they contend that even if the President had the authority to issue an order that would detain them for the indefinite period between now and the completion of the war, their continued detention violates: (1) each non-resident alien's rights under the United States Constitution; (2) certain federal laws; (3) certain treaties to which the United States is a signatory State; and (4) certain customary international law provisions that have been incorporated into this country's common law. In the final analysis, petitioners contend that at least one of these alleged violations constitutes a legal theory which provides this Court with a viable basis to not only issue a writ of habeas corpus, but to ultimately find their detention unlawful. For the following reasons, the Court disagrees and finds no viable legal theory under which it could issue the writ they each seek.

. . .

The Supreme Court majority in *Rasul* expressly limited its inquiry to whether non-resident aliens detained at Guantanamo have a right to a judicial review of the legality of their detention under the habeas statute, *Rasul,* ___ U.S. at ___, 124 S.Ct. at 2693 ("The question now before us is whether the *habeas statute* confers a right to judicial review of the legality of Executive detention of aliens in a territory over which the United States exercises plenary and exclusive jurisdiction, but not 'ultimate sovereignty.'"), and, therefore, did not concern itself with whether the petitioners had any independent constitutional rights. Indeed, the *Rasul* majority went on to distinguish *Eisentrager* on grounds that *Eisentrager* was primarily concerned with whether the prisoners had any *constitutional* rights that could be vindicated via a writ of habeas corpus. *Id.* at 2693–94 ("The [*Eisentrager*] Court had far less to say on the question of the petitioners' *statutory* entitlement to habeas review.") (emphasis in original). Thus, by focusing on the petitioners' statutory *right* to file a writ of habeas corpus, the *Rasul* majority left intact the holding in *Eisentrager* and its progeny.

. . . The *Rasul* majority thereafter further emphasized the limitations on its holding in the concluding paragraph of the opinion by stating "[w]hat is presently at stake is only whether the federal courts have *jurisdiction* to determine the legality of the Executive's potentially indefinite detention of individuals who claim to be wholly innocent of wrongdoing." Thus, in its own words, the Supreme Court chose to only answer the question of jurisdiction, and not the question of whether these same individuals possess any substantive rights on the merits of their claims. Indeed, the *Rasul* Court expressly acknowledged that it expected that its decision would cause "further proceedings" among the lower courts to consider the very issue that it had not: the "merits of petitioners' claims."

Accordingly, for all of these reasons the Court concludes that the petitioners lack any viable theory under the United States Constitution to challenge the lawfulness of their continued detention at Guantanamo.

. . .

The petitioners, however, have not offered any viable theory relating to any existing federal laws or treaties that could serve as the basis for the issuance of a writ. By and large, their petitions do not contain detainee-specific allegations of mistreatment at the hands of the respondents. Instead, the petitioners have essentially cast their grievances in generalized terms. . . .

The mere fact that the petitioners are in custody, of course, does not violate any specific federal statutory law because Congress has not, to-date, enacted any legislation restricting the President's ability to capture and detain alien combatants in the manner applicable to these petitioners. To the contrary, as discussed previously, Congress has authorized the President to use "all necessary and appropriate force" through the AUMF. *See* AUMF § 2. Here, as conceded by the parties, the capture and detention of each petitioner was executed pursuant to a *lawful* military order, even if it were based upon flawed or incomplete intelligence. (wherein petitioners assert that they believe that the "continued detention" and the "capture under the circumstances under which it occurred" made the detention unlawful, but not that the order to capture the petitioners was itself unlawful). And with respect to their allegations that the *conditions* of their custody might violate existing United States law, such alleged conduct, even if it had occurred, and there is no specific allegation that it did, does not support the issuance of a writ because, though deplorable if true, it does not render the *custody* itself unlawful.

. . .

It is not surprising that the petitioners have been unable to cite any case in which a federal court has engaged in the substantive review and evaluation they seek of either the military's decision to capture and detain a non-citizen as an enemy combatant, or the conditions under which that combatant was being held. The leading cases dealing with applications for habeas relief *brought by an alien* during a time of war clearly hold that judicial review is limited to the question of whether Congress has given the military the authority to detain or charge the individual as an enemy combatant, rather than whether the military's decision was correct or otherwise supported by the facts. *See, e.g., Ex parte Quirin,* 317 U.S. at 25; *Application of Yamashita,* 327 U.S. 1, 66 S.Ct. 340, 90 L.Ed. 499 (1946); *Eisentrager,* 339 U.S. at 786.

Indeed, the Supreme Court itself in *Yamashita* articulated the governing rule, the underlying rationale, and the resulting limitation on this Court's inquiry in the instant proceedings as follows:

> [W]e consider here only the lawful power of the commission to try the petitioner for the offense charged. In the present cases it must be recognized throughout that the military tribunals which Congress has sanctioned by the Articles of War are not courts whose rulings and judgments are made subject to review by this Court. . . . They are tribunals whose determinations are reviewable by the military authorities either as provided in the military orders constituting such tribunals or as provided by the Articles of War. Congress conferred on the courts no power to review their determinations save only as it has granted judicial power 'to grant writs of habeas corpus for the purpose of an inquiry into the cause of the restraint of liberty.' *The courts may inquire whether the detention complained of is within the authority of those detaining the petitioner. If the*

military tribunals have lawful authority to hear, decide and condemn, their action is not subject to judicial review merely because they have made a wrong decision on disputed facts. Correction of their errors of decision is not for the courts but for the military authorities which are alone authorized to review their decisions. Yamashita (emphasis added).

. . .

In the final analysis, the Court's role in reviewing the military's decision to capture and detain a non-resident alien is, and must be, highly circumscribed. The Court is well aware of the measures that have been adopted by the political branches—Congress and the Executive—to ensure that abuse does not occur and to ensure these petitioners are given the treatment that they are deserved. Indeed, Congress recently enacted the Reagan Act to ensure that all United States personnel clearly understand their obligations with respect to the treatment of detainees. *See* Reagan Act, § 1091(b)(3). Conspicuous in its absence in the Reagan Act is any reference by Congress to federal court review where United States personnel engages in impermissible treatment of a detainee. Indeed, any enforcement and/or punishment for impermissible conduct under the Act remains, as it always has, with the Department of Defense and appropriate military authorities. *E.g.,* Reagan Act, § 1091(a)(4) ("[T]he *Armed Forces* are moving swiftly and decisively to identify, try, and, if found guilty, punish persons who perpetrated such abuse[.]") (emphasis added); *id.* § 1091(a)(5) ("[T]he *Department of Defense* and *appropriate military authorities* must continue to undertake corrective action, as appropriate, to address chain-of-command deficiencies and the systemic deficiencies identified in the incidents in question[.]") (emphasis added). In fact, the Act will soon be codified in Title 10 of the United States Code, which is the Title governing the Armed Forces. *See generally* Reagan Act, Pub.L. 108–375, 118 Stat. 1811.

. . .

Thus, to the extent these non-resident detainees have rights, they are subject to both the military review process already in place and the laws Congress has passed defining the appropriate scope of military conduct towards these detainees. The extent to which these rights and conditions should be modified or extended is a matter for the political branches to determine and effectuate through either Constitutional amendments, appropriate international entities [sic?]. Thus, until Congress and the President act further, there is similarly no viable legal theory under international law by which a federal court could issue a writ.

Accordingly, for this and all the reasons stated above, the respondents' motion to dismiss must be GRANTED.

Notes and Questions

1.   Rasul seemed to give the Guantanamo detainees the right to seek habeas corpus relief in U.S. courts. Judge Leon in Khalid concludes, however, that neither Rasul nor any other source provides a legal basis for obtaining relief despite the fact that the U.S. courts have been determined to have jurisdiction in such cases. Accordingly, the jurisdiction that Rasul established would appear to be an empty vessel—not a basis for obtaining any relief. Do you agree with Judge Leon's reading of Rasul?

2.   Consider the language of footnote 1 in Hamdi:

> The legal category of enemy combatant has not been elaborated upon in great detail. The permissible bounds of the category will be defined by the lower courts as subsequent cases are presented to them.

The Supreme Court in this footnote in Hamdi seems to have contemplated consideration of the enemy combatant category by the federal courts. If the legal category is not to be considered in the type of action brought by Khalid, in what kinds of actions might it be an issue?

* * *

4.   The second case, post-Hamdi and Rasul, presenting the substantive claims of Guantanamo detainees produced a very different result from that in Khalid v. Bush, supra.

IN RE GUANTANAMO DETAINEE CASES

355 F.Supp.2d 443 (D.D.C. 2005).

RESPONDENTS' MOTION TO DISMISS OR FOR JUDGMENT AS A MATTER OF LAW

GREEN, Joyce Hen, District J.

These eleven coordinated *habeas* cases were filed by detainees held as "enemy combatants" at the United States Naval Base at Guantanamo Bay, Cuba. Presently pending is the government's motion to dismiss or for judgment as a matter of law regarding all claims filed by all petitioners, including claims based on the United States Constitution, treaties, statutes, regulations, the common law, and customary international law. Counsel filed numerous briefs addressing issues raised in the motion and argued their positions at a hearing in early December 2004. Upon consideration of all filings submitted in these cases and the arguments made at the hearing, and for the reasons stated below, the Court concludes that the petitioners have stated valid claims under the Fifth Amendment to the United States Constitution and that the procedures implemented by the government to confirm that the petitioners are "enemy combatants" subject to indefinite detention violate the petitioners' rights to due process of law. The Court also holds that at least some of the petitioners have stated valid claims under the Third Geneva Convention. Finally, the Court holds that the government is entitled to the dismissal of the petitioners' remaining claims.

Because this Memorandum Opinion references classified material, it is being issued in two versions. The official version is unredacted and is being filed with the Court Security Officer at the U.S. Department of Justice responsible for the management of classified information in these cases. The Court Security Officer will maintain possession of the original, distribute copies to counsel with the appropriate security clearances in accordance with the procedures earlier established in these cases, and ensure that the document is transmitted to the Court of Appeals should an appeal be taken. Classified information in the official version is highlighted in gray to alert the reader to the specific material that may not be released to the public. The other version of the Memorandum Opinion contains redactions of all classified information and, in an abundance of caution, portions of any discussions that might lead to the discovery of classified information. The redacted version is being posted in the electronic dockets of the cases and is available for public review.

. . .

In addition to belligerents captured during the heat of war in Afghanistan, the U.S. authorities are also detaining at Guantanamo Bay pursuant to the AUMF numerous individuals who were captured hundreds or thousands of miles from a battle zone in the traditional sense of that term. For example, detainees at Guantanamo Bay who are presently seeking *habeas* relief in the United States District Court for the District of Columbia include men who were taken into custody as far away from Afghanistan as Gambia, Zambia, Bosnia, and Thailand. Some have already been detained as long as three years while others have been captured as recently as September 2004. Although many of these individuals may never have been close to an actual battlefield and may never have raised conventional arms against the United States or its allies, the military nonetheless has deemed them detainable as "enemy combatants" based on conclusions that they have ties to al Qaeda or other terrorist organizations.

All of the individuals who have been detained at Guantanamo Bay have been categorized to fall within a general class of people the administration calls "enemy combatants." It is the government's position that once someone has been properly designated as such, that person can be held indefinitely until the end of America's war on terrorism or until the military determines on a case by case basis that the particular detainee no longer poses a threat to the United States or its allies. Within the general set of "enemy combatants" is a subset of individuals whom the administration decided to prosecute for war crimes before a military commission established pursuant to a Military Order issued by President Bush on November 13, 2001. Should individuals be prosecuted and convicted in accordance with the Military Order, they would be subject to sentences with fixed terms of incarceration or other specific penalties. Since the beginning of the military's detention operations at Guantanamo Bay in early 2002, detainees subject to criminal prosecution have been bestowed with more rights than detainees whom the military did not intend to prosecute formally for war crimes. . . .

The first of these coordinated cases challenging the legality of the detention of alleged "enemy combatants" at Guantanamo Bay and the terms and conditions of that detention commenced nearly three years ago on February 19, 2002. *Rasul v. Bush,* 02–CV–0299 (CKK). The action, brought by relatives on behalf of one Australian and two British nationals as their "next friends," was styled as a petition for writ of *habeas corpus* pursuant to 28 U.S.C. §§ 2241 and 2242. The initial relief sought included an order requiring the release of the detainees, an order permitting counsel to meet with the detainees in private and without government monitoring, and an order directing the cessation of interrogations of the detainees during the pendency of litigation. The asserted substantive bases for the requested relief ultimately included the Fifth, Sixth, Eighth, and Fourteenth Amendments to the United States Constitution, the International Covenant on Civil and Political Rights, the American Declaration on the Rights and Duties of Man, and customary international law.

. . .

The Supreme Court reversed the D.C. Circuit's decision and held that the District Court did have jurisdiction to hear the detainees' *habeas* claims. *Rasul v. Bush,* ___ U.S.___, 124 S.Ct. 2686, 159 L.Ed.2d 548 (2004). The majority opinion, issued June 28, 2004, noted several facts that distinguished the Guantanamo detainees from the petitioners in *Eisentrager* more than fifty years earlier:

. . .

The Supreme Court expressly acknowledged that the allegations contained in the petitions for writs of *habeas corpus* "unquestionably describe 'custody in violation of the Constitution or laws or treaties of the United States' " as required by the *habeas* statute, and concluded by instructing:

> Whether and what further proceedings may become necessary after respondents make their response to the merits of petitioners' claims are matters that we need not address now. What is presently at stake is only whether the federal courts have jurisdiction to determine the legality of the Executive's potentially indefinite detention of individuals who claim to be wholly innocent of wrongdoing. Answering that question in the affirmative, we reverse the judgment of the Court of Appeals and remand for the District Court to consider in the first instance the merits of petitioners' claims.

. . .

Although most of the detainees had already been held as "enemy combatants" for more than two years and had been subjected to unspecified "multiple levels of review," the respondents chose to submit as factual support for their detention of the petitioners the records from the CSRT proceedings, which had only commenced in late August or early September 2004. Those factual returns were filed with the Court on a rolling basis as the CSRT proceedings were completed, with the earliest submitted on September 17, 2004 and the latest on December 30, 2004. Because every complete CSRT record contained classified information, respondents filed redacted, unclassified versions on the public record, submitted the full, classified versions for the Court's *in camera* review, and served on counsel for the petitioners with appropriate security clearances versions containing most of the classified information disclosed in the Court's copies but redacting some classified information that respondents alleged would not exculpate the detainees from their "enemy combatant" status.

. . .

The petitioners in these eleven cases allege that the detention at Guantanamo Bay and the conditions thereof violate a variety of laws. All petitions assert violations of the Fifth Amendment, and a majority claim violations of the Alien Tort Claims Act, [the Administrative Procedure Act, and the Geneva Conventions. In addition, certain petitions allege violations of the Sixth, Eighth, and Fourteenth Amendments; the War Powers Clause; the Suspension Clause; Army Regulation 190–8, entitled "Enemy Prisoners of War, Retained Personnel, Civilian Internees and Other Detainees;" the International Covenant on Civil and Political Rights ("ICCPR"); the American Declaration on the Rights and Duties of Man ("ADRDM"); the Optional Protocol to the Convention on the Rights of the Child on the Involvement of Children in Armed Conflict; the International Labour Organization's Convention 182, Concerning the Prohibition and Immediate Action for the Elimination of the Worst Forms of Child Labour; and customary international law. The respondents contend that none of these provisions constitutes a valid basis for any of the petitioners' claims and seek dismissal of all counts as a matter of law . . . for failing to state a claim upon which relief can be granted. . . .

In addressing a motion to dismiss for failure to state a claim upon which relief can be granted . . . the Court must accept as true all factual allegations contained in a petition and must resolve every factual inference in the petitioner's favor.

Notwithstanding the Supreme Court's decision in *Rasul* that the District Court's dismissal of the petitioners' claims was incorrect as a matter of law, the respondents argue in their October 2004 motion that the *Rasul* decision resolved only whether individuals detained at Guantanamo Bay had the right merely to *allege* in a United States District Court under the *habeas* statute that they are being detained in violation of the Constitution and other laws. Respondents argue that the decision was silent on the issue of whether the detainees actually *possess* any underlying substantive rights, and they further contend that earlier Supreme Court precedent and the law of this Circuit make clear that the detainees do not hold any such substantive rights. Accordingly, it is the respondents' position that although *Rasul* clarified that a detainee has every right to file papers in the Clerk's Office alleging violations of the Constitution, statutes, treaties and other laws, and although the Court has jurisdiction to accept the filing and to consider those papers, the Court must not permit the case to proceed beyond a declaration that no underlying substantive rights exist. While the Court would have welcomed a clearer declaration in the *Rasul* opinion regarding the specific constitutional and other substantive rights of the petitioners, it does not interpret the Supreme Court's decision as narrowly as the respondents suggest it should. To the contrary, the Court interprets *Rasul,* in conjunction with other precedent, to require the recognition that the detainees at Guantanamo Bay possess enforceable constitutional rights.

The significance and scope of the *Rasul* decision is best understood after a review of earlier case law addressing the applicability of the Constitution outside of the United States and to individuals who are not American citizens. . . .

[Judge Green here conducted a detailed review of the case law pertinent to that issue, and then continued. . . .]

* * *

. . .

. . . [P]erhaps the strongest basis for recognizing that the detainees have fundamental rights to due process rests at the conclusion of the *Rasul* majority opinion. In summarizing the nature of these actions, the Court recognized:

> Petitioners' allegations—that, although they have engaged neither in combat nor in acts of terrorism against the United States, they have been held in Executive detention for more than two years in territory subject to the long-term, exclusive jurisdiction and control of the United States, without access to counsel and without being charged with any wrongdoing—unquestionably describe "custody in violation of the Constitution or laws or treaties of the United States." 28 U.S.C. § 2241(c)(3). __ U.S. at __ n. 15, 124 S.Ct. at 2698 n. 15.

. . . Given the *Rasul* majority's careful scrutiny of *Eisentrager,* it is difficult to imagine that the Justices would have remarked that the petitions "unquestionably describe 'custody in violation of the Constitution or laws or treaties of the United States' " unless they considered the petitioners to be within a territory in which constitutional rights are guaranteed. Indeed, had the Supreme Court intended to uphold the D.C. Circuit's rejection in *Al Odah* of underlying constitutional rights, it is reasonable to assume that the majority would have included in its opinion at least a brief statement to that effect, rather than delay the ultimate resolution of this litigation and require the expenditure of additional judicial resources in the lower courts.

. . .

There would be nothing impracticable and anomalous in recognizing that the detainees at Guantanamo Bay have the fundamental right to due process of law under the Fifth Amendment. Recognizing the existence of that right at the Naval Base would not cause the United States government any more hardship than would recognizing the existence of constitutional rights of the detainees had they been held within the continental United States. American authorities are in full control at Guantanamo Bay, their activities are immune from Cuban law, and there are few or no significant remnants of native Cuban culture or tradition remaining that can interfere with the implementation of an American system of justice.

* * *

In sum, there can be no question that the Fifth Amendment right asserted by the Guantanamo detainees in this litigation—the right not to be deprived of liberty without due process of law—is one of the most fundamental rights recognized by the U.S. Constitution. In light of the Supreme Court's decision in *Rasul,* it is clear that Guantanamo Bay must be considered the equivalent of a U.S. territory in which fundamental constitutional rights apply. Accordingly ... , the respondents' contention that the Guantanamo detainees have no constitutional rights is rejected, and the Court recognizes the detainees' rights under the Due Process Clause of the Fifth Amendment.

Having found that the Guantanamo detainees are entitled to due process under the Fifth Amendment to the United States Constitution, the Court must now address the exact contours of that right as it applies to the government's determinations that they are "enemy combatants." Due process is an inherently flexible concept, and the specific process due in a particular circumstance depends upon the context in which the right is asserted....

Although the detainees in the cases before this Court are aliens and are therefore not being detained by their own governments, that fact does not lessen the significance of their interests in freedom from incarceration and from being held virtually *incommunicado* from the outside world. There is no practical difference between incarceration at the hands of one's own government and incarceration at the hands of a foreign government; significant liberty is deprived in both situations regardless of the jailer's nationality.

As was the case in *Hamdi,* the potential length of incarceration is highly relevant to the weighing of the individual interests at stake here. The government asserts the right to detain an "enemy combatant" until the war on terrorism has concluded or until the Executive, in its sole discretion, has determined that the individual no longer poses a threat to national security. The government, however, has been unable to inform the Court how long it believes the war on terrorism will last. *See* December 1, 2004 Transcript of Motion to Dismiss (hereinafter "Transcript") at 22–23. Indeed, the government cannot even articulate at this moment how it will determine when the war on terrorism has ended. At a minimum, the government has conceded that the war could last several generations, thereby making it possible, if not likely, that "enemy combatants" will be subject to terms of life imprisonment at Guantanamo Bay. Short of the death penalty, life imprisonment is the ultimate deprivation of liberty, and the uncertainty of whether the war on terror—and thus the period of incarceration—will last a lifetime may be even worse than if the detainees had been tried, convicted, and definitively sentenced to a fixed term.

It must be added that the liberty interests of the detainees cannot be minimized for purposes of applying the *Mathews v. Eldridge* balancing test by the government's allegations that they are in fact terrorists or are affiliated with terrorist organizations. The purpose of imposing a due process requirement is to prevent mistaken characterizations and erroneous detentions, and the government is not entitled to short circuit this inquiry by claiming *ab initio* that the individuals are alleged to have committed bad acts. . . . Moreover, all petitioners in these cases have asserted that they are not terrorists and have not been involved in terrorist activities, and under the standards provided by the applicable rules of procedure, those allegations must be accepted as true for purposes of resolving the government's motion to dismiss.

On the other side of the *Mathews v. Eldridge* analysis is the government's significant interest in safeguarding national security. Having served as the Chief Judge of the United States Foreign Intelligence Surveillance Court (also known as "the FISA Court"), the focus of which involves national security and international terrorism, this Judge is keenly aware of the determined efforts of terrorist groups and others to attack this country and to harm American citizens both at home and abroad. Utmost vigilance is crucial for the protection of the United States of America. Of course, one of the government's most important obligations is to safeguard this country and its citizens by ensuring that those who have brought harm upon U.S. interests are not permitted to do so again. . . . Without doubt, our Constitution recognizes that core strategic matters of warmaking belong in the hands of those who are best positioned and most politically accountable for making them." *Id.* Indeed, a majority of the Court affirmed the Executive's authority to seize and detain Taliban fighters as long as the conflict in Afghanistan continues, regardless of how indefinite the length of that war may be. . . .

Given the existence of competing, highly significant interests on both sides of the equation—the liberty of individuals asserting complete innocence of any terrorist activity versus the obligation of the government to protect this country against terrorist attacks—the question becomes what procedures will help ensure that innocents are not indefinitely held as "enemy combatants" without imposing undue burdens on the military to ensure the security of this nation and its citizens. The four member *Hamdi* plurality answered this question in some detail, and although the two concurring members of the Court, Justice Souter and Justice Ginsburg, emphasized a different basis for ruling in favor of Mr.

Hamdi, they indicated their agreement that, at a minimum, he was entitled to the procedural protections set forth by the plurality.

According to the plurality in *Hamdi,* an individual detained by the government on the ground that he is an "enemy combatant" "must receive notice of the factual basis for his classification, and a fair opportunity to rebut the Government's factual assertions before a neutral decisionmaker." Noting the potential burden these requirements might cause the government at a time of ongoing military conflict, the plurality stated that it would not violate due process for the decision maker to consider hearsay as the most reliable available evidence. In addition, the plurality declared it permissible to adopt a presumption in favor of "enemy combatant" status, "so long as that presumption remained a rebuttable one and fair opportunity for rebuttal were provided." For that presumption to apply and for the onus to shift to the detainee, however, the plurality clarified that the government first would have to "put[ ] forth credible evidence that the [detainee] meets the enemy-combatant criteria."

After setting forth these standards, the plurality suggested the "possibility" that constitutional requirements of due process could be met by an "appropriately authorized and properly constituted military tribunal" and referenced the military tribunals used to determine whether an individual is entitled to prisoner of war status under the Geneva Convention. In the absence of a tribunal following constitutionally mandated procedures, however, the plurality declared that it was the District Court's obligation to provide those procedural rights to the detainee in a *habeas* action.... *Hamdi* was decided before the creation of the Combatant Status Review Tribunal, and the respondents contend in their motion to dismiss that were this Court to conclude that the detainees are entitled to due process under the Fifth Amendment, the CSRT proceedings would fully comply with all constitutional requirements. More specifically, the respondents claim that the CSRT regulations were modeled after Army Regulation 190–8 governing the determination of prisoner of war status, referenced in *Hamdi,* and actually exceed the requirements set forth by the *Hamdi* plurality. For example, respondents cite the facts that under CSRT rules, tribunal members must certify that they have not been involved in the "apprehension, detention, interrogation, or previous determination of status of the detainee[s]," that detainees are provided a "Personal Representative" to assist in the preparation of their cases, that the "Recorder"—that is, the person who presents evidence in support of "enemy combatant" status— must search for exculpatory evidence, that the detainee is entitled to an unclassified summary of the evidence against him, and that the tribunal's decisions are reviewed by a higher authority. Notwithstanding the procedures cited by the respondents, the Court finds that the procedures provided in the CSRT regulations fail to satisfy constitutional due process requirements in several respects.

The constitutional defects in the CSRT procedures can be separated into two categories. The first category consists of defects which apply across the board to all detainees in the cases before this Judge. Specifically, those deficiencies are the CSRT's failure to provide the detainees with access to material evidence upon which the tribunal affirmed their "enemy combatant" status and the failure to permit the assistance of counsel to compensate for the government's refusal to disclose classified information directly to the detainees. The second category of defects involves those which are detainee specific and may or may not apply to every petitioner in this litigation. Those defects include the manner in which the CSRT handled accusations of torture and the vague and potentially overbroad definition of "enemy combatant" in the CSRT regulations. While additional specific defects may or may not exist, further inquiry is unnecessary at this stage of the litigation given the fundamental deficiencies detailed below.

1.   General Defects Existing in All Cases Before the Court: Failure to Provide Detainees Access to Material Evidence Upon Which the CSRT Affirmed "Enemy Combatant" Status and Failure to Permit the Assistance of Counsel

The CSRT reviewed classified information when considering whether each detainee presently before this Court should be considered an "enemy combatant," and it appears that all of the CSRT's decisions substantially relied upon classified evidence. No detainee, however, was ever permitted access to any classified information nor was any detainee permitted to have an advocate review and challenge the classified evidence on his behalf. Accordingly, the CSRT failed to provide any detainee with sufficient notice of the factual basis for which he is being detained and with a fair opportunity to rebut the government's evidence supporting the determination that he is an "enemy combatant."

The inherent lack of fairness of the CSRT's consideration of classified information not disclosed to the detainees is perhaps most vividly illustrated in the following unclassified colloquy, which, though taken from a case not presently before this Judge, exemplifies the practical and severe disadvantages faced by all Guantanamo prisoners. In reading a list of allegations forming the basis for the detention of Mustafa Ait Idr, a petitioner in *Boumediene v. Bush,* 04–CV–1166 (RJL), the Recorder of the CSRT asserted, "While living in Bosnia, the Detainee associated with a known Al Qaida operative." In response, the following exchange occurred:

Detainee: Give me his name.

Tribunal President: I do not know.

Detainee: How can I respond to this?

Tribunal President: Did you know of anybody that was a member of Al Qaida?

Detainee: No, no.

Tribunal President: I'm sorry, what was your response?

Detainee: No.

Tribunal President: No?

Detainee: No. This is something the interrogators told me a long while ago. I asked the interrogators to tell me who this person was. Then I could tell you if I might have known this person, but not if this person is a terrorist. Maybe I knew this person as a friend. Maybe it was a person that worked with me. Maybe it was a person that was on my team. But I do not know if this person is Bosnian, Indian or whatever. If you tell me the name, then I can respond and defend myself against this accusation.

Tribunal President: We are asking you the questions and we need you to respond to what is on the unclassified summary.

Respondents' Factual Return to Petition for Writ of Habeas Corpus by Petitioner Mustafa Ait Idir, filed October 27, 2004, Enclosure (3) at 13. Subsequently, after the Recorder read the allegation that the detainee was arrested because of his alleged involvement in a plan to attack the U.S. Embassy in Sarajevo, the detainee expressly asked in the following colloquy to see the evidence upon which the government's assertion relied:

Detainee: . . . The only thing I can tell you is I did not plan or even think of [attacking the Embassy]. Did you find any explosives with me? Any weapons? Did you find me in front of the embassy? Did you find me in contact with the Americans? Did I threaten anyone? I am prepared now to tell you, if you have anything or any evidence, even if it is just very little, that proves I went to the embassy and looked like that [Detainee made a gesture with his head and neck as if he were looking into a building or a window] at the embassy, then I am ready to be punished. I can just tell you that I did not plan anything. Point by point, when we get to the point that I am associated with Al Qaida, but we already did that one.

Recorder: It was [the] statement that preceded the first point.

Detainee: If it is the same point, but I do not want to repeat myself. These accusations, my answer to all of them is I did not do these things. But I do not have anything to prove this. The only thing is the citizenship. I can tell you where I was and I had the papers to prove so. But to tell me I planned to bomb, I can only tell you that I did not plan.

Tribunal President: Mustafa, does that conclude your statement?

Detainee: That is it, but I was hoping you had evidence that you can give me. If I was in your place—and I apologize in advance for these words—but if a supervisor came to me and showed me accusations like these, I would take these accusations and I would hit him in the face with them. Sorry about that.

[Everyone in the Tribunal room laughs.]

Tribunal President: We had to laugh, but it is okay.

Detainee: Why? Because these are accusations that I can't even answer. I am not able to answer them. You tell me I am from Al Qaida, but I am not an Al Qaida. I don't have any proof to give you except to ask you to catch Bin Laden and ask him if I am a part of Al Qaida. To tell me that I thought, I'll just tell you that I did not. I don't have proof regarding this. What should be done is you should give me evidence regarding these accusations because I am not able to give you any evidence. I can just tell you no, and that is it.

The laughter reflected in the transcript is understandable, and this exchange might have been truly humorous had the consequences of the detainee's "enemy combatant" status not been so terribly serious and had the detainee's criticism of the process not been so piercingly accurate.

. . .

The Court fully appreciates the strong governmental interest in not disclosing classified evidence to individuals believed to be terrorists intent on causing great harm to the United States. Indeed, this Court's protective order prohibits the disclosure of any classified information to any of the petitioners in these *habeas* cases. Amended Protective Order and Procedures for Counsel Access to Detainees at the United States Naval Base in Guantanamo Bay, Cuba, 344 F.Supp.2d 174 (D.D.C.2004). To compensate for the resulting hardship to the petitioners and to ensure due process in the litigation of these cases, however, the protective order requires the disclosure of all relevant classified information to the petitioners' counsel who have the appropriate security clearances. Although counsel are not permitted to share any classified information with their clients, they at least have the opportunity to examine all evidence relied upon by the government in making an "enemy combatant" status determination and to investigate and ensure the accuracy, reliability and relevance of that evidence. Thus, the governmental and private interests have been fairly balanced in a manner satisfying constitutional due process requirements. In a similar fashion, the rules regulating the military commission proceedings for aliens—rules which the government so vigorously defended in *Hamdan v. Rurnsfeld*—expressly provide that although classified evidence may be withheld from the defendant, it may not be withheld from defense counsel. Procedures for Trials by Military Commissions of Certain Non–United States Citizens in the War Against Terrorism, 32 C.F.R. § 9.6(b)(3) ("A decision to close a proceeding or portion thereof may include a decision to exclude the Accused, Civilian Defense Counsel, or any other person, but Detailed Defense Counsel may not be excluded from any trial proceeding or portion thereof."). In contrast, the CSRT regulations do not properly balance the detainees' need for access to material evidence considered by the tribunal against the government's interest in protecting classified information.

The CSRT regulations do acknowledge to some extent the detainees' need for assistance during the tribunal process, but they fall far short of the procedural protections that would have existed had counsel been permitted to participate. The implementing regulations create the position of "Personal Representative" for the purpose of "assist[ing] the detainee in reviewing all relevant unclassified information, in preparing and presenting information, and in questioning witnesses at the CSRT." But notwithstanding the fact that the Personal Representative may review classified information considered by the tribunal, that person is neither a lawyer nor an advocate and thus cannot be considered an effective surrogate to compensate for a detainee's inability to personally review and contest classified evidence against him. Additionally, there is no confidential relationship between the detainee and the Personal Representative, and the Personal Representative is obligated to disclose to the tribunal any relevant inculpatory information he obtains from the detainee. *Id.* Consequently, there is inherent risk and little corresponding benefit should the detainee decide to use the services of the Personal Representative.

. . .

In sum, the CSRT's extensive reliance on classified information in its resolution of "enemy combatant" status, the detainees' inability to review that information, and the prohibition of assistance by counsel jointly deprive the detainees of sufficient notice of the factual bases for their detention and deny them a fair opportunity to challenge their incarceration. These grounds alone are sufficient to find a violation of due process rights and to require the denial of the respondents' motion to dismiss these cases.

* * *

b.   Vague and Overly Broad Definition of "Enemy Combatant"

Although the government has been detaining individuals as "enemy combatants" since the issuance of the AUMF in 2001, it apparently did not formally define the term until the July 7, 2004 Order creating the CSRT. The lack of a formal definition seemed to have troubled at least the plurality of the Supreme Court in *Hamdi,* but for purposes of resolving the issues in that case, the plurality considered the government's definition to be an individual who was " 'part of or supporting forces hostile to the United States or coalition partners' in Afghanistan *and* who 'engaged in an armed conflict against the United States' there." (*quoting* Brief for the Respondents) (emphasis added). The Court agreed with the government that the AUMF authorizes the Executive to detain individuals falling within that limited definition, *id.,* with the plurality explaining that "[b]ecause detention to prevent a combatant's return to the battlefield is a fundamental incident of waging war, in permitting the use of 'necessary and appropriate force,' Congress has clearly and unmistakably authorized detention in the narrow circumstances considered here." The plurality cautioned, however, "that indefinite detention for the purpose of interrogation is not authorized" by the AUMF, and added that a congressional grant of authority to the President to use "necessary and appropriate force" might not be properly interpreted to include the authority to detain individuals for the duration of a particular conflict if that conflict does not take a form that is based on "longstanding law-of-war principles." *Id.*

The definition of "enemy combatant" contained in the Order creating the CSRT is significantly broader than the definition considered in *Hamdi*. According to the definition currently applied by the government, an "enemy combatant" "shall mean an individual who was part of or supporting Taliban or al Qaeda forces, or associated forces that are engaged in hostilities against the United States or its coalition partners. This *includes* any person who has committed a belligerent act or has directly supported hostilities in aid of enemy armed forces." July 7, 2004 Order at 1 (emphasis added). Use of the word "includes" indicates that the government interprets the AUMF to permit the indefinite detention of individuals who never committed a belligerent act or who never directly supported hostilities against the U.S. or its allies. This Court explored the government's position on the matter by posing a series of hypothetical questions to counsel at the December 1, 2004 hearing on the motion to dismiss. In response to the hypotheticals, counsel for the respondents argued that the Executive has the authority to detain the following individuals until the conclusion of the war on terrorism: "[a] little old lady in Switzerland who writes checks to what she thinks is a charity that helps orphans in Afghanistan but [what] really is a front to finance al-Qaeda activities,", a person who teaches English to the son of an al Qaeda member, and a journalist who knows the location of Osama Bin Laden but refuses to disclose it to protect her source.

The Court can unequivocally report that no factual return submitted by the government in this litigation reveals the detention of a Swiss philanthropist, an English teacher, or a journalist. The Court can also acknowledge the existence of specific factual returns containing evidence indicating that certain detainees fit the narrower definition of "enemy combatant" approved by the Supreme Court in *Hamdi*. The petitioners have argued in opposition to the respondents' motion to dismiss, however, that at least with respect to some detainees, the expansive definition of "enemy combatant" currently in use in the CSRT proceedings violates long standing principles of due process by permitting the detention of individuals based solely on their membership in anti-American organizations rather than on actual activities supporting the use of violence or harm against the United States. Al Odah Petitioners' Reply to the Government's "Response to Petitions for Writ of Habeas Corpus and Motion to Dismiss" at 25–26

Whether the detention of each individual petitioner is authorized by the AUMF and satisfies the mandates of due process must ultimately be determined on a detainee by detainee basis. At this stage of the litigation, however, sufficient allegations have been made by at least some of the petitioners and certain evidence exists in some CSRT factual returns to warrant the denial of the respondents' motion to dismiss on the ground that the respondents have employed an overly broad definition of "enemy combatant."

. . .

It may well turn out that after the detainee is given a fair opportunity to challenge his detention in a *habeas* proceeding, the legality of his detention as an "enemy combatant" will be upheld and he will continue to be held at Guantanamo Bay until the end of the war on terrorism or until the government determines he no longer poses a threat to U.S. security. It is also possible, however, that once given a fair opportunity to litigate his case, the detainee will establish that he is being indefinitely detained not because of anything he has done and not to prevent his return to any "battlefield," metaphorical or otherwise, but simply because _____ such detention is not permissible _____ and the respondents' motion to dismiss must therefore be denied.

Nothing written above should be interpreted to require the immediate release of any detainee, nor should the conclusions reached be considered to have fully resolved whether or not sufficient evidence exists to support the continued detention of any petitioner. The respondents' motion to dismiss asserted that no evidence exists and that the petitioners could make no factual allegations which, if taken as true, would permit the litigation of these *habeas* cases to proceed further. For the reasons stated above, the Court has concluded otherwise. . . .

D.   CLAIMS BASED ON THE GENEVA CONVENTIONS

* * *

Although the Court rejects the primary basis argued by the respondents for dismissal of claims based on the Geneva Conventions, it does accept one of the alternative grounds put forth in their motion, namely that the Geneva Conventions do not apply to al Qaeda. * * *

This does not end the analysis for purposes of resolving the respondents' motion to dismiss, however, because some of the petitioners in the above-captioned cases are being detained either solely because they were Taliban fighters or because they were associated with both the Taliban and al Qaeda. Significantly, the respondents concede that the Geneva Conventions apply to the Taliban detainees in light of the fact that Afghanistan is a High Contracting Party to the Conventions. Motion to Dismiss at 70–71 n.80 (*citing* White House Fact Sheet (Feb. 7, 2002), available at http:// www.whitehouse.gov/news/releases/2002/02/20020207–13.html). They argue in their motion to dismiss, however, that notwithstanding the *application* of the Third Geneva Convention to Taliban detainees, the treaty does not *protect* Taliban detainees because the President has declared that no Taliban fighter is a "prisoner of war" as defined by the Convention. *Id.* The respondents' argument in this regard must be rejected, however, for the Third Geneva Convention does not permit the determination of prisoner of war status in such a conclusory fashion.

Article 4 of the Third Geneva Convention defines who is considered a "prisoner of war" under the treaty. Paragraph (1) provides that the term "prisoners of war" includes "[m]embers of the armed forces of a Party to the conflict, as well as members of militias or volunteer corps forming part of such armed forces." As provided in Paragraph (2), the definition of "prisoners of war" also includes "[m]embers of other militias and members of other volunteer corps, including those of organized resistance movements," but only if they fulfill the following conditions: "(a) that of being commanded by a person responsible for his subordinates; (b) that of having a fixed distinctive sign recognizable at a distance; (c) that of carrying arms openly; (d) that of conducting their operations in accordance with the laws and customs of war." If there is any doubt as to whether individuals satisfy the Article 4 prerequisites, Article 5 entitles them to be treated as prisoners of war "until such time as their status has been determined by a competent tribunal." Army Regulation 190–8 created the rules for the "competent tribunal" referenced in Article 5 of the Third Geneva Convention, and the CSRT was established in accordance with that provision. *See* Army Regulation 190–8 § 1–1.b, Motion to Dismiss at 32.

Nothing in the Convention itself or in Army Regulation 190–8 authorizes the President of the United States to rule by fiat that an entire group of fighters covered by the Third Geneva Convention falls outside of the Article 4 definitions of "prisoners of war." To the contrary, . . . the President's broad characterization of how the Taliban generally fought the war in Afghanistan cannot substitute for an Article 5 tribunal's determination on an individualized basis of whether a particular fighter complied with the laws of war or otherwise falls within an exception denying him prisoner of war status. Clearly, had an appropriate determination been properly made by an Article 5 tribunal that a petitioner was not a prisoner of war, that petitioner's claims based on the Third Geneva Convention could not survive the respondents' motion to dismiss. But although numerous petitioners in the above-captioned cases were found by the CSRT to have been Taliban fighters, nowhere do the CSRT records for many of those petitioners reveal specific findings that they committed some particular act or failed to satisfy some defined prerequisite entitling the respondents to deprive them of prisoner of war status. Accordingly, the Court denies that portion of the respondents' motion to dismiss addressing the Geneva Convention claims of those petitioners who were found to be Taliban fighters but who were not specifically determined to be excluded from prisoner of war status by a competent Article 5 tribunal.

* * *

Notes and Questions

1. With Khalid v. Bush and In re Guanatanamo Detainees Cases having reached opposite conclusions, the split will have to be resolved by the U.S. Court of Appeals, and perhaps, ultimately by the Supreme Court. How do you think the Court of Appeals will rule? The Supreme Court?

2. Are there practical problems with the implementation of Judge Green's opinion? Given over 500 detainees, how burdensome are the procedures that her opinion will require? How significant is it that only 60–70 detainees have thus far filed habeas petitions?

* * *

D. Conditions and terms of detention

1. Methods of interrogation: the torture controversy

Notes and Questions

1. In 2003 and 2004, reports and pictures of abusive treatment of prisoners in Iraq and reports of some abuse of prisoners in Guantanamo made headlines and stirred up enormous controversy and soul-searching. There was a question whether the abusive treatment had been authorized, condoned or fostered by actions or statements of the administration.

* * *

f. On December 30, 2004, shortly before Alberto R. Gonzales was to testify in connection with his nomination to be Attorney General of the United States, see LA Times, January 5, 2005, at A20, a memorandum was made public that had been sent from the Acting Assistant Attorney General for the Office of Legal Counsel to Deputy Attorney General James B. Comey. It included the following statements:

> Torture is abhorrent both to American law and values and to international norms . . . . .

> Questions have since been raised, both by this Office and by others, about the appropriateness and relevance of the non-statutory discussion in the August 2002 Memorandum [Ed. See a. above], and also about various aspects of the statutory analysis, in particular the statement that "severe" pain under the statute was limited to pain "equivalent in intensity to the pain accompanying serious physical injury, such as organ failure, impairment of bodily function, or even death." . . . We decided to withdraw the August 2002 Memorandum, a decision you announced in June 2004. At that time, you directed this Office to prepare a replacement memorandum. . . .

> This Memorandum supersedes the August 2002 Memorandum in its entirety. Because the discussion in that memorandum concerning the President's Commander-in-Chief power and the potential defenses to liability was—and remains—unnecessary, it has been eliminated from the analysis that follows. Consideration of the bounds of any such authority would be inconsistent with the President's unequivocal directive that United States personnel not engage in torture.

* * *

5. The reports of actual torture in Iraq and Guantanamo and the government memoranda on the subject triggered a significant amount of scholarly and quasi-scholarly discussion and debate in the law journals, op ed pages and magazines. Many of the authorities and issues are developed in Marcy Strauss, Torture, 48 N.Y.L. Sch. L.Rev. 201 (2003) and Alan M. Dershowitz, The Torture Warrant: A Response to Professor Strauss, 48 N.Y.L. Sch. L.Rev. 275 (2003).

6. Consider the following two scholarly views. Which has the better of the argument? What factors need to be taken into account or need to be known in choosing between them?

a. "I am generally against torture as a *normative* matter, and I would like to see its use minimized.... I think that if we ever confronted an actual case of imminent mass terrorism that could be prevented by the infliction of torture, we would use torture (even lethal torture)....

... I pose the issue as follows: If torture is in fact being and/or would in fact be used in an actual ticking bomb mass terrorism case, would it be normatively better or worse to have such torture regulated by some kind of warrant.... Dershowitz , op. cit. supra, note 5 at 277.

b. "Dershowitz believes that the occasions for the use of torture should be regularized—by requiring a judicial warrant.... But he overlooks an argument for leaving such things to executive discretion. If rules are promulgated permitting torture in defined circumstances, some officials are bound to want to explore the outer bounds of the rules. Better to leave in place the formal and customary prohibitions, but with the understanding that that they will not be enforced in extreme circumstances." Richard A. Posner, The Best Offense, The New Republic, Sept 2, 2002, 28, quoted in Dershowitz, op. cit. supra note 5 at 279.

7. The stronger the prohibitions against torture and their enforcement, the more likely that methods may be developed for using foreign surrogates. See Editorial, Blood on Our Hands, LA Times, Oct. 6, 2004, B10, condemning the fact that the House of Representatives might take up provisions as part of the Intelligence Reform bill that would permit U.S. officials to send terror suspects to countries that permit torture. In fact the provisions were dropped from the bill as enacted. Also see LA Times, January 13, 2005, A1, reporting a story that a Guantanamo detainee with Australian citizenship claimed that he had been shipped to Egypt where he was tortured. And see Strauss, op. cit. supra, note 5. at footnote 227. Also see Wash. Post, Dec. 27, 2004 A01 reporting on a story about a jet aircraft that purportedly the CIA uses clandestinely to fly "captured terrorists from one country to another for detention and interrogation."

* * *

Chapter 8

MILITARY TRIBUNALS

A. Introduction

On November 13, 2001, two months after September 11, 2001, President Bush issued a Military Order that provided for the detention and trial by "military commission" of certain categories of persons involved in acts of international terrorism. In issuing the Order, the government expressly relied on the President's authority as Commander in Chief of the Armed Forces; on the Joint Resolution of the Congress, (Authorization for Use of Military Force Joint Resolution) (Public Law 107–40, 115 Stat. 224) which appears in Chapter 5, supra, at p. ___; and on two long-standing legislative provisions 10 U.S.C §§ 821 and 836. The Military Order and the two legislative provisions appear below.

NOTICE

Detention, Treatment, and Trial of Certain Non–Citizens in the War Against Terrorism.
66 Fed. Reg. 57833

By the authority vested in me as President and as Commander in Chief of the Armed Forces of the United States by the Constitution and the laws of the United States of America, including the Authorization for Use of Military Force Joint Resolution (Public Law 107–40, 115 Stat. 224) and sections 821 and 836 of title 10, United States Code, it is hereby ordered as follows:

Section 1. Findings.

(a) International terrorists, including members of al Qaida, have carried out attacks on United States diplomatic and military personnel and facilities abroad and on citizens and property within the United States on a scale that has created a state of armed conflict that requires the use of the United States Armed Forces.

(b) In light of grave acts of terrorism and threats of terrorism, including the terrorist attacks on September 11, 2001, on the headquarters of the United States Department of Defense in the national capital region, on the World Trade Center in New York, and on civilian aircraft such as in Pennsylvania, I proclaimed a national emergency on September 14, 2001 (Proc. 7463, Declaration of National Emergency by Reason of Certain Terrorist Attacks).

(c) Individuals acting alone and in concert involved in international terrorism possess both the capability and the intention to undertake further terrorist attacks against the United States that, if not detected and prevented, will cause mass deaths, mass injuries, and massive destruction of property, and may place at risk the continuity of the operations of the United States Government.

(d) The ability of the United States to protect the United States and its citizens, and to help its allies and other cooperating nations protect their nations and their citizens, from such further terrorist attacks depends in significant part upon using the United States Armed Forces to identify terrorists and those who support them, to disrupt their activities, and to eliminate their ability to conduct or support such attacks.

(e) To protect the United States and its citizens, and for the effective conduct of military operations and prevention of terrorist attacks, it is necessary for individuals subject to this order pursuant to section 2 hereof to be detained, and, when tried, to be tried for violations of the laws of war and other applicable laws by military tribunals.

(f) Given the danger to the safety of the United States and the nature of international terrorism, and to the extent provided by and under this order, I find consistent with section 836 of title 10, United States Code, that it is not practicable to apply in military commissions under this order the principles of law and the rules of evidence generally recognized in the trial of criminal cases in the United States district courts.

(g) Having fully considered the magnitude of the potential deaths, injuries, and property destruction that would result from potential acts of terrorism against the United States, and the probability that such acts will occur, I have determined that an extraordinary emergency exists for national defense purposes, that this emergency constitutes an urgent and compelling government interest, and that issuance of this order is necessary to meet the emergency.

Sec. 2. Definition and Policy.

(a) The term "individual subject to this order" shall mean any individual who is not a United States citizen with respect to whom I determine from time to time in writing that:

    (1) there is reason to believe that such individual, at the relevant times,

        (i) is or was a member of the organization known as al Qaida;

        (ii) has engaged in, aided or abetted, or conspired to commit, acts of international terrorism, or acts in preparation therefor, that have caused, threaten to cause, or have as their aim to cause, injury to or adverse effects on the United States, its citizens, national security, foreign policy, or economy; or

(iii) has knowingly harbored one or more individuals described in subparagraphs (i) or (ii) of subsection 2(a)(1) of this order; and

(2) it is in the interest of the United States that such individual be subject to this order.

(b) It is the policy of the United States that the Secretary of Defense shall take all necessary measures to ensure that any individual subject to this order is detained in accordance with section 3, and, if the individual is to be tried, that such individual is tried only in accordance with section 4.

(c) It is further the policy of the United States that any individual subject to this order who is not already under the control of the Secretary of Defense but who is under the control of any other officer or agent of the United States or any State shall, upon delivery of a copy of such written determination to such officer or agent, forthwith be placed under the control of the Secretary of Defense.

Sec. 3. Detention Authority of the Secretary of Defense. Any individual subject to this order shall be—

(a) detained at an appropriate location designated by the Secretary of Defense outside or within the United States;

(b) treated humanely, without any adverse distinction based on race, color, religion, gender, birth, wealth, or any similar criteria;

(c) afforded adequate food, drinking water, shelter, clothing, and medical treatment;

(d) allowed the free exercise of religion consistent with the requirements of such detention; and

(e) detained in accordance with such other conditions as the Secretary of Defense may prescribe.

Sec. 4. Authority of the Secretary of Defense Regarding Trials of Individuals Subject to this Order.

(a) Any individual subject to this order shall, when tried, be tried by military commission for any and all offenses triable by military commission that such individual is alleged to have committed, and may be punished in accordance with the penalties provided under applicable law, including life imprisonment or death.

(b) As a military function and in light of the findings in section 1, including subsection (f) thereof, the Secretary of Defense shall issue such orders and regulations, including orders for the appointment of one or more military commissions, as may be necessary to carry out subsection (a) of this section.

(c) Orders and regulations issued under subsection (b) of this section shall include, but not be limited to, rules for the conduct of the proceedings of military commissions, including pretrial, trial, and post-trial procedures, modes of proof, issuance of process, and qualifications of attorneys, which shall at a minimum provide for—

(1) military commissions to sit at any time and any place, consistent with such guidance regarding time and place as the Secretary of Defense may provide;

(2) a full and fair trial, with the military commission sitting as the triers of both fact and law;

(3) admission of such evidence as would, in the opinion of the presiding officer of the military commission (or instead, if any other member of the commission so requests at the time the presiding officer renders that opinion, the opinion of the commission rendered at that time by a majority of the commission), have probative value to a reasonable person;

(4) in a manner consistent with the protection of information classified or classifiable under Executive Order 12958 of April 17, 1995, as amended, or any successor Executive Order, protected by statute or rule from unauthorized disclosure, or otherwise protected by law, (A) the handling of, admission into evidence of, and access to materials and information, and (B) the conduct, closure of, and access to proceedings;

(5) conduct of the prosecution by one or more attorneys designated by the Secretary of Defense and conduct of the defense by attorneys for the individual subject to this order;

(6) conviction only upon the concurrence of two-thirds of the members of the commission present at the time of the vote, a majority being present;

(7) sentencing only upon the concurrence of two-thirds of the members of the commission present at the time of the vote, a majority being present; and

(8) submission of the record of the trial, including any conviction or sentence, for review and final decision by me or by the Secretary of Defense if so designated by me for that purpose.

Sec. 5. Obligation of Other Agencies to Assist the Secretary of Defense.

Departments, agencies, entities, and officers of the United States shall, to the maximum extent permitted by law, provide to the Secretary of Defense such assistance as he may request to implement this order.

Sec. 6. Additional Authorities of the Secretary of Defense.

(a) As a military function and in light of the findings in section 1, the Secretary of Defense shall issue such orders and regulations as may be necessary to carry out any of the provisions of this order.

(b) The Secretary of Defense may perform any of his functions or duties, and may exercise any of the powers provided to him under this order (other than under section 4(c)(8) hereof) in accordance with section 113(d) of title 10, United States Code.

Sec. 7. Relationship to Other Law and Forums.

(a) Nothing in this order shall be construed to—

(1) authorize the disclosure of state secrets to any person not otherwise authorized to have access to them;

(2) limit the authority of the President as Commander in Chief of the Armed Forces or the power of the President to grant reprieves and pardons; or

(3) limit the lawful authority of the Secretary of Defense, any military commander, or any other officer or agent of the United States or of any State to detain or try any person who is not an individual subject to this order.

(b) With respect to any individual subject to this order—

(1) military tribunals shall have exclusive jurisdiction with respect to offenses by the individual; and

(2) the individual shall not be privileged to seek any remedy or maintain any proceeding, directly or indirectly, or to have any such remedy or proceeding sought on the individual's behalf, in

(i) any court of the United States, or any State thereof,

(ii) any court of any foreign nation, or

(iii) any international tribunal.

(c) This order is not intended to and does not create any right, benefit, or privilege, substantive or procedural, enforceable at law or equity by any party, against the United States, its departments, agencies, or other entities, its officers or employees, or any other person.

(d) For purposes of this order, the term "State" includes any State, district, territory, or possession of the United States.

(e) I reserve the authority to direct the Secretary of Defense, at any time hereafter, to transfer to a governmental authority control of any individual subject to this order. Nothing in this order shall be construed to limit the authority of any such governmental authority to prosecute any individual for whom control is transferred.

Sec. 8. Publication.

This order shall be published in the Federal Register.

GEORGE W. BUSH
THE WHITE HOUSE,

November 13, 2001

TITLE 10—UNITED STATES CODE (ARMED FORCES)
SUBTITLE A—GENERAL MILITARY LAW PART II— PERSONNEL CHAPTER 47—UNIFORM CODE OF MILITARY JUSTICE—SUBCHAPTER IV—COURT–MARTIAL JURISDICTION

Section 821. Art. 21. Jurisdiction of courts-martial not exclusive

The provisions of this chapter conferring jurisdiction upon courts-martial do not deprive military commissions, provost courts, or other military tribunals of concurrent jurisdiction with respect to offenders or offenses that by statute or by the law of war may be tried by military commissions, provost courts, or other military tribunals.

Section 836. Art. 36. President may prescribe rules

(a) Pretrial, trial, and post-trial procedures, including modes of proof, for cases arising under this chapter triable in courts-martial, military commissions and other military tribunals, and procedures for courts of inquiry, may be prescribed by the President by regulations which shall, so far as he considers practicable, apply the principles of law and the rules of evidence generally recognized in the trial of criminal cases in the United States district courts, but which may not be contrary to or inconsistent with this chapter.

(b) All rules and regulations made under this article shall be uniform insofar as practicable

B.   The question of legal authority

The issuance of the Presidential Military Order generated a great deal of commentary, both in law reviews and the general media. Much of the commentary attacked the Order as being either an unconstitutional or unwise assertion of authority by the President. The main constitutional argument made against the Order was that the President did not have the authority to issue the order without congressional authorization. The response of the administration and the administration's defenders was that the President had such authority as Commander in Chief. If further congressional authorization was needed, the post-Sept. 11 Joint Resolution (Public Law 107–40) and the two long-standing Title 10 sections provided such authority. The government also cited as authority, the decision of the Supreme Court in Ex parte Quirin, 317 U.S. 1 (1942).

EX PARTE QUIRIN
317 U.S. 1 (1942).

Mr. Chief Justice STONE delivered the opinion of the Court.

These cases are brought here by petitioners' several applications for leave to file petitions for habeas corpus in this Court, and by their petitions for certiorari to review orders of the District Court for the District of Columbia, which denied their applications for leave to file petitions for habeas corpus in that court.

The question for decision is whether the detention of petitioners by respondent for trial by Military Commission, appointed by Order of the President of July 2, 1942, on charges preferred against them purporting to set out their violations of the law of war and of the Articles of War, is in conformity to the laws and Constitution of the United States.

After denial of their applications by the District Court, 47 F.Supp. 431, petitioners asked leave to file petitions for habeas corpus in this Court. In view of the public importance of the questions raised by their petitions and of the duty which rests on the courts, in time of war as well as in time of peace, to preserve unimpaired the constitutional safeguards of civil liberty, and because in our opinion the public interest required that we consider and decide those questions without any avoidable delay, we directed that petitioners' applications be set down for full oral argument at a special term of this Court, convened on July 29, 1942. The applications for leave to file the petitions were presented in open court on that day and were heard on the petitions, the answers to them of respondent, a stipulation of facts by counsel, and the record of the testimony given before the Commission.

While the argument was proceeding before us, petitioners perfected their appeals from the orders of the District Court to the United States Court of Appeals for the District of Columbia and thereupon filed with this Court petitions for certiorari to the Court of Appeals before judgment, pursuant to Section 240(a) of the Judicial Code, 28 U.S.C. § 347(a). We granted certiorari before judgment for the reasons which moved us to convene the special term of Court. In accordance with the stipulation of counsel we treat the record, briefs and arguments in the habeas corpus proceedings in this Court as the record, briefs and arguments upon the writs of certiorari.

On July 31, 1942, after hearing argument of counsel and after full consideration of all questions raised, this Court affirmed the orders of the District Court and denied petitioners' applications for leave to file petitions for habeas corpus. By per curiam opinion, . . . we announced the decision of the Court, and that the full opinion in the causes would be prepared and filed with the Clerk.

The following facts appear from the petitions or are stipulated. Except as noted they are undisputed.

All the petitioners were born in Germany; all have lived in the United States. All returned to Germany between 1933 and 1941. All except petitioner Haupt are admittedly citizens of the German Reich, with which the United States is at war. Haupt came to this country with his parents when he was five years old; it is contended that he became a citizen of the United States by virtue of the naturalization of his parents during his minority and that he has not since lost his citizenship. The Government, however, takes the position that on attaining his majority he elected to maintain German allegiance and citizenship or in any case that he has by his conduct renounced or abandoned his United States citizenship. See Perkins v. Elg, 307 U.S. 325, 334, 59 S.Ct. 884, 889, 83

L.Ed. 1320; United States ex rel. Rojak v. Marshall, D.C., 34 F.2d 219; United States ex rel. Scimeca v. Husband, 2 Cir., 6 F.2d 957, 958; 8 U.S.C.§ 801, and compare 8 U.S.C. § 808. For reasons presently to be stated we do not find it necessary to resolve these contentions.

After the declaration of war between the United States and the German Reich, petitioners received training at a sabotage school near Berlin, Germany, where they were instructed in the use of explosives and in methods of secret writing. Thereafter petitioners, with a German citizen, Dasch, proceeded from Germany to a seaport in Occupied France, where petitioners Burger, Heinck and Quirin, together with Dasch, boarded a German submarine which proceeded across the Atlantic to Amagansett Beach on Long Island, New York. The four were there landed from the submarine in the hours of darkness, on or about June 13, 1942, carrying with them a supply of explosives, fuses and incendiary and timing devices. While landing they wore German Marine Infantry uniforms or parts of uniforms. Immediately after landing they buried their uniforms and the other articles mentioned and proceeded in civilian dress to New York City.

The remaining four petitioners at the same French port boarded another German submarine, which carried them across the Atlantic to Ponte Vedra Beach, Florida. On or about June 17, 1942, they came ashore during the hours of darkness wearing caps of the German Marine Infantry and carrying with them a supply of explosives, fuses, and incendiary and timing devices. They immediately buried their caps and the other articles mentioned and proceeded in civilian dress to Jacksonville, Florida, and thence to various points in the United States. All were taken into custody in New York or Chicago by agents of the Federal Bureau of Investigation. All had received instructions in Germany from an officer of the German High Command to destroy war industries and war facilities in the United States, for which they or their relatives in Germany were to receive salary payments from the German Government. They also had been paid by the German Government during their course of training at the sabotage school and had received substantial sums in United States currency, which were in their possession when arrested. The currency had been handed to them by an officer of the German High Command, who had instructed them to wear their German uniforms while landing in the United States.

The President, as President and Commander in Chief of the Army and Navy, by Order of July 2, 1942, appointed a Military Commission and directed it to try petitioners for offenses against the law of war and the Articles of War, and prescribed regulations for the procedure on the trial and for review of the record of the trial and of any judgment or sentence of the Commission. On the same day, by Proclamation, the President declared that 'all persons who are subjects, citizens or residents of any nation at war with the United States or who give obedience to or act under the direction of any such nation, and who during time of war enter or attempt to enter the United States * * * through coastal or boundary defenses, and are charged with committing or attempting or preparing to commit sabotage, espionage, hostile or warlike acts, or violations of the law of war, shall be subject to the law of war and to the jurisdiction of military tribunals'.

The Proclamation also stated in terms that all such persons were denied access to the courts.

Pursuant to direction of the Attorney General, the Federal Bureau of Investigation surrendered custody of petitioners to respondent, Provost Marshal of the Military District of Washington, who was directed by the Secretary of War to receive and keep them in custody, and who thereafter held petitioners for trial before the Commission.

On July 3, 1942, the Judge Advocate General's Department of the Army prepared and lodged with the Commission the following charges against petitioners, supported by specifications:

1. Violation of the law of war.

2. Violation of Article 81 of the Articles of War, defining the offense of relieving or attempting to relieve, or corresponding with or giving intelligence to, the enemy.

3. Violation of Article 82, defining the offense of spying.

4. Conspiracy to commit the offenses alleged in charges 1, 2 and 3.

The Commission met on July 8, 1942, and proceeded with the trial, which continued in progress while the causes were pending in this Court. On July 27th, before petitioners' applications to the District Court, all the evidence for the prosecution and the defense had been taken by the Commission and the case had been closed except for arguments of counsel. It is conceded that ever since petitioners' arrest the state and federal courts in Florida, New York, and the District of Columbia, and in the states in which each of the petitioners was arrested or detained, have been open and functioning normally.

. . .

Petitioners' main contention is that the President is without any statutory or constitutional authority to order the petitioners to be tried by military tribunal for offenses with which they are charged; that in consequence they are entitled to be tried in the civil courts with the safeguards, including trial by jury, which the Fifth and Sixth Amendments guarantee to all persons charged in such courts with criminal offenses. In any case it is urged that the President's Order, in prescribing the procedure of the Commission and the method for review of its findings and sentence, and the proceedings of the Commission under the Order, conflict with Articles of War adopted by Congress—particularly Articles 38, 43, 46, 50 1/2 and 70—and are illegal and void.

The Government challenges each of these propositions. But regardless of their merits, it also insists that petitioners must be denied access to the courts, both because they are enemy aliens or have entered our territory as enemy belligerents, and because the President's Proclamation undertakes in terms to deny such access to the class of persons defined by the Proclamation, which aptly describes the character and conduct of petitioners. It is urged that if they are enemy aliens or if the Proclamation has force no court may afford the petitioners a hearing. But there is certainly nothing in the Proclamation to preclude access to the courts for determining its applicability to the particular case. And neither the Proclamation nor the fact that they are enemy aliens forecloses consideration by the courts of petitioners' contentions that the Constitution and laws of the United States constitutionally enacted forbid their trial by military commission. As announced in our per curiam opinion we have resolved those questions by our conclusion that the Commission has jurisdiction to try the charge preferred against petitioners. There is therefore no occasion to decide contentions of the parties unrelated to this issue. We pass at once to the consideration of the basis of the Commission's authority.

We are not here concerned with any question of the guilt or innocence of petitioners. Constitutional safeguards for the protection of all who are charged with offenses are not to be disregarded in order to inflict merited punishment on some who are guilty. Ex parte Milligan, 4 Wall. 119, 132, 18 L.Ed. 281; Tumey v. Ohio, 273 U.S. 510, 535, 47 S.Ct. 437, 445, 71 L.Ed. 749, 50 A.L.R. 1243; Hill v. Texas, 316 U.S. 400, 62 S.Ct. 1159, 1161, 1162, 86 L.Ed. 1559. But the detention and trial of petitioners—ordered by the President in the declared exercise of his powers as Commander in Chief of the Army in time of war and of grave public danger—are not to be set aside by the courts without the clear conviction that they are in conflict with the Constitution or laws of Congress constitutionally enacted.

Congress and the President, like the courts, possess no power not derived from the Constitution. But one of the objects of the Constitution, as declared by its preamble, is to 'provide for the common defence'. As a means to that end the Constitution gives to Congress the power to 'provide for the common Defence', Art. I, § 8, cl. 1; 'To raise and support Armies', 'To provide and maintain a Navy', Art. I, § 8, cls. 12, 13; and 'To make Rules for the Government and Regulation of the land and naval Forces', Art. I, § 8, cl. 14. Congress is given authority 'To declare War, grant Letters of Marque and Reprisal, and make Rules concerning Captures on Land and Water', Art. I, § 8, cl. 11; and 'To define and punish Piracies and Felonies committed on the high Seas, and Offenses against the Law of Nations', Art. I, § 8, cl. 10. And finally the Constitution authorizes Congress 'To make all Laws which shall be necessary and proper for carrying into Execution the foregoing Powers, and all other Powers vested by this Constitution in the Government of the United States, or in any Department or Officer thereof.' Art. I, § 8, cl. 18.

The Constitution confers on the President the 'executive Power', Art II, § 1, cl. 1, and imposes on him the duty to 'take Care that the Laws be faithfully executed'. Art. II, § 3. It makes him the Commander in Chief of the Army and Navy, Art. II, § 2, cl. 1, and empowers him to appoint and commission officers of the United States. Art. II, § 3, cl. 1.

The Constitution thus invests the President as Commander in Chief with the power to wage war which Congress has declared, and to carry into effect all laws passed by Congress for the conduct of war and for the government and regulation of the Armed Forces, and all laws defining and punishing offences against the law of nations, including those which pertain to the conduct of war.

By the Articles of War, 10 U.S.C. §§ 1471–1593, Congress has provided rules for the government of the Army. It has provided for the trial and punishment, by courts martial, of violations of the Articles by members of the armed forces and by specified classes of persons associated or serving with the Army. Arts. 1, 2. But the Articles also recognize the 'military commission' appointed by military command as an appropriate tribunal for the trial and punishment of offenses against the law of war not ordinarily tried by court martial. See Arts. 12, 15. Articles 38 and 46 authorize the President, with certain limitations, to prescribe the procedure for military commissions. Articles 81 and 82 authorize trial, either by court martial or military commission, of those charged with relieving, harboring or corresponding with the enemy and those charged with spying. And Article 15 declares that 'the provisions of these articles conferring jurisdiction upon courts-martial shall not be construed as depriving military commissions * * * or other military tribunals of concurrent jurisdiction in respect of offenders or offenses that by statute or by the law of war may be triable by such military commissions * * * or other military tribunals'. Article 2 includes among those persons subject to military law the personnel of our own military establishment. But this, as Article 12 provides, does not exclude from that class 'any other person who by the law of war is subject to trial by military tribunals' and who under Article 12 may be tried by court martial or under Article 15 by military commission.

Similarly the Espionage Act of 1917, which authorizes trial in the district courts of certain offenses that tend to interfere with the prosecution of war, provides that nothing contained in the act 'shall be deemed to limit the jurisdiction of the general courts-martial, military commissions, or naval courts-martial'. 50 U.S.C. § 38.

From the very beginning of its history this Court has recognized and applied the law of war as including that part of the law of nations which prescribes, for the conduct of war, the status, rights and duties of enemy nations as well as of enemy individuals. By the Articles of War, and especially Article 15, Congress has explicitly provided, so far as it may constitutionally do so, that military tribunals shall have jurisdiction to try offenders or offenses against the law of war in appropriate cases. Congress, in addition to making rules for the government of our Armed Forces, has thus exercised its authority to define and punish offenses against the law of nations by sanctioning, within constitutional limitations, the jurisdiction of military commissions to try persons for offenses which, according to the rules and precepts of the law of nations, and more particularly the law of war, are cognizable by such tribunals. And the President, as Commander in Chief, by his Proclamation in time of war has invoked that law. By his Order creating the present Commission he has undertaken to exercise the authority conferred upon him by Congress, and also such authority as the Constitution itself gives the Commander in Chief, to direct the performance of those functions which may constitutionally be performed by the military arm of the nation in time of war.

An important incident to the conduct of war is the adoption of measures by the military command not only to repel and defeat the enemy, but to seize and subject to disciplinary measures those enemies who in their attempt to thwart or impede our military effort have violated the law of war. It is unnecessary for present purposes to determine to what extent the President as Commander in Chief has constitutional power to create military commissions without the support of Congressional legislation. For here Congress has authorized trial of offenses against the law of war before such commissions. We are concerned only with the question whether it is within the constitutional power of the national government to place petitioners upon trial before a military commission for the offenses with which they are charged. We must therefore first inquire whether any of the acts charged is an offense against the law of war cognizable before a military tribunal, and if so whether the Constitution prohibits the trial. We may assume that there are acts regarded in other countries, or by some writers on international law, as offenses against the law of war which would not be triable by military tribunal here, either because they are not recognized by our courts as violations of the law of war or because they are of that class of offenses constitutionally triable only by a jury. It was upon such grounds that the Court denied the right to proceed by military tribunal in Ex parte Milligan, supra. But as we shall show, these petitioners were charged with an offense against the law of war which the Constitution does not require to be tried by jury.

It is no objection that Congress in providing for the trial of such offenses has not itself undertaken to codify that branch of international law or to mark its precise boundaries, or to enumerate or define by statute all the acts which that law condemns. An Act of Congress punishing 'the crime of piracy as defined by the law of nations' is an appropriate exercise of its constitutional authority, Art. I, § 8, cl. 10, 'to define and punish' the offense since it has adopted by reference the sufficiently precise definition of international law. United States v. Smith, 5 Wheat. 153, 5 L.Ed. 57; see The Marianna Flora, 11 Wheat. 1, 40, 41, 6 L.Ed. 405; United States v. The Malek Adhel, 2 How. 210, 232, 11 L.Ed. 239; The Ambrose Light, D.C., 25 F. 408, 423, 428; 18 U.S.C. § 481. Similarly by the reference in the 15th Article of War to 'offenders or offenses that * * * by the law of war may be triable by such military commissions', Congress has incorporated by reference, as within the jurisdiction of military commissions, all offenses which are defined as such by the law of war (compare Dynes v. Hoover, 20 How. 65, 82, 15 L.Ed. 838), and which may constitutionally be included within that jurisdiction. Congress had the choice of crystalizing in permanent form and in minute detail every offense against the law of war, or of adopting the system of common law applied by military tribunals so far as it should be recognized and deemed applicable by the courts. It chose the latter course.

By universal agreement and practice the law of war draws a distinction between the armed forces and the peaceful populations of belligerent nations and also between those who are lawful and unlawful combatants. Lawful combatants are subject to capture and detention as prisoners of war by opposing military forces. Unlawful combatants are likewise subject to capture and detention, but in addition they are subject to trial and punishment by military tribunals for acts which render their belligerency unlawful. The spy who secretly and without uniform passes the military lines of a belligerent in time of war, seeking to gather military information and communicate it to the enemy, or an enemy combatant who without uniform comes secretly through the lines for the purpose of waging war by destruction of life or property, are familiar examples of belligerents who are generally deemed not to be entitled to the status of prisoners of war, but to be offenders against the law of war subject to trial and punishment by military tribunals. See Winthrop, Military Law, 2d Ed., pp. 1196–1197, 1219–1221; Instructions for the Government of Armies of the United States in the Field, approved by the President, General Order No. 100, April 24, 1863, sections IV and V.

Such was the practice of our own military authorities before the adoption of the Constitution, and during the Mexican and Civil Wars.

. . .

Our Government, by thus defining lawful belligerents entitled to be treated as prisoners of war, has recognized that there is a class of unlawful belligerents not entitled to that privilege, including those who though combatants do not wear 'fixed and distinctive emblems'. And by Article 15 of the Articles of War Congress has made provision for their trial and punishment by military commission, according to 'the law of war'.

By a long course of practical administrative construction by its military authorities, our Government has likewise recognized that those who during time of war pass surreptitiously from enemy territory into our own, discarding their uniforms upon entry, for the commission of hostile acts involving destruction of life or property, have the status of unlawful combatants punishable as such by military commission. This precept of the law of war has been so recognized in practice both here and abroad, and has so generally been accepted as valid by authorities on international law that we think it must be regarded as a rule or principle of the law of war recognized by this Government . . .

Specification 1 of the First charge is sufficient to charge all the petitioners with the offense of unlawful belligerency, trial of which is within the jurisdiction of the Commission, and the admitted facts affirmatively show that the charge is not merely colorable or without foundation.

Specification 1 states that petitioners 'being enemies of the United States and acting for * * * the German Reich, a belligerent enemy nation, secretly and covertly passed, in civilian dress, contrary to the law of war, through the military and naval lines and defenses of the United States * * * and went behind such lines, contrary to the law of war, in civilian dress * * * for the purpose of committing * * * hostile acts, and, in particular, to destroy certain war industries, war utilities and war materials within the United States'.

This specification so plainly alleges violation of the law of war as to require but brief discussion of petitioners' contentions. As we have seen, entry upon our territory in time of war by enemy belligerents, including those acting under the direction of the armed forces of the enemy, for the purpose of destroying property used or useful in prosecuting the war, is a hostile and war-like act. It subjects those who participate in it without uniform to the punishment prescribed by the law of war for unlawful belligerents. It is without significance that petitioners were not alleged to have borne conventional weapons or that their proposed hostile acts did not necessarily contemplate collision with the Armed Forces of the United States. Paragraphs 351 and 352 of the Rules of Land Warfare, already referred to, plainly contemplate that the hostile acts and purposes for which unlawful belligerents may be punished are not limited to assaults on the Armed Forces of the United States. Modern warfare is directed at the destruction of enemy war supplies and the implements of their production and transportation quite as much as at the armed forces. Every consideration which makes the unlawful belligerent punishable is equally applicable whether his objective is the one or the other. The law of war cannot rightly treat those agents of enemy armies who enter our territory, armed with explosives intended for the destruction of war industries and supplies, as any the less belligerent enemies than are agents similarly entering for the purpose of destroying fortified places or our Armed Forces. By passing our boundaries for such purposes without uniform or other emblem signifying their belligerent status, or by discarding that means of identification after entry, such enemies become unlawful belligerents subject to trial and punishment.

Citizenship in the United States of an enemy belligerent does not relieve him from the consequences of a belligerency which is unlawful because in violation of the law of war. Citizens who associate themselves with the military arm of the enemy government, and with its aid, guidance and direction enter this country bent on hostile acts are enemy belligerents within the meaning of the Hague Convention and the law of war. Cf. Gates v. Goodloe, 101 U.S. 612, 615, 617, 618, 25 L.Ed. 895. It is as an enemy belligerent that petitioner Haupt is charged with entering the United States, and unlawful belligerency is the gravamen of the offense of which he is accused.

Nor are petitioners any the less belligerents if, as they argue, they have not actually committed or attempted to commit any act of depredation or entered the theatre or zone of active military operations. The argument leaves out of account the nature of the offense which the Government charges and which the Act of Congress, by incorporating the law of war, punishes. It is that each petitioner, in circumstances which gave him the status of an enemy belligerent, passed our military and naval lines and defenses or went behind those lines, in civilian dress and with hostile purpose. The offense was complete when with that purpose they entered—or, having so entered, they remained upon—our territory in time of war without uniform or other appropriate means of identification. For that reason, even when committed by a citizen, the offense is distinct from the crime of treason defined in Article III, § 3 of the Constitution, since the absence of uniform essential to one is irrelevant to the other.

But petitioners insist that even if the offenses with which they are charged are offenses against the law of war, their trial is subject to the requirement of the Fifth Amendment that no person shall be held to answer for a capital or otherwise infamous crime unless on a presentment or indictment of a grand jury, and that such trials by Article III, § 2, and the Sixth Amendment must be by jury in a civil court. Before the Amendments, § 2 of Article III, the Judiciary Article, had provided: 'The Trial of all Crimes, except in Cases of Impeachment, shall be by Jury', and had directed that 'such Trial shall be held in the State where the said Crimes shall have been committed'.

Presentment by a grand jury and trial by a jury of the vicinage where the crime was committed were at the time of the adoption of the Constitution familiar parts of the machinery for criminal trials in the civil courts. But they were procedures unknown to military tribunals, which are not courts in the sense of the Judiciary Article, Ex parte Vallandigham, 1 Wall. 243, 17 L.Ed. 589; In re Vidal, 179 U.S. 126, 21 S.Ct. 48, 45 L.Ed. 118; cf. Williams v. United States, 289 U.S. 553, 53 S.Ct. 751, 77 L.Ed. 1372, and which in the natural course of events are usually called upon to function under conditions precluding resort to such procedures. As this Court has often recognized, it was not the purpose or effect of § 2 of Article III, read in the light of the common law, to enlarge the then existing right to a jury trial. The object was to preserve unimpaired trial by jury in all those cases in which it had been recognized by the common law and in all cases of a like nature as they might arise in the future, District of Columbia v. Colts, 282 U.S. 63, 51 S.Ct. 52, 75 L.Ed. 177, but not to bring within the sweep of the guaranty those cases in which it was then well understood that a jury trial could not be demanded as of right.

. . .

In the light of this long-continued and consistent interpretation we must conclude that § 2 of Article III and the Fifth and Sixth Amendments cannot be taken to have extended the right to demand a jury to trials by military commission, or to have required that offenses against the law of war not triable by jury at common law be tried only in the civil courts.

. . .

Section 2 of the Act of Congress of April 10, 1806, 2 Stat. 371, derived from the Resolution of the Continental Congress of August 21, 1776, imposed the death penalty on alien spies 'according to the law and usage of nations, by sentence of a general court martial'. This enactment must be regarded as a contemporary construction of both Article III, § 2, and the Amendments as not foreclosing trial by military tribunals, without a jury, of offenses against the law of war committed by enemies not in or associated with our Armed Forces. It is a construction of the Constitution which has been followed since the founding of our government, and is now continued in the 82nd Article of War. Such a construction is entitled to the greatest respect. Stuart v. Laird, 1 Cranch, 299, 309, 2 L.Ed. 115; Field v. Clark, 143 U.S. 649, 691, 12 S.Ct. 495, 504, 36 L.Ed. 294; United States v. Curtiss–Wright Corp., 299 U.S. 304, 328, 57 S.Ct. 216, 224, 81 L.Ed. 255. It has not hitherto been challenged, and so far as we are advised it has never been suggested in the very extensive literature of the subject that an alien spy, in time of war, could not be tried by military tribunal without a jury.

The exception from the Amendments of 'cases arising in the land or naval forces' was not aimed at trials by military tribunals, without a jury, of such offenses against the law of war. Its objective was quite different—to authorize the trial by court martial of the members of our Armed Forces for all that class of crimes which under the Fifth and Sixth Amendments might otherwise have been deemed triable in the civil courts. The cases mentioned in the exception are not restricted to those involving offenses against the law of war alone, but extend to trial of all offenses, including crimes which were of the class traditionally triable by jury at common law.

Since the Amendments, like § 2 of Article III, do not preclude all trials of offenses against the law of war by military commission without a jury when the offenders are aliens not members of our Armed Forces, it is plain that they present no greater obstacle to the trial in like manner of citizen enemies who have violated the law of war applicable to enemies. Under the original statute authorizing trial of alien spies by military tribunals, the offenders were outside the constitutional guaranty of trial by jury, not because they were aliens but only because they had violated the law of war by committing offenses constitutionally triable by military tribunal.

We cannot say that Congress in preparing the Fifth and Sixth Amendments intended to extend trial by jury to the cases of alien or citizen offenders against the law of war otherwise triable by military commission, while withholding it from members of our own armed forces charged with infractions of the Articles of War punishable by death. It is equally inadmissible to construe the Amendments—whose primary purpose was to continue unimpaired presentment by grand jury and trial by petit jury in all those cases in which they had been customary—as either abolishing all trials by military tribunals, save those of the personnel of our own armed forces, or what in effect comes to the same thing, as imposing on all such tribunals the necessity of proceeding against unlawful enemy belligerents only on presentment and trial by jury. We conclude that the Fifth and Sixth Amendments did not restrict whatever authority was conferred by the Constitution to try offenses against the law of war by military commission, and that petitioners, charged with such an offense not required to be tried by jury at common law, were lawfully placed on trial by the Commission without a jury.

Petitioners, and especially petitioner Haupt, stress the pronouncement of this Court in the Milligan case, 4 Wall. page 121, 18 L.Ed. 281, that the law of war 'can never be applied to citizens in states which have upheld the authority of the government, and where the courts are open and their process unobstructed'.

Elsewhere in its opinion, 4 Wall. at pages 118, 121, 122, and 131, 18 L.Ed. 281, the Court was at pains to point out that Milligan, a citizen twenty years resident in Indiana, who had never been a resident of any of the states in rebellion, was not an enemy belligerent either entitled to the status of a prisoner of war or subject to the penalties imposed upon unlawful belligerents. We construe the Court's statement as to the inapplicability of the law of war to Milligan's case as having particular reference to the facts before it. From them the Court concluded that Milligan, not being a part of or associated with the armed forces of the enemy, was a non-belligerent, not subject to the law of war save as—in circumstances found not there to be present and not involved here— martial law might be constitutionally established.

The Court's opinion is inapplicable to the case presented by the present record. We have no occasion now to define with meticulous care the ultimate boundaries of the jurisdiction of military tribunals to try persons according to the law of war. It is enough that petitioners here, upon the conceded facts, were plainly within those boundaries, and were held in good faith for trial by military commission, charged with being enemies who, with the purpose of destroying war materials and utilities, entered or after entry remained in our territory without uniform—an offense against the law of war. We hold only that those particular acts constitute an offense against the law of war which the Constitution authorizes to be tried by military commission.

. . .

Accordingly, we conclude that Charge I, on which petitioners were detained for trial by the Military Commission, alleged an offense which the President is authorized to order tried by military commission; that his Order convening the Commission was a lawful order and that the Commission was lawfully constituted; that the petitioners were held in lawful custody and did not show cause for their discharge. It follows that the orders of the District Court should be affirmed, and that leave to file petitions for habeas corpus in this Court should be denied.

Mr. Justice MURPHY took no part in the consideration or decision of these cases.

Orders of District Court affirmed and leave to file petitions for habeas corpus in the Supreme Court denied.

Notes and Questions

1. Does Quirin provide adequate support for the issuance of the Military Order by the President?

2. Consider the following commentary on the President's legal authority to establish the military commissions.

* * *

b. Neal K. Katyal and Laurence H. Tribe, Waging War, Deciding Guilt: Trying the Military Tribunals, 111 Yale L.J. 1259, 1269–1270 (2002):

> ... [T]he Bush Administration has sought to convert the singular Commander-in-Chief Clause into a textual warrant for exceptional unilateralism.... In the theatre of a war, the President does not need congressional permission to decide how and when, within the laws of war and other applicable rules of international law, to take custody of enemy combatants upon their capture or surrender for the purpose of detention until the war ends and repatriation is possible. That much is implicit in the commander-in-chief function itself.

> The moment the President moves beyond detaining enemy combatants as war prisoners to actually adjudicating their guilt and meting out punishment, however, he has moved outside the perimeter of his role as Commander-in-Chief of our armed forces and entered a zone that involves judging and punishing alleged violations of the laws, including the law of nations.... In that adjudicatory and punitive zone, the fact that the President entered wearing his military garb should not blind us to the fact that he is now pursuing a different goal—assessing guilt and meting out retrospective justice rather than waging war.

c. Jonathan J. Paust, Antiterrorism Military Commissions: Courting Illegality, 23 Michigan Mich. J. Int'l L. 1, 5–9 (2001):

> The President's Commander-in-Chief power to set up military commissions applies only during actual war within a war zone or relevant occupied territory and apparently ends when peace is finalized. ...

* * *

d. Curtis A. Bradley and Jack L. Goldsmith, The Constitutional Validity of Military Commissions, 5 Green Bag 2d 249, 252, Spring 2002:

> A strong argument can be made that President Bush has independent power as Commander in Chief, to establish military commissions to try

war crimes violations, even in the absence of affirmative congressional authorization. Presidents have long claimed that their constitutional authority to manage the war effort includes the power to create military commissions, and they have exercised such a power throughout U.S. history.The Supreme Court in Quirin appeared to agree with this claim in dicta, but, because it found congressional authorization, the Court concluded that it was unnecessary to determine the extent of the President's independent power to create military commissions.

e.   In his article, The Threat to Patriotism, The New York Review of Books, February 28, 2002, Ronald Dworkin draws a connection between the USA PATRIOT Act, the tightening of U.S. immigration enforcement, and promulgation of the President's military tribunal order and argues that Al Qaeda has succeeded in unleashing an attack on the U.S. Constitution itself, and that America ought to fight every temptation to change its Constitutional system in order to meet this terrorist threat.

3.   Other criticisms and concerns regarding the establishment of military tribunals under the President's Military Order have been expressed. Consider, for example, the following:

a.   Harold Hongju Koh, The Case against Military Commissions, 96 Am. J. Int'l L 337, 339–342 (2002):

> Fundamentally, the Military Order undermines the constitutional principle of separation of power. For under the order, the president directs his subordinates to create military commissions, to determine who shall be tried before them, and to choose the finders of fact, law, and guilt. However, detailed its rules and procedures may be, a military commission is not an independent court, and is commissioners are not genuinely independent decisionmakers. Historically, a military commission is neither a court nor a tribunal, but "an advisory board of officers, convened for the purpose of informing the conscience of the commanding officer, in cases where he might act for himself if he chose." Commissioners are not independent judges, but usually military officers who are ultimately answerable to the secretary of defense and the president, who prosecute the cases. 'Such blending of functions in one branch of government,' Justice Black recognized, 'is the objectionable thing which the draftsmen of the Constitution endeavored to prevent by providing for the separation of governmental powers.'

> . . .

> These specific legal deficiencies stand atop a much broader rule-of-law concern. International law permits the United States to redress the unprovoked killing of thousands on September 11, 2001, by itself engaging in an armed attack upon the Al Qaeda perpetrators. But should those culprits be captured, the United States must try, not lynch, them to promote four legal values higher than vengeance: holding them accountable for their crimes against humanity; telling the world the truth about those crimes; reaffirming that such acts violate all norms of civilized society; and demonstrating that law-abiding societies, unlike terrorists, respect human rights by channeling retribution into criminal punishment for even the most heinous outlaws.

The Military Order undermines each of these values. . . .

. . .

The use of military commissions potentially endangers Americans overseas by undermining the U.S. government's ability to protest effectively when other countries use such tribunals. But just as troubling, espousing military commissions undermines U.S. moral leadership abroad when that leadership is needed the most. The United States regularly takes other countries to task for military proceedings that violate basic civil rights. How, then, can the United States be surprised when its European allies refuse to extradite captured terrorist suspects to U.S. military justice?

b.   In Jack Goldsmith and Cass R. Sunstein, "Military Tribunals And Legal Culture: What A Difference Sixty Years Makes," 19 Const. Comment. 261, Spring 2001, the authors argue that the difference in the reactions to President Roosevelt's use of military tribunals and President Bush's tribunal order (that is, the fact that the World War II use of tribunals was not controversial) owes to social changes, including the "decreased trust of executive and military authority, and a strengthened commitment to individual rights in the legal system and broader culture."

c.   Also see George P. Fletcher, The Military Tribunal Order: On Justice and War: Contradictions in the Proposed Military Tribunals, 25 Harv. J.L. & Pub. Pol'y 635, 639 (2002):

Through invoking the language of war, the President has ignored an important principle of the law that has always governed our military conflicts. If the "individuals" detained as combatants engaged in fighting for the enemy, they are entitled to treatment as prisoners of war. They cannot be tried for acts of violence that are normal and standard in fighting wars, and they must be released when hostilities cease. As combatants they may be liable for war crimes but not for violations of the criminal code of the country they have attacked. Yet one can imagine the Administration's response to this critique: "this is not really a war; this is bringing them to justice." This is the great advantage of conceptual confusion. When it suits its purposes, the administration justifies its actions as the pursuit of justice; if the justice argument fails, the move is to think in the language of war and collective self-defense.

C.   Procedures used in the military tribunals—Due Process concerns

As some of the comments indicate, criticisms were directed against the prospect of prosecution before a military commission, reflecting concerns about the lack of procedural protections—"the United States must try, not lynch, them . . . ," see Koh, supra, at 340. On March 21, 2002, the Department of Defense issued regulations under the authority of the Military Order. These regulations can be found at *http://www.defenselink.mil/news/Mar2002/d20020321ord.pdf*.

* * *

Notes and Questions

1. At least some of the concerns about the adequacy of procedural guarantees before the commissions were allayed by the Department of Defense regulations. Among other provisions, the regulations provide: a) for the detailing of military counsel to the accused but they also provide that the accused may select a military officer who is a judge advocate to replace the detailed defense counsel or the accused may retain the services of a civilian attorney of the accused's choosing and at no expense to the United States; b) the accused is be furnished in advance with a statement of the charges; c) the accused shall be presumed innocent until proven guilty. d) the standard of proof is to be proof beyond a reasonable doubt; e) the accused is not required to testify and no adverse inference is to be drawn from the failure to testify; f) the accused through counsel has a right to cross examine prosecution's witnesses; g) the accused shall be given access to the evidence the prosecution intends to produce at both the trial and at the sentencing proceedings; h) the proceedings will be open to public except where there are grounds for closure—for example, to protect classified information; and the accused may not be tried again on a charge that has become final. The regulations also provide for what would have probative value to a reasonable person as the standard of admissibility for evidence. Hearsay evidence may be considered by the Commission. A finding of guilt may be made by two thirds vote while a death sentence requires a unanimous vote. The record of the trial is to be reviewed by a review panel appointed by the Secretary of Defense, then by the Secretary of Defense, and then by the President.

2. Consider the following commentary on the DoD regulations.

Eric M. Freedman, The Bush Military Tribunals: Where Have We Been? Where Are We Going?" ABA, Crim J. Section, 17 Crim Justice 14, 17 (2002):

... [T]he tribunal regulations that the government eventually published ... seemed to ameliorate some of the key constitutional concerns....

Ronald Dworkin, The Trouble with Tribunals, The New York Review of Books, April 25, 2002 criticizes the rules established in March 2002 for military tribunals, saying they fail to uphold some of the key procedural safeguards necessary for justice and promised by the President in his original order, such as public access and release of detainees in the event of a not-guilty verdict.

Harold J. Koh, op cit. supra, note 3 p. ___, at 338–339 :

On its face the [President's Military] [O]rder authorizes the Department of Defense to dispense with the basic procedural guarantees required by the Bill of Rights, the International Covenant on Civil and Political Rights and the Third Geneva Convention of 1949. Insofar as any of these guarantees—which include the presumption of innocence, the rights to be informed of charges and equal treatment before the courts, public hearings, independent and impartial decision makers, the rights to speedy trial, confrontation, and counsel of one's own choosing, the privilege against self-incrimination, and review by a higher tribunal according to law—are subject to suspension in time of emergency, the Bush administration has taken no formal steps to enable it to derogate from them.

Koh, supra, at footnote 9:

While the regulations issued by the Department of Defense . . . respond to the heated criticism of the Military Order by providing more courtlike guarantees, they pointedly omit any opportunity for judicial review before a civilian court. The irony . . . is that proceedings before these commissions will now be likely to suffer from many of the inefficiencies associated with judicial proceedings, but without garnering in return the global respect that genuine, credible judicial proceedings are accorded.

3.   While the DOD regulations do not provide for judicial review, they do provide for review by a panel and ultimate review by the Secretary of Defense and President. Why are these provisions for review not adequate? Is the problem with this arrangement the fact that the reviewing panel is within the military establishment and thus subject to the authority of the Secretary of Defense? Does review by the President ameliorate these concerns? Does review by the judiciary guarantee a kind of independence from superior authority that is needed to guarantee impartiality and freedom from undue influence? Under conventional military law, defendants can appeal to the U.S. Court of Appeals for the Armed Forces, and ultimately to the U.S. Supreme Court. Why not for commissions?

4.   Probably to respond to the type of concerns reflected in the previous note, four distinguished individuals from outside the military (including a former US circuit judge and Attorney General, another former cabinet official, a former congressman and a former justice of a state supreme court) were appointed to the reviewing panel. As for the comparison with the Uniform Code of Military Justice and the notion that only review by the judiciary adequately protects the rights of the accused, consider the following comment of Judge Robertson in Hamdan v. Rumsfeld, (the case is reproduced, infra p. ___):

And, as for the President's naming himself or the Secretary of Defense as the final reviewing authority, that, after all, is what a military commission is. If Hamdan is triable by any military tribunal, the fact that final review of a finding of guilt would reside in the President or his designee is not "contrary to or inconsistent with" the UCMJ.

5.   Are there other important procedural and other protections that accrue to criminal defendants in the civilian courts that are not provided for under the terms of the Military Order or the DOD regulations, apart from the opportunity for judicial review mentioned by Professor Koh? What might they be? Consider, for example, whether there is any speedy trial guarantee? Or, for that matter, guarantee of any trial? Relate the absence of such a protection back to the issues regarding extended detention discussed in Chapter 7, supra. How significant is the absence of such protections? Could the government hold a defendant indefinitely without any trial in the civilian system? Could the government hold a terrorist suspect indefinitely without trial under this system?

6.   The regulations also make the standard of admissibility of evidence what would have probative value to a reasonable person. This is the type of admissibility standard usually used in administrative proceedings. In such proceedings, other detailed rules of evidence, e.g. regulating the admissibility of hearsay and character evidence are not applicable. Before the military tribunals, too, it would appear that there would be no specific bar to the admissibility of hearsay evidence unless it amounted to the type of evidence that would not have probative value to a reasonable person. Is the absence of rules addressing the admissibility of hearsay a serious defect in the tribunal process? Does it mean that an accused could be convicted based on affidavits, without the witnesses appearing before the tribunal? How much protection is afforded by the fact that a conviction must be based on proof beyond a reasonable doubt?

7.   The issue that concerned Judge Robertson in Hamdan v. Rumsfeld, infra, p. at p. , was the fact that the accused could be excluded from the courtroom when classified information was being presented (although under the Commission Procedures, his Detailed Defense Counsel who would have security clearance would be present). How significant is the exclusion of the defendant if his counsel is allowed to be present? See Judge Robertson's comments on this issue, infra, p. ___.

8.   On February 28, 2003, the Pentagon released a draft, Crimes and Elements for Trials by Military Commission—seeking public comment before finalizing the document. Recall that section 4 of the President's Military Order authorizing the military commissions had referred to "any and all offenses triable by military commission." On April, 30, 2003, the draft was finalized [It can be found at 32 CFR 11.1 et seq.].

* * *

Notes and Questions

1.   In an article titled War Crimes Proceedings in Iraq? The Bush Administration's Dilemma, posted on Findlaw.com on April 4, 2003, Professor George Fletcher made the following comments regarding the February 28, 2003 draft of Military Commission Instruction No. 2, Crimes and Elements for Trials by Military Commission. Professor Fletcher viewed Instruction No. 2 as aimed at use in prosecutions in post-war Iraq. (Whether or not he is correct in that view, the Crimes and Elements provide the substantive crime foundation for prosecutions of the Guantanamo detainees before military commissions):

> The Instruction's subject matter is described as "Crimes and Elements for Trials by Military Commission." The document defines twenty-four crimes that the government could prosecute against suspected foreign terrorists. The list of crimes is revealing, for it demonstrates that the Administration is contemplating the use of military tribunals in occupied Iraq to prosecute the Iraqi leadership for war crimes.

> Most of the crimes described in the Instruction come straight from the Geneva Conventions, and run parallel to the war crimes defined in the Rome Statute [that] established the International Criminal Court. These

include the crimes of killing civilians, taking hostages, using poisonous weapons, and killing or injuring treacherously.

But, significantly, the list includes some new offenses—crimes not now recognized under American law. For example, the term "terrorism" is used, much like the phrase "organized crime," to refer to a category of offenses, rather than a single offense. No crime by the name of "terrorism" is to be found in either the Rome Statute or U.S. federal law.

. . .

The crime of "terrorism," as defined by the Instruction, has some unusual characteristics. Most of these conform to the usual federal definition of terrorism, which stresses that the perpetrator must have a political purpose of influencing a government by "intimidation or coercion." In addition, however, the terrorism must be associated with an "armed conflict" and it must be committed by persons who do not enjoy "combat immunity."

A perfect example of conduct targeted by this latter provision is the recent suicide bombing committed by Iraqi personnel wearing civilian clothes, and resulting in the death of four American soldiers.

. . .

The debate that will occur when the Administration actually announces its intention to use tribunals is predictable. Those who supported military tribunals when the President issued his executive order in November 2001, will still support them. Those who opposed them then, will still oppose them now.

Opponents will have good reason for continuing their opposition: The tribunals infringe basic guarantees of due process. They permit secret hearings; the death penalty can be imposed by the unanimous vote of three military judges; there is no appeal to civilian courts. The standards of fairness fall far short not only of constitutional guarantees but of the simplified procedures allowed in general courts martial.

Nevertheless, we should acknowledge some positive points in the Instruction. It attempts to reach precision in the definition of offenses. It also employs the concepts of "combat immunity" and "belligerent immunity"—thus avoiding the confusing phrase "unlawful combatant." Understanding the significance of this shift in vocabulary requires a brief explanation.

The point of the new definition of "belligerent immunity" is to make it clear that fighters who qualify as combatants under Geneva Convention III—those who wear uniforms, carry their arms openly, and fight under a chain of command—are not going to be considered terrorists. They will not be subject to prosecution unless they exceed the privileges of warfare by killing civilians or committing some other well-defined war crime. Otherwise, they enjoy immunity and cannot be prosecuted for killing soldiers and destroying the instruments of warfare belonging to the enemy.

The unfortunate expression "unlawful combatant" used in the leading U.S. Supreme Court case of *Ex parte Quirin* has fostered misconceptions about the punishability of combatants in civilian clothes. For instance, it has led many otherwise thoughtful commentators to think that merely crossing enemy lines without wearing a uniform should be considered a punishable war crime.

According to the Instruction, however, no unlawful combatant commits a crime merely by failing to qualify for immunity under the Geneva Convention. The relevant crime, these new regulations make clear, is not failing to enjoy combat immunity in itself. Rather, the crime occurs when someone who does not qualify as a combatant under international law commits a homicidal or destructive act against military personnel.

2. As of this writing, four men had been charged under the Crimes and Elements, supra, and their trials had begun before military commissions: Salim Ahmed Hamdan; Ibrahim Ahmed Mahmoud Al Qosi; Ali Hamza Ahmad Sulayman Al Bahlul; and David Hicks. Each of the first three was charged with conspiracy to commit various offenses including attacking civilians, murder by an unprivileged belligerent, and terrorism. In addition to being charged with a similar conspiracy offense, David Hicks was also charged with the substantive offenses of attempted murder by an unprivileged belligerent and aiding the enemy. Various overt acts were alleged against each of the three. It appears from the charge sheets that among other al Qaeda-linked activities, it is alleged that Hamdan served as Osam Bin Laden's driver; al Bahlul engaged in various media-related activities in support of al Qaeda and served as Bin Laden's body guard; al Qosi served as an accountant and financial official in various al Qaeda-linked enterprises and also served as one of Bin Laden's drivers and body guards; and Hicks received military training in al Qaeda training camps and fought in combat against Coalition forces.

3. A Department of Defense news release dated Aug. 27, 2004 (No. 839–04) reported that an additional eleven detainees have been deemed eligible for similar trials for violations of the law of war.

4. Various military commissions proceedings involving the defendants described in note 2 supra were conducted in the late summer and early fall, 2004. News reports regarding these proceedings reported that "officials acknowledge that the process is in turmoil." NY Times, Sept. 26, 2004, Pt I, 26. Among other problems, some of the trial panel's members were successfully challenged for bias or conflict of interest, and the translation system was inadequate. Ibid.

5. After the decision in Hamdan v. Rumsfeld, below, an order was issued holding in abeyance the four cases that had begun, pending the appeal in the Hamdan case.

HAMDAN v. RUMSFELD

344 F.Supp.2d 152 (D.D.C.2004).

ROBERTSON, District Judge.

Salim Ahmed Hamdan petitions for a writ of habeas corpus, challenging the lawfulness of the Secretary of Defense's plan to try him for alleged war crimes before a military commission convened under special orders issued by the President of the United States, rather than before a court-martial convened under the Uniform Code of Military Justice. The government moves to dismiss. Because Hamdan has not been determined by a competent tribunal to be an offender triable under the law of war, 10 U.S.C. § 821, and because in any event the procedures established for the Military Commission by the President's order are "contrary to or inconsistent" with those applicable to courts-martial, 10 U.S.C. § 836, Hamdan's petition will be **granted** in part. The government's motion will be **denied**. The reasons for these rulings are set forth below.

Hamdan was captured in Afghanistan in late 2001, during a time of hostilities in that country that followed the terrorist attacks in the United States on September 11, 2001 mounted by al Qaeda, a terrorist group harbored in Afghanistan. He was detained by American military forces and transferred sometime in 2002 to the detention facility set up by the Defense Department at Guantanamo Bay Naval Base, Cuba. On July 3, 2003, acting pursuant to the Military Order he had issued on November 13, 2001, and finding "that there is reason to believe that [Hamdan] was a member of al Qaida or was otherwise involved in terrorism directed against the United States," the President designated Hamdan for trial by military commission. Press Release, Dep't of Defense, President Determines Enemy Combatants Subject to His Military Order (July 3, 2003), http://www.defenselink.mil/releases/2003/nr20030703–0173.html. In December 2003, Hamdan was placed in a part of the Guantanamo Bay facility known as Camp Echo, where he was held in isolation. On December 18, 2003, military counsel was appointed for him. On February 12, 2004, Hamdan's counsel filed a demand for charges and speedy trial under Article 10 of the Uniform Code of Military Justice. On February 23, 2004, the legal advisor to the Appointing Authority ruled that the UCMJ did not apply to Hamdan's detention. On April 6, 2004, in the United States District Court for the Western District of Washington, Hamdan's counsel filed the petition for mandamus or habeas corpus that is now before this court. On July 9, 2004, Hamdan was formally charged with conspiracy to commit the following offenses: "attacking civilians; attacking civilian objects; murder by an unprivileged belligerent; destruction of property by an unprivileged belligerent; and terrorism." Dep't of Defense, Military Commission List of Charges for Salim Ahmed Hamdan, http:// www.defenselink.mil/news/Jul2004/d20040714hcc.pdf. Following the Supreme Court's decision on June 28, 2004, that federal district courts have jurisdiction of habeas petitions filed by Guantanamo Bay detainees, *Rasul v. Bush*, ___ U.S. ___, 124 S.Ct. 2686, 159 L.Ed.2d 548 (2004), and the Ninth Circuit's decision on July 8, 2004, that all such cases should be heard in the District of the District of Columbia, *Gherebi v. Bush*, 374 F.3d 727 (9th Cir.2004), the case was transferred here. . . .

Hamdan's petition is stated in eight counts. It alleges the denial of Hamdan's speedy trial rights in violation of Article 10 of the Uniform Code of Military Justice, 10 U.S.C. § 810 (count 1); challenges the nature and length of Hamdan's pretrial detention as a violation of the Third Geneva Convention (count 2) and of Common Article 3 of the Geneva Conventions (count 3); challenges the order establishing the Military Commission as a violation of the separation of powers doctrine (count 4) and as purporting to invest the Military Commission with authority that exceeds the law of war (count 7); challenges the creation of the Military Commission as a violation of the equal protection guarantees of the Fifth Amendment (count 5) and of 42 U.S.C. § 1981 (count 6); and argues that the Military Order does not, on its face, apply to Hamdan (count 8).

. . . The issues before me will be resolved as a matter of law. The only three facts that are necessary to my disposition of the petition for habeas corpus and of the cross-motion to dismiss are that Hamdan was captured in Afghanistan during hostilities after the 9/11 attacks, that he has asserted his entitlement to prisoner-of-war status under the Third Geneva Convention, and that the government has not convened a competent tribunal to determine whether Hamdan is entitled to such status. All of those propositions appear to be undisputed. . . .

. . .

The major premise of the government's argument that the President has untrammeled power to establish military tribunals is that his authority emanates from Article II of the Constitution and is inherent in his role as commander-in-chief. . . . In *Quirin* the Supreme Court located the power in Article I, § 8, emphasizing the President's *executive* power as commander-in-chief "to wage war which *Congress* has declared, and to carry into effect all laws passed by *Congress* for the conduct of war and for the government and regulation of the Armed Forces, and all laws defining and punishing offences against the law of nations, including those which pertain to the conduct of war." *Quirin,* 317 U.S. at 26, 63 S.Ct. at 10 *Quirin* stands for the proposition that the authority to appoint military commissions is found, not in the inherent power of the presidency, but in the Articles of War (a predecessor of the Uniform Code of Military Justice) by which *Congress* provided rules for the government of the army. *Id.* Thus, *Congress* provided for the trial by courts-martial of members of the armed forces and specific classes of persons associated with or serving with the army, *id.,* and "the *Articles [of War]* also recognize the 'military commission' appointed by military command as an appropriate tribunal for the trial and punishment of offenses against the law of war not ordinarily tried by court martial." *Id.* The President's authority to prescribe procedures for military commissions was conferred by Articles 38 and 46 of the Articles of War. *Id.* The *Quirin* Court sustained the President's order creating a military commission, because "[b]y his Order creating the . . . Commission [the President] has undertaken to exercise the authority conferred upon him by *Congress.* . . . " *Id.* at 28, 63 S.Ct. at 11. This sentence continues with the words " . . . and also such authority as the Constitution itself gives the Commander in Chief, to direct the performance of those functions which may constitutionally be performed by the military arm of the nation in time of war." *Id.* at 28, 63 S.Ct. at 11. That dangling idea is not explained—in *Quirin* or in later cases. The Court expressly found it unnecessary in *Quirin* "to determine to what extent the President as Commander in Chief has constitutional power to create military commissions without the support of Congressional legislation. For here Congress has authorized trial of offenses against the law of war before such commissions." *Id.*

. . .

If the President does have inherent power in this area, it is quite limited. Congress has the power to amend those limits and could do so tomorrow. Were the President to act outside the limits now set for military commissions now set for military commissions by [10 U.S.C. § 821], however, his actions would fall into the most restricted category of cases identified by Justice Jackson in his concurring opinion in *Youngstown Sheet & Tube Co. v. Sawyer,* 343 U.S. 579, 637, 72 S.Ct. 863, 96 L.Ed. 1153 (1952), in which "the President takes measures incompatible with the expressed or implied will of Congress," and in which the President's power is "at its lowest ebb."

. . . The United States has ratified the Geneva Convention Relative to the Treatment of Prisoners of War of August 12, 1949, 6 U.S.T. 3316, 74 U.N.T.S. 135 (the Third Geneva Convention). Afghanistan is a party to the Geneva Conventions. The Third Geneva Convention is acknowledged to be part of the law of war, 10/25/04 Tr. at 55; Military Commission Instruction No. 2, § (5)(G) (Apr. 30, 2003); 32 C.F.R. § 11.5(g), http://www.defensel ink.mil/news/May2003/d20030430milcom-instno2.pdf. It is applicable by its terms in "all cases of declared war or of any other armed conflict which may arise between two or more of the High Contracting Parties, even if the state of war is not recognized by one of them." Third Geneva Convention, art. 2. That language covers the hostilities in Afghanistan that were ongoing in late 2001, when Hamdan was captured there. If Hamdan is entitled to the protections accorded prisoners of war under the Third Geneva Convention, one need look no farther than Article 102 for the rule that requires his habeas petition to be granted:

> A prisoner of war can be validly sentenced only if the sentence has been pronounced by the same courts according to the same procedure as in the case of members of the armed forces of the Detaining Power, and if, furthermore, the provisions of the present Chapter have been observed.

The Military Commission is not such a court. Its procedures are not such procedures. The government does not dispute the proposition that prisoners of war may not be tried by military tribunal. Its position is that Hamdan is not entitled to the protections of the Third Geneva Convention at all, and certainly not to prisoner-of-war status, and that in any event the protections of the Third Geneva Convention are not enforceable by way of habeas corpus. (1) The government's first argument that the Third Geneva Convention does not protect Hamdan asserts that Hamdan was captured, not in the course of a conflict between the United States and Afghanistan, but in the course of a "separate" conflict with al Qaeda. That argument is rejected. The government apparently bases the argument on a Presidential "finding" that it claims is "not reviewable." The finding is set forth in Memorandum from the President, to the Vice President *et al.*, Humane Treatment of al Qaeda and Taliban Detainees(February 7, 2002), http:// www.library.law.pace.edu/research/020207_bushmemo.pdf, stating that the Third Geneva Convention applies to the Taliban detainees, but not to the al Qaeda detainees captured in Afghanistan, because al Qaeda is not a state party to the Geneva Conventions.

Notwithstanding the President's view that the United States was engaged in two separate conflicts in Afghanistan (the common public understanding is to the contrary, *see* Joan Fitzpatrick, Jurisdiction of Military Commissions and the Ambiguous War on Terrorism, 96 Am. J. Int'l. L. 345, 349 (2002) (conflict in Afghanistan was international armed conflict in which Taliban and al Qaeda joined forces against U.S. and its Afghan allies)), the government's attempt to separate the Taliban from al Qaeda for Geneva Convention purposes finds no support in the structure of the Conventions themselves, which are triggered by the place of the conflict, and not by what particular faction a fighter is associated with. Thus at some level—whether as a prisoner-of-war entitled to the full panoply of Convention protections or only under the more limited protections afforded by Common Article 3—the Third Geneva Convention applies to all persons detained in Afghanistan during the hostilities there.

The government next argues that, even if the Third Geneva Convention might theoretically apply to anyone captured in the Afghanistan theater, members of al Qaeda such as Hamdan are not entitled to POW status because they do not satisfy the test established by Article 4(2) of the Third Geneva Convention—they do not carry arms openly and operate under the laws and customs of war. Gov't Resp. at 35. *See also* The White House, Statement by the Press Secretary on the Geneva Convention (May 7, 2003), http:// www.whitehouse.gov/news/releases/2003/05/20030507–18.html. We know this, the government argues, because the President himself has determined that Hamdan was a member of al Qaeda or otherwise involved in terrorism against the United States. *Id.* Presidential determinations in this area, the government argues, are due "extraordinary deference.". Moreover (as the court was advised for the first time at oral argument on October 25, 2004) a Combatant Status Review Tribunal (CSRT) found, after a hearing on October 3, 2004, that Hamdan has the status of an enemy combatant "as either a member of or affiliated with Al Qaeda."

Article 5 of the Third Geneva Convention provides:

Should any doubt arise as to whether persons, having committed a belligerent act and having fallen into the hands of the enemy, belong to any of the categories enumerated in Article 4 such persons shall enjoy the protection of the present Convention until such time as their status has been determined by a competent tribunal.

. . . Hamdan has asserted his entitlement to POW status, and the Army's regulations provide that whenever a detainee makes such a claim his status is "in doubt." Army Regulation 190–8, § 1–6(a); . . . The Army's regulation is in keeping with general international understandings of the meaning of Article 5. Thus the government's position that no doubt has arisen as to Hamdan's status does not withstand scrutiny, and neither does the government's position that, if a hearing is required by Army regulations, "it was provided,". There is nothing in this record to suggest that a competent tribunal has determined that Hamdan is not a prisoner-of-war under the Geneva Conventions. Hamdan has appeared before the Combatant Status Review Tribunal, but the CSRT was not established to address detainees' status under the Geneva Conventions. It was established to comply with the Supreme Court's mandate in *Hamdi, supra,* to decide "whether the detainee is properly detained as an enemy combatant" for purposes of continued detention.

The government's legal position is that the CSRT determination that Hamdan was a member of or affiliated with al Qaeda is also determinative of Hamdan's prisoner-of-war status, since the President has already determined that detained al Qaeda members are not prisoners-of-war under the Geneva Conventions, . . . The President is not a "tribunal," however. The government must convene a competent tribunal (or address a competent tribunal already convened) and seek a specific determination as to Hamdan's status under the Geneva Conventions. Until or unless such a tribunal decides otherwise, Hamdan has, and must be accorded, the full protections of a prisoner-of-war.

. . .

The government has asserted a position starkly different from the positions and behavior of the United States in previous conflicts, one that can only weaken the United States' own ability to demand application of the Geneva Conventions to Americans captured during armed conflicts abroad. * * *

The government's putative trump card is that Hamdan's rights under the Geneva Conventions, if any, and whatever they are, are not enforceable by this Court—that, in effect, Hamdan has failed to state a claim upon which relief can be granted—because the Third Geneva Convention is not "self-executing" and does not give rise to a private cause of action. As an initial matter, it should be noted Hamdan has not asserted a "private right of action" under the Third Geneva Convention. The Convention is implicated in this case by operation of the statute that limits trials by military tribunal to "offenders . . . triable under the law of war." 10 U.S.C. § 821. The government's argument thus amounts to the assertion that no federal court has the authority to determine whether the Third Geneva Convention has been violated, or, if it has, to grant relief from the violation.

Treaties made under the authority of the United States are the supreme law of the land. United States courts are bound to give effect to international law and to international agreements of the United States unless such agreements are "non-self-executing." . . . . A treaty is "non-self-executing" if it manifests an intention that it not become effective as domestic law without enactment of implementing legislation; or if the Senate in consenting to the treaty requires implementing legislation; or if implementing legislation is constitutionally required.

The Geneva Conventions, of course, are all about prescribing rules by which the rights of individuals may be determined. Moreover, as petitioner and several of the *amici* have pointed out, it is quite clear from the legislative history of the ratification of the Geneva Conventions that Congress carefully considered what further legislation, if any, was deemed "required to give effect to the provisions contained in the four conventions," and found that only four provisions required implementing legislation. Articles 5 and 102, which are dispositive of Hamdan's case, *supra,* were not among them. What did require implementing legislation were Articles 129 and 130, providing for additional criminal penalties to be imposed upon those who engaged in "grave" violations of the Conventions, such as torture, medical experiments, or "wilful" denial of Convention protections, none of which is involved here. Third Geneva Convention, art. 130. . . . "Some provisions of an international agreement may be self-executing and others non-self-executing." Restatement (Third) of Foreign Relations Law of the United States § 111 cmt. h.

Because the Geneva Conventions were written to protect individuals, because the Executive Branch of our government has implemented the Geneva Conventions for fifty years without questioning the absence of implementing legislation, because Congress clearly understood that the Conventions did not require implementing legislation except in a few specific areas, and because nothing in the Third Geneva Convention itself manifests the contracting parties' intention that it not become effective as domestic law without the enactment of implementing legislation, I conclude that, insofar as it is pertinent here, the Third Geneva Convention is a self-executing treaty.[11] I further conclude that it is at least a matter of some doubt as to whether or not Hamdan is entitled to the protections of the Third Geneva Convention as a prisoner of war and that accordingly he must be given those protections unless and until the "competent tribunal" referred to in Article 5 concludes otherwise. It follows from those conclusions that Hamdan may not be tried for the war crimes he is charged with except by a court-martial duly convened under the Uniform Code of Military Justice.

There is an argument that, even if Hamdan does not have prisoner-of-war status, Common Article 3 would be violated by trying him for his

---

11. Hamdan is a citizen of Yemen. The government has refused permission for Yemeni diplomats to visit Hamdan at Guantanamo Bay. Decl. of Lieutenant Commander Charles Swift at 4 (May 3, 2004). It ill behooves the government to argue that enforcement of the Geneva Convention is only to be had through diplomatic channels.

alleged war crimes in this Military Commission. Abstention is appropriate, and perhaps required, on that question, because, unlike Article 102, which unmistakably mandates trial of POW's only by general court-martial and thus implicates the jurisdiction of the Military Commission, the Common Article 3 requirement of trial before a "regularly constituted court affording all the judicial guarantees which are recognized as indispensable by civilized peoples" has no fixed, term-of-art meaning. A substantial number of rights and procedures conferred by the UCMJ are missing from the Military Commission's rules. I am aware of no authority that defines the word "guarantees" in Common Article 3 to mean that all of these rights must be guaranteed in advance of trial. Only Hamdan's right to be present at every phase of his trial and to see all the evidence admitted against him is of immediate pretrial concern. That right is addressed in the next section of this opinion.

3.   In at least one critical respect, the procedures of the Military Commission are fatally contrary to or inconsistent with those of the Uniform Code of Military Justice.

In most respects, the procedures established for the Military Commission at Guantanamo under the President's order define a trial forum that looks appropriate and even reassuring when seen through the lens of American jurisprudence. The rules laid down by Military Commission Order No. 1, 32 C.F.R. § 9.3, provide that the defendant shall have appointed military counsel, that he may within reason choose to replace "detailed" counsel with another military officer who is a judge advocate if such officer is available, that he may retain a civilian attorney if he can afford it, that he must receive a copy of the charges in a language that he understands, that he will be presumed innocent until proven guilty, that proof of guilt must be beyond a reasonable doubt, that he must be provided with the evidence the prosecution intends to introduce at trial and with any exculpatory evidence known to the prosecution, with important exceptions discussed below, that he is not required to testify at trial and that the Commission may not draw an adverse inference from his silence, that he may obtain witnesses and documents for his defense to the extent necessary and reasonably available, that he may present evidence at trial and cross-examine prosecution witnesses, and that he may not be placed in jeopardy twice for any charge as to which a finding has become final.

The Military Commission is remarkably different from a court-martial, however, in two important respects. The first has to do with the structure of the reviewing authority after trial; the second, with the power of the appointing authority or the presiding officer to exclude the accused from hearings and deny him access to evidence presented against him.[12]

---

12. A great many other differences are identified and discussed in David Glazier, Kangaroo Court or Competent Tribunal? Judging the 21st Century Military Commis- sion, 89 Va. L.Rev. 2005, 2015–2020 (2003). Differences include (not an exhaustive list):

Article 16 requires that every court-martial consist of a military judge and no

Petitioner's challenge to the first difference is unsuccessful. It is true that the President has made himself, or the Secretary of Defense acting at his direction, the final reviewing authority, whereas under the Uniform Code of Military Justice there would be two levels of independent review by members of the Third Branch of government—an appeal to the Court of Appeals for the Armed Forces, whose active bench consists of five civilian judges, and possible review by the Supreme Court on writ of *certiorari*. The President has, however, established a Review Panel that will review the trial record and make a recommendation to the Secretary of Defense, or, if the panel finds an error of law, return the case for further proceedings. The President has appointed to that panel some of the most distinguished civilian lawyers in the country (who may receive temporary commissions to fulfill the requirement that they be "officers," *see* Military Commission Order No. 1(6)(H); 32 C.F.R. § 9.6(h)).[13] And, as for the President's naming himself or the Secretary of Defense as the final reviewing authority, that, after all, is what a

less than five members, as opposed to the Military Commission rules that require only three members. Military Commission Order No. 1 (4)(A); Article 10 of the UCMJ provides a speedy trial right, while the Military Commission rules provide none. Article 13 states that pre-trial detention should not be more rigorous than required to ensure defendant's presence, while the Commission rules contain no such provision and, in fact, Hamdan was held in solitary confinement in Camp Echo for over 10 months. Article 30 states that charges shall be signed by one with personal knowledge of them or who has investigated them. The Military Commission rules include no such requirement. Article 31 provides that the accused must be informed before interrogation of the nature of the accusation, his right not to make any statement, and that statements he makes may be used in proceedings against him, and further provides that statements taken from the accused in violation of these requirements may not be received in evidence at a military proceeding. The Military Commission rules provide that the accused may not be forced to testify at his own trial, but the rule does not "preclude admission of evidence of prior statements or conduct of the Accused." Military Commission Order No. 1(5)(F). Article 33 states that the accused will receive notice of the charges against him within eight days of being arrested or confined unless written reason is given why this is not practicable. The Military Commission rules include no such requirement, and in fact, Hamdan, after being moved to Camp Echo for pre-commission detainment, was not notified of

the charges against him for over 6 months. Article 38 provides the accused with certain rights before charges brought against him may be "referred" for trial, which include the right to counsel and the right to present evidence on his behalf. The Military Commission rules provide for no pre-trial referral process at all. Article 41 gives each side one peremptory challenge, while the Military Commission rules provide for none. Article 42 requires all trial participants to take an oath to perform their duties faithfully. The Military Commission rules allow witnesses to testify without taking an oath. Military Commission Order No. 1(6)(D). Article 52 requires three-fourths concurrence to impose a life sentence. The Military Commission rules only require two-thirds concurrence of the members to impose such a sentence. Military Commission Order No. 1 (6)(F). Article 26 provides that military judges do not vote on guilt or innocence. Under the Military Commission rules, the Presiding Officer is a voting member of the trial panel. Military Commission Order No. 1 (4)(A).

13. Griffin B. Bell, a former United States Circuit Judge and Attorney General; William T. Coleman, Jr., a former Secretary of Transportation; Edward George Biester, Jr., a former Congressman, former Pennsylvania Attorney General, and current Pennsylvania Judge; and Frank J. Williams, Chief Justice of the Rhode Island Supreme Court. *See* Dep't of Defense, Military Commission Biographies, http:// www.defenselink.mil/news/Aug2004/commissions_biographies.html

military commission is. If Hamdan is triable by any military tribunal, the fact that final review of a finding of guilt would reside in the President or his designee is not "contrary to or inconsistent with" the UCMJ.

The second difference between the procedures adopted for the Military Commission and those applicable in a court-martial convened under the Uniform Code of Military Justice is far more troubling. That difference lies in the treatment of information that is classified; information that is otherwise "protected"; or information that might implicate the physical safety of participants, including witnesses, or the integrity of intelligence and law enforcement sources and methods, or "other national security interests." *See* Military Commission Order No. 1(6)(B)(3); 32 C.F.R. § 9.6(b). Under the Secretary of Defense's regulations, the Military Commission must "[h]old open proceedings except where otherwise decided by the Appointing Authority or the Presiding Officer." *Id.* Detailed military defense counsel may not be excluded from proceedings, nor may evidence be received that has not been presented to detailed defense counsel, Military Commission Order No. 1 (6)(B)(3), (6)(D)(5); 32 C.F.R. §§ 9.6(b)(3), (d)(5). *The accused himself may be excluded from proceedings,* however, and evidence may be adduced that he will never see (because his lawyer will be forbidden to disclose it to him).

Thus, for example, testimony may be received from a confidential informant, and Hamdan will not be permitted to hear the testimony, see the witness's face, or learn his name. If the government has information developed by interrogation of witnesses in Afghanistan or elsewhere, it can offer such evidence in transcript form, or even as summaries of transcripts. *See* Military Commission Order No. 1(6)(D); 32 C.F.R. § 9.6(d). The Presiding Officer or the Appointing Authority may receive it in evidence if it meets the "reasonably probative" standard but forbid it to be shown to Hamdan. *See id.* As counsel for Hamdan put it at oral argument, portions of Mr. Hamdan's trial can be conducted "outside his presence. He can be excluded, not for his conduct, [but] because the government doesn't want him to know what's in it. They make a great big deal out of I can be there, but anybody who's practiced trial law, especially criminal law, knows that where you get your cross examination questions from is turning to your client and saying, 'Did that really happen? Is that what happened?' I'm not permitted to do that."

It is obvious beyond the need for citation that such a dramatic deviation from the confrontation clause could not be countenanced in any American court, particularly after Justice Scalia's extensive opinion in his decision this year in *Crawford v. Washington,* 541 U.S. 36, 124 S.Ct. 1354, 158 L.Ed.2d 177 (2004). It is also apparent that the right to trial "in one's presence" is established as a matter of international humanitarian and human rights law. But it is unnecessary to consider whether Hamdan can rely on any American constitutional notions of fairness, or whether the nature of these proceedings really is, as counsel asserts, akin to the Star Chamber, 10/25/04 Tr. at 97 (and violative of

Common Article 3), because—at least in this critical respect—the rules of the Military Commission are fatally "contrary to or inconsistent with" the statutory requirements for courts-martial convened under the Uniform Code of Military Justice, and thus unlawful.

In a general court-martial conducted under the UCMJ, the accused has the right to be present during sessions of the court:

> When the members of a court-martial deliberate or vote, only the members may be present. *All other proceedings,* including any other consultation of the members of the court with counsel or the military judge, shall be made a part of the record and *shall be in the presence of the accused,* the defense counsel, the trial counsel, and, in cases in which a military judge has been detailed to the court, the military judge. UCMJ Article 39(b), 10 U.S.C. § 839(b) (emphasis added).

Article 36 of the Uniform Code of Military Justice, 10 U.S.C. § 836(a), provides:

> Pretrial, trial, and post-trial procedures, including modes of proof, for cases arising under this chapter triable in courts-martial, military commissions and other military tribunals, and procedures for courts of inquiry, may be prescribed by the President by regulations which shall, so far as he considers practicable, apply the principles of law and the rules of evidence generally recognized in the trial of criminal cases in the United States district courts, but which may not be *contrary to or inconsistent with* this chapter. (Emphasis added.)

The government argues for procedural "flexibility" in military commission proceedings, asserting that construing Article 36 rigidly to mean that there can be no deviation from the UCMJ ... would have resulted in having virtually all of the UCMJ provisions apply to the military commissions, which would clearly be in conflict with historical practice, as recognized by the Supreme Court, ... and also inconsistent with Congress' intent, as reflected in Articles 21 and 36, and other provisions of the UCMJ that specifically mention commissions when a particular rule applies to them.But the language of Article 36 does not require rigid adherence to all of the UCMJ's rules for courts-martial. It proscribes only procedures and modes of proof that are "contrary to or inconsistent with" the UCMJ.

* * * Neither the President in his findings and determinations nor the government in its briefs has explained what "need" calls forth the abandonment of the right Hamdan would have under the UCMJ to be present at every stage of his trial and to confront and cross-examine all witnesses and challenge all evidence brought against him. Presumably the problems of dealing with classified or "protected" information underlie the President's blanket finding that using the regular rules is "not practicable." The military has not found it impracticable to deal with classified material in courts-martial, however. An extensive and elaborate process for dealing with classified material has evolved in the

Military Rules of Evidence. Mil. R. Evid. 505; *see* 10/25/04 Tr. 131–32. Alternatives to full disclosure are provided, Mil. R. Evid. 505(i)(4)(D). Ultimately, to be sure, the government has a choice to make, if the presiding military judge determines that alternatives may not be used and the government objects to disclosure of information. At that point, the conflict between the government's need to protect classified information and the defendant's right to be present becomes irreconcilable, and the only available options are to strike or preclude the testimony of a witness, or declare a mistrial, or find against the government on any issue as to which the evidence is relevant and material to the defense, or dismiss the charges (with or without prejudice), Mil. R. Evid. 505(i)(4)(E). The point is that the rules of the Military Commission resolve that conflict, not in favor of the defendant, but in favor of the government.

Unlike the other procedural problems with the Commission's rules that are discussed elsewhere in this opinion, this one is neither remote nor speculative: Counsel made the unrefuted assertion at oral argument that Hamdan has already been excluded from the *voir dire* process and that "the government's already indicated that for two days of his trial, he won't be there. And they'll put on the evidence at that point." Counsel's appropriate concern is not only for the established right of his client to be present at his trial, but also for the adequacy of the defense he can provide to his client. The relationship between the right to be present and the adequacy of defense is recognized by military courts, which have interpreted Article 39 of the UCMJ in the light of Confrontation Clause jurisprudence. . . .

A tribunal set up to try, possibly convict, and punish a person accused of crime that is configured in advance to permit the introduction of evidence and the testimony of witnesses out of the presence of the accused is indeed substantively different from a regularly convened court-martial. If such a tribunal is not a "regularly constituted court affording all the judicial guarantees which are recognized as indispensable by civilized peoples," it is violative of Common Article 3. That is a question on which I have determined to abstain. In the meantime, however, I cannot stretch the meaning of the Military Commission's rule enough to find it consistent with the UCMJ's right to be present. 10 U.S.C. § 839. A provision that permits the exclusion of the accused from his trial for reasons other than his disruptive behavior or his voluntary absence is indeed directly contrary to the UCMJ's right to be present. I must accordingly find on the basis of the statute that, so long as it operates under such a rule, the Military Commission cannot try Hamdan.

CONCLUSION

It is now clear, by virtue of the Supreme Court's decision in *Hamdi*, that the detentions of enemy combatants at Guantanamo Bay are not unlawful per se. The granting (in part) of Hamdan's petition for habeas corpus accordingly brings only limited relief. The order that accompanies this opinion provides: (1) that, unless and until a competent tribunal determines that Hamdan is not entitled to POW status, he may be tried for the offenses with which he is charged only by court-martial under the Uniform Code of Military Justice; (2) that, unless and until the Military Commission's rule permitting Hamdan's exclusion from commission sessions and the withholding of evidence from him is amended so that it is consistent with and not contrary to UCMJ Article 39, Hamdan's trial before the Military Commission would be unlawful; and (3) that Hamdan must be released from the pre-Commission detention wing of Camp Delta and returned to the general population of detainees, unless some reason other than the pending charges against him requires different treatment. Hamdan's remaining claims are in abeyance.

Notes and Questions

1. Judge Robertson found the procedure before the military commission flawed because the defendant could be excluded from the hearing room when classified evidence was presented and would not be informed of the nature of that evidence. He concluded that the fact that Detailed Defense Counsel (who would have security clearance) could be present and hear the classified evidence was not enough to protect the defendant's rights. Compare Judge Green's position in In re Guantanamo Detainees Cases, supra, p. , where she views the procedure provided for in the military commission cases—that is, counsel has access to the classified evidence—as a procedure that ought to be added to the CSRT process. What might account for the different views of the military commission provisions on this issue?

* * *

Chapter 9

CLASSIFIED INFORMATION IN ADJUDICATORY PROCEEDINGS: THE CLASSIFIED INFORMATION PROCEDURES ACT (CIPA) AND OTHER APPROACHES

A. Various approaches to dealing with classified information in adjudicatory proceedings

1. Introduction

As we have moved through the chapters in this volume, we have encountered a variety of different ways for dealing with classified information in trials and other adjudicatory proceedings.

a. One approach, typically provided for by statute or regulation, authorizes, without more, consideration of the classified information when offered by the government, without making it available to the other party whose status is under consideration. An example is found in the procedures governing the alien Removal Court, 8 U.S.C. §§ 1531 et seq., especially see § 1533. p. ___ (Note: the procedures established by § 1531 et seq. have not yet been utilized by the government.) A second illustration, with provision for consideration of the classified information by the decisionmaker and the reviewing court *in camera*, but with no access provided to the affected party is 8 U.S.C. § 1189, which governs the procedure for designating an organization as a foreign terrorist organization, see supra, p. ___. Still a third example is the procedure established for the Combatant Status Review Tribunals (CSRT) which gives the personal representative of the detainee access to the classified information, but the representative is not the detainee's attorney and does not have an attorney-client relationship with him and is obligated to provide inculpatory information to the tribunal. See In re Guantanamo Detainee Cases, 355 F.Supp.2d 443 (D.D.C. 2005).

b.   A second approach is to disclose the confidential information to the defendant's counsel but prohibit disclosure to the defendant. In some instances this approach is found in statutory form or in regulations but, on occasion, it is established ad hoc, by a judge's protective order or the promulgation of a Special Administrative Measure for a detainee. An example in the form of a regulation is contained in the provisions governing the procedures for the military commissions established by the President's Military Order of Nov. 13, 2001. Those provisions in Military Commission Order No. 1 provide for a Detailed Defense Counsel for the accused who: 1) is required to have security clearance; 2) has an attorney-client relationship with the accused; 3) has access to all of the classified information taken into account in the proceeding; and 4) is barred from disclosing the classified information to his client, which imposes some limits on the utility of having the information. Arrangements generally similar have been established ad hoc under protective orders and/or SAM's, for example, issued by Judge Green for the Guantanamo detainees, see In re Guantanamo Detainee Cases, 344 F.Supp.2d 174 (D.D.C. 2004) and by Judge Carr in the case of Ali Saleh Kahlah Al–Marri v. Hanft.

* * *

c.   The third approach is that taken under the Classified Information Procedures Act (CIPA) which tries to strike a balance between notions of fair trial and protection of the confidentiality of classified information by the use of summaries and like, and if these do not suffice, putting the government to a choice whether to strike specific testimony or dismiss charges, on the one hand or disclose the classified information to the defendant, on the other. Here, too, there are instances of non-statutory implementation of this kind of approach.

* * *

B.   The Classified Information Procedures Act—Introduction

The material in section A above, indicates that the Classified Information Procedures Act is not the only approach to dealing with classified information in trials and other adjudicatory proceedings. Some of the questions that have been raised suggest making a comparative assessment of the different approaches to dealing with classified information. Certainly, however, the CIPA has been the dominant approach for many years. As suggested by the preceding materials, the terrorism case context is beginning to shift some of the focus away from CIPA.

Even though the applications of the Classified Information Procedures Act (CIPA) are not restricted to terrorism prosecutions, the Act plays a central role in such cases. Terrorism prosecutions are often developed through intelligence information that the government is reluctant to reveal for fear of compromising sources or methods of obtaining the information, or where the information itself has a national security dimension. The purpose of CIPA is to strike a balance between protecting the rights of a criminal defendant to know the evidence being used against him or her and the government's need to protect against disclosure of certain types of information, generally captured by the adjective "classified."

Prior to the enactment of CIPA in 1980, the government often found itself in a dilemma—either disclose information to the defendant that the government believed should not be disclosed, or face dismissal of the prosecution on the ground that the right of the defendant to access said information was being denied. A defendant's putting the government in this kind of bind came to be known as the use of "graymail" (i.e. I shall disclose the information if you prosecute me or, alternatively, give me the information or else face dismissal of the prosecution). CIPA was intended to resolve this tension in a way that adequately protected the rights of the criminal defendant while not requiring the government either to permit or make full disclosure or give up the prosecution. An important question that you should consider in light of the materials in this chapter is whether CIPA has largely eliminated graymail, or whether the recurring nature of the phenomenon persists.

While not attempting to delve into all of the nooks and crannies of CIPA law, we shall focus here on several of its salient features. Where relevant classified information is at issue, CIPA makes provision for several possible alternative remedies, the most important of which is providing a summary as a substitution for the information itself. We examine the standard(s) used in determining the relevancy of the classified information; issues relating to the use of a summary as a means of resolving the recurring dilemma; the extent to which in camera, or in camera and ex parte, proceedings may be used under CIPA; whether a requirement of obtaining security clearance may be imposed on defense counsel in CIPA cases, and the constitutionality of CIPA.

One view of CIPA is that it tracks Rule 16 of the Federal Rules of Criminal Procedure, which deals with criminal discovery by the defendant, and simply adds the summary to the possible remedies in criminal discovery. To the extent that CIPA operates in a discovery context, this observation is essentially correct. However, CIPA issues can arise in contexts other than criminal discovery by the defendant. For example, CIPA issues are raised when a criminal defendant proposes to disclose at trial classified information to which he already has access. CIPA issues can also arise at the instance of the government when the prosecutor anticipates that a discovery request for classified information will be made by the defendant or that the defendant is preparing to disclose classified information in his possession. Similarly, the government itself may wish to use at trial information that is classified, and in order to do so, may propose to introduce a summary under the terms of CIPA.

The full text of CIPA is to found at 18 U.S.C. App 3, §§ 1–16. These provisions are set forth below:

TITLE 18, UNITED STATES CODE (CRIMES AND CRIMINAL PROCEDURE)
APPENDIX 3. CLASSIFIED INFORMATION PROCEDURES ACT
Public Law 96–456 (94 Stat. 2025), Oct. 15, 1980

§ 1. Definitions.

(a) "Classified information", as used in this Act, means any information or material that has been determined by the United States Government pursuant to an Executive order, statute, or regulation, to require protection against unauthorized disclosure for reasons of national security and any restricted data, as defined in paragraph r. of section 11 of the Atomic Energy Act of 1954 (42 U.S.C. 2014(y)).

(b) "National security", as used in this Act, means the national defense and foreign relations of the United States.

§ 2. Pretrial Conference.

At any time after the filing of the indictment or information, any party may move for a pretrial conference to consider matters relating to classified information that may arise in connection with the prosecution. Following such motion, or on its own motion, the court shall promptly hold a pretrial conference to establish the timing of requests for discovery, the provision of notice required by section 5 of this Act, and the initiation of the procedure established by section 6 of this Act. In addition, at the pretrial conference the court may consider any matters which relate to classified information or which may promote a fair and expeditious trial. No admission made by the defendant or by any attorney for the defendant at such a conference may be used against the defendant unless the admission is in writing and is signed by the defendant and by the attorney for the defendant.

§ 3. Protective Orders

Upon motion of the United States, the court shall issue an order to protect against the disclosure of any classified information disclosed by the United States to any defendant in any criminal case in a district court of the United States.

§ 4. Discovery of classified information by defendants

The court, upon a sufficient showing, may authorize the United States to delete specified items of classified information from documents to be made available to the defendant through discovery under the Federal Rules of Criminal Procedure, to substitute a summary of the information for such classified documents, or to substitute a statement admitting relevant facts that the classified information would tend to prove. The court may permit the United States to make a request for such authorization in the form of a written statement to be inspected by the court alone. If the court enters an order granting relief following such an ex parte showing, the entire text of the statement of the United

States shall be sealed and preserved in the records of the court to be made available to the appellate court in the event of an appeal.

§ 5. Notice of defendant's intention to disclose classified information

(a) Notice by defendant

If a defendant reasonably expects to disclose or to cause the disclosure of classified information in any manner in connection with any trial or pretrial proceeding involving the criminal prosecution of such defendant, the defendant shall, within the time specified by the court or, where no time is specified, within thirty days prior to trial, notify the attorney for the United States and the court in writing. Such notice shall include a brief description of the classified information. Whenever a defendant learns of additional classified information he reasonably expects to disclose at any such proceeding, he shall notify the attorney for the United States and the court in writing as soon as possible thereafter and shall include a brief description of the classified information. No defendant shall disclose any information known or believed to be classified in connection with a trial or pretrial proceeding until notice has been given under this subsection and until the United States has been afforded a reasonable opportunity to seek a determination pursuant to the procedure set forth in section 6 of this Act, and until the time for the United States to appeal such determination under section 7 has expired or any appeal under section 7 by the United States is decided.

(b) Failure to comply

If the defendant fails to comply with the requirements of subsection (a) the court may preclude disclosure of any classified information not made the subject of notification and may prohibit the examination by the defendant of any witness with respect to any such information.

§ 6. Procedure for cases involving classified information

(a) Motion for hearing

Within the time specified by the court for the filing of a motion under this section, the United States may request the court to conduct a hearing to make all determinations concerning the use, relevance, or admissibility of classified information that would otherwise be made during the trial or pretrial proceeding. Upon such a request, the court shall conduct such a hearing. Any hearing held pursuant to this subsection (or any portion of such hearing specified in the request of the Attorney General) shall be held in camera if the Attorney General certifies to the court in such petition that a public proceeding may result in the disclosure of classified information. As to each item of classified information, the court shall set forth in writing the basis for its determination. Where the United States' motion under this subsection is filed prior to the trial or pretrial proceeding, the court shall rule prior to the commencement of the relevant proceeding.

(b) Notice

(1) Before any hearing is conducted pursuant to a request by the United States under subsection (a), the United States shall provide the defendant with notice of the classified information that is at issue. Such notice shall identify the specific classified information at issue whenever that information previously has been made available to the defendant by the United States. When the United States has not previously made the information available to the defendant in connection with the case, the information may be described by generic category, in such form as the court may approve, rather than by identification of the specific information of concern to the United States.

(2) Whenever the United States requests a hearing under subsection (a), the court, upon request of the defendant, may order the United States to provide the defendant, prior to trial, such details as to the portion of the indictment or information at issue in the hearing as are needed to give the defendant fair notice to prepare for the hearing.

(c) Alternative procedure for disclosure of classified information

(1) Upon any determination by the court authorizing the disclosure of specific classified information under the procedures established by this section, the United States may move that, in lieu of the disclosure of such specific classified information, the court order—

(A) the substitution for such classified information of a statement admitting relevant facts that the specific classified information would tend to prove; or

(B) the substitution for such classified information of a summary of the specific classified information.

The court shall grant such a motion of the United States if it finds that the statement or summary will provide the defendant with substantially the same ability to make his defense as would disclosure of the specific classified information. The court shall hold a hearing on any motion under this section. Any such hearing shall be held in camera at the request of the Attorney General.

(2) The United States may, in connection with a motion under paragraph (1), submit to the court an affidavit of the Attorney General certifying that disclosure of classified information would cause identifiable damage to the national security of the United States and explaining the basis for the classification of such information. If so requested by the United States, the court shall examine such affidavit in camera and ex parte.

(d) Sealing of records of in camera hearings

If at the close of an in camera hearing under this Act (or any portion of a hearing under this Act that is held in camera) the court determines that the classified information at issue may not be disclosed or elicited at the trial or pretrial proceeding, the record of such in camera hearing shall be sealed and preserved by the court for use in the event of an appeal. The defendant may seek reconsideration of the court's determination prior to or during trial.

(e) Prohibition on disclosure of classified information by defendant, relief for defendant when United States opposes disclosure

(1) Whenever the court denies a motion by the United States that it issue an order under subsection (c) and the United States files with the court an affidavit of the Attorney General objecting to disclosure of the classified information at issue, the court shall order that the defendant not disclose or cause the disclosure of such information.

(2) Whenever a defendant is prevented by an order under paragraph (1) from disclosing or causing the disclosure of classified information, the court shall dismiss the indictment or information; except that, when the court determines that the interests of justice would not be served by dismissal of the indictment or information, the court shall order such other action, in lieu of dismissing the indictment or information, as the court determines is appropriate. Such action may include, but need not be limited to—

(A) dismissing specified counts of the indictment or information;

(B) finding against the United States on any issue as to which the excluded classified information relates; or

(C) striking or precluding all or part of the testimony of a witness.

An order under this paragraph shall not take effect until the court has afforded the United States an opportunity to appeal such order under section 7, and thereafter to withdraw its objection to the disclosure of the classified information at issue.

(f) Reciprocity

Whenever the court determines pursuant to subsection (a) that classified information may be disclosed in connection with a trial or pretrial proceeding, the court shall, unless the interests of fairness do not so require, order the United States to provide the defendant with the information it expects to use to rebut the classified information. The court may place the United States under a continuing duty to disclose such rebuttal information. If the United States fails to comply with its obligation under this subsection, the court may exclude any evidence not made the subject of a required disclosure and may prohibit the examination by the United States of any witness with respect to such information.

§ 7. Interlocutory appeal

* * *

§ 8. Introduction of classified information

(a) Classification status

Writings, recordings, and photographs containing classified information may be admitted into evidence without change in their classification status.

(b) Precautions by court

The court, in order to prevent unnecessary disclosure of classified information involved in any criminal proceeding, may order admission into evidence of only part of a writing, recording, or photograph, or may order admission into evidence of the whole writing, recording, or photograph with excision of some or all of the classified information contained therein, unless the whole ought in fairness be considered.

(c) Taking of testimony

During the examination of a witness in any criminal proceeding, the United States may object to any question or line of inquiry that may require the witness to disclose classified information not previously found to be admissible. Following such an objection, the court shall take such suitable action to determine whether the response is admissible as will safeguard against the compromise of any classified information. Such action may include requiring the United States to provide the court with a proffer of the witness' response to the question or line of inquiry and requiring the defendant to provide the court with a proffer of the nature of the information he seeks to elicit.

§ 9. Security procedures

(a) Within one hundred and twenty days of the date of the enactment of this Act, the Chief Justice of the United States, in consultation with the Attorney General, the Director of Central Intelligence, and the Secretary of Defense, shall prescribe rules establishing procedures for the protection against unauthorized disclosure of any classified information in the custody of the United States district courts, courts of appeal, or Supreme Court. Such rules, and any changes in such rules, shall be submitted to the appropriate committees of Congress and shall become effective forty-five days after such submission.

(b) Until such time as rules under subsection (a) first become effective, the Federal courts shall in each case involving classified information adopt procedures to protect against the unauthorized disclosure of such information.

§ 10. Identification of information related to national defense

In any prosecution in which the United States must establish that material relates to the national defense or constitutes classified information, the United States shall notify the defendant, within the time before trial specified by the court, of the portions of the material that it reasonably expects to rely upon to establish the national defense or classified information element of the offense.

. . .

§ 12. Attorney General guidelines

(a) Within one hundred and eighty days of enactment of this Act, the Attorney General shall issue guidelines specifying the factors to be used by the Department of Justice in rendering a decision whether to prosecute a violation of Federal law in which, in the judgment of the Attorney General, there is a possibility that classified information will be revealed. Such guidelines shall be transmitted to the appropriate committees of Congress.

(b) When the Department of Justice decides not to prosecute a violation of Federal law pursuant to subsection (a), an appropriate official of the Department of Justice shall prepare written findings detailing the reasons for the decision not to prosecute. The findings shall include—

(1) the intelligence information which the Department of Justice officials believe might be disclosed,

(2) the purpose for which the information might be disclosed,

(3) the probability that the information would be disclosed, and

(4) the possible consequences such disclosure would have on the national security.

. . .

C. Determining relevancy and related issues

UNITED STATES v. YUNIS
867 F.2d 617 (D.C.Cir.1989).

Before SILBERMAN, WILLIAMS, and SENTELLE, Circuit Judges.

SENTELLE, Circuit Judge:

This is an interlocutory appeal by the United States seeking review of a District Court order releasing classified information under the Classified Information Procedures Act ("CIPA"), 18 U.S.C.App. §§ 1–16 (1982). Section 7 of CIPA, 18 U.S.C.App. § 7, provides for the instant interlocutory appeal. The order in question permits discovery of fourteen transcripts of taped conversations between an informant and the defendant/appellee, Fawaz Yunis, whose trial for crimes allegedly committed during an international hijacking is now pending. After reviewing the transcripts in camera, we hold that the contents of the transcripts were on the whole not relevant to the defendant's guilt or innocence and the few statements that were even marginally relevant were not sufficiently helpful or beneficial to the defense to overcome the classified information privilege. We conclude that the District Court abused its discretion in ordering the disclosure of the transcripts to the defense.

I. FACTUAL BACKGROUND

A. Incident, Investigation, Informant, and Apprehension.

Appellee Fawaz Yunis ("Yunis" or "appellee") is a Lebanese citizen awaiting trial for air piracy, conspiracy, and hostage taking, inter alia, arising out of the June 11, 1985, hijacking of Royal Jordanian Airlines flight number 402. On that date, five armed men boarded the aircraft at Beirut International Airport, taking hostage the crew and approximately sixty passengers, including three Americans. The hijackers ordered the pilot to fly to Tunis. After Tunisian officials twice refused to permit the aircraft to land, the hijackers ordered the aircraft to Damascus, Syria, after brief stops in Cyprus and Sicily for food and fuel. When Syrian officials refused to permit the aircraft to land at Damascus, the hijackers ordered the aircraft to return to Beirut, more than thirty hours after its initial departure. In Beirut, the hijackers exited the aircraft and held a press conference. Yunis allegedly read a statement. The hijackers evacuated the crew and passengers, blew up the aircraft, and escaped into the Lebanese countryside.

Immediately after the hijacking, several United States agencies, led by the Federal Bureau of Investigation, sought to identify, locate and capture the hijackers. Government efforts after several months of investigation focused on Yunis as the probable ringleader of the five hijackers. The FBI then recruited as a government informant Jamal Hamdan, a Lebanese acquaintance of Yunis. Over the next several months, Hamdan and Yunis met on many occasions. Conversations between the two were intercepted by some undisclosed law enforcement intelligence-gathering source or method. As old friends and in order for Hamdan to make Yunis feel relaxed, the two discussed many matters, most of which were completely unrelated to the hijacking or any other terrorist operation or criminal activity. Even the District Court characterized the transcripts of these conversations as something "interesting for an Ann Landers column or Dorothy Dixon [sic] or someone of that sort . . . just pure trivia."

After the investigation had produced sufficient evidence, the FBI obtained a warrant for Yunis's arrest. Hamdan lured Yunis from Lebanon to international waters off the coast of Cyprus under the ruse of conducting a narcotics deal. On September 13, 1987, Hamdan and Yunis traveled on a small motor boat to a yacht manned by FBI agents who apprehended Yunis shortly after he boarded the yacht. From the yacht, they transferred Yunis to a United States Navy munitions ship, the U.S.S. Butte, which carried him to the aircraft carrier, the U.S.S. Saratoga. A military aircraft transported Yunis from the U.S.S. Saratoga to Andrews Air Force Base outside of Washington, D.C. He was subsequently arraigned in the United States District Court for the District of Columbia. On October 1, 1987, a District of Columbia grand jury returned a nine count superseding indictment for crimes arising out of the hijacking.

B. Discovery Proceedings and District Court Decision.

After arraignment, counsel for Yunis on November 10, 1987, filed several motions, including Defendant's Motion to Compel Discovery

Under Rule 16 and for Production Under Brady v. Maryland. Joint Appendix ("J.A.") at 69. The motion requested, inter alia:

1. Documents generated by other federal agencies, to include military and intelligence organizations in connection with this case. . . . This is to include any foreign governments who assisted.

. . .

12. Copies of all tapes or documentation of conversations between Jamal Hamdan and Mr. Yunis.

. . .

22. Any and all information concerning any tapes or wire taps used in this case. The request includes, but is not limited to, any intercepted wire, oral or electronic communications, mobile tracking devices, pen registers and trap and trace devices. The breadth of the request covers past or present operations whether domestic (warrant required) or national security in nature and authorization.

J.A. at 70, 71 & 73.

The United States filed an omnibus response to all of Yunis's motions. Government's Omnibus Response to Defendant's Pretrial Motions, J.A. at 78. This response argued that Yunis had failed "to explain the relevance of each portion of his broad request and ha[d] failed to state the provision of law which entitles him to discovery of each item." Id. at 79. In particular, the government argued that "a criminal defendant is not entitled to know everything that the government's investigation has unearthed if it is not used at trial." Id. at 80. Regarding Yunis's request for tapes or documentations of conversations between him and the informant, the government stated:

"We have provided tapes and transcripts of the conversations between Hamdan and Yunis which will be offered in evidence. . . . [A] multi-agency search was initiated to locate other materials pertaining to surveillance of the defendant. . . . These will be the subject of an ex parte in camera submission to the [District] Court pursuant to Section 4 of CIPA and Rule 16(d) of the Federal Rules of Criminal Procedure." Id. at 87. Simultaneously the government filed a motion for a pretrial conference under Section 2 of CIPA to consider matters relating to classified information.

Pursuant to Section 4 of CIPA and Federal Rule of Criminal Procedure 16(d), on December 28, 1987, the government filed the first of several ex parte in camera pleadings. These pleadings, filed over the next ten months, argued that disclosure of the transcripts would harm national security. The first ex parte in camera pleading included a declaration from a senior government official describing the national security implications of complying with Yunis's broad discovery request, particularly the risk of disclosing intelligence sources and methods.

On January 25, 1988, the District Court ordered the government to furnish an index and summary of the contents of all the recordings of the conversations between Hamdan and Yunis which had not already been furnished to Yunis. Pretrial Memorandum Order No. 2, United States v. Yunis, Criminal No. 87–0377 (D.D.C. Jan. 25, 1988) (J.A. at 237, 241–42). In an ex parte in camera filing, the government furnished the Court the indices of all the transcripts on February 1 and supplied eight of the transcripts on February 3. The government also submitted the declarations of two more senior government officials explaining the national security implications that would likely result from disclosure. On June 6, the government filed yet another declaration from a government official discussing the national security implications of compliance with Yunis's discovery motion.

Unsatisfied with the government's ex parte in camera filings regarding the risk to national security of disclosure, the District Court ordered the government to provide defendant's counsel with, inter alia, "[a]ll audio and video tapes and/or transcripts of conversations between defendant and Jamal Hamdan."

. . .

In ruling on Yunis's request for discovery and the government's assertion of privilege as to the classified information, the District Court applied a three-step analysis: first, inquiring as to whether the evidence was relevant, second, if relevant, determining if it was material, and finally, balancing the defendant's need for access to the information in the preparation of his defense against the government's need to keep the information from disclosure by reason of its potential harm to our country's national security interests. Id. at 275–79. The Court initially concluded that the transcripts were relevant because several of the recorded conversations would aid the defendant in reconstructing the events surrounding the hijacking and the apprehension of the defendant. Id. at 276. It next concluded that the transcripts were material in that they "may . . . go to some very crucial issues, such as motive, intent, prejudice, credibility, or even the possibility of exposing duress or entrapment." Id. The Court next found the balance favored the defendant. Having found all three steps favored the defendant, the Court ordered the disclosure of the transcripts.

In an attempt to avoid the disclosure of the transcripts, the government notified the Court and the defense counsel that it would not call Hamdan as a witness. Thus, the government argued, conversations between the informant and the defendant after the crime and before the arrest were no longer relevant to any issue in the case. That is, if Hamdan was not a witness, then his alleged bias as a paid informant no longer lent relevance to the transcripts as impeachment material. The government therefore sought modification of the District Court's pretrial order releasing it from disclosing this classified information.

The District Court rejected the government's argument . . . [8]

---

8. In so specifying what to release, the District Court inadvertently disclosed classified information. The original Pretrial Memorandum Order No. 7 was redacted

II. STATUTORY BACKGROUND

Section 4 of CIPA, 18 U.S.C.App. § 4, titled "Discovery of classified information by defendants," provides:

> The court, upon a sufficient showing, may authorize the United States to delete specified items of classified information from documents to be made available to the defendant through discovery under the Federal Rules of Criminal Procedure. . . .

This Section creates no new rights of or limits on discovery of a specific area of classified information. Rather it contemplates an application of the general law of discovery in criminal cases to the classified information area with limitations imposed based on the sensitive nature of the classified information. In this case the relevant discovery procedure arises from Rule 16(a)(1)(A) of the Federal Rules of Criminal Procedure, which entitles a defendant to discover "any relevant written or recorded statements made by the defendant."

The requirement that statements made by the defendant be relevant has not generally been held to create a very high threshold. Generally speaking, the production of a defendant's statements has become "practically a matter of right even without a showing of materiality." United States v. Haldeman, 559 F.2d 31, 74 n. 80 (D.C.Cir.1976) (en banc), cert. denied, 431 U.S. 933, 97 S.Ct. 2641, 53 L.Ed.2d 250 (1977).

CIPA, on the other hand, as noted above, provides procedures governing the defendant's access to classified information sought to be discovered from the government. It is against the background of general discovery rules and specific limitations designed to protect classified information that the District Court and now this Court must determine the availability of the classified transcripts containing statements by the defendant.

. . . District Court quite properly conducted a relevance analysis as the first step in its consideration of the discovery request in this case. As that Court noted, relevance is determined under the definition contained

and republished but only after the disclosure had occurred. The Chief Justice of the United States has directed courts in all criminal proceedings involving classified information to appoint a court security officer to assist with the proper handling of such information. In any proceeding in a criminal case or appeal therefrom in which classified information is within, or reasonably expected to be within, the custody of the court, the court shall designate a court security officer. The court security officer shall be an individual with demonstrated competence in security matters, and shall, prior to designation, have been certified to the court in writing by the Department of Justice Security Officer as cleared for the level and category of classified information that will be involved. The court security officer shall be responsible to the court for document, physical, personnel and communications security, and shall take measures reasonably necessary to fulfill these responsibilities. Security Procedures Established Pursuant to Pub.L. 96–456, 94 Stat. 2025, By the Chief Justice of the United States for the Protection of Classified Information § 2, 18 U.S.C.App. § 9 Historical Note (1985).

Because members of the federal judiciary and their staffs are generally not familiar with security procedures, we think it wise that judges within this Circuit direct their respective court security officers to review orders, decisions, and memoranda before they are released. As an appointee of a court, the court security officer is bound to the same ethical and confidentiality standards as other staff members of a court.

in Federal Rule of Evidence 401, which defines "relevant evidence" as any "evidence having any tendency to make the existence of any fact that is of consequence to the determination of the action more probable or less probable than it would be without the evidence."

We have, however, reviewed in camera the classified information which is the subject of the instant controversy and find that only two, or at most three, sentences or sentence fragments in the transcribed conversations of defendant and Jamal Hamdan have even the remotest relevance to any issue in this cause. Were this not classified information this might give us pause, since matters of discovery are ordinarily within the discretion of the District Court, and our review of such matters would normally focus only on an abuse of that discretion. See, e.g., United States v. Clegg, 740 F.2d 16, 18 (9th Cir.1984). However, in this case determination of relevance does not close the inquiry.

As the District Court correctly noted, a further inquiry is in order before discovery of classified information should be ordered. See J.A. at 275. Where the government asserts a privilege, a trial court abuses its discretion if it orders disclosure "absent a showing of materiality." United States v. Grisham, 748 F.2d 460, 463 (8th Cir.1984) (per curiam). See also United States v. Skeens, 449 F.2d 1066, 1070 (D.C.Cir.1971). This second step of the inquiry is firmly established in Roviaro v. United States, 353 U.S. 53, 77 S.Ct. 623, 1 L.Ed.2d 639 (1957), and cases following it. In Roviaro, the Supreme Court dealt with the so-called informant's privilege, which permits the government to withhold disclosure of an informant's identity or the contents of a communication which would endanger the secrecy of that information. This privilege exists to further "the obligation of citizens to communicate their knowledge of the commission of crimes to law-enforcement officials and, by preserving their anonymity, encourages them to perform that obligation." Id. at 59, 77 S.Ct. at 627. Roviaro held that this privilege must give way when disclosure of the information "is relevant and helpful to the defense of an accused."

Similarly sensitive considerations underlie the classified information privilege asserted here. The Supreme Court has long recognized that a legitimate government privilege protects national security concerns. In C. & S. Air Lines v. Waterman S.S. Corp., 333 U.S. 103, 111, 68 S.Ct. 431, 436, 92 L.Ed. 568 (1948), the Court wrote: "[The executive branch] has available intelligence services whose reports are not and ought not to be published to the world," . . .

While CIPA creates no new rule of evidence regarding admissibility, the procedures it mandates protect a government privilege in classified information similar to the informant's privilege identified in Roviaro. United States v. Smith, 780 F.2d 1102, 1108 (4th Cir.1985) (en banc).
* * *

In reviewing the material for the purpose of establishing the facial validity of the government's claim of privilege, we note that the District Judge, in his review, conducted at the third or "balancing" stage of his analysis, apparently misapprehended, at least in part, the nature of the sensitive information the government sought to protect. Our own review of the government's affidavits and transcripts reveals that much of the government's security interest in the conversation lies not so much in the contents of the conversations, as in the time, place, and nature of the government's ability to intercept the conversations at all. Things that did not make sense to the District Judge would make all too much sense to a foreign counter-intelligence specialist who could learn much about this nation's intelligence-gathering capabilities from what these documents revealed about sources and methods. Implicit in the whole concept of an informant-type privilege is the necessity that information-gathering agencies protect from compromise "intelligence sources and methods." The Supreme Court has expressly recognized the legitimacy of this concern in construing the National Security Act of 1947, 61 Stat. 498, 50 U.S.C. § 403(d)(3), in CIA v. Sims, 471 U.S. 159, 105 S.Ct. 1881, 85 L.Ed.2d 173 (1985). " 'The government has a compelling interest in protecting both the secrecy of information important to our national security and the appearance of confidentiality so essential to the effective operation of our foreign intelligence service.' " * * *

We hold, in short, that classified information is not discoverable on a mere showing of theoretical relevance in the face of the government's classified information privilege, but that the threshold for discovery in this context further requires that a defendant seeking classified information, like a defendant seeking the informant's identity in Roviaro, is entitled only to information that is at least "helpful to the defense of [the] accused."

We recognize that the defendant and his counsel in CIPA cases are hampered by the fact that the information they seek is not available to them until such a showing is made. Thus, it might be said, they cannot show the helpfulness of contents, because they do not know their nature. This apparent Catch–22 is more apparent than real. The Supreme Court dealt with a similar problem in United States v. Valenzuela–Bernal, 458 U.S. 858, 102 S.Ct. 3440, 73 L.Ed.2d 1193 (1982). In that case, defendant had been found guilty of illegally transporting an alien in the United States in violation of 8 U.S.C. § 1324(a)(2). Two of the alien passengers in the defendant's vehicle had been deported to Mexico by the United States before Valenzuela's trial. The Ninth Circuit held that the government, by making the alien witnesses unavailable to the defendant for interview or trial testimony, had violated his Fifth and Sixth Amendment rights. United States v. Valenzuela–Bernal, 647 F.2d 72 (9th Cir.1981). The Supreme Court reversed. In so doing, it noted that the Circuit Court had applied to the unavailable testimony a test requiring only that the evidence be of some " 'conceivable benefit' " to the defense. 458 U.S. at 862, 102 S.Ct. at 3444. See also United States v. Valenzuela–Bernal, 647 F.2d at 73–75; United States v. Mendez–Rodriguez, 450 F.2d 1, 4–5 (9th Cir.1971). * * *

Of especial relevance to the present case are the Court's observations on the defendant's difficulty in arguing the "materiality" of testimony from a witness whom he has had no opportunity to interview. As the Court noted, while a defendant in such circumstances may face a difficult task in making a showing of materiality, the task is not an impossible one. In such circumstances it is of course not possible to make any avowal of how a witness may testify. But the events to which a witness may testify, and the relevance of those events to the crime charged, may well demonstrate either the presence or absence of the required materiality. In addition, it should be remembered that respondent was present throughout the commission of this crime. No one knows better than he what the deported witnesses actually said to him, or in his presence, that might bear upon [his defense in the case]. Like the defendant in Valenzuela–Bernal, Yunis was present during all the relevant conversations. It does not impose upon him any burden of absolute memory, omniscience, or superhuman mental capacity to expect some specificity as to what benefit he expects to gain from the evidence sought here.

In any event, we have reviewed the information in question ex parte and in camera. The relevance found by the District Court is no more than theoretical. Nothing in the classified documents in fact goes to the innocence of the defendant vel non, impeaches any evidence of guilt, or makes more or less probable any fact at issue in establishing any defense to the charges. Therefore, it is at least arguable that even the relevance hurdle is not met. But affording the defendant the near presumption of relevance of his own statements recognized in Haldeman, 559 F.2d at 74 n. 80, we still find that the ex parte showing falls far short of establishing the helpful or beneficial character necessary to meet the second step of the test. Cf. United States v. Grisham, 748 F.2d at 463–64. We do not intend by our characterization of the second phase as requiring that the evidence be "helpful or beneficial" to direct a new test separate from the second step employed by the District Judge, styled by him as determining the "materiality" of the evidence. We recognize that that term is drawn directly from the Supreme Court's language in Roviaro and Valenzuela–Bernal. However, in practical application of the test, the frequent confusion of the terms "materiality" and "relevance" in evidentiary law leads us to the conclusion that the Supreme Court's alternate phrasing of "helpful to the defense of an accused," provides more guidance in a trial context. Roviaro, 353 U.S. at 60–61, 77 S.Ct. at 628. Since our review discloses nothing of this sort, we hold that the District Court abused its discretion by ordering discovery of the statements in the face of the government's colorable claim of the classified information privilege.

As to the third step of the analysis employed by the District Judge, that is the balancing of the defendant's interest in disclosure against the government's need to keep the information secret, we need not reach this question. We recognize that the language in Roviaro suggests such a balancing test, and that two of our sister circuits have applied such a test in the CIPA context. But this circuit has not yet faced that question, nor, in light of disposition of the present appeal, do we now. Thus, we neither adopt nor reject the balancing test set forth in Smith, referenced in United States v. Sarkissian, 841 F.2d 959, 965 (9th Cir.1988), and followed by the District Court in the present case. The resolution of that inquiry can await the day when we face a case in which a defendant seeks colorably privileged information with more than theoretical relevance which is genuinely helpful to his defense. This is not the case.

* * *

D. Adjudging the adequacy of substitutions for classified information

* * *

It would seem that defense counsel has a difficult task in challenging the adequacy of substitutions. First, he or she often does not have access to the original classified documents. The inquiry regarding adequacy is conducted in camera. Query, can it also be ex parte? See below. Second, the courts generally defer to any claim by the government that national security is implicated. See United States v. Fernandez, 913 F.2d 148 (4th Cir.1990): "We are not asked, and we have no authority, to consider judgments made by the Attorney General concerning the extent to which the information in issue here implicates national security." Compare the treatment of the adequacy-of-substitutions issue in the following two cases.

UNITED STATES v. REZAQ

134 F.3d 1121 (D.C.Cir. 1998).

Before Wald, Sentelle and Henderson, Circuit Judges.

Opinion for the Court filed by Circuit Judge WALD.

WALD, Circuit Judge:

Omar Mohammed Ali Rezaq appeals his conviction on one count of aircraft piracy under 49 U.S.C. app. § 1472(n) (1994). In 1985, Rezaq hijacked an Air Egypt flight shortly after takeoff from Athens, and ordered it to fly to Malta. On arrival, Rezaq shot a number of passengers, killing two of them, before he was apprehended. Rezaq pleaded guilty to murder charges in Malta, served seven years in prison, and was released in February 1993. Shortly afterwards, he was taken into custody in Nigeria by United States authorities and brought to the United States for trial . . .

I. BACKGROUND

Rezaq did not deny committing the hijacking at trial, relying instead on the defenses of insanity and obedience to military orders. Thus, the following account of the hijacking was not contested at Rezaq's trial.

Rezaq is Palestinian, and was, at the time of the hijacking, a member of a Palestinian terrorist organization, which planned and ordered the hijacking. On the evening of November 23, 1985, Rezaq boarded Air Egypt Flight 648 in Athens. He was accompanied by two other hijackers; one of his confederates, named Salem, was the leader of the operation, and the name of the other is unknown. Shortly after the plane took off, the three produced weapons, announced that they were seizing the plane, and demanded that the captain fly it to Malta. A gun battle ensued between the hijackers and an Egyptian plainclothes sky marshal stationed on the plane, as a result of which Salem was killed and the sky marshal was wounded.

Rezaq then took charge of the hijacking. After the plane arrived in Malta, he separated the Israeli and American passengers from the others, and moved them to the front of the plane. He released a number of Egyptian and Filipino female passengers, as well as two wounded flight attendants. He then demanded that the aircraft be refueled; when the authorities refused, he announced that he would shoot a passenger every fifteen minutes until his demand was met.

Rezaq carried out his threat. He first shot Israeli national Tamar Artzi. Although he shot her twice, once in the head, she survived. Fifteen minutes later, he shot her companion, Nitzan Mendelson, also an Israeli; Ms. Mendelson died of her injuries nine days later. Rezaq then shot Patrick Baker, an American, but only succeeded in grazing his head. Two or three hours later, Rezaq shot Scarlett Rogenkamp—a United States citizen and an employee of the United States Air Force—in the head, killing her. Some time later, he shot Jackie Pflug, also an American, in the head, injuring her very seriously. Rezaq shot his victims near the front door of the plane, and either threw them or let them fall onto the tarmac; this may explain why three of the five were able to survive, either by escaping (Artzi and Baker), or by feigning death (Pflug).

In the evening of November 24th—about a day after the hijacking began—Egyptian commandos stormed the plane. The operation seems to have been a singularly incompetent one. The commandos fired indiscriminately, and set off an explosive device of some kind, as a result of which the aircraft burst into flames. Fifty-seven passengers were killed, as was the third hijacker. Rezaq was injured, and was taken, with a multitude of injured passengers, to a hospital. There, he was identified as the hijacker by passengers, members of the crew, and several of his victims.

The authorities in Malta charged Rezaq with murder, attempted murder, and hostage taking. He pled guilty, and was sentenced to 25 years' imprisonment. For reasons unclear, Maltese authorities released him some seven years later, in February 1993, and allowed him to board a plane to Ghana. Rezaq's itinerary was to carry him from there to Nigeria, and then to Ethiopia, and finally to Sudan. Ghanaian officials detained Rezaq for several months, but eventually allowed him to proceed to Nigeria. When Rezaq's plane landed in Nigeria, Nigerian authorities placed him in the custody of FBI agents, who transported him on a waiting aircraft to the United States.

Rezaq was indicted and tried for air piracy in the District Court for the District of Columbia. At trial, Rezaq invoked the defenses of insanity and obedience to military orders. In support of his insanity defense, Rezaq presented evidence that he suffered from post-traumatic stress disorder ("PTSD"). As witnesses, he called several members of his own family and three psychiatric experts; Rezaq himself also testified at length. Rezaq asserted that his PTSD sprang from numerous traumatic events he had experienced, first in the Jordanian refugee camp in which he spent much of his youth, and later in Lebanon, where he was active in Palestinian revolutionary organizations from 1978 to 1985. The Lebanese experiences he described included witnessing the killing of hundreds of refugees by Israeli forces in Beirut in 1982; witnessing the killings of the populations of entire villages; and nearly being killed in a car bombing. Rezaq's family testified that when he left Jordan he was normal, friendly, and extroverted, but that when he returned from Lebanon he was pale, inattentive, prone to nightmares, antisocial, and had lost his sense of humor. Rezaq's psychiatric experts said that these changes in behavior were symptomatic of PTSD, and, based on their examination of Rezaq and on the testimony of other witnesses, they concluded that Rezaq was suffering from PTSD when he committed the hijacking in November 1985. The United States presented two psychiatric experts of its own, who testified that Rezaq's symptoms were not as intense as those usually associated with PTSD, and that Rezaq was able to reason and make judgments normally at the time he hijacked the plane.

The jury did not credit Rezaq's defenses, and found him guilty of the one count with which he was charged, aircraft piracy in violation of 49 U.S.C. app. § 1472(n) (1994).

* * *

Because death resulted from Rezaq's commission of the offense, § 1472(n)(1)(B) applied, and the district court sentenced Rezaq to life imprisonment. (The United States had not sought the death sentence.) The district court also ordered Rezaq to pay a total of $254,000 in restitution, an amount which it found to represent the financial cost to the victims of his crime.

. . .

When classified materials may be relevant to criminal proceedings, the Classified Information Procedures Act ("CIPA"), 18 U.S.C. app. III (1994), provides procedures designed to protect the rights of the defendant while minimizing the associated harm to national security. In the course of preparing for trial, the United States identified a number of arguably discoverable classified materials, and obtained permission from the district court to file an *ex parte, in camera* motion for a protective order. After reviewing this motion and the accompanying documents, the district court ordered the United States to prepare an index listing the contents of each document, whether it believed the document to be subject to discovery, and why. This document, too, was submitted *ex parte* and *in camera*; the district court subjected this document to detailed review, and prepared a list of the materials that it considered discoverable.

Under CIPA, the court may allow the United States to disclose "a statement admitting relevant facts that the classified information would tend to prove," in lieu of disclosing the information itself. 18 U.S.C. app. III § 4 (1994). The United States sought, and obtained, permission to substitute admissions for all of the documents that the district court had identified as discoverable. The district court reviewed the United States's proposed substitutions, and concluded that they fairly stated the relevant elements of the classified documents. The substitutions were then disclosed to Rezaq's attorney

Rezaq's request on appeal is very limited. He does not ask us to review the district court's determination as to which documents were discoverable in the first instance. Instead, he asks only that we review the documents that the district court found to be discoverable, and decide whether the summaries that the court furnished to him were as helpful to his defense as the original documents would have been. He is particularly concerned that the summaries may have omitted important information, or that the process of transforming the documents into desiccated statements of material fact might have hampered the "evidentiary richness and narrative integrity" of the defense he was able to present.

We found in *Yunis* that a defendant seeking classified information is not entitled to receive it "on a mere showing of theoretical relevance," but "is entitled only to information that is at least 'helpful to the defense of the accused.'" 867 F.2d at 623 (quoting *Roviaro v. United States,* 353 U.S. 53, 60–61, 77 S.Ct. 623, 627–28, 1 L.Ed.2d 639 (1957)). This principle applies to sub-elements of individual documents; if some portion or aspect of a document is classified, a defendant is entitled to receive it only if it may be helpful to his defense. A court applying this rule should, of course, err on the side of protecting the interests of the defendant. In some cases, a court might legitimately conclude that it is necessary to place a fact in context in order to ensure that the jury is able to give it its full weight. For instance, it might be appropriate in some circumstances to attribute a statement to its source, or to phrase it as a quotation.

The district court's substitution decisions turned on the relevance of the facts contained in the discoverable documents, and are therefore reviewed, like other relevance decisions under CIPA, for abuse of discretion. *See United States v. Yunis,* 867 F.2d 617, 625 (D.C.Cir.1989). We are obliged to consider the district court's substitution decisions very carefully, as Rezaq's counsel is unable to consult the original documents, and so cannot present arguments on his client's behalf. We have accordingly conducted a detailed *in camera* comparison of the originals of the discoverable documents with the summaries approved by the district court. We find that the district court did a commendable job of discharging its obligations under CIPA, and in particular that its orders protected Rezaq's rights very effectively despite the fact that Rezaq's attorney was unable to participate in the CIPA proceedings. No information was omitted from the substitutions that might have been helpful to Rezaq's defense, and the discoverable documents had no unclassified features that might have been disclosed to Rezaq.

UNITED STATES v. FERNANDEZ

913 F.2d 148 (4th Cir. 1990).

Before Chapman, Wilkinson, and Wilkins, Circuit Judges.

WILKINSON, Circuit Judge:

Independent Counsel, who is prosecuting this case for the United States pursuant to the Ethics in Government Act, 28 U.S.C. § 594(a), appeals under § 7(a) of the Classified Information Procedures Act (CIPA), 18 U.S.C.App. § 7(a), from the district court's dismissal of the indictment against defendant Joseph Fernandez. The district court dismissed the case with prejudice after the Attorney General of the United States filed an affidavit under § 6(e)(1) of CIPA prohibiting the disclosure of classified evidence that the district court had previously ruled to be relevant and admissible.

On appeal, the government contends that the district court abused its discretion in ruling certain classified evidence to be admissible, in rejecting the government's proposals for substituted versions of the evidence, and in dismissing the case with prejudice after the Attorney General prohibited disclosure of the evidence. After thoroughly reviewing the record, we cannot say that any of the district court rulings constitute an abuse of discretion. We thus affirm its judgment.

I.

On November 25, 1986, the Attorney General of the United States announced that proceeds from arms transfers from the United States to Iran may have been diverted to assist the Nicaraguan resistance forces known as the Contras. This disclosure led to two investigations pertinent to this case: In late November 1986, the CIA's Office of Inspector General began an investigation into the CIA's military and paramilitary support of the Contras; and on December 1, 1986, the President of the United States established a Special Review Board, known as the Tower Commission, to examine the proper role of the National Security Council and the circumstances surrounding the Iran–Contra affair.

In January and February 1987, the two investigative bodies interviewed appellee Joseph Fernandez concerning his activities as the CIA's Chief of Station in San Jose, Costa Rica, from 1984–1986, a time during which the Boland Amendment prohibited CIA officers from supporting military and paramilitary operations by the Contras. The investigators questioned Fernandez about, *inter alia*, (1) his activities relating to the construction of an airstrip in northwestern Costa Rica in 1985, (2) his role in a 1986 operation by so-called "private benefactors" to resupply the Contras from the airstrip, and (3) his relationship with several individuals involved in the resupply operation—including Colonel Oliver North, then a member of the National Security Council staff, and Rafael Quintero, one of North's representatives in Central America. The investigators never questioned Fernandez under oath, and they failed to record or to transcribe any of his answers.

On April 24, 1989, Fernandez was indicted on two counts of making false official statements to the two investigative bodies in violation of 18 U.S.C. § 1001, and on two counts of obstructing the investigators' proceedings in violation of 18 U.S.C. § 1505. The indictment was obtained by an Independent Counsel appointed pursuant to the Ethics in Government Act, 28 U.S.C.A. §§ 591 *et seq.* That Act transfers from the Department of Justice to Independent Counsel all prosecutorial and investigative authority in cases that come within Independent Counsel's jurisdiction. *See Appeal of the United States by the Attorney General,* 887 F.2d 465, 468 (4th Cir.1989). Thus, this case is being prosecuted by Independent Counsel rather than the Attorney General of the United States. Nonetheless, the Attorney General retains responsibility under CIPA for protection of national security secrets. *Id.* at 471. Accordingly, his office has worked closely with Independent Counsel "to ensure that national security secrets are safeguarded," and has "participated in framing both the initial charges and the substitution proposals." *Id.* at 467.

Counts One and Two of the indictment charge Fernandez with misrepresentations to the Inspector General of the CIA about the genesis and purpose of the Costa Rican airstrip project. The indictment states that the airstrip project was initiated by Fernandez and was designed to assist in the resupply of the Contras. It also states that Fernandez had numerous contacts with Rafael Quintero concerning the construction of the airstrip. It alleges that Fernandez lied and obstructed proceedings when he stated that the airstrip was initiated by the Costa Rican government and that the airstrip was to be used for training activities by Costa Rican forces in preparation for a feared invasion by Nicaragua. It also alleges that Fernandez misrepresented the nature of his contacts with Quintero.

. . .

To defend himself against these charges, Fernandez intended to show that he did not make some of the allegedly false statements, and that others were actually true. With respect to Counts One and Two, he intended to establish the truth of his allegedly false statements concerning the origin and purpose of the airstrip by demonstrating that the airstrip was part of a comprehensive * * * * initiative designed to repel a potential invasion by Nicaragua. . . .

To present this defense, Fernandez claimed the need to introduce as evidence certain classified documents. Accordingly, following his indictment he invoked the procedures of the Classified Information Procedures Act .

Fernandez filed notices under § 5 of CIPA on June 23, 1989, identifying nearly 5000 documents containing classified information that he proposed to disclose at trial. The government moved to strike the § 5 notice, complaining that the defendant had merely listed documents rather than proffering the specific classified information that he planned to disclose. At a hearing on June 27, 1989, the trial judge suggested, and both parties agreed, that the government should provide Fernandez's attorneys with the specific documents it planned to use in its case-in-chief so that the defense could narrow the scope of the classified information it would reasonably need to use at trial. In addition, the parties agreed that Fernandez should recast his CIPA notice in the form of categories of classified information organized by subject matter rather than as a mere listing of classified documents. The parties believed that this organizational scheme would enable the government to make an informed assessment of the danger of disclosing the information and would allow the trial court to rule intelligently and efficiently on the information's relevance and admissibility. Accordingly, on July 3 Fernandez filed a second notice under § 5 of CIPA setting forth summaries, organized by subject matter, of the categories of classified information that he reasonably expected to disclose at trial.

On July 10, the district court conducted a hearing under § 6(a) of CIPA to determine the "use, relevance, or admissibility" of the classified information. At the government's request, the trial court went through each subject matter category of classified information to determine each category's relevance and admissibility. In the course of two days of CIPA hearings, the trial court ruled that several categories of classified information were irrelevant and thus not admissible. It also ruled, however, that two categories of classified information were material to Fernandez's defense and could be disclosed at trial.

The first category of classified information admitted by the trial judge concerned three intelligence projects undertaken jointly by the United States and Costa Rica: (1) * * * *, (2) * * * *, and (3) * * * * (collectively referred to as the "projects"). The district court agreed with Fernandez that classified information concerning these programs would corroborate his claim that the airstrip project was part of a larger Costa Rican effort to protect itself against a Nicaraguan invasion, which would in turn support the truth of his allegedly false statements about the origin and purpose of, and his involvement in, the airstrip project.

. . .

Following the district court's order authorizing the disclosure of information about the locations and the projects, the United States submitted a series of proposed substitutions under § 6(c) of CIPA. The government's proposed substitutions were introduced on July 12, and revised on July 14, 21, and 24. As explained below, the district court rejected these various substitution proposals over the course of several days as inadequate to "provide the defendant with substantially the same ability to make his defense as would disclosure of the specific classified information." 18 U.S.C.App. § 6(c).

. . .

Before the trial commenced in district court, on November 22, 1989, the Attorney General filed an affidavit under § 6(e)(1) of CIPA prohibiting the disclosure at trial of any classified information concerning the * * * * or the three projects. The Attorney General's affidavit, corroborated by affidavits of the Director of the CIA, the Deputy Director for Operations of the CIA, and * * * *, detailed the serious damage to national security that would result from disclosure of the classified information.

In response to the § 6(e)(1) affidavit, Independent Counsel filed a memorandum concerning sanctions in which it requested the trial court not to dismiss the indictment. Instead, it urged the trial court to make adverse findings against the government and to narrow the indictment in a manner previously proposed (and rejected) on July 21. After a sanctions hearing on November 24, the district court rejected Independent Counsel's suggestions and dismissed the indictment. The court reasoned that because the information concerning the stations and projects was "essential for the defendant to put forth a defense in this case and to receive a fair trial," and because the "6(e) affidavit prevents the disclosure of all that information," the entire case had to be dismissed with prejudice.

Our earlier decision in this case stated that § 7(a) of CIPA allows Independent Counsel to appeal the district court's relevancy and substitution rulings together with its appeal from the district court's sanction. Accordingly, the United States now appeals from (1) the district court's rulings that the information concerning the projects and stations was relevant and admissible, (2) the district court's rejections of the government's proposed substitutions, and (3) the district court's sanction of dismissal. The government does not seek a remand for further findings or further factual development. Rather, it requests that we either reverse the district court's admission of the classified evidence, or order the district court to accept the government's substitution proposals, or require the district court to accept the government's proposed sanctions.

Our role in this appeal is circumscribed. We are not asked, and we have no authority, to consider judgments made by the Attorney General concerning the extent to which the information in issue here implicates national security. Similarly, neither the prosecutorial decisions in this case nor the possibility of graymail—the "practice whereby a criminal defendant threatens to reveal classified information during the course of his trial in the hope of forcing the government to drop the criminal charge against him,"—comes within our purview. Instead, we are faced with a series of very narrow, fact-specific evidentiary determinations and with the question whether the defendant could receive a fair trial without the aid of certain evidence.

Of course, the evidentiary rulings here were made under the procedural guidelines in CIPA, and we must ensure that CIPA's statutory requirements have been followed. Section 6(c) of CIPA provides for the district court to rule on the "use, relevance, or admissibility" of classified information that a defendant requests to use at trial. In *United States v. Smith*, 780 F.2d at 1106–08, this court considered the standard a court must follow in making a determination under § 6(c). *Smith* held that although the relevance of classified information under § 6(c) should be governed by Fed.R.Evid. 401, all relevant evidence is not automatically admissible under CIPA. *Id.* at 1106. Specifically, we ruled that the admissibility of relevant evidence under § 6(c) of CIPA involves a further balancing of "the public interest in nondisclosure against the defendant's right to prepare a defense." *Id.* at 1107.

Smith does not, however, set forth a mechanical balancing rule. Rather, it simply ensures that before admitting classified evidence, the trial court takes cognizance of both the state's interest in protecting national security and the defendant's interest in receiving a fair trial. Although *Smith* requires a court to take into account the government's interest in protecting national security, it also stresses that this interest cannot override the defendant's right to a fair trial. Thus, *Smith* requires the admission of classified information that is "helpful to the defense of an accused, or is essential to a fair determination of a cause." *Id.* at 1107 Were it otherwise, CIPA would be in tension with the defendant's fundamental constitutional right to present a complete defense. . . . Here, the government is simultaneously prosecuting the defendant and attempting to restrict his ability to use information that he feels is necessary to defend himself against the prosecution. Although CIPA contemplates that the use of classified information be streamlined, courts must not be remiss in protecting a defendant's right to a full and meaningful presentation of his claim to innocence.

The standard of review of the district court's evidentiary rulings is a deferential one. "The trial court has wide discretion [in ruling on relevance and admissibility], . . . and its determination will not be overturned except under the most 'extraordinary' circumstances." The trial court was immersed in the complicated facts of this case for several months, and its familiarity with the particulars of this prosecution far exceeds our own. Accordingly, we must review the trial court's § 6(a) admissibility rulings, as with any other determination of relevance and admissibility, under an abuse of discretion standard. The abuse of discretion standard also applies to the trial court's decision to reject a proposed substitution under § 6(c). With these principles in mind, we turn to consider the trial court's evidentiary rulings under CIPA.

We first review the trial court's admission of information pertaining to the three * * * * projects in Costa Rica, as well as its rejection of the government's proposed substitutions for this information. We conclude that the court did not abuse its discretion either in admitting this evidence or in rejecting the government's proposed substitutions for this evidence.

A.

Fernandez is charged in Counts One and Two with representing to the CIA Inspector General that the airstrip project was initiated by the Costa Rican authorities to enhance their national security. The indictment alleges that this representation was false and misleading because in fact Fernandez initiated the airstrip as a base for resupply of the Contras. Fernandez's primary defense to this charge is that his statements to the Inspector General about the genesis and purpose of the airstrip were true. In order to demonstrate the truth of his assertions that the airstrip was designed by the Costa Ricans to promote their security concerns, Fernandez claims that he needs to introduce evidence about three classified * * * * projects—* * * *. Fernandez maintains that these * * * * projects were all undertaken as part of a joint United States–Costa Rican effort to address the military threat posed to Costa Rica by Nicaragua, and that the airstrip project was part of this broader Costa Rican national security effort. Thus, evidence about the three projects and their relationship to the airstrip supports the truth of his allegedly false statements about the airstrip.

The district court agreed with Fernandez, ruling that information relating to these three projects was central to the charges against him and was thus admissible. With regard to the admissibility of the * * * *, the court stated:

* * * * *

I think [Fernandez] is entitled to that kind of evidence. I think positive steps that were taken that shows the concern of the Costa Ricans for that airstrip is the guts of his case. . . .

* * * * This is right at the heart of the allegations [the government has] made. And I think that [Fernandez] is entitled to use the facts that support the [Costa Rican's] concern. Simply standing up and saying that they are concerned isn't sufficient.

. . .

The government raises three objections to the admission of this evidence. First, it reargues the relevancy of the projects to the charges against Fernandez. Second, it contends that the district court failed to examine specific classified documents and ruled too broadly that everything pertaining to the three programs was relevant to Fernandez's defense. Third, the government argues that the trial court failed to apply the balancing test of *United States v. Smith*. We address each contention in turn.

The district court clearly did not abuse its discretion in determining information about the projects to be relevant. Fernandez is accused of falsely stating that the airstrip project was a Costa Rican initiative designed to address the Nicaraguan threat. Fernandez claims that the airstrip project, like the three classified projects he wanted to disclose at trial, was part of a joint U.S.-Costa Rican project designed to address the danger to Costa Rican national security posed by the Nicaraguan military. Information about the three projects thus directly substantiates the truth of his alleged false statements. It also shows that he lacked either the motive or the intent to lie to the Inspector General of the agency— the CIA—that he was working for and that was closely involved in the projects. Whether a jury would believe Fernandez is, of course, uncertain, but to rule this evidence irrelevant under § 6(a) of CIPA would be to vitiate much of the force of the defense. Accordingly, the district court correctly ruled, and in any event did not abuse its discretion in ruling, that the information on the three * * * * projects in Costa Rica was central to Fernandez's defense.

. . .

Finally, we find no merit in the government's contention that the district court failed to follow the dictates of *United States v. Smith*. While the government laments what it perceives as the failure of the trial court to perform an "express balancing" of the various interests involved, the transcripts of the CIPA hearings reveal that the trial judge's CIPA rulings were informed by a sensitivity both to the costs of disclosure and to the requirements of a fair trial. When the government invoked *Smith* at the CIPA hearing on July 13 the trial court acknowledged its awareness of these facts and stated:

> [W]hat I have been doing [during two days of CIPA hearings] is weighing the interests of security against the necessity for the defendant to have certain information in order to receive a fair trial in this case.

Furthermore, *Smith* makes clear that a finding that particular classified information is necessary to the defense is enough to defeat the contrary interest in protecting national security. *Smith*, 780 F.2d at 1107. In addition to the balancing inherent in all of the trial court's deliberations, the court twice made specific findings that the projects were necessary to the defense:

> I think positive steps that were taken that shows the concern of the Costa Ricans for that airstrip is the guts of [the defendant's] case. . . . This is right at the heart of the allegations you all have made.

. . .

And the other projects that were ongoing at the same time that [the defendant] was involved in [the airstrip project] I find are very relevant and necessary to his defense in this case. Clearly, then, the trial court fulfilled the requirements of *Smith*.

The government next argues that even if the classified information concerning the three projects was properly admitted, the trial court abused its discretion in rejecting the government's proposed substitutions. CIPA contemplates that the government may propose substitutions for relevant classified information, and that the trial court shall accept these substitution proposals if they "provide the defendant with substantially the same ability to make his defense as would disclosure of the specific classified information." 18 U.S.C.App. § 6(c)(1). We recognize that substitutions play an important part in the CIPA scheme, and we accordingly review them with some care. The government made two substitution proposals concerning the projects. The original proposals spoke very generally about Costa Rican concerns regarding the Nicaraguan threat. It also stated in general terms that Costa Rica sought and received assistance from the United States in the form of several projects in which Fernandez was involved. The district court rejected these proposals as inadequate to allow Fernandez to put on the kind of defense that the court had previously determined to be necessary:

> [I]t seems to me [that] for you to expect to indict and accuse the defendant of lying about who instigated this airstrip and then to prevent him from showing the serious undertakings of that Government in other areas that would tend to corroborate this undertaking, and reduce him to a simple general statement that, oh yeah, people were concerned, really doesn't allow this man to defend himself.

> . . . . .

> [W]hat you have prevented the defendant from doing by this substitution is to show the seriousness with which the Costa Rican government took the situation and got other specific programs started.

> . . . . .

If all [the Costa Ricans] had was a general concern about the situation, for this defendant to say, oh, they instigated the airstrip, that is the only specific thing they did because of their general concern, well, that leaves him in a very poor position to defend his case. The government's revised substitutions fared no better. The new substitutions spoke in general terms about * * * *. The trial court rejected these new proposals as similarly inadequate to the prior ones:

> I find that this stipulation does not meet what the defendant should be allowed to show. . . . I think the defendant must have the latitude of showing how these projects were instigated, who requested them, how they came about, to show the basic magnitude of the programs so that he can show the concerns of the Costa Rican government. And this submission that I have here just simply doesn't meet that.

We do not think the district court abused its discretion in ruling that the substitutions failed to "provide the defendant with substantially the same ability to make his defense as would disclosure of the specific classified information." 18 U.S.C.App. § 6(c)(1). The proposed substitutions fell far short of informing the jury about that which the trial judge had already determined to be essential to Fernandez's defense, namely, information about the origin, purpose, and scope of the three projects.

The substitutions would have precluded the defense from demonstrating the integral relationship between the airstrip project about which he is accused of lying and the other three projects whose purposes support his version of events. Fernandez himself would have been unable to testify about his understanding of the projects and their relationship to one another, and would have been precluded from introducing numerous classified CIA communication cables that he authored that would flesh out the common purpose of the projects (including the airstrip operation). In addition, the substitutions would have hampered Fernandez's ability to demonstrate the intimate involvement of the Costa Rican government in the projects and the closeness of U.S.-Costa Rican cooperation concerning them. For example, the substitution proposal which concedes that * * * * does not begin to capture the continuous and intimate interaction between Fernandez and * * * * with regard to all four projects and their relationship to Costa Rica's concern about the Nicaraguan threat.

The charge that Fernandez misrepresented the purpose of the airstrip project essentially calls into question his version of the truth about what he did as CIA station chief in Costa Rica. To address this charge requires Fernandez to paint a concrete and detailed picture of his working environment as he saw it. We agree with Fernandez's contention that the substitutions would preclude the defense from "present[ing] a coherent case of its own, since it would be shackled to a script written by the prosecution." If the vague, extremely abbreviated descriptions of the projects were accepted as exclusive substitutes for Fernandez's own testimony about his role in and understanding of the projects, for classified cables written by him that corroborated his understanding, and for his direct and cross-examination of witnesses involved in these projects, Fernandez's constitutionally guaranteed ability to present a defense would be severely compromised. The substitutions would have required the jury to judge Fernandez's role in the airstrip project, and thus the truth of his statements about it, in a contextual vacuum. They would not have provided Fernandez with "substantially the same ability to make his defense," and the court below did not abuse its discretion in rejecting them.

Nor, finally, did it abuse its discretion in ruling that the government's proposed narrowing of the indictment failed to satisfy Fernandez's need to introduce classified information about the three projects. . . .

E. Ex parte and in camera versus in camera

Notes and Questions

1. The flavor and amount detail found in the Fernandez ruling on the adequacy of the substitutions differs considerably from that of the Rezaq opinion. There are a number of things that might account for the differences. Might one of the factors be the fact that Rezaq involved an ex parte determination where the judge made his ruling essentially without any input from the defendant's counsel, while in Fernandez, the issues were addressed in an adversary proceeding?

What accounts for this procedural difference? Rezaq proceeded under sec. 4 of CIPA while Fernandez proceeded under sec. 6. Sec. 4 provides for an in camera ex parte proceeding while sec. 6 in subsec. (a) provides only for an in camera hearing. (Compare, however, sec. 6(c)(2).) Note, too, that Fernandez was a former CIA station chief who had probably earlier had full access to the documents involved and was probably generally familiar with them. Given those likelihoods, why was the government so insistent on not permitting the introduction of the original documents into evidence? We must assume that this was an instance where it was not a concern about disclosing the information to the defendant, but rather disclosing it to the jury, and, ultimately, to the public.

2.   Note, too, that in the Yunis case, supra, the government had filed "several ex parte in camera pleadings" under sec. 4 of CIPA. Consider the choice between these different forms of proceeding in light of the following excerpt from Brian Z. Tamanaha, a Critical Review of the Classified Information Procedures Act, 13 Am.J.Crim.L. 277, 307–308 (1987):

> ... [T]he creation of substitutions is the only feature unique to CIPA which effectively inhibits graymail. Substitutions are also powerful weapons for the prosecution with a high potential for abuse. They are used where the defendant's right to a fair trial most directly conflicts with the government's need to protect national security information. . . .

> The standard in section 6(c) that substitutions are not permissible unless substantially equivalent to the nondisclosed information, was included in fairness to the defendant. Likewise, to ensure that substitutions did not violate constitutional requirements, Congress provides in section 6 that substitutions may be approved only after a full adversary hearing in which the defendant has access to all the underlying documents.

> Not all substitutions, however, are created with the protection contained in section 6. Section 4 of CIPA allows the government to submit an ex parte request for the substitution of discoverable information in lieu of producing the actual documents. Since the substitution is formulated and approved ex parte, the defendant cannot oppose it and never has access to the underlying documents. The defendant has no way of knowing whether the substitution contains all the discoverable information, or whether it correctly states this information. . . .

> More troublesome, section 4 threatens to swallow the protections contained in section 6. To circumvent the adversary hearing in section 6, where the defendant has access to all the underlying information and is able to contest the adequacy of each substitution, the government may simply produce all or most of the discoverable information in the form of ex parte approved substitutions. Nothing in CIPA prohibits this approach and, indeed, a prosecutor would be remiss if this strategy were not adopted because it significantly reduces the amount of classified information that will be disclosed to the defendant. Following this strategy, the only substitutions subject to the adversary process will be those containing information already possessed by the defendant inde-

pendent of discovery. Relevant classified information not possessed by the defendant may be substituted without input from the defense.

Congress was aware that substitutions are approved ex parte in section 4 and not in section 6. The rationale for this different treatment is that 'since the government is seeking to withhold classified information from the defendant, an adversary hearing with defense knowledge would defeat the very purpose of the discovery rules.'

* * *

Chapter 10

THE FOREIGN INTELLIGENCE SURVEILLANCE ACT

A. Introduction

1. A brief history

Electronic surveillance of private conversations and physical searches of private premises by government agents must comply with the requirements of the Fourth Amendment. In the federal system, "normal" electronic surveillance must also comply with relevant federal statutes. The statutory requirements establishing a warrant procedure for "normal" electronic surveillance are set down in 18 U.S.C. § 2518, enacted as part of Title III of the Omnibus Crime Control and Safe Streets Act of 1968.

In 1978, the Foreign Intelligence Surveillance Act was enacted: It gave the Attorney General a broad power to authorize, without court order, electronic surveillance to acquire foreign intelligence information if it is directed solely at communications exclusively between or among foreign powers. However, if the surveillance is directed at agents of foreign powers or is likely to acquire the contents of foreign intelligence communications involving a United States person (defined as a U.S. citizen or a permanent resident alien), the FISA established a procedure for obtaining approval by a special court. This approval procedure involved the application of standards that differed from those provided in section 2518, supra.

Before describing the procedures involving the special court, a little historical background may be in order. Until 1968, there was no federal legislation on the books providing a judicial authorization procedure for electronic surveillance by federal law agents. However, beginning probably with the presidency of Franklin D. Roosevelt and until the FISA was enacted in 1978, some electronic surveillance without court approval was conducted by government agents under the authority of the Executive Branch, that is, the President, in aid of "national security." It was thought that there were not very many of these surveillances conducted and that they usually involved surveillance of foreign government activi-

230

ty. Thus, until 1968, to the extent that electronic surveillance by federal agents occurred with any colorable claim to being lawful, it was taking place without judicial authorization and usually in the context of a legal claim that there was a national security exception to the Fourth Amendment.

Beginning with the Kennedy administration in the early 1960's, Congress each year considered legislative bills that would have established a judicial authorization procedure for electronic surveillance based on a probable cause standard, modeled generally after the procedure and standards used to obtain warrants for physical searches. It was not until 1968, however, that legislation on this subject was finally enacted. 18 U.S.C. §§ 2510–2522 established a judicial approval procedure for "normal" electronic surveillance. However, in one of those provisions, § 2511(3), it was provided that nothing in this statute "shall limit the constitutional power of the President" to protect the national security of the United States. Subsequently, the Supreme Court in United States v. United States District Court, 407 U.S. 297 (1972) ruled that the government lacked the power to conduct electronic surveillance without judicial approval in "domestic security" cases. The Court left open, however, whether the government could engage in surveillance of foreign governments or their agents without judicial approval. Six years later, enactment of the FISA established procedures for judicial authorization of electronic surveillance by government agents to obtain foreign intelligence information. Viewed against this historical backdrop, rather than expanding federal authority, the FISA can be seen as a statute that reined in the Executive Branch, regulating a kind of electronic eavesdropping that previously had been uncontrolled by the judiciary.

2. The FISA statute

The FISA in 50 U.S.C. § 1803 provides for appointment by the Chief Justice of a court of seven district judges to hear applications and approve orders for foreign intelligence electronic surveillance anywhere in the United States. Section 1803 also provides for appointment of a three judge court to review denials of applications made under the Act and for review of the decisions of that court through a petition for a writ of certiorari to the Supreme Court. Excerpts from the FISA statute are set forth below.

§ 1801. Definitions

As used in this subchapter:

(a) "Foreign power" means—

(1) a foreign government or any component thereof, whether or not recognized by the United States;

(2) a faction of a foreign nation or nations, not substantially composed of United States persons;

(3) an entity that is openly acknowledged by a foreign government or governments to be directed and controlled by such foreign government or governments;

(4) a group engaged in international terrorism or activities in preparation therefor;

* * *

(b) ''Agent of a foreign power'' means—

(1) any person other than a United States person, who—

(A) acts in the United States as an officer or employee of a foreign power, or as a member of a foreign power as defined in subsection (a)(4) of this section;

(B) acts for or on behalf of a foreign power which engages in clandestine intelligence activities in the United States contrary to the interests of the United States, when the circumstances of such person's presence in the United States indicate that such person may engage in such activities in the United States, or when such person knowingly aids or abets any person in the conduct of such activities or knowingly conspires with any person to engage in such activities;

(C) engages in international terrorism or activities in preparation therefore;* or

(2) any person who—

(A) knowingly engages in clandestine intelligence gathering activities for or on behalf of a foreign power, which activities involve or may involve a violation of the criminal statutes of the United States;

(B) pursuant to the direction of an intelligence service or network of a foreign power, knowingly engages in any other clandestine intelligence activities for or on behalf of such foreign power, which activities involve or are about to involve a violation of the criminal statutes of the United States;

(C) knowingly engages in sabotage or international terrorism, or activities that are in preparation therefor, for or on behalf of a foreign power;

(D) knowingly enters the United States under a false or fraudulent identity for or on behalf of a foreign power or, while in the United States, knowingly assumes a false or fraudulent identity for or on behalf of a foreign power; or

(E) knowingly aids or abets any person in the conduct of activities described in subparagraph (A), (B), or (C) or knowingly conspires with any person to engage in activities described in subparagraph (A), (B), or (C).

* This subparagraph was added in December, 2004 through an amendment contained in the Intelligence Reform and Terrorism Prevention Act of 2004 (sec. 6001).

(c) "International terrorism" means activities that—

(1) involve violent acts or acts dangerous to human life that are a violation of the criminal laws of the United States or of any State, or that would be a criminal violation if committed within the jurisdiction of the United States or any State;

(2) appear to be intended—

(A) to intimidate or coerce a civilian population;

(B) to influence the policy of a government by intimidation or coercion; or

(C) to affect the conduct of a government by assassination or kidnapping; and

(3) occur totally outside the United States, or transcend national boundaries in terms of the means by which they are accomplished, the persons they appear intended to coerce or intimidate, or the locale in which their perpetrators operate or seek asylum.

. . .

(e) "Foreign intelligence information" means—

(1) information that relates to, and if concerning a United States person is necessary to, the ability of the United States to protect against—

(A) actual or potential attack or other grave hostile acts of a foreign power or an agent of a foreign power;

(B) sabotage or international terrorism by a foreign power or an agent of a foreign power; or

(C) clandestine intelligence activities by an intelligence service or network of a foreign power or by an agent of a foreign power; or

(2) information with respect to a foreign power or foreign territory that relates to, and if concerning a United States person is necessary to—

(A) the national defense or the security of the United States; or

(B) the conduct of the foreign affairs of the United States.

* * *

(i) "United States person" means a citizen of the United States, an alien lawfully admitted for permanent residence (as defined in section 1101(a)(20) of Title 8), an unincorporated association a substantial number of members of which are citizens of the United States or aliens lawfully admitted for permanent residence, or a corporation which is incorporated in the United States, but does not include a corporation or an association which is a foreign power, as defined in subsection (a)(1), (2), or (3) of this section.

* * *

§ 1802. Electronic surveillance authorization without court order; certification by Attorney General; reports to Congressional committees; transmittal under seal; duties and compensation of communication common carrier; applications; jurisdiction of court

(a)(1) Notwithstanding any other law, the President, through the Attorney General, may authorize electronic surveillance without a court order under this subchapter to acquire foreign intelligence information for periods of up to one year if the Attorney General certifies in writing under oath that—

(A) the electronic surveillance is solely directed at—

(i) the acquisition of the contents of communications transmitted by means of communications used exclusively between or among foreign powers, as defined in section 1801(a)(1), (2), or (3) of this title; or

(ii) the acquisition of technical intelligence, other than the spoken communications of individuals, from property or premises under the open and exclusive control of a foreign power, as defined in section 1801(a)(1), (2), or (3) of this title;

(B) there is no substantial likelihood that the surveillance will acquire the contents of any communication to which a United States person is a party; and

(C) the proposed minimization procedures with respect to such surveillance meet the definition of minimization procedures under section 1801(h) of this title. * * *

(2) An electronic surveillance authorized by this subsection may be conducted only in accordance with the Attorney General's certification and the minimization procedures adopted by him. The Attorney General shall assess compliance with such procedures and shall report such assessments to the House Permanent Select Committee on Intelligence and the Senate Select Committee on Intelligence under the provisions of section 1808(a) of this title.

* * *

(b) Applications for a court order under this subchapter are authorized if the President has, by written authorization, empowered the [Attorney] General to approve applications to the court having jurisdiction under section 1803 of this title, and a judge to whom an application is made may, notwithstanding any other law, grant an order, in conformity with section 1805 of this title, approving electronic surveillance of a foreign power or an agent of a foreign power for the purpose of obtaining foreign intelligence information, except that the court shall not have jurisdiction to grant any order approving electronic surveillance directed solely as described in paragraph (1)(A) of subsection (a) of this section unless such surveillance may involve the acquisition of communications of any United States person.

§ 1803. Designation of judges

(a) Court to hear applications and grant orders; record of denial; transmittal to court of review.

The Chief Justice of the United States shall publicly designate 11 district court judges from seven of the United States judicial circuits of whom no fewer than 3 shall reside within 20 miles of the District of Columbia who shall constitute a court which shall have jurisdiction to hear applications for and grant orders approving electronic surveillance anywhere within the United States under the procedures set forth in this Act, except that no judge designated under this subsection shall hear the same application for electronic surveillance under this Act which has been denied previously by another judge designated under this subsection. If any judge so designated denies an application for an order authorizing electronic surveillance under this Act, such judge shall provide immediately for the record a written statement of each reason for his decision and, on motion of the United States, the record shall be transmitted, under seal, to the court of review established in subsection (b).

(b) Court of review; record, transmittal to Supreme Court.

The Chief Justice shall publicly designate three judges, one of whom shall be publicly designated as the presiding judge, from the United States district courts or courts of appeals who together shall comprise a court of review which shall have jurisdiction to review the denial of any application made under this Act. If such court determines that the application was properly denied, the court shall immediately provide for the record a written statement of each reason for its decision and, on petition of the United States for a writ of certiorari, the record shall be transmitted under seal to the Supreme Court, which shall have jurisdiction to review such decision.

(c) Expeditious conduct of proceedings; security measures for maintenance of records.

Proceedings under this Act shall be conducted as expeditiously as possible. The record of proceedings under this Act, including applications made and orders granted, shall be maintained under security measures established by the Chief Justice in consultation with the Attorney General and the Director of Central Intelligence.

(d) Tenure.

Each judge designated under this section shall so serve for a maximum of seven years and shall not be eligible for redesignation, except that the judges first designated under subsection (a) shall be designated for terms of from one to seven years so that one term expires each year, and that judges first designated under subsection (b) shall be designated for terms of three, five, and seven years.

§ 1804. Applications for court orders

(a) Submission by Federal officer; approval of Attorney General; contents.

Each application for an order approving electronic surveillance under this subchapter shall be made by a Federal officer in writing upon oath or affirmation to a judge having jurisdiction under section 1803 of this title. Each application shall require the approval of the Attorney General based upon his finding that it satisfies the criteria and requirements of such application as set forth in this subchapter. It shall include—

(1) the identity of the Federal officer making the application;

(2) the authority conferred on the Attorney General by the President of the United States and the approval of the Attorney General to make the application;

(3) the identity, if known, or a description of the target of the electronic surveillance;

(4) a statement of the facts and circumstances relied upon by the applicant to justify his belief that—

(A) the target of the electronic surveillance is a foreign power or an agent of a foreign power; and

(B) each of the facilities or places at which the electronic surveillance is directed is being used, or is about to be used, by a foreign power or an agent of a foreign power;

(5) a statement of the proposed minimization procedures;

(6) a detailed description of the nature of the information sought and the type of communications or activities to be subjected to the surveillance;

(7) a certification or certifications by the Assistant to the President for National Security Affairs or an executive branch official or officials designated by the President from among those executive officers employed in the area of national security or defense and appointed by the President with the advice and consent of the Senate—

(A) that the certifying official deems the information sought to be foreign intelligence information;

(B) that a significant purpose of the surveillance is to obtain foreign intelligence information;

(C) that such information cannot reasonably be obtained by normal investigative techniques;

(D) that designates the type of foreign intelligence information being sought according to the categories described in section 1801(e) of this title; and

(E) including a statement of the basis for the certification that—

(i) the information sought is the type of foreign intelligence information designated; and

(ii) such information cannot reasonably be obtained by normal investigative techniques;

(8) a statement of the means by which the surveillance will be effected and a statement whether physical entry is required to effect the surveillance;

(9) a statement of the facts concerning all previous applications that have been made to any judge under this subchapter involving any of the persons, facilities, or places specified in the application, and the action taken on each previous application;

(10) a statement of the period of time for which the electronic surveillance is required to be maintained, and if the nature of the intelligence gathering is such that the approval of the use of electronic surveillance under this subchapter should not automatically terminate when the described type of information has first been obtained, a description of facts supporting the belief that additional information of the same type will be obtained thereafter;

* * *

§ 1805. Issuance of order.

(a) Necessary findings.

Upon an application made pursuant to section 1804 of this title, the judge shall enter an ex parte order as requested or as modified approving the electronic surveillance if he finds that—

(1) the President has authorized the Attorney General to approve applications for electronic surveillance for foreign intelligence information;

(2) the application has been made by a Federal officer and approved by the Attorney General;

(3) on the basis of the facts submitted by the applicant there is probable cause to believe that—

(A) the target of the electronic surveillance is a foreign power or an agent of a foreign power: Provided, That no United States person may be considered a foreign power or an agent of a foreign power solely upon the basis of activities protected by the first amendment to the Constitution of the United States; and

(B) each of the facilities or places at which the electronic surveillance is directed is being used, or is about to be used, by a foreign power or an agent of a foreign power;

(4) the proposed minimization procedures meet the definition of minimization procedures under section 1801(h) of this title; and

(b) Probable cause.

In determining whether or not probable cause exists for purposes of an order under subsection (a)(3), a judge may consider past activities of the target, as well as facts and circumstances relating to current or future activities of the target.

. . .

(e) Duration of order; extensions; review of circumstances under which information was acquired, retained or disseminated.

(1) An order issued under this section may approve an electronic surveillance for the period necessary to achieve its purpose, or for ninety days, whichever is less, except that

(A) an order under this section shall approve an electronic surveillance targeted against a foreign power, as defined in section 1801(a)(1), (2), or (3) of this title, for the period specified in the application or for one year, whichever is less, and

(B) an order under this chapter for a surveillance targeted against an agent of a foreign power, as defined in section 1801(b)(1)(A) of this title may be for the period specified in the application or for 120 days, whichever is less.

(2) Extensions of an order issued under this subchapter may be granted on the same basis as an original order upon an application for an extension and new findings made in the same manner as required for an original order, except that

(A) an extension of an order under this chapter for a surveillance targeted against a foreign power, as defined in section 1801(a)(5) or (6) of this title, or against a foreign power as defined in section 1801(a)(4) of this title that is not a United States person, may be for a period not to exceed one year if the judge finds probable cause to believe that no communication of any individual United States person will be acquired during the period, and

(B) an extension of an order under this chapter for a surveillance targeted against an agent of a foreign power as defined in section 1801 (b)(1)(A) of this title may be for a period not to exceed 1 year.

(3) At or before the end of the period of time for which electronic surveillance is approved by an order or an extension, the judge may assess compliance with the minimization procedures by reviewing the circumstances under which information concerning United States persons was acquired, retained, or disseminated.

(f) Emergency orders.

Notwithstanding any other provision of this subchapter, when the Attorney General reasonably determines that—

(1) an emergency situation exists with respect to the employment of electronic surveillance to obtain foreign intelligence information before an order authorizing such surveillance can with due diligence be obtained; and

(2) the factual basis for issuance of an order under this subchapter to approve such surveillance exists; he may authorize the emergency employment of electronic surveillance if a judge having jurisdiction under section 1803 of this title is informed by the Attorney General or his designee at the time of such authorization that the decision has been made to employ emergency electronic surveillance and if an application in accordance with this subchapter is made to that judge as soon as practicable, but not more than 72 hours after the Attorney General authorizes such surveillance. If the Attorney General authorizes such emergency employment of electronic surveillance, he shall require that the minimization procedures required by this subchapter for the issuance of a judicial order be followed. In the absence of a judicial order approving such electronic surveillance, the surveillance shall terminate when the information sought is obtained, when the application for the order is denied, or after the expiration of 72 hours from the time of authorization by the Attorney General, whichever is earliest. In the event that such application for approval is denied, or in any other case where the electronic surveillance is terminated and no order is issued approving the surveillance, no information obtained or evidence derived from such surveillance shall be received in evidence or otherwise disclosed in any trial, hearing, or other proceeding in or before any court, grand jury, department, office, agency, regulatory body, legislative committee, or other authority of the United States, a State, or political subdivision thereof, and no information concerning any United States person acquired from such surveillance shall subsequently be used or disclosed in any other manner by Federal officers or employees without the consent of such person, except with the approval of the Attorney General if the information indicates a threat of death or serious bodily harm to any person. A denial of the application made under this subsection may be reviewed as provided in section 1803 of this title.

Notes and Questions

1. The FISA statute was amended in December, 2004 by language contained in the Intelligence Reform and Terrorism Prevention Act of 2004, as indicated in the asterisked footnote to § 1801(b)(1)(C). What is the effect of this amendment on the scope of authority that the FBI has to invoke FISA in terrorism investigations? Consider in this connection also how § 1801(a)(4) and § 1801(b)(2)(C) relate to the new provision. Does the new

provision broaden the FBI's FISA terrorism authority to any significant extent?

2. Problem: Five African–American converts to Islam along with a sixth individual who is a native of Jordan, living in the United States, attempt to travel to Afghanistan in 2001 to join with al Qaeda and Taliban forces against the U.S. military They reach China but never make it to their destination and are turned back. Learning of their plans and their travels, in 2002, the FBI alleges the foregoing facts as the basis for its application to obtain a FISA warrant to conduct electronic surveillance and listen in on their conversations. Should the warrant application be approved? Suppose the application for the warrant is made in January, 2005. Is the legal basis for obtaining the warrant stronger in 2005 than it was in 2002? The facts are taken from United States v. Battle as described in an article by Anita Ramasastry posted at http://writ.news.findlaw.com/ramasastry/20030305.html on Mar. 5, 2003.

3. Problem: Compare with the facts presented in 2. above the following:

Hizballah is an organization founded by Lebanese Shi'a Muslims in response to the 1982 invasion of Lebanon by Israel. Hizballah provides various forms of humanitarian aid to Shi'a Muslims in Lebanon. However, it is also a strong opponent of Western presence in the Middle East, and it advocates the use of terrorism in support of its agenda. Hizballah is particularly opposed to the existence of Israel and to the activities of the American government in the Middle East. Hizballah's general secretary is Hassan Nasserallah, and its spiritual leader is Sheikh Fadlallah.

In 1992, Hammoud, a citizen of Lebanon, attempted to enter the United States on fraudulent documents. After being detained by the INS, Hammoud sought asylum. While the asylum application was pending, Hammoud moved to Charlotte, North Carolina, where his brothers and cousins were living. Hammoud ultimately obtained permanent resident status by marrying a United States citizen.

At some point in the mid–1990s, Hammoud, his wife, one of his brothers, and his cousins all became involved in a cigarette smuggling operation. The conspirators purchased large quantities of cigarettes in North Carolina, smuggled them to Michigan, and sold them without paying Michigan taxes. . . .

. . .

Hammoud concedes that Hizballah is a foreign power under FISA, but he argues that the Government did not have probable cause to believe that he was an agent of Hizballah. Hammoud's motion to suppress the FISA evidence was referred to a magistrate judge, who reviewed the FISA applications and supporting materials in camera and concluded that there was probable cause to believe that Hammoud was an agent of a foreign power. . . .

Based on the facts alleged above, is there probable cause to meet the FISA standard?

The facts are taken from United States v. Hammoud, 381 F.3d 316 (4th Cir. 2004). . . .

4.   The amendment that added § 1801(b)(1)(C) to the FISA statute also provided that the amendment would sunset, that is, cease to have effect on December 31, 2005 (unless, of course, renewed by Congress) along with certain other provisions enacted in the USA PATRIOT Act. Does making this amendment subject to a sunset provision—especially one that was at the time of enactment just one year away—make any sense? What might be the explanation?

* * *

C.   Comparing FISA surveillance rules and "normal" surveillance rules under 18 U.S.C. § 2510 et seq.

An important issue relating to FISA surveillances is how far they permit the government to depart from the "normal" Fourth Amendment judicial approval requirements. In this connection, a detailed comparison of the probable cause, duration and informing-the-target requirements, as well as other features of both categories of surveillances is useful.

1.   The probable cause requirement

a.   Before an order approving electronic surveillance can be issued under 18 U.S.C. § 2518, the judge must find that there is probable cause for belief that an individual is committing, has committed, or is about to commit a particular offense. There must also be probable cause for belief that particular communications concerning that offense will be obtained and that the facilities are being or are about to be used in connection with the commission of the offense.

b.   Under FISA, there is also a probable cause requirement, but on its face it does not require probable cause as to the commission of a crime. Rather under 50 U.S.C. § 1805, there must be probable cause that the target is a foreign power or the agent of a foreign power. (Under 1802(a) (1) (A), the President acting through the Attorney General, can without a judicial order authorize surveillance of communications solely between foreign powers provided that there is no substantial likelihood that communications to which a United States person is a party may be overheard.)

The issue of what the probable cause specified under 1805 relates to under FISA is somewhat more complicated than at first appears. True, it relates to whether the target is a foreign power or agent of a foreign power, but how are those terms defined? Foreign power is defined to include foreign governments or government-like or-related entities. No mention of criminality here but a foreign government can hardly claim the benefit of the probable cause requirement of the Fourth Amendment. The definition also includes: a group engaged in international terrorism or in activities in preparation therefor. Insofar as the probable cause is that the target is such a group, the probable cause would seem to refer to a criminal behavior component.

Suppose the probable cause relates to an agent of a foreign power. How is that phrase defined? Does it include a criminal conduct component? The definition of agent of a foreign power found in section 1801 is repeated below. It is a multi-part definition, and it is not easy to work one's way through it. Given this definition, to what extent does probable cause that a person is an agent of a foreign power include a criminal conduct component? With the December, 2004 addition to § 1801 of subsection (b)(1)(C), probable cause that an individual "engages in international terrorism or activities in preparation therefore" will suffice. While under the new language, the probable cause may relate to the conduct of an individual rather than a group, it still requires probable cause relating to terrorist activity or preparations therefore—again, it would seem requiring some measure of criminal activity-related behavior. How does it compare with the probable cause that an individual is committing a crime formula under 18 U.S.C § 2518? Is there more of a criminal conduct component to the FISA probable cause determination than initially appeared? Is it, however, less than what is required under 2518?

* * *

2. Duration of the intercept; time period within which target must be notified about the interception

a. Under 2518, the duration of the interception is limited to 30 days. Extensions can be granted by the judge but for not more than another 30 days per extension. Not later than 90 days after the period of the interception is terminated, the person named in the order approving the interception and such other parties to intercepted communications as the judge in his discretion determines, are to be provided information about the interception.

b. Under FISA, section 1805, the duration of the interception may be 90 days or 120 days, or in some circumstances as much as one year, and extensions may be for the period originally authorized or in certain cases for one year.

There is no requirement under FISA that the persons whose communications were intercepted be notified later about the interception.

3. Other aspects of FISA and "normal" surveillances

The FISA permits surveillance under some circumstances even though the target has not been identified, 50 U.S.C. § 1804(a)(3), which would seem inconsistent with the Fourth Amendment requirement that the place to be searched and the person and things to be seized be described with particularity. Minimization procedures under the FISA should also be compared with those required under Title III. Also, under the FISA, if the case ripens into a criminal prosecution, the application and orders may be reviewed by the district judge in camera and ex parte, without giving the surveilled party access to them. The Attorney General has authority under 50 U.S.C. § 1805 to issue surveillance orders in "emergency situations." See p. ___, supra.

4. Physical searches

While not part of the original FISA, provisions authorizing judicial approval of FISA physical searches under roughly the same standards that are used for electronic surveillance were subsequently added to the statute, 50 U.S.C. §§ 1822, 1823. The rules governing "normal" physical searches are found in Rule 41, Federal Rules of Criminal Procedure.

5. Statistical comparison of FISA and "normal" electronic surveillances

Since it first went into operation in 1979, there have been more than 10,000 applications for judicial approval of FISA surveillances. Until 2003, reportedly, no FISA application for judicial approval of a surveillance had been denied in the almost 25 year history of the Act although some had been modified. The actual numbers between 1978 and 1995 averaged more than 500 each year. Since 1995, as reported in annual letters from the Attorney General to the Administrative Office of the Courts and to the Speaker of the House, there has been a gradual increase in the annual numbers: in 1995, 697; 1996, 839; 1997, 749; 1998, 796; 1999, 886; 2000, 1005; 2001, 932; 2002, 1228. The letter for 2003, dated April 20, 2004, reported a significant spike in the number of applications, 1727. These include those applications for approval of searches which were solely electronic, solely physical or a combination of both electronic surveillance and physical search. For the first time, too, the report indicated that the FISA court had turned down some applications, four in all, but as a result of modification and resubmission, the court approved a total of 1724 applications. The letter also reported that the court had made substantial modifications in 79 applications.

At first, the foregoing numbers seem truly extraordinary—in the year, 2000, for example, an average of almost 3 applications a day and in 2003, the number jumps to almost 5 a day! Can there really be so much foreign intelligence surveillance going on? These numbers are tempered somewhat, however, when one realizes that the numbers include both initial applications and applications for extensions. There is thus a kind of double counting if one is trying to determine how many surveillances are on-going (as opposed to how many judicial determinations have occurred). Nevertheless, the numbers are quite large. If we assume that approximately one half of the FISA numbers are extensions, for the past five years, there were between 500 and 600 new applications each year—still a very significant number.

What is the comparable number of "normal" surveillances? Looking at the data since 1991, the number of intercept applications requested under 18 U.S.C. § 2518 ranged from 856 in 1991 to 1491 in 2001, averaging about 1100 per year. Extensions are reported separately and they ranged from 601 in 1991 to 1008 in 2001.

The sheer numbers, of course, do not necessarily indicate abuse of the FISA process. Still and all, the numbers give one pause.

Only the foregoing FISA statistics are reported publicly. More extensive reports are made to the Intelligence Committees but these are not reported publicly. A bill was introduced that would have required more information to be disclosed publicly. What came out of Congress, however, was legislation (sec. 6002 of the Intelligence Reform and Terrorism Prevention Act of 2004) that imposed these more detailed reporting obligations on the Attorney General, but only in reports to the Intelligence Committees and Judiciary Committees of the two Houses of Congress.

D. Gathering foreign intelligence information versus gathering information with a view to criminal prosecution

1. Background

The original notion behind the FISA statute may have been that intelligence gathering can be done entirely separate and insulated from criminal investigation and prosecution. Thus, for example, the notion may have been that the gathering of foreign intelligence usefully can serve many purposes that are not dependent on, or involve criminal prosecution—e.g., it can inform foreign policy; be used on occasion to expel foreign diplomats engaged in intelligence work; and help to protect the national security through the forestalling of plots directed against the United States.

Whatever the original conception may have been, while in the implementation of the FISA a distinction was drawn between gathering information for intelligence purposes and gathering it for use by law enforcement for prosecution purposes, in the statute itself no hard lines were drawn. The FISA did not bar the use by law enforcement personnel of information gathered for foreign intelligence purposes; indeed it seemed to contemplate such use, but it did single out such use for special treatment and generally did not seem to encourage it. For example, see 50 U.S.C. § 1806(a) and (b) as originally enacted.

§ 1806. Use of information

(a) Compliance with minimization procedures; privileged communications; lawful purposes

Information acquired from an electronic surveillance conducted pursuant to this subchapter concerning any United States person may be used and disclosed by Federal officers and employees without the consent of the United States person only in accordance with the minimization procedures required by this subchapter. No otherwise privileged communication obtained in accordance with, or in violation of, the provisions of this subchapter shall lose its privileged character. No information acquired from an electronic surveillance pursuant to this subchapter may be used or disclosed by Federal officers or employees except for lawful purposes.

(b) Statement for disclosure

No information acquired pursuant to this subchapter shall be disclosed for law enforcement purposes unless such disclosure is accompanied by a statement that such information, or any information derived therefrom, may only be used in a criminal proceeding with the advance authorization of the Attorney General.

Provisions recently incorporated into the FISA by the USA PATRIOT Act (Public Law 107–56, 115 Stat. 272) and the Homeland Security Act (Public Law 107–296, 116 Stat. 2135) appear to have been aimed at shifting the emphasis and moving the FISA in a different direction. These amendments appear to encourage the sharing of information between foreign intelligence personnel and law enforcement personnel. Issues of statutory interpretation are present, however. How far do the new provisions in the FISA, added by the USA PATRIOT Act, go in permitting the intermixing of the foreign intelligence and law enforcement functions? The USA PATRIOT Act added language that authorized the sharing by foreign intelligence personnel from their side, 50 U.S.C. § 403–5 (note the phrase "obtained as part of a criminal investigation,"), and similarly sharing by law enforcement personnel from their side, 18 U.S.C. § 2517.

* * *

The issues go beyond the sharing of information, however. Ultimately the question is whether it should be permissible to undertake a foreign intelligence-type surveillance that also has a law enforcement, that is, a criminal prosecution, purpose; and whether it should be permissible to have such investigations led by law enforcement rather than foreign intelligence personnel? Those who favor these types of undertakings see no harm in them and argue that otherwise law enforcement is frustrated in their efforts to deal with terrorists and terrorist activity and the foreign intelligence personnel are not able to do their job properly. Those who oppose it argue that permitting the use of foreign intelligence surveillance, with its watered down standards, secrecy and lack of protection for the U.S. person is a way to get around the requirements of the Fourth Amendment, that it will lead to abuses whereby a foreign intelligence purpose will be inappropriately used to obtain judicial authorization to eavesdrop or search, and that ultimately, it establishes a slippery slope leading to the undermining of Fourth Amendment protections.

* * *

§ 1804. Applications for court orders

(a) Submission by Federal officer; approval of Attorney General; contents

Each application for an order approving electronic surveillance under this subchapter shall be made by a Federal officer in writing upon oath or affirmation to a judge having jurisdiction under section 1803 of this title. Each application shall require the approval of the Attorney General based upon his finding that it satisfies the criteria and requirements of such application as set forth in this subchapter. It shall include—

. . .

(7) a certification . . .

(A) that the certifying official deems the information sought to be foreign intelligence information;

(B) that a significant purpose of the surveillance is to obtain foreign intelligence information;

(C) that such information cannot reasonably be obtained by normal investigative techniques;

. . .

Previously (a)(7)(B) of 50 U.S.C. § 1804 had provided that the obtaining of foreign intelligence information be "the purpose of the surveillance."

Does changing the language from "the purpose" to "a significant purpose," open the door to a contention that the primary purpose of the surveillance could be a law enforcement purpose, provided only that foreign intelligence information gathering was also a significant purpose of the endeavor?

Further, does the language of section (k)(1) added to § 1806, as delineated above, support the undertaking of a coordinated foreign intelligence and criminal investigation?

2. An opinion of the Foreign Intelligence Surveillance Court of Review

The proceedings of the Foreign Intelligence Surveillance Court are secret. Normally none of its opinions are published. On Thursday, August 22, 2002, for the first time in the history of the court, one of its opinions was made available to the Congress, the media and the public, an opinion actually filed on May 17, 2002 in a matter titled, In re All Matters Submitted to the Foreign Intelligence Surveillance Court. The opinion of all seven judges of the lower FISA court (subsequent to the development of this matter, the number of judges was increased to eleven) provided a fascinating window into the ongoing tension between the foreign intelligence information gathering function and the law enforcement-prosecution function. The government than appealed from the lower FISA court decision to the FISA Court of Review, as provided in 50 U.S.C § 1803. Since this was the first appeal to this Court, the opinion handed down, which is reproduced in pertinent part below, is this Court's first-ever opinion.

IN RE: SEALED CASE No.'s 02–001, 02–002

United States Foreign Intelligence Surveillance Court of Review.
310 F.3d 717 (2002).

Before: Guy, Senior Circuit Judge, Presiding; Silberman and Leavy, Senior Circuit Judges.

Per Curiam:

This is the first appeal from the Foreign Intelligence Surveillance Court to the Court of Review since the passage of the Foreign Intelligence Surveillance Act (FISA), 50 U.S.C. §§ 1801–1862, in 1978. This appeal is brought by the United States from a FISA court surveillance order which imposed certain restrictions on the government. Since the government is the only party to FISA proceedings, we have accepted briefs filed by the American Civil Liberties Union (ACLU) and the National Association of Criminal Defense Lawyers (NACDL) as amici curiae.

Not surprisingly this case raises important questions of statutory interpretation, and constitutionality. After a careful review of the briefs filed by the government and amici, we conclude that FISA, as amended by the Patriot Act, supports the government's position, and that the restrictions imposed by the FISA court are not required by FISA or the Constitution. We therefore remand for further proceedings in accordance with this opinion.

The court's decision from which the government appeals imposed certain requirements and limitations accompanying an order authorizing electronic surveillance of an "agent of a foreign power" as defined in FISA. There is no disagreement between the government and the FISA court as to the propriety of the electronic surveillance; the court found that the government had shown probable cause to believe that the target is an agent of a foreign power and otherwise met the basic requirements of FISA. The government's application for a surveillance order contains detailed information to support its contention that the target, who is a United States person, is aiding, abetting, or conspiring with others in international terrorism. The FISA court authorized the surveillance, but imposed certain restrictions, which the government contends are neither mandated nor authorized by FISA. Particularly, the court ordered that law enforcement officials shall not make recommendations to intelligence officials concerning the initiation, operation, continuation or expansion of FISA searches or surveillances. Additionally, the FBI and the Criminal Division [of the Department of Justice] shall ensure that law enforcement officials do not direct or control the use of the FISA procedures to enhance criminal prosecution, and that advice intended to preserve the option of a criminal prosecution does not inadvertently result in the Criminal Division's directing or controlling the investigation using FISA searches and surveillances toward law enforcement objectives.

To ensure the Justice Department followed these strictures the court also fashioned what the government refers to as a "chaperone requirement"; that a unit of the Justice Department, the Office of Intelligence Policy and Review (OIPR) (composed of 31 lawyers and 25 support staff), "be invited" to all meetings between the FBI and the Criminal Division involving consultations for the purpose of coordinating efforts "to investigate or protect against foreign attack or other grave hostile acts, sabotage, international terrorism, or clandestine intelligence activities by foreign powers or their agents." If representatives of OIPR are unable to attend such meetings, "OIPR shall be apprized of the substance of the meetings forthwith in writing so that the Court may be notified at the earliest opportunity."

We think it fair to say, however, that the May 17 opinion of the FISA court does not clearly set forth the basis for its decision. It appears to proceed from the assumption that FISA constructed a barrier between counterintelligence/intelligence officials and law enforcement officers in the Executive Branch—indeed, it uses the word "wall" popularized by certain commentators (and journalists) to describe that supposed barrier. Yet the opinion does not support that assumption with any relevant language from the statute.

The "wall" emerges from the court's implicit interpretation of FISA. The court apparently believes it can approve applications for electronic surveillance only if the government's objective is not primarily directed toward criminal prosecution of the foreign agents for their foreign intelligence activity. But the court neither refers to any FISA language supporting that view, nor does it reference the Patriot Act amendments, which the government contends specifically altered FISA to make clear that an application could be obtained even if criminal prosecution is the primary counter mechanism.

Instead the court relied for its imposition of the disputed restrictions on its statutory authority to approve "minimization procedures" designed to prevent the acquisition, retention, and dissemination within the government of material gathered in an electronic surveillance that is unnecessary to the government's need for foreign intelligence information. 50 U.S.C. § 1801(h).

The government makes two main arguments. The first, it must be noted, was not presented to the FISA court; indeed, insofar as we can determine it has never previously been advanced either before a court or Congress. That argument is that the supposed pre-Patriot Act limitation in FISA that restricts the government's intention to use foreign intelligence information in criminal prosecutions is an illusion; it finds no support in either the language of FISA or its legislative history. The government does recognize that several courts of appeals, while upholding the use of FISA surveillances, have opined that FISA may be used only if the government's primary purpose in pursuing foreign intelligence information is not criminal prosecution, but the government argues that those decisions, which did not carefully analyze the statute, were incorrect in their statements, if not incorrect in their holdings.

Alternatively, the government contends that even if the primary purpose test was a legitimate construction of FISA prior to the passage of the Patriot Act, that Act's amendments to FISA eliminate that concept. And as a corollary, the government insists the FISA court's construction of the minimization procedures is far off the mark both because it is a misconstruction of those provisions per se, as well as an end run around the specific amendments in the Patriot Act designed to deal with the real issue underlying this case. The government, moreover, contends that the FISA court's restrictions, which the court described as minimization procedures, are so intrusive into the operation of the Department of Justice as to exceed the constitutional authority of Article III judges.

We turn first to the statute as enacted in 1978. ... As is apparent, the definitions of agent of a foreign power and foreign intelligence information are crucial to an understanding of the statutory scheme. The latter means

> (1) information that relates to, and if concerning a United States person is necessary to, the ability of the United States to protect against—
>
>> A) actual or potential attack or other grave hostile acts of a foreign power or an agent of a foreign power;
>>
>> B) sabotage or international terrorism by a foreign power or an agent of a foreign power; or
>>
>> C) clandestine intelligence activities by an intelligence service or network of a foreign power or by an agent of a foreign power.

Id. § 1801(e)(1).

The definition of an agent of a foreign power, if it pertains to a U.S. person (which is the only category relevant to this case), is closely tied to criminal activity. The term includes any person who "knowingly engages in clandestine intelligence gathering activities ... which activities involve or may involve a violation of the criminal statutes of the United States," or "knowingly engages in sabotage or international terrorism, or activities that are in preparation therefor." Id. §§ 1801(b)(2)(A), (C) (emphasis added). International terrorism refers to activities that "involve violent acts or acts dangerous to human life that are a violation of the criminal laws of the United States or of any State, or that would be a criminal violation if committed within the jurisdiction of the United States or any State." Id. § 1801(c)(1). Sabotage means activities that "involve a violation of chapter 105 of [the criminal code], or that would involve such a violation if committed against the United States." Id. § 1801(d). For purposes of clarity in this opinion we will refer to the crimes referred to in section 1801(a)-(e) as foreign intelligence crimes.

In light of these definitions, it is quite puzzling that the Justice Department, at some point during the 1980s, began to read the statute as limiting the Department's ability to obtain FISA orders if it intended to prosecute the targeted agents—even for foreign intelligence crimes. To be sure, section 1804, which sets forth the elements of an application for an order, required a national security official in the Executive Branch—typically the Director of the FBI—to certify that "the purpose" of the surveillance is to obtain foreign intelligence information (amended by the Patriot Act to read "a significant purpose"). But as the government now argues, the definition of foreign intelligence information includes evidence of crimes such as espionage, sabotage or terrorism. Indeed, it is virtually impossible to read the 1978 FISA to exclude from its purpose the prosecution of foreign intelligence crimes, most importantly because, as we have noted, the definition of an agent of a foreign power—if he or she is a U.S. person—is grounded on criminal conduct. It does not seem that FISA, at least as originally enacted, even contemplated that the FISA court would inquire into the government's purpose in seeking foreign intelligence information. ... The government argues persuasively that arresting and prosecuting terrorist agents of, or spies for, a foreign power may well be the best technique to prevent them from successfully continuing their terrorist or espionage activity. The government might wish to surveil the agent for some period of time to discover other participants in a conspiracy or to uncover a foreign power's plans, but typically at some point the government would wish to apprehend the agent and it might be that only a prosecution would provide sufficient incentives for the agent to cooperate with the government. Indeed, the threat of prosecution might be sufficient to "turn the agent."

* * *

The origin of what the government refers to as the false dichotomy between foreign intelligence information that is evidence of foreign intelligence crimes and that which is not appears to have been a Fourth Circuit case decided in 1980. United States v. Truong Dinh Hung, 629 F.2d 908 (4th Cir.1980). That case, however, involved an electronic surveillance carried out prior to the passage of FISA and predicated on the President's executive power. In approving the district court's exclusion of evidence obtained through a warrantless surveillance subsequent to the point in time when the government's investigation became "primarily" driven by law enforcement objectives, the court held that the Executive Branch should be excused from securing a warrant only when "the object of the search or the surveillance is a foreign power, its agents or collaborators," and "the surveillance is conducted 'primarily' for foreign intelligence reasons." Id. at 915. Targets must "receive the protection of the warrant requirement if the government is primarily attempting to put together a criminal prosecution." Id. at 916. Although the Truong court acknowledged that "almost all foreign intelligence investigations are in part criminal" ones, it rejected the government's assertion that "if surveillance is to any degree directed at gathering foreign intelligence, the executive may ignore the warrant requirement of the Fourth Amendment." Id. at 915.

Several circuits have followed Truong in applying similar versions of the "primary purpose" test, despite the fact that Truong was not a FISA decision. * * *

⟨ . . .

The government's overriding concern is to stop or frustrate the agent's or the foreign power's activity by any means, but if one considers the actual ways in which the government would foil espionage or terrorism it becomes apparent that criminal prosecution analytically cannot be placed easily in a separate response category. It may well be that the government itself, in an effort to conform to district court holdings, accepted the dichotomy it now contends is false. Be that as it may, since the cases that "adopt" the dichotomy do affirm district court opinions permitting the introduction of evidence gathered under a FISA order, there was not much need for the courts to focus on the issue with which we are confronted.

In sum, we think that the FISA as passed by Congress in 1978 clearly did not preclude or limit the government's use or proposed use of foreign intelligence information, which included evidence of certain kinds of criminal activity, in a criminal prosecution. In order to understand the FISA court's decision, however, it is necessary to trace developments and understandings within the Justice Department post-Truong as well as after the passage of the Patriot Act. As we have noted, some time in the 1980s—the exact moment is shrouded in historical mist—the Department applied the Truong analysis to an interpretation of the FISA statute. What is clear is that in 1995 the Attorney General adopted "Procedures for Contacts Between the FBI and the Criminal Division Concerning Foreign Intelligence and Foreign Counterintelligence Investigations." Apparently to avoid running afoul of the primary purpose test used by some courts, the 1995 Procedures limited contacts between the FBI and the Criminal Division in cases where FISA surveillance or searches were being conducted by the FBI for foreign intelligence (FI) or foreign counterintelligence (FCI) purposes. The procedures state that "the FBI and Criminal Division should ensure that advice intended to preserve the option of a criminal prosecution does not inadvertently result in either the fact or the appearance of the Criminal Division's directing or controlling the FI or FCI investigation toward law enforcement objectives." 1995 Procedures at 2, ¶ 6 (emphasis added). Although these procedures provided for significant information sharing and coordination between criminal and FI or FCI investigations, based at least in part on the "directing or controlling" language, they eventually came to be narrowly interpreted within the Department of Justice, and most particularly by OIPR, as requiring OIPR to act as a "wall" to prevent the FBI intelligence officials from communicating with the Criminal Division regarding ongoing FI or FCI investigations. . . . Thus, the focus became the nature of the underlying investigation, rather than the general purpose of the surveillance. Once prosecution of the target was being considered, the procedures, as interpreted by OIPR in light of the case law, prevented the Criminal Division from providing any meaningful advice to the FBI. Id.

The Department's attitude changed somewhat after the May 2000 report by the Attorney General and a July 2001 Report by the General Accounting Office both concluded that the Department's concern over how the FISA court or other federal courts might interpret the primary purpose test has inhibited necessary coordination between intelligence and law enforcement officials. General Accounting Office, FBI Intelligence Investigations: Coordination Within Justice on Counterintelligence Criminal Matters is Limited (July 2001) (GAO–01–780) (GAO Report) at 3. The AGRT Report also concluded, based on the text of FISA and its legislative history, that not only should the purpose of the investigation not be inquired into by the courts, but also that Congress affirmatively anticipated that the underlying investigation might well have a criminal as well as foreign counterintelligence objective. In response to the AGRT Report, the Attorney General, in January 2000, issued additional, interim procedures designed to address coordination problems identified in that report. In August 2001, the Deputy Attorney General issued a memorandum clarifying Department of Justice policy governing intelligence sharing and establishing additional requirements. (These actions, however, did not replace the 1995 Procedures.) But it does not appear that the Department thought of these internal procedures as "minimization procedures" required under FISA. Nevertheless, the FISA court was aware that the procedures were being followed by the Department and apparently adopted elements of them in certain cases.

The passage of the Patriot Act altered and to some degree muddied the landscape. In October 2001, Congress amended FISA to change "the purpose" language in 1804(a)(7)(B) to "a significant purpose." It also added a provision allowing "Federal officers who conduct electronic surveillance to acquire foreign intelligence information" to "consult with Federal law enforcement officers to coordinate efforts to investigate or protect against" attack or other grave hostile acts, sabotage or international terrorism, or clandestine intelligence activities, by foreign powers or their agents. 50 U.S.C. § 1806(k)(1). And such coordination "shall not preclude" the government's certification that a significant purpose of the surveillance is to obtain foreign intelligence information, or the issuance of an order authorizing the surveillance. Id. § 1806(k)(2). Although the Patriot Act amendments to FISA expressly sanctioned consultation and coordination between intelligence and law enforcement officials, in response to the first applications filed by OIPR under those amendments, in November 2001, the FISA court for the first time adopted the 1995 Procedures, as augmented by the January 2000 and August 2001 Procedures, as "minimization procedures" to apply in all cases before the court.

The Attorney General interpreted the Patriot Act quite differently. On March 6, 2002, the Attorney General approved new "Intelligence

Sharing Procedures" to implement the Act's amendments to FISA. The 2002 Procedures supersede prior procedures and were designed to permit the complete exchange of information and advice between intelligence and law enforcement officials. They eliminated the "direction and control" test and allowed the exchange of advice between the FBI, OIPR, and the Criminal Division regarding "the initiation, operation, continuation, or expansion of FISA searches or surveillance." On March 7, 2002, the government filed a motion with the FISA court, noting that the Department of Justice had adopted the 2002 Procedures and proposing to follow those procedures in all matters before the court. The government also asked the FISA court to vacate its orders adopting the prior procedures as minimization procedures in all cases and imposing special "wall" procedures in certain cases.

Unpersuaded by the Attorney General's interpretation of the Patriot Act, the court ordered that the 2002 Procedures be adopted, with modifications, as minimization procedures to apply in all cases. The court emphasized that the definition of minimization procedures had not been amended by the Patriot Act, and reasoned that the 2002 Procedures "cannot be used by the government to amend the Act in ways Congress has not." The court explained:

> Given our experience in FISA surveillances and searches, we find that these provisions in sections II.B and III [of the 2002 Procedures], particularly those which authorize criminal prosecutors to advise FBI intelligence officials on the initiation, operation, continuation or expansion of FISA's intrusive seizures, are designed to enhance the acquisition, retention and dissemination of evidence for law enforcement purposes, instead of being consistent with the need of the United States to "obtain, produce, and disseminate foreign intelligence information" ... as mandated in § 1801(h) and § 1821(4).

The FISA court also adopted a new rule of court procedure, Rule 11, which provides that "[a]ll FISA applications shall include informative descriptions of any ongoing criminal investigations of FISA targets, as well as the substance of any consultations between the FBI and criminal prosecutors at the Department of Justice or a United States Attorney's Office."

Undeterred, the government submitted the application at issue in this appeal on July 19, 2002, and expressly proposed using the 2002 Procedures without modification. In an order issued the same day, the FISA judge hearing the application granted an order for surveillance of the target but modified the 2002 Procedures consistent with the court's May 17, 2002 en banc order. It is the July 19, 2002 order that the government appeals, along with an October 17, 2002 order granting, with the same modifications as the July 19 order, the government's application for renewal of the surveillance in this case. Because those orders incorporate the May 17, 2002 order and opinion by reference, however, that order and opinion are before us as well.

. . .

Essentially, the FISA court took portions of the Attorney General's augmented 1995 Procedures—adopted to deal with the primary purpose standard—and imposed them generically as minimization procedures. In doing so, the FISA court erred. It did not provide any constitutional basis for its action—we think there is none—and misconstrued the main statutory provision on which it relied. The court mistakenly categorized the augmented 1995 Procedures as FISA minimization procedures and then compelled the government to utilize a modified version of those procedures in a way that is clearly inconsistent with the statutory purpose.

* * *

We also think the refusal by the FISA court to consider the legal significance of the Patriot Act's crucial amendments was error. The government, in order to avoid the requirement of meeting the "primary purpose" test, specifically sought an amendment to section 1804(a)(7)(B) which had required a certification "that the purpose of the surveillance is to obtain foreign intelligence information" so as to delete the article "the" before "purpose" and replace it with "a." The government made perfectly clear to Congress why it sought the legislative change. Congress, although accepting the government's explanation for the need for the amendment, adopted language which it perceived as not giving the government quite the degree of modification it wanted. Accordingly, section 1804(a)(7)(B)'s wording became "that a significant purpose of the surveillance is to obtain foreign intelligence information." There is simply no question, however, that Congress was keenly aware that this amendment relaxed a requirement that the government show that its primary purpose was other than criminal prosecution.

No committee reports accompanied the Patriot Act but the floor statements make congressional intent quite apparent. The Senate Judiciary Committee Chairman Senator Leahy acknowledged that "[p]rotection against these foreign-based threats by any lawful means is within the scope of the definition of 'foreign intelligence information,' and the use of FISA to gather evidence for the enforcement of these laws was contemplated in the enactment of FISA." 147 Cong. Rec. S11004 (Oct. 25, 2001). "This bill . . . break[s] down traditional barriers between law enforcement and foreign intelligence. This is not done just to combat international terrorism, but for any criminal investigation that overlaps a broad definition of 'foreign intelligence.'" 147 Cong. Rec. S10992 (Oct. 25, 2001) (statement of Sen. Leahy). And Senator Feinstein, a "strong support[er]," was also explicit.

The ultimate objective was to make it easier to collect foreign intelligence information under the Foreign Intelligence Surveillance Act, FISA. Under current law, authorities can proceed with surveillance under FISA only if the primary purpose of the investigation is to collect foreign intelligence.

But in today's world things are not so simple. In many cases, surveillance will have two key goals—the gathering of foreign intelligence, and the gathering of evidence for a criminal prosecution. Determining which purpose is the "primary" purpose of the investigation can be difficult, and will only become more so as we coordinate our intelligence and law enforcement efforts in the war against terror.

Rather than forcing law enforcement to decide which purpose is primary—law enforcement or foreign intelligence gathering, this bill strikes a new balance. It will now require that a "significant" purpose of the investigation must be foreign intelligence gathering to proceed with surveillance under FISA. The effect of this provision will be to make it easier for law enforcement to obtain a FISA search or surveillance warrant for those cases where the subject of the surveillance is both a potential source of valuable intelligence and the potential target of a criminal prosecution. Many of the individuals involved in supporting the September 11 attacks may well fall into both of these categories.

147 Cong. Rec. S10591 (Oct. 11, 2001).

To be sure, some Senate Judiciary Committee members including the Chairman were concerned that the amendment might grant too much authority to the Justice Department—and the FISA court.

* * *

Accordingly, the Patriot Act amendments clearly disapprove the primary purpose test. And as a matter of straightforward logic, if a FISA application can be granted even if "foreign intelligence" is only a significant—not a primary—purpose, another purpose can be primary. One other legitimate purpose that could exist is to prosecute a target for a foreign intelligence crime. We therefore believe the Patriot Act amply supports the government's alternative argument but, paradoxically, the Patriot Act would seem to conflict with the government's first argument because by using the term "significant purpose," the Act now implies that another purpose is to be distinguished from a foreign intelligence purpose.

The government heroically tries to give the amended section 1804(a)(7)(B) a wholly benign interpretation. It concedes that "the 'significant purpose' amendment recognizes the existence of the dichotomy between foreign intelligence and law enforcement," but it contends that "it cannot be said to recognize (or approve) its legitimacy." We are not persuaded. The very letter the Justice Department sent to the Judiciary Committee in 2001 defending the constitutionality of the significant purpose language implicitly accepted as legitimate the dichotomy in FISA that the government now claims (and we agree) was false.

It said, "it is also clear that while FISA states that 'the' purpose of a search is for foreign surveillance, that need not be the only purpose. Rather, law enforcement considerations can be taken into account, so long as the surveillance also has a legitimate foreign intelligence purpose." The senatorial statements explaining the significant purpose amendments which we described above are all based on the same understanding of FISA which the Justice Department accepted—at least until this appeal.

In short, even though we agree that the original FISA did not contemplate the "false dichotomy," the Patriot Act actually did—which makes it no longer false. The addition of the word "significant" to section 1804(a)(7)(B) imposed a requirement that the government have a measurable foreign intelligence purpose, other than just criminal prosecution of even foreign intelligence crimes. Although section 1805(a)(5), as we discussed above, may well have been intended to authorize the FISA court to review only the question whether the information sought was a type of foreign intelligence information, in light of the significant purpose amendment of section 1804 it seems section 1805 must be interpreted as giving the FISA court the authority to review the government's purpose in seeking the information.

That leaves us with something of an analytic conundrum. On the one hand, Congress did not amend the definition of foreign intelligence information which, we have explained, includes evidence of foreign intelligence crimes. On the other hand, Congress accepted the dichotomy between foreign intelligence and law enforcement by adopting the significant purpose test. Nevertheless, it is our task to do our best to read the statute to honor congressional intent. The better reading, it seems to us, excludes from the purpose of gaining foreign intelligence information a sole objective of criminal prosecution. We therefore reject the government's argument to the contrary. Yet this may not make much practical difference. Because, as the government points out, when it commences an electronic surveillance of a foreign agent, typically it will not have decided whether to prosecute the agent (whatever may be the subjective intent of the investigators or lawyers who initiate an investigation). So long as the government entertains a realistic option of dealing with the agent other than through criminal prosecution, it satisfies the significant purpose test.

The important point is—and here we agree with the government—the Patriot Act amendment, by using the word "significant," eliminated any justification for the FISA court to balance the relative weight the government places on criminal prosecution as compared to other counterintelligence responses. If the certification of the application's purpose articulates a broader objective than criminal prosecution—such as stopping an ongoing conspiracy—and includes other potential non-prosecutorial responses, the government meets the statutory test. Of course, if the court concluded that the government's sole objective was merely to gain evidence of past criminal conduct—even foreign intelligence crimes—to punish the agent rather than halt ongoing espionage or terrorist activity, the application should be denied.

The government claims that even prosecutions of non-foreign intelligence crimes are consistent with a purpose of gaining foreign intelligence information so long as the government's objective is to stop espionage or terrorism by putting an agent of a foreign power in prison. That interpretation transgresses the original FISA. It will be recalled that Congress intended section 1804(a)(7)(B) to prevent the government from targeting a foreign agent when its "true purpose" was to gain non-foreign intelligence information—such as evidence of ordinary crimes or scandals. (If the government inadvertently came upon evidence of ordinary crimes, FISA provided for the transmission of that evidence to the proper authority. 50 U.S.C. § 1801(h)(3).) It can be argued, however, that by providing that an application is to be granted if the government has only a "significant purpose" of gaining foreign intelligence information, the Patriot Act allows the government to have a primary objective of prosecuting an agent for a non-foreign intelligence crime. Yet we think that would be an anomalous reading of the amendment. For we see not the slightest indication that Congress meant to give that power to the Executive Branch. Accordingly, the manifestation of such a purpose, it seems to us, would continue to disqualify an application. That is not to deny that ordinary crimes might be inextricably intertwined with foreign intelligence crimes. For example, if a group of international terrorists were to engage in bank robberies in order to finance the manufacture of a bomb, evidence of the bank robbery should be treated just as evidence of the terrorist act itself. But the FISA process cannot be used as a device to investigate wholly unrelated ordinary crimes.

One final point; we think the government's purpose as set forth in a section 1804(a)(7)(B) certification is to be judged by the national security official's articulation and not by a FISA court inquiry into the origins of an investigation nor an examination of the personnel involved. It is up to the Director of the FBI, who typically certifies, to determine the government's national security purpose, as approved by the Attorney General or Deputy Attorney General. This is not a standard whose application the FISA court legitimately reviews by seeking to inquire into which Justice Department officials were instigators of an investigation. All Justice Department officers—including those in the FBI—are under the control of the Attorney General. If he wishes a particular investigation to be run by an officer of any division, that is his prerogative. There is nothing in FISA or the Patriot Act that suggests otherwise. That means, perforce, if the FISA court has reason to doubt that the government has any real non-prosecutorial purpose in seeking foreign intelligence information it can demand further inquiry into the certifying officer's purpose—or perhaps even the Attorney General's or Deputy Attorney General's reasons for approval. The important point is that the relevant purpose is that of those senior officials in the Executive Branch who have the responsibility of appraising the government's national security needs.

* * *

Although the Court ... [has] cautioned that the threat to society is not dispositive in determining whether a search or seizure is reasonable, it certainly remains a crucial factor. Our case may well involve the most serious threat our country faces. Even without taking into account the President's inherent constitutional authority to conduct warrantless foreign intelligence surveillance, we think the procedures and government showings required under FISA, if they do not meet the minimum Fourth Amendment warrant standards, certainly come close. We, therefore, believe firmly, applying the balancing test drawn from Keith, that FISA as amended is constitutional because the surveillances it authorizes are reasonable.

Accordingly, we reverse the FISA court's orders in this case to the extent they imposed conditions on the grant of the government's applications, vacate the FISA court's Rule 11, and remand with instructions to grant the applications as submitted and proceed henceforth in accordance with this opinion.

Notes and Questions

1. Reportedly, government investigations of terrorist activity have been energized by the decision in the principal case; that prosecutors had assumed that FISA information was off limits in criminal cases. See Glenn R. Simpson and Jess Bravin, New Powers Fuel Legal Assault on Suspected Terror Supporters, Wall Street Journal, Jan. 21, 2003.

2. a. The FBI has information that members of a motorcycle gang involved in illegal drug trafficking who have been under law enforcement investigation have been in touch with foreign agents who the Bureau believes are plotting a terrorist action. The FBI believes that the foreign agents are exploring the possibility of importing drugs, selling them to the motorcycle gang and using the profits to help finance the terrorist plot. The Justice Department wishes to obtain judicial approval under FISA for electronic surveillance and physical searches directed against members of the motorcycle gang as well as the foreign agents. Should the FISA court approve an order authorizing the surveillance?

b. The FBI has been investigating a drug ring. It learns that there is a new member of the ring who in the past has had ties to al Qaeda. It requests an order under FISA approving electronic surveillance of all members of the ring. What result?

c. A member of a terrorist group now defunct has slipped into the United States surreptitiously. The FBI wishes to obtain a judicial order under FISA to listen in to his telephone conversations. Their purpose is: a) to determine whether he is currently planning any terrorist activity; and b) to gather evidence about a past terrorist bomb planting in which they believe he was involved. What result?

3. What does the court of review opinion have to say, if anything about the following subjects?

a. the propriety of a sharing of information between personnel with a law enforcement-prosecution mission and those with a foreign intelligence mission during the course of an investigation;

b. the permissibility of consultation and advice-seeking and advice-giving among these two sets of personnel during the course of an investigation; and,

c. the permissibility of law enforcement personnel's initiating, supervising and directing of an investigation conducted using surveillance and search authority obtained under the terms of FISA.

4. In an investigation of a suspected terrorist cell, the FBI obtains a FISA search warrant to search the homes of the cell members and also obtains judicial approval for electronic surveillance of these same individuals. Clearly the FBI wishes to prevent any planned terrorist attacks. But if they get evidence of planning of these attacks, they will wish also to prosecute these individuals. At some point law enforcement personnel and prosecutors concerned with prosecution will need to be brought into the picture? Does it make sense, did it ever make sense to try to build a wall between intelligence and law enforcement personnel in the context of this kind of scenario?

5. The concern about an undermining of Fourth Amendment protections through the use of FISA in inappropriate situations is a legitimate worry. Did the approach which the FISA Court of Review rejected really serve Fourth Amendment interests? Now that that approach has been rejected, what needs to be done to assure that FISA is not being misused?

6. The In re Sealed Case, supra, triggered much law review commentary, most of it expressing concern about the watering down of Fourth Amendment protections that would result from the PATRIOT Act amendments of the FISA statute and the FISA Review Court's decision in the matter. See, e.g., George P. Varghese, A Sense of Purpose: The Role of Law Enforcement in Foreign Intelligence Surveillance, 152 U.Pa. L.Rev. 385 (2003); Nola K. Breglio, Note: Leaving FISA Behind: The Need to Return to Warrantless Foreign Intelligence Surveillance, 113 Yale L.J. 179 (2003); David Hardin, The Fuss over Two Small Words: The Unconstitutionality of the USA PATRIOT Act Amendments to FISA Under the Fourth Amendment, 71 Geo. Wash.L.Rev. 291 (2003); John E. Branch III, Statutory Misinterpretation: The Foreign Intelligence Court of Review's Interpretation of the "Significant Purpose" Requirement of the Foreign Intelligence Surveillance Act, 81 N.C.L.Rev. 2075 (2003).

* * *

Chapter 13

U.S. AGENTS ACTING ABROAD

A. Introduction

In the previous chapters, we have focused on issues raised by governmental actions directed against terrorism occurring mainly in the territorial United States, but terrorism is now a global affair, and terrorist planning and actions directed against the United States or U.S. interests can occur anywhere in the world. As revealed in Chapter 3, *supra*, many of our anti-terrorism criminal statutes have provisions that expressly provide for extra-territorial jurisdiction over criminal conduct abroad that harms specified U.S. interests.

Accordingly, in fighting terrorism, the government is trying to attack terrorists and their infrastructure in all parts of the world. These efforts raise issues somewhat different from those posed by governmental actions in the United States. The basic questions are, how far does U.S. law, both statutory and constitutional, reach? Should the extension of the reach of U.S. criminal laws carry with it an extension of the application of rights protected by the Constitution or by statute? Are U.S. agents limited in the actions they can engage in while abroad to the same extent as in the territorial United States? Or are our agents freer to engage in actions abroad that would not be lawful if done here? What kinds of factors bear on what our agents can or cannot lawfully (i.e. lawful under U.S. law) do? Does it matter whether we are working in cooperation with official personnel of the host country or complying with the laws of the host country? Are there limits imposed by international law that bear on these issues? Are we bound in our actions by international law?

Accordingly, in this chapter, we address questions growing out of various kinds of actions by U.S. agents, usually FBI or CIA, acting in foreign lands. For a survey of many of these issues, see Ronald J. Sievert, War on Terrorism or Global Law Enforcement Operation?, 78 Notre Dame L.Rev. 307 (2003).

B.   Investigation and information-gathering

Investigation and information gathering can take various forms. The kind that focuses on specific individuals usually is considered under one or more of several legal categories—physical searches, electronic surveillance, and interrogation.

* * *

Notes and Questions

1.   As mentioned in the introductory comments to this section, the issues of governmental action abroad in an investigatory mode typically arise in the context of physical searches, electronic surveillance and interrogations. More of the caselaw has involved electronic surveillance but the law of such cases, insofar as it is based in constitutional doctrine, generally would be applicable to the physical search area, too.

* * *

9.   In December, 2002, a detailed report appeared in the Washington Post describing interrogations of terrorist suspects—some involving extreme physical techniques that amount to physical torture. According to the story, U.S. agents, reportedly from the CIA, either are undertaking the interrogations themselves or are managing the questioning by foreign officials, with varying degrees of involvement. Dana Priest and Barton Gellman, U.S. Decries Abuse but Defends Interrogations; 'Stress and Duress' Tactics Used on Terrorism Suspects Held in Secret Overseas Facilities, The Washington Post, Dec. 26, 2002, at A01.

In response to the Washington Post story, a military spokesman at the location in Afghanistan where the CIA was supposed to be conducting the interrogations stated that the Post article was false. White House spokesman Scott McClellan responded by saying that "we believe we are in full compliance with domestic and international law, including domestic and international law dealing with torture." Wherever U.S. forces are holding combatants, they are being held "humanely, in a manner consistent with the third Geneva Convention," McClellan said. See Alan Cooperman, CIA Interrogation Under Fire; Human Rights Groups Say Techniques Could Be Torture, The Washington Post, Dec. 28, 2002, at A09.

Also according to a news report, the federal government has trained interrogators on the use of various interrogation techniques that arguably tread on the line between interviewing and torture. See Jess Bravin, Interrogation School Tells Army Recruits How Grilling Works; 30 Techniques in 16 Weeks, Just Short of Torture; Do They Yield Much?, The Wall Street Journal, April 26, 2002, at A1.

10.   Also see the material in Chapter 7, . . . relating to discussions and memoranda within the government regarding the legality of the use of torture in interrogation. Given the September 11th attacks and the continuing threat that al Qaeda poses, is the use of extreme measures to gain information legally justified? Morally justified? See Emanuel Gross, Legal Aspects of Tackling Terrorism: the The Balance between the Right of a Democracy to Defend Itself and the Protection of Human Rights, 6 UCLA J. Int'l L. and & Foreign Aff. 89 (2001).

11.   . . . On the one hand, it is clear that these interrogations are being conducted in part for intelligence information purposes—that is, to acquire information to be used to apprehend other terrorists and to prevent acts of terrorism. On the other hand, once the information is obtained, it seems likely that there will be occasions where the information will be introduced in criminal trials. Thus, for example, in the military commission trials that are currently being initiated, issues relating to the use of evidence allegedly obtained by torture are likely to be raised by the defendants. . . . Compare the prosecution of John Walker Lindh. . . . Lindh's lawyer complained that Lindh had been mistreated in Afghanistan and that there had been interrogation improprieties. In the end, Lindh pleaded guilty.

12.   The question arises whether a non-resident alien with no connection to the U.S. can claim the benefit of Fifth Amendment protections in a federal criminal prosecution in this country. Consult Mark A. Godsey, The New Frontier of Constitutional Confession Law—The The International Arena: Exploring the Admissibility of Confessions Taken by U.S. Investigators from Non–Americans Abroad, 91 Geo. L.J. 851 (2003); Adam Shedd, The Fifth Amendment Privilege Against Self–Incrimination–Does It Exist Extra-Territorially?, 77 Tul.L.Rev. 767 (2003), and consider the following case:

UNITED STATES v. BIN LADEN

132 F.Supp. 2d 168 (S.D.N.Y. 2001).

SAND, District Judge:

. . .

From the outset, Al-'Owhali was considered by his interrogators to be a suspect in the embassy bombing, a violation of both U.S. and Kenyan law. S.A. Gaudin understood that he was, at all times, involved in a criminal investigation.

. . .

Subsequent to August 12, interrogation of Al-'Owhali took place on eight other days: August 13 (approx. 4 hours), 14 (approx. 2 to 2.5 hours), 17 (approx. 3.5 hours), and 21–25.

. . .

Our analysis of Defendants' motions to suppress statements turns chiefly on the constitutional standard we adopt today, as a matter of first impression, concerning the admissibility of a defendant's admissions at his criminal trial in the United States, where that defendant is a non-resident alien and his statements were the product of an interrogation conducted abroad by U.S. law enforcement representatives. We conclude that such a defendant, insofar as he is the present subject of a domestic criminal proceeding, is indeed protected by the privilege against self-incrimination guaranteed by the Fifth Amendment, notwithstanding the fact that his only connections to the United States are his alleged violations of U.S. law and his subsequent U.S. prosecution. Additionally, we hold that courts may and should apply the familiar warning/waiver framework set forth in *Miranda v. Arizona,* 384 U.S. 436, 86 S.Ct. 1602, 16 L.Ed.2d 694 (1966), to determine whether the government, in its case-in-chief, may introduce against such a defendant evidence of his custodial statements—even if that defendant's interrogation by U.S. agents occurred wholly abroad and while he was in the physical custody of foreign authorities.

The predicate issue is as follows: Is the Government correct that a criminal defendant on trial in the United States does not enjoy the privilege against self-incrimination because he is a non-resident alien whose only connections to the United States are his alleged violations of U.S. law and his subsequent U.S. prosecution? We regard this narrow reading of the Constitution as being at odds with the text of the Fifth Amendment, overarching notions of fundamental fairness, relevant case-law, and the policy goals supporting the privilege against self-incrimination. Therefore, we reject the Government's interpretive contention and find that defendants in the position of Al-'Owhali and K.K. Mohamed may properly invoke the privilege against self-incrimination as a basis for suppressing custodial statements made to U.S. law enforcement representatives during overseas interrogation. . . .

To begin, it bears noting that the Government incorrectly frames the legal inquiry as one dependent on the extraterritorial application of the Fifth Amendment. Whether or not Fifth Amendment rights reach out to protect individuals while they are situated outside the United States is beside the point. This is because any violation of the privilege against self-incrimination occurs, not at the moment law enforcement officials coerce statements through custodial interrogation, but when a defendant's involuntary statements are actually used against him at an American criminal proceeding.[9] . . . Indeed, were the opposite the case—

---

9. Limited support for this reasoning can further be found in cases where courts have addressed efforts by defendants to suppress statements resulting from overseas interrogation *by foreign police.* These decisions refuse to suppress statements on the sole ground that foreign police failed to administer pre-interrogational *Miranda* warnings; the deterrent rationale of the exclusionary rule, it is posited, has little force with respect to a foreign sovereign. However, the same courts then go on to determine whether the challenged statement is nonetheless involuntary and should thus be suppressed pursuant to the privilege against self-incrimination. This added layer of review assumes implicitly what we state explicitly above: that the extraterritorial situs of interrogation is not dispositive since the Constitution is violated when a defendant's compelled statement is used against him as evidence, and not when he is coerced into making it in the first place. . . .

that is, if instead the Fifth Amendment injury resulted from the forcible extraction of a statement and not its later evidentiary use—then no statute compelling witness testimony under grants of immunity could withstand constitutional challenge. The violation of Defendants' rights here, if any, is clearly prospective, and so the relevant question is the scope of the privilege against self-incrimination as to non-resident aliens presently inside the United States and subject to domestic criminal proceedings.

We turn first to the expansive language used in the Fifth Amendment itself. . . . The crucial phrase is "no person" and it neither denotes nor connotes any limitation in scope, in marked contrast to the use of "the people" in most of the other Amendments contained within the Bill of Rights. From the outset, then, these protections seemingly apply with equal vigor to all defendants facing criminal prosecution at the hands of the United States, and without apparent regard to citizenship or community connection.

In the face of the Amendment's inclusive text, however, the Government insists that "any assessment of the extent to which constitutional rights may vest in a non-American in a given instance is significantly influenced by the degree to which he has sought to insert himself into the fabric of our society."

Whatever the validity of this proposition in unrelated contexts (e.g., immigration), it is unsupportable in its intimation that criminal defendants on trial in a U.S. court should receive differing levels of Fifth Amendment procedural protection depending on their level of "insertion" into American society. It is true that the Supreme Court has yet to rule affirmatively that the three remaining Fifth Amendment procedural guarantees—indictment by grand jury, bar on double jeopardy, and privilege against self-incrimination—apply to criminal defendants who are non-citizens. But we find that circumstance to be emblematic, not of doctrinal reticence, but of widespread acceptance that these strictures apply universally to any criminal prosecution brought by the United States within its own borders... And even in the context of this particular case, we note that the parties have proceeded as if Defendants indeed possessed these three rights: The Government has sought a grand jury indictment nine times; the Court has reviewed the charging instrument for multiplicitous counts; and the desire by some defendants not to testify at various hearings, whenever so expressed, has been scrupulously honored. In sum, we are not at all surprised that courts rarely, if ever, face the scenario wherein the United States, acting domestically, attempts to convict non-resident aliens without following the procedural framework of the Fifth Amendment.

. . .

Of great significance is the Supreme Court's own explicit treatment of the privilege against self-incrimination as a "fundamental trial right of criminal defendants."

. . .

Lastly, we believe that the policies undergirding the Fifth Amendment privilege against self-incrimination are no less relevant when the criminal defendant at issue is an unconnected, non-resident alien. While these policies may arguably lose their force when the fear of compelled self-incrimination points to a prospective foreign prosecution ... when the defendant is, as here, prosecuted within the United States, before a United States court, for alleged violations of United States law, having been previously and thoroughly interrogated by U.S. law enforcement— then the Government's use of a coerced confession against him would still have the debilitating effect of infecting our criminal justice system. Such a system will undoubtedly, "in the long run, be less reliable and more subject to abuses."

We hold that Defendants ..., as the present subjects of a U.S. criminal proceeding, are protected by the Fifth Amendment's privilege against self-incrimination, despite their status as non-resident aliens whose only connections to this country are their alleged crimes and their domestic prosecution therefor.

Our next inquiry focuses on an issue imbued with significant consequence, not the least of which is its inevitable impact on U.S. law enforcement officials who, in furtherance of their duties and with increasing regularity, are dispatched and stationed beyond our national borders. Assume for purposes of this discussion these generalized facts: An individual held in the custody of foreign police is suspected of having violated both local and U.S. criminal law. As a matter of global comity, U.S. law enforcement representatives are permitted inside the foreign stationhouse to pose their own questions to the suspect. U.S. agents eventually succeed in extracting inculpatory statements, and the suspect is thereafter transported to the United States for prosecution, with the consent of foreign authorities. By what standards should a domestic court admit the above statements as governmental evidence at trial? We believe that a principled, but realistic application of *Miranda's* familiar warning/waiver framework, in the absence of a constitutionally-adequate alternative, is both necessary and appropriate under the Fifth Amendment. Only by doing so can courts meaningfully safeguard from governmental incursion the privilege against self-incrimination afforded to all criminal defendants in this country—wherever in the world they might initially be apprehended—while at the same time imposing manageable costs on the transnational investigatory capabilities of America's law enforcement personnel.

Contrary to the Government's apocalyptic protestations, we are not dissuaded from applying *Miranda* to overseas interrogations conducted by U.S. law enforcement, even if the interrogational target is in the physical custody of foreign authorities. After all, the inherent coerciveness of that police technique is clearly no less troubling when carried out beyond our borders and under the aegis of a foreign stationhouse. It is, on the contrary, far more likely that a custodial interrogation held in such conditions will present greater threats of compulsion since all that happens to the accused cannot be controlled by the Americans. For instance, the laws of the host nation might permit lengthy incommunicado detention subsequent to arrest, thereby leaving the accused isolated and without assistance for a duration not seen today in America. Substandard detention conditions could further contribute to the toll. Worst yet, local authorities may privately engage in aggressive practices, both legal and illegal in their own nation, but certainly not tolerated within the United States. As such, by the time U.S. agents are finally on hand to ask questions of their own, strong countervailing forces will already have run head first into the free will of the accused.

None of this is to say that American law enforcement representatives, who have behaved conscientiously and with great sensitivity, should always be responsible for the acts of a foreign sovereign. Rather, our point is—as is that of the Supreme Court in *Miranda*—that the inherent coercion associated with any custodial interrogation is a specter that haunts all confessions later gleaned therefrom, even apart from the added externalities of oppressive detention and improper police behavior. The great wisdom of *Miranda*—that American law … For purposes of safeguarding the Fifth Amendment privilege against self-incrimination, the *Miranda* warning/waiver framework still provides, even in the overseas context, a necessary and workable solution. We therefore hold that a defendant's statements, if extracted by U.S. agents acting abroad, should be admitted as evidence at trial only if the Government demonstrates that the defendant was first advised of his rights and that he validly waived those rights. Suppression in the absence of either requirement will protect that defendant insofar as he is the present subject of a domestic criminal proceeding, while additionally deterring U.S. law enforcement from again committing similar omissions.[13]

Our conclusion in this regard is further reinforced by the line of cases involving the suppression of statements elicited during overseas interrogation *by foreign police*. These decisions uniformly recognize an exception to the usual rule that the failure to provide *Miranda* warnings is not dispositive of the motion to suppress whenever questioning is conducted by foreign authorities. Referred to as the "joint venture" exception, it provides that the lack of *Miranda* warnings will still lead to suppression if U.S. law enforcement themselves actively participated in the questioning, or if U.S. personnel, despite asking no questions directly, used the foreign officials as their interrogational agents in order to circumvent the requirements of *Miranda*. Whatever the precise formulation, the existence of the exception itself is based on the assumption that *Miranda* must apply to any portion of an overseas interrogation that is,

---

13. The Government calls it "positively perverse" that the admissibility of Defendants' statements would not require any *Miranda* warnings at all if those statements were instead the product of questioning by foreign police. (Gov't Post–Hr'g Memo. in Opp. to Al-'Owhali's and Odeh's Mots. at 48–49.) Yet we see nothing at all anomalous in requiring *our own* Government to abide by the strictures of *our own* Constitution whenever it seeks to convict an accused, in *our own* courts, on the basis of admissions culled via an inherently coercive interrogation conducted by *our own* law enforcement.

in fact or form, conducted by U.S. law enforcement. This is perfectly consistent with our holding today.

It now remains to be decided what specific warnings should be administered by U.S. agents prior to their overseas interrogation of a suspect not in U.S. custody. Clearly, he must be told that he has the right to remain silent, effective even if he has already spoken to the foreign authorities. He must also be told that anything he does say may be used against him in a court in the United States or elsewhere. This much is uncontroversial. But what about the right to the assistance and presence of counsel, either privately retained or publicly appointed? Unlike the previous two admonitions, this one may often be affected by the fact that the suspect is being interrogated overseas and that he is in the physical custody of a foreign nation. We agree with the Government that *Miranda* does not require law enforcement to promise that which they cannot guarantee or that which is in fact impossible to fulfill. No constitutional purpose is served by compelling law enforcement personnel to lie or mislead subjects of interrogation. Nor does *Miranda* mandate that U.S. agents compel a foreign sovereign to accept blind allegiance to American criminal procedure, at least when U.S. involvement in the foreign investigation is limited to mutual cooperation. However, if the particular overseas context actually presents *no* obvious hurdle to the implementation of an accused's right to the assistance and presence of counsel, due care should be taken not to foreclose an opportunity that in fact exists. To the maximum extent reasonably possible, efforts must be made to replicate what rights would be present if the interrogation were being conducted in America.

We thus believe that the fair and correct approach under *Miranda* is for U.S. law enforcement simply to be clear and candid as to both the existence of the right to counsel and the possible impediments to its exercise. The goal is to convey to a suspect that, with respect to any questioning by U.S. agents, his ability to exercise his right to the presence and assistance of counsel—a right ordinarily unqualified—hinges on two external considerations arising from the fact of his foreign custody. First, since there exists no institutional mechanism for the international provision of an American court-appointed lawyer, the availability of public counsel overseas turns chiefly on foreign law. Second, foreign law may also ban all manner of defense counsel from even entering the foreign stationhouse, and such law necessarily trumps American procedure. Given these eventualities, U.S. law enforcement can only do the best they can to give full effect to a suspect's right to the presence and assistance of counsel, while still respecting the ultimate authority of the foreign sovereign. And if an attorney, whether appointed or retained, is truly and absolutely unavailable, and that result remains unsatisfactory to the suspect, he should be told that he need not speak to the Americans so long as he is without legal representation. Moreover, even if the suspect opts to speak without a lawyer present, he should know that he still has the right to stop answering questions at any time.

. . .

The foregoing reading of *Miranda* renders baseless the Government's claims that a warning/waiver requirement will impose intolerable costs to both international investigatory cooperation and America's own ability to deter transnational crime. As described above, if foreign law indeed bans all counsel from the stationhouse entirely, then we do not require U.S. law enforcement to violate such laws. Rather, only if the foreign authorities themselves permit the assistance and presence of counsel will that right be given effect during interrogation by U.S. agents. Even less persuasive is the alleged inability of the United States to counter transnational crime when constrained by *Miranda* overseas. We doubt that the simple recitation of an advice of rights to a criminal suspect questioned abroad, when such warnings are already required domestically, will in any way shift the tide in favor of global lawlessness. To the extent that a suspect's *Miranda* rights allegedly impede foreign intelligence collection, we note that *Miranda* only prevents an unwarned or involuntary statement from being used as evidence in a domestic criminal trial; it does not mean that such statements are never to be elicited in the first place.

It bears reiteration that the issues addressed by this Opinion relate solely to the admissibility of statements in an American court. This is *not* the same question as the ability of American law enforcement or intelligence officials to obtain intelligence formation from non-citizens abroad, information which may be vital to national security interests. What we find impermissible is not intelligence gathering by agents of the U.S. government empowered to do so, but rather the use in a domestic criminal trial of statements extracted in violation of the Fifth Amendment.

* * *

D.   Targeted killing abroad by U.S. agents

EXECUTIVE ORDER 11905 (UNITED STATES FOREIGN INTELLIGENCE ACTIVITIES)

February 18, 1976 [signed by President Gerald Ford].
41 FR 7703, 1976 WL 21308.

Sec. 5. Restrictions on Intelligence Activities

. . .

g) Prohibition of Assassination. No employee of the United States Government shall engage in, or conspire to engage in, political assassination.

. . .

EXECUTIVE ORDER 12333 (UNITED STATES INTELLIGENCE ACTIVITIES)

December 4, 1981 [signed by President Ronald Reagan].
46 FR 59941, 1981 WL 76054.

Part 2

. . .

2.11   Prohibition on Assassination. No person employed by or acting on behalf of the United States Government shall engage in, or conspire to engage in, assassination.

2.12   Indirect Participation. No agency of the Intelligence Community shall participate in or request any person to undertake activities forbidden by this Order.

Notes and Questions

1.   The Gerald Ford Executive Order prohibition on political assassination was reaffirmed by President Carter. Note that the Ford prohibition speaks of "political assassination" while the Reagan Order simply prohibits "assassination." Is this difference significant? How would you define "political assassination"? Note that during the Reagan administration the U.S. dropped bombs on the home of Libyan leader Colonel Muammar Gaddafi, the Libyan leader, in retaliation for a terrorist bombing in Germany directed against a place frequented by American soldiers. During the Clinton administration, the U.S. fired cruise missiles at suspected guerilla camps in Afghanistan after the bombings of two U.S. embassies in Africa. *See* U.S. Policy on Assassination, CNN transcript, November 4, 2002, 6:38 p.m. Should these events be viewed as breaches of the policy or as a guide to how the assassination ban is being (should be?) interpreted?

2.   It was reported by CNN, *supra* note 1, that after the September 11 attacks, the White House said that the prohibition against assassinations would not prevent the U.S from acting in self-defense. Other administration sources have indicated that the ban on assassination does not apply in wartime. Senate Joseph Biden was quoted as saying: "These are combatants of war. And I find no difficulty with it." *See* Senators Support CIA Anti–Terror Effort, Reuters, December 15, 2002, 4:18 p.m.

3.   Apart from the executive orders quoted above, there is no publicly available statement of policy in this area. News reports have indicated that after September 11, the President signed a secret finding that authorizes the CIA to covertly attack al Qaeda members anywhere in the world; contains no exemption for American citizens, and does not require that the President approve specific operations. Reportedly also, the administration has prepared a list of terrorist leaders the CIA is authorized to kill, but the CIA's authority to kill is not limited to those on the list. *See* James Risen and David Johnston, Threats and Responses: Hunt for al Qaeda: Bush Has Widened Authority of CIA To Kill Terrorists, NY Times, December 15, 2002.

4.   On November 3, 2002, a missile fired by a U.S. unmanned aerial vehicle killed a carload of suspected operatives in Yemen. The principal

target of the attack was a man named Qaed Salim Sinan al-Harethi, who was allegedly an al Qaeda operative in Yemen. He was suspected of having been involved in the terrorist attack on the U.S.S. Cole. Reportedly, an American citizen was also in the car which was totally destroyed.

5. Immediately after the attack, many legal commentators criticized such targeting and killing of persons suspected of terrorist acts. *See* Laura K. Donohue, The "Good Guy" Turns Assassin, LA Times, Nov. 17, 2002, Sunday Opinion Section. Professor Donohue argues, *inter alia*: 1) how can we claim to be a protector of human rights when we engage in extrajudicial killings; 2) is it better to kill individuals whose guilt is unproved than for lives of Americans to be put at risk? 3) if we are at war, it should be a just war and we must be careful in the force that we use; 4) we need to provide immunity for innocents whenever possible; 5) assassination erodes national security by undermining our image and our moral authority before the world community. Also see Daniel B. Pickard, Legalizing Assassination? Terrorism, The Central Intelligence Agency and International Law, 39 Ga. J. Int'l & Comp.L. 1 (2001); Patricia Zengel, Assassination and the Law of Armed Conflict, 45 Mercer L. Rev. 615 (1992).

6. Is the argument that "we are at war and killing the enemy in wartime is acceptable" a sufficient answer to the kind of arguments articulated in the previous note? If you were in a position of authority in the administration, what position would you take on this issue?

7. Assume that in fact you are employed in the administration. Your superior asks you to prepare a set of policies and procedures governing the subject of target killings? Assume, too, that you have grave doubts about the morality and/or the efficacy of such a policy. What would you do?

8. Same case as note 7, *supra*, but assume that you do not have any qualms about developing policies and procedures on the subject of targeted killings and therefore set to work on your assignment. What position would you recommend should be taken on the following issues?

a. At what level of government should the specific determination to target an individual suspected terrorist be made? Absent urgency, should the President be involved in each such case? Should the Secretary of Defense? Anyone else? Note: news reports have indicated that the President has issued a finding authorizing such killings, but is not consulted in the individual case.

b. What kind of terrorist involvement, al Qaeda membership, leadership role in al Qaeda, and/or specific terrorist acts should be required, before a targeting order is approved?

c. What kind of evidence of the involvements described in b. above should be required? Suppose all of the information is based on informants' reports? How would you formulate the standard of proof?

d. Should there be a kind of formal fact-finding process? What kinds of formalities, if any? Any process of review of the fact-finding determination? By whom? How many?

e. Under what circumstances should a targeted killing be considered an acceptable option? For example, should there be a specific determination that the option of capturing the suspect would be too dangerous or logistically impossible? Note that it is reported that Harethi was living in a remote area of Yemen that was a lawless region where the Yemeni government had little control. See NY Times, December 15, 2002, *supra*, note 3.

f. Targeted killings have occurred on the battlefield, that is, in Afghanistan and in Yemen. Should the policies distinguish between the kinds of settings?

g. Should the consent of the host country's government be required, before undertaking such an action? Note that news reports indicated that unofficially the Yemeni government actually assisted in the Harethi killing by providing intelligence. Suppose the host country is one that tacitly or actively supports the terrorist organizations?

h. Should the policies distinguish between the killing of leaders and those who are lower down in the terrorist organizational hierarchy?

i. Should the policies require input from U.S. law enforcement agencies involved in the anti-terrorism effort, before a determination to target an individual is made?

j. Should the policies prohibit targeted killings on U.S. soil?

k. What kind of assurance should be required in the policies that innocent bystanders will not be injured? What kind of "collateral damage" should be deemed acceptable?

9. A feature of this area is that the actual policy(ies) we are applying and any procedures connected thereto are not publicly available. Nor is this an area where it seems feasible to obtain judicial review that would inquire into the applications of the policy. In other words, almost all of what we know is derived from the news media and the occasional interview or statement emanating from an administration official. The policy and practice is essentially unknown and unreviewable outside of the Executive Branch. Would it be desirable to change these features of the situation? How might this be done?

10. The New York Times (David Johnston and David E. Sanger, Yemen Killing Based on Rules Set Out by Bush, NY Times, Nov. 6, 2002) reported that the CIA did not "seek input from or consult law enforcement officials" prior to the killing by missile of Mr. Harethi and his companions in Yemen, *supra* note 4. Law enforcement officials indicated they had wanted to question Harethi about the Cole attack, but they were not unhappy that he had been killed. This would appear to be an area where coordination between the law enforcement and intelligence-military operation is not occurring, even after the post September 11 congressional and administration efforts to improve communication and coordination between these governmental functions. Do you think efforts should be made also to introduce greater coordination into this arena of anti-terrorist activity?

*

Chapter 14

Epilogue

In the preceding chapters, we examined a series of new applications and extensions of the criminal law, enforcement methods and adjudicative process that have been triggered by the government's very active program of anti-terrorism. Having taken up these various subjects seriatim, it may be useful to take a step back and make some general observations about what appears to be going on in the U.S. legal system as a result of the anti-terrorist efforts of the government.

It is obvious, and perhaps not surprising, that the government in aid of its anti-terrorism activities has consistently opted for laws, process, procedures and investigatory methods that are designed to make its efforts more efficient, effective, and, the government hopes, more successful.

Thus, invoking the general notion that "we are at war," the government has mustered legal support and justification for the lengthy (and in some instances, indefinite) detention of individuals using material witness doctrine; immigration laws and status-as-aliens; and enemy combatant status in specific doctrinal reliance on the "at war" concept. It has established a set of military commissions that will, if they survive the legal challenges now being directed against them, provide less procedural protection for individuals than our regular civilian court system.

With the assistance of the Congress, it has largely eliminated the previously-existing separation between intelligence and law enforcement information gathering. While that separation, when it was maintained, may not have bee particularly effective in protecting Fourth Amendment interests, it at least reflected an effort in that direction. Neither the government nor the courts have put anything concrete in its place, to ensure that there is not an erosion in the direction of using FISA warrants in ordinary criminal investigations. Also with Congress' assistance, the government has broadened significantly its electronic surveillance authority, made previously secret grand jury information more readily available and broadened its authority to detain people under the immigration laws.

In the realm of privacy and First Amendment interests, the government, again with the assistance of new legislation, has received broadened authority to obtain information regarding individuals. Similarly, through a simple change in administrative policy, the government has regained authority it once exercised to have undercover informants attend meetings of organizations, churches, mosques and synagogues, trolling for information that might be relevant to anti-terrorism enforcement.

Further, the government is actively using new kinds of anti-terrorist crimes as well as civil enforcement legislation against organizations and individuals in the United States. Abroad, the government is wielding a big stick: It, of course, has recently functioned in a military manner on the battlefield where at least some of the enemy were members of al Qaeda, but it is also using other methods that do not directly involve the battlefield. It may, for example, be using extreme measures in interrogating suspected terrorists, whether directly or through surrogates, and it has, at least on one occasion, reportedly exercised its presidentially-granted authority to engage in targeted killing of suspected terrorists.

We recount these various steps that have been taken, most of them in the wake of the attacks on September 11, not because we think any one of them necessarily lacks legal justification. We appreciate the national security concerns that led the government to these various actions. Reasonable persons, however, can disagree about the extent of the danger, whether we are truly at war, and whether any specific action of those listed is truly warranted by real national security concerns.

Taking note of the impact of these various actions as a totality is a rather startling experience. Each of the steps taken on the home front, in its own way, has decreased somewhat our liberties, privacy, and traditional procedural protections to some discernible degree. Taken in their totality, these domestic actions arguably have effected a substantial change in the relationship between the individual and the government of the United States. While these actions may not have been felt yet by most of us directly, they are affecting individual members of our society in specific instances—It behooves us to keep in mind that "There but for . . . go I." These actions are surely also affecting our moral image and status in the world.

What is also striking is the speed with which these changes have occurred and the relative lack of public outcry about them. The absence of much protest probably reflects the fact that the changes have not had a direct impact on much of the population at large, the changes are very new, and, given the trauma that September 11 wreaked on the psyche of America, the general public is receptive to the notion of "doing what needs to be done" to deal with the threat.

Two other topics merit attention in a general review of what has been happening in anti-terrorism criminal enforcement and related topics since September 11—the executive branch's penchant for secrecy, that is, making much less information available to the public; and the role of the courts in the current circumstances. We have seen a number of instances where government lawyers declined to provide information and then fought efforts made in the courts to require them to disclose. Thus, the government declined to provide the names of those who were detained in the immediate aftermath of September 11 and other related information. Similarly, they made strenuous legal efforts to keep closed immigration hearings that had a anti-terrorism link. Regarding actions by U.S. agents abroad, the administration discloses very little, so it is hard to resolve the conflicting statements regarding the use of torture in interrogation of terrorist suspects. Similarly, the administration has acknowledged that in October, 2003, the President made an official finding that authorized targeted killings, but the finding is secret, and we know very little about its exact terms.

Over the course of the past half century, the general trend has been toward less government secrecy and toward more transparency. The Freedom of Information Act was the centerpiece of this historical trend. However, among the many casualties of September 11, this historical movement toward openness in government arguably has been stopped and reversed.

Another historical pattern may also have changed since September 11. In the past half century, the courts functioned as a primary protector of the individual against the powers of government. Since September 11, we have seen a number of ways in which that modern judicial function may be changing. First, because of notions of justiciability and standing, there are various actions of the government regarding which it has been hard to mount a judicial challenge. On some issues, for example, the interrogations conducted abroad and the targeted killing policy, it would seem that there are insuperable legal obstacles to mounting any kind of attack in the courts.

Recent Supreme Court decisions have rejected some of the government's more extreme claims for unreviewable executive authority, but it remains to be seen how much real protection is being provided by the processes that have been put in place and whether these processes will in the end win judicial approval. On the secrecy front, while there have been a few decisions, upholding challenges to government secrecy, a fairly strong pattern has begun to emerge of decisions sustaining government actions through the adoption of a judicial posture of deference or non-interference where the issues involve claims of national security. If the pattern holds, we may not be able rely on the courts as a way to curb government claims of a need for secrecy.

We have not yet mentioned the Congress in this general summation. Thus far, the Congress has deferred to the executive branch by positively responding to most of the administration's requests for new legislation. The politics at work are very much like the politics that attend issues of crime legislation. Members of the national legislative bodies do not wish to be seen as "soft on terrorism."

A final note. Many have observed on numerous occasions that if we are in a "war," it is a war that may not have an ending. This observation obviously has important implications for the changes in the relation between government and individual that are justified as "wartime measures." Are we witnessing legal changes in the essential nature of the U.S. society that are to be with us for the indefinite future? It is a sobering thought.

Index

†